Andrew I

CW01643533

A

Concordance to Shakespeare

Elibron Classics
www.elibron.com

Elibron Classics series.

ISBN 1-4021-5173-X (paperback)
ISBN 1-4212-7770-0 (hardcover)

This Elibron Classics Replica Edition is an unabridged facsimile of the edition published in 1787 in London.

A CONCORDANCE TO SHAKESPEARE:

SUITED TO ALL THE EDITIONS,

IN WHICH

THE DISTINGUISHED AND PARALLEL PASSAGES IN THE PLAYS OF THAT JUSTLY ADMIRED WRITER ARE METHODICALLY ARRANGED.

TO WHICH ARE ADDED,

THREE HUNDRED NOTES AND ILLUSTRATIONS,

ENTIRELY NEW.

LONDON:
PRINTED FOR G. G. J. AND J. ROBINSON,
PATERNOSTER-ROW.

M.DCC.LXXXVII.

ADVERTISEMENT.

SHAKESPEARE is deservedly placed at the head of our Dramatic Writers. There is not, however, at this time, any necessity for inquiring into his several merits and excellencies: they have been already particularly pointed out by his very numerous commentators. The design of the present publication, is to bring into one view the parallel passages of the poet, so as to form a kind of Concordance to his works. The utility of such a compilation must be obvious, and indeed especially so, when it is considered, as is observed by Dr. Johnson,—"that the plays "of Shakespeare are filled with practical axioms and domestic wisdom; and that a system of civil and economical prudence may "be collected from them." The Editor is therefore in hope, as it has been his study, in the following selection, to make choice of such particular passages of his author, as might serve to confirm the justness and propriety of the preceding remark, that he may ſtand acquitted in the opinion of the public, as to any error in judgment, with regard to the undertaking now before them. In a word, he wiſhes it to be remembered, that the plan is not entirely his own, but that he has in a great meaſure fallen in with, and adopted the ſentiments of the eminent writer already named.

The method purſued throughout the work, will be ſeen in the following ſketch or example:

HONOUR.

—— For life, I prize it
As I weigh grief, which I would ſpare: for honour,
'Tis a derivative from me to mine,
And only that I ſtand for. *Winter's Tale*, A. 3, S. 2.

—— This thou ſhouldſt have done,
And not have ſpoken of it! In me 'tis villainy;
In thee it had been good ſervice. Thou muſt know,
'Tis not my profit that does lead mine honour:
Mine honour it. *Antony and Cleopatra*, A. 2, S. 7.

—— Rightly, to be great
Is not to ſtir without great argument;
But greatly to find quarrel in a ſtraw,
When Honour's at the ſtake. *Hamlet*, A. 4, S. 4.

A ſcar nobly got, or a noble ſcar, is a good livery of honour. *All's well that ends well*, A. 4, S. 5.

Mine

Mine honour keeps the weather of my fate:
Life every man holds dear; but the dear man
Holds honour far more precious dear than life.

Troilus and Cressida, A. 5, S. 3.

——— Honour but of danger wins a scar;
As oft it loses all. *All's well that ends well*, A. 3, S. 2.

Set Honour in one eye and Death i' the other,
And I will look on both indifferently:
For let the gods so speed me, as I love
The name of Honour more than I fear Death.

Julius Cæsar, A. 1, S. 2.

—— Let higher Italy see that you come,
Not to woo Honour, but to wed it.

All's well that ends well, A. 2, S. 1.

——— His honour,
Clock to itself, knew the true minute when
Exception bid him speak, and, at that time,
His tongue obey'd his hand.

All's well that ends well, A. 1, S. 2.

A jewel in a ten-times barr'd up chest,
Is—a bold spirit in a loyal breast.
Mine honour is my life; both grow in one:
Take honour from me, and my life is done.

Richard II. A. 1, S. 1.

——— I am not covetous for gold;
Nor care I, who doth feed upon my cost;
Such outward things dwell not in my desires:
But, if it be a sin to covet honour,
I am the most offending soul alive. *Henry V.* A. 4, S. 3.

Well, 'tis no matter; Honour pricks me on. Yea, but how

how if Honour prick me off when I come on? Can Honour ſet to a leg? No. Or an arm? No. Or take away the grief of a wound? No. Honour hath no ſkill in ſurgery then? No. *Henry IV.* P. 1, A. 5, S. 1.

In like manner with the above, the Editor has endeavoured to exhibit the moſt ſtriking ſentiments of the "*great poet of nature*," cleared of all impurities, of all "eye-offending" droſs*. He has broken and disjointed ſeveral of the ſpeeches, but this muſt not be urged againſt him as a fault:---The nature of the work demanded it; and as the reader is referred to the act and ſcene of every play, in which the more beautiful of ſuch ſpeeches are to be found, and as there are likewiſe innumerable compilations in which they are given entire, there is conſequently the leſs occaſion for apology. It is hoped, moreover, that no one will object to the arrangement of any of the paſſages, by ſaying, "I would "have diſpoſed them in a different manner," but rather remember, that there is no particular rule or ſtandard by which to be governed

* It muſt not be imagined, from what is here ſaid, that the Editor has at any time preſumed to alter a ſingle expreſſion of Shakeſpeare; but only, that he has occaſionally omitted an exceptionable line or two.

in ſuch a matter. The Editor, indeed, is ſenſible that the order in which they are placed, is not always ſtrictly proper. This, however, is not occaſioned by negligence, but from an unwillingneſs to multiply the heads, or diviſions, which are already ſufficiently numerous. In fine, he has regulated them in the way which to him appeared the beſt. The Editor repeats---The intention in the preſent ſelection is, to make the poet ſometimes ſpeak in *maxims* or *ſentences*, according to the idea of Dr. Johnſon; and at other times to give his deſcription of one and the ſame affection or paſſion, as it is ſeen in different perſons and at different ſeaſons: or, as it may be called forth by accidental, by foreign and oppoſed circumſtances *.

With reſpect to the notes, which are to be met with in the following pages, and which are diſtinguiſhed by the initials A. B. they are the efforts of a young, but zealous critic; of one who is deſirous of rendering Shake-

* Such particular paſſages, however, as are intimately connected with the fable and characters, or which, from the train of the dialogue, would ſcarcely be underſtood when ſtanding alone, are not to be expected here.

ſpeare as clear and perſpicuous as poſſible*. The indulgence of the reader is requeſted for them; and if the writer ſhall be found to have thrown a light on ſome of the obſcurities of a favourite author, the world will no doubt readily acknowledge it, and amply reward him for his labours.

LONDON,
October 31, 1787.

* He has likewiſe in his poſſeſſion a conſiderable number of obſervations on ſuch paſſages of the poet as come not within the plan of the preſent work. If duly encouraged, he means to publiſh them without delay.

A
CONCORDANCE
TO
SHAKESPEARE.

ABSTINENCE.

HE doth with holy abſtinence ſubdue
That in himſelf, which he ſpurs on his power
To qualify in others. *Meaſ. for Meaſ.* A. 4, S. 2.

ACQUAINTANCE.

[1] Talk logick with acquaintance that you have,
And practiſe rhetorick in your common talk.
Taming of the Shrew, A. 1, S. 1.

[1] *Talk logick.*] The old copies read *Balcke* logick, &c. MALONE.
"Balke logick" is right: *Balke*, with the writers of Shakeſpeare's time is *omit*.—"Never regard truth, ſays Tranio, in "your worldly tranſactions; but be flouriſhing and rhetorical "in your ordinary diſcourſe." This is the language of a man who knows the world. A. B.

ACT, ACTION, ACTIONS.

——— Each your doing,
So ſingular in each particular,
Crowns what you are doing in the preſent deeds,
That all your acts are queens. *Wint. Tale*, A. 4, S. 3.

——— If powers divine
Behold our human actions (as they do),
I doubt not then, but innocence ſhall make
Falſe accuſation bluſh, and tyranny
Tremble at patience. *Winter's Tale*, A. 3, S. 2.

——— Give thy thoughts no tongue,
Nor any unproportion'd thought his act.
Be thou familiar, but by no means vulgar.
Hamlet, A. 1, S. 3.

——— Such an act,
That blurs the grace and bluſh of modeſty;
Calls virtue, hypocrite; [1] takes off the roſe
From the fair forehead of an innocent love,
And ſets a bliſter there; makes marriage vows
As falſe as dicers' oaths. *Hamlet*, A. 3, S. 4.

——— Her actions ſhall be holy, as,
You hear, my ſpell is lawful: do not ſhun her,
Until you ſee her die again: for then
You kill her double. *Winter's Tale*, A. 5, S. 3.

——— The rarer action is
In virtue than in vengeance. *Tempeſt*, A. 5, S. 1.

[1] *Takes off the roſe.*] Alluding to the cuſtom of wearing roſes on the ſide of the face. WARBURTON.

I believe Dr. Warburton is miſtaken; for it muſt be allowed that there is a material difference between an ornament worn on the *forehead*, and one exhibited *on the ſide of the face*. STEEVENS.

It is not a little extraordinary that the commentators ſhould be for conſidering literally, expreſſions that are purely metaphorical. Roſe is beauty, and bliſter is deformity. The meaning plainly is, *renders love, which is naturally beautiful, ugly and deformed.*

A. B.

——Look

——— Look you, how pale he glares!
His form and cauſe conjoin'd, preaching to ſtones,
Would make them capable.—Do not look upon me,
Leſt with this piteous action, you convert
My ſtern effects. *Hamlet*, A. 3, S. 4.

Either our hiſtory ſhall, with full mouth,
Speak freely of our acts; or elſe our grave,
Like Turkiſh mute, ſhall have a tongueleſs mouth,
Not worſhipp'd with a waxen epitaph[1].
Henry V. A. 1, S. 2.

As many ſeveral ways meet in one town;
As many freſh ſtreams run in one ſelf ſea;
As many lines cloſe in the dial's center;
So may a thouſand actions, once a-foot,
End in one purpoſe, and be all well borne
Without defeat. *Henry V.* A. 1, S. 2.

My lord of Hereford, whom you call king,
Is a foul traitor to proud Hereford's king:
And if you crown him, let me propheſy,—
The blood of Engliſh ſhall manure the ground,

[1] *With a waxen epitaph.*] The quarto, 1608, reads with a *paper* epitaph.

Either a *waxen* or *paper* epitaph, is an epitaph eaſily obliterated or deſtroyed; one which can confer no laſting honour on the dead. STEEVENS.

"Waxen" is hardly right; for to ſay that his tomb ſhould *not* have a waxen epitaph, *i. e.* one that is eaſily obliterated, is entirely adverſe to the meaning of Henry. We muſt, therefore, read,

"Not worſhipp'd with a *wiſſen* epitaph."

To *wiſſe* is to *teach*, to *inſtruct*.

The meaning is, *without an epitaph, to ſet forth his virtues or his deeds in arms.*

After all, however, "a paper epitaph" may be right. But *paper epitaph* muſt not be interpreted literally: it means not an epitaph written on paper to be placed on a tomb—but an *hiſtory*, the memoirs of Henry's life. Unleſs we effect the buſineſs in hand (ſays the king), we wiſh not to be honoured, or to have our memory reſpected. Thus the reaſoning is juſt and pertinent. A. B.

And future ages groan for this foul act.
Richard II. A. 4, S. 1.

There is not a dangerous action can peep out his head but I am thrust upon it: Well, I cannot last ever: but it was always yet the trick of our English nation, if they have a good thing, to make it too common. *Henry IV.* P. 2, A. 1, S. 2.

Though now we must appear bloody and cruel,
As by our hands, and this our present act,
You see we do; yet see you but our hands,
And this the bleeding business they have done:
Our hearts you see not, they are pitiful.
Julius Cæsar, A. 3, S. 1.

But wherefore do you droop? why look you sad?
Be great in act, as you have been in thought;
Let not the world see fear, and sad distrust,
Govern the motion of a kingly eye.
King John, A. 5, S. 1.

——— If thou didst but consent
To this most cruel act, do but despair,
And, if thou want'st a cord, the smallest thread
That ever spider twisted from her womb,
Will serve to strangle thee. *K. John*, A. 4, S. 3.

——— What we oft do best,
[1] By sick interpreters, once weak ones, is
Not ours, or not allow'd; what worst, as oft,
Hitting a grosser quality, is cry'd up
For our best act. *Henry VIII.* A. 1, S. 2.

——— We must not stint
Our necessary actions, in the fear

[1] *By sick, &c.*] The modern editors read, *or* weak ones; but *once* is not unfrequently used for *sometime*, or at *one time or other*, among our ancient writers. STEEVENS.

The disjunctive particle *or* is certainly wrong; *once* is not, in this place, to be taken in the sense which Mr. S. would willingly affix to it. The meaning is, "interpreters who are at once sick "and weak." We may read, perhaps,

"By sick interpreters *and* weak ones, is" A. B.

To

To cope malicious cenſurers; which ever,
As ravenous fiſhes, do a veſſel follow
That is new trimm'd. *Henry VIII.* A. 1, S. 2.

My lords, I care not, if my actions
Were try'd by every tongue, every eye ſaw 'em,
Envy and baſe opinion ſet againſt 'em,
I know my life ſo even. *Henry VIII.* A. 3, S. 1.

I have done as you have done; that's what I can:
Induc'd, as you have been; that's for my country:
He, that has but effected his good will,
Hath overta'en mine act. *Coriolanus,* A. 1, S. 9.

Go to them, with this bonnet in thy hand;
And thus far having ſtretch'd it (here be with them),
Thy knee buſſing the ſtones, for in ſuch buſineſs
Action is eloquence, and the eyes of the ignorant
More learned than the ears. *Coriolanus,* A. 3, S. 2.

Why, univerſal plodding priſons up
The nimble ſpirits in the arteries;
As motion, and long-during action, tires
The ſinewy vigour of the traveller.
Love's Labour Loſt, A. 4, S. 3.

—— We are oft to blame in this—
'Tis too much prov'd—that, with devotion's viſage,
And pious action, we do ſugar o'er
The devil himſelf. *Hamlet,* A. 3, S. 1.

Hear me profeſs ſincerely:—Had I a dozen ſons, each in my love alike, and none leſs dear than thine and my good Marcius—I had rather have eleven die nobly for their country, than one voluptuouſly ſurfeit out of action. *Coriolanus,* A. 1, S. 3.

A C T O R.

Pol. The actors are come hither, my lord.
Ham. Buz, buz![1]
Pol. Upon mine honour,—— *Hamlet,* A. 2, S. 2.

[1] *Buz, buz!*] Mere idle talk; the buz of the vulgar. Johnson.

ADVANTAGE.

Thus ſays my king:—Say thou to Harry of England, though we ſeemed dead, we did but ſleep: Advantage is a better ſoldier, than raſhneſs; Tell him, we cou'd have rebuked him at Harfleur; but that we thought not good to bruiſe an injury, till it were full ripe. *Henry* V. A. 3, S. 6.

ADVERSITY.

A wretched ſoul, bruis'd with adverſity,
We bid be quiet, when we hear it cry;
But were we burden'd with like weight of pain,
As much or more, we ſhould ourſelves complain.
Comedy of Errors, A. 2, S. 1.

Sweet are the uſes of adverſity;
Which, like the toad, ugly and venomous,
Wears yet a precious jewel in his head.
As you like it, A. 2, S. 1.

AFFECTIONS.

—When his headſtrong riot hath no curb,
When rage and hot blood are his counſellors,
When means and laviſh manners meet together,

Buzzer, in a ſubſequent ſcene of this play, is uſed for a *buſy talker*.

"And wants not *buzzers* to infect his ear."

It is therefore probable, from the anſwer of Polonius, that *buz* was uſed, as Dr. Johnſon ſuppoſes, for an idle rumour, without foundation. MALONE.

When Hamlet ſays "buz, buz!" he cannot mean by it *mere idle talk*, becauſe he had already been informed by Guildernſtern that the players were actually arrived. I underſtand the expreſſion thus:—The Prince is vexed at the officious intruſion of Polonius into his preſence, and exclaims, "buz, buz!—now ſhall I be tormented with your chattering." Polonius miſtaking Hamlet, and thinking that he doubts the truth of his news, replies—"upon mine honour," &c. A. B.

O, with

O, with what wings ſhall his affections fly,
Towards fronting peril and oppos'd decay!
Henry IV. P. 2, A. 4. S. 4.

I ſaw Baſſanio and Anthonio part:
Baſſanio told him, he would make ſome ſpeed
Of his return; he anſwer'd—Do not ſo,
And even there, his eye being big with tears,
And with affection wond'rous ſenſible
He wrung Baſſanio's hand, and ſo they parted.
Merchant of Venice, A. 2, S. 8.

What he hath taken away from thy father per-force, I will render thee again in affection; by mine honour, I will; and when I break that oath, let me turn monſter. *As you like it*, A. 1, S. 2.

My wife comes foremoſt; then the honour'd mould
Wherein this trunk was fram'd, and in her hand
The grandchild to her blood. But, out, affection!
All bond and privilege of nature, break!
Let it be virtuous to be obſtinate. *Coriolan.* A. 5, S. 3.

—Brave conquerors!—for ſo you are,
That war againſt your own affections,
And the huge army of the world's deſires.
Love's Labour Loſt, A. 1, S. 1.

If drawing my ſword againſt the humour of affection would deliver me from the reprobate thought of it, I would take deſire priſoner, and ranſom him to any French courtier for a new deviſed court'ſy.
Love's Labour Loſt, A. 1. S. 2.

——Beſeech you, let her will
Have a free way. [1]I therefore beg it not
To pleaſe the palate of my appetite;

Nor

[1] ———*I therefore beg it not*
To pleaſe the palate of my appetite;
Nor to comply with heat, (the young affects,
In me defunct) and proper ſatisfaction;
But, &c.]

 Very

Nor to comply with heat, (the young affects,
In me defunct) and proper satisfaction;
But to be free and bounteous to her mind:
And heaven defend your good souls, that you think
I will your serious and great business scant,
For she is with me. *Othello*, A. 1, S. 3.

I remember, one said, there were no sallets in the lines[2], to make the matter savoury; nor no matter in the phrase, that might indite the author of affection[3]: but called it an honest method; as wholesome as sweet, and by very much more handsome than fine. *Hamlet*, A. 2, S. 2.

O, she, that hath a heart of that fine frame,
To pay this debt of love but to a brother,
How will she love, when the rich golden shaft
Hath kill'd the flock of all affections else
That live in her! *Twelfth Night*, A. 1. S. 1.

Very many notes have been written on these seemingly difficult lines, but without discovering the poet's meaning. A very slight change will give sufficient clearness to the passage, and consistency to Othello's speech. I read,

(the young affects,
In me conjunct), &c.

The meaning will therefore be,—I beg it not to comply with heat, nor yet in consideration of the young affections (alluding to his recent marriage), which may very naturally be supposed to be *conjunct*, or joining, in this my request; but, &c. A. B.

[2] *There were no sallets in the lines.*] Such is the reading of the old copies. I know not why the latter editors have adopted the alteration of Mr. Pope, and read, no *salt*, &c. STEEVENS.

"No *sallets* in the lines" is nonsense; and no *salt* in the lines is not right. The poet has here, as is very common with him, adopted a French word, viz. *saletés*, i. e. *smut*, or *smuttiness*. *Dire des saletés*, is, *to talk lewdly*. *Saletés* having been at first printed without the accent, was read *saletes*, and thence arose the mistake. A. B.

[3] — *indite the author of affection.*] *i. e.* Convict the author of being a fantastical, affected writer. STEEVENS.

"Affection" is not, in this place, I believe, *affected* or *fantastical*. "No matter in the phrase that might indite the author of "affection," seems to mean, *that he was a cold, uninteresting writer, that he did not speak from the heart.* A. B

AFFLICTION

AFFLICTION.

——Tell my friends,
Tell Athens, in the ſequence of degree,
From high to low throughout, that whoſo pleaſe
To ſtop affliction, let him take his haſte,
Come hither, ere my tree hath felt the axe,
And hang himſelf. *Timon*, A. 5, S. 2.

——Had it pleas'd heaven
To try me with affliction; had he rain'd
All kind of ſores, and ſhames, on my bare head,
Steep'd me in poverty to the very lips;
Given to captivity me and my utmoſt hopes;
I ſhould have found in ſome place of my ſoul
A drop of patience. *Othello*, A. 4, S. 2.

——O, you mighty Gods!
This world I do renounce; and, in your ſights,
Shake patiently my great affliction off:
If I could bear it longer, and not fall
To quarrel with your great oppoſeleſs wills,
My ſnuff, and loathed part of nature, ſhould
Burn itſelf out. *Lear*, A. 4, S. 6.

——Henceforth, I'll bear
Affliction, till it do cry out itſelf,
Enough, enough, and die. *Lear*, A. 4, S. 6.

Proſperity's the very bond of love;
Whoſe freſh complexion, and whoſe heart together,
Affliction alters. *Winter's Tale*, A. 4, S. 3.

——What's gone, and what's paſt help,
Should be paſt grief: Do not receive affliction
At my petition, I beſeech you!
Winter's Tale, A. 3, S. 2.

I think, affliction may ſubdue the check,
But not take in the mind.
Winter's Tale, A. 4, S. 3.

——Nay,

——Nay, forsooth, my friends,
They that must weigh out my afflictions[1],
They that my trust must grow to, live not here.
King Henry VIII. A. 3, S. 1.

AGE.

—— The sixth age shifts
Into the lean and slipper'd pantaloon;
With spectacles on nose, and pouch on side;
And his big manly voice,
Turning again towards childish treble, pipes
And whistles in his sound.
As you like it, A. 2, S. 7.

AIR.

—— When he speaks,
The air, a charter'd libertine, is still,
And the mute wonder lurketh in men's ears,
To steal his sweet and honey'd sentences.
Henry V. A. 1, S. 1.

—— Thou art
As glorious to this night, being o'er my head,
As is a winged messenger of heaven
Unto the white, up-turned wond'ring eyes

[1] ———— *weigh out my afflictions.*] This phrase is obscure. To *weigh out*, is, in modern language, *to deliver by weight*; but this sense cannot be here admitted. *To weigh* is likewise to *deliberate upon*, to *consider* with *due attention*. This may perhaps be meant. Or the phrase, *to weigh out*, may signify *to counterbalance*, *to counteract* with equal force. JOHNSON.

To *weigh out*, is the same as to *outweigh*. STEEVENS.

I understand the passage thus: The Queen would insinuate that she is the child of affliction, as we would say; and that such she must be content to remain. She at the same time hints, however, that her friends, who in such a case would *weigh out*, or *apportion her afflictions*, and who would consequently make them as easy and light as possible, were absent; and that she has nothing to hope for from the Cardinals, who would rather endeavour to heap misfortunes on her head. A. B.

Of

Of mortals, that fall back to gaze on him,
When he beſtrides the lazy-pacing clouds,
And ſails upon the boſom of the air.

Romeo, A. 2, S. 2.

Look, as I blow this feather from my face,
And as the air blows it to me again,
Obeying with my wind when I do blow,
And yielding to another when it blows,
Commanded always by the greater guſt;
Such is the lightneſs of you common men.

Henry VI. P. 3, A. 3, S. 1.

—— You leaden meſſengers,
That ride upon the violent ſpeed of fire,
Fly with falſe aim; move the ſtill-piercing air,
That ſings with piercing.[1]

All's well that ends well, A. 3, S. 2.

All thoſe which were his fellows but of late,
Follow his ſtrides, his lobbies fill with tendance,
Rain ſacrificial whiſperings in his ear,
Make ſacred even his ſtirrup, and through him
Drink the free air. *Timon*, A. 1, S. 1.

[1] ——— *move the ſtill-piercing air,*
That ſings with piercing.]
The words are here oddly ſhuffled into nonſenſe. We ſhould read,

"——— pierce the ſtill-moving air,
"This ſings with piercing."

i. e. pierce the air, which is in perpetual motion, and ſuffers no injury by piercing. WARBURTON.

Perhaps we might better read, "The ſtill-piecing air," *i. e.* the air that cloſes immediately. STEEVENS.

"Still-piecing air" is very harſh. The old copy reads, "Still peering air."——*Peering*, I think, may have been printed in miſtake for *fleering*, and the words which immediately follow ("that ſings with piercing") ſomewhat ſtrengthens my conjecture. "Pierce," ſays Helena, "the air, that regards not your "attack—that *fleers*, that mocks, that laughs, in ſhort, at your "power, but do not touch Bertram." A. B.

—— What,

—— What, think'ſt
That the bleak air, thy boiſterous chamberlain,
Will put thy ſhirt on warm? Will theſe moiſt trees,
That have out-liv'd the eagle, page thy heels,
And ſkip when thou point'ſt out? Will the cold brook,
Candied with ice, caudle thy morning taſte
To cure thy o'er-night's ſurfeit? *Timon*, A. 4, S. 3.

—— The bleſſed gods
Purge all infection from our air, whilſt you
Do climate here! *Winter's Tale*, A. 5, S. 1.

—— The air
Nimbly and ſweetly recommends itſelf
Unto our gentle ſenſes[1]. *Macbeth*, A. 1, S. 6.

AMBITION.

As Cæſar lov'd me, I weep for him; as he was fortunate, I rejoice at it; as he was valiant, I honour him: but, as he was ambitious, I ſlew him: There are tears, for his love; joy, for his fortune; honour, for his valour; and death, for his ambition.

Julius Cæſar, A. 3, S. 2.

He hath brought many captives home to Rome,

[1] *Unto our gentle ſenſes*] How odd a character is this of the air, that it *recommends itſelf* to all the ſenſes, not excepting the ſight and hearing. Without doubt we ſhould read "Unto our general "ſenſe," meaning the *touch* or *feeling*, which not being confined to one part, like the reſt of the ſenſes, but extended over the whole body, the poet, by a fine periphraſis, calls the *general ſenſe*. WARBURTON.

Senſes are nothing more than each *man's ſenſe*. Gentle ſenſe is very elegant, as it means *placid*, *calm*, *compoſed*, and intimates the peaceable delight of a fine day. JOHNSON.

There is no neceſſity for Dr. Warburton's alteration. As to Dr. Johnſon's explanation of the preſent reading, it is no way ſatisfactory. I read,

—— The air
Nimbly and ſweetly recommends itſelf:—
Gentle unto our ſenſe.

i. e. Soft, bland, pleaſing to the ſenſe. A. B.

Whoſe

Whoſe ranſoms did the general coffers fill:
Did this in Cæſar ſeem ambitious?
When that the poor have cry'd, Cæſar hath wept;
Ambition ſhould be made of ſterner ſtuff:
Yet Brutus ſays, he was ambitious;
And Brutus is an honourable man!

Julius Cæſar, A. 3, S. 2.

—— [1] 'Tis a common proof,
That lowlineſs is young ambition's ladder,
Whereto the climber upwards turns his face:
But when he once attains the upmoſt round,
He then unto the ladder turns his back;
Looks in the clouds, ſcorning the baſe degrees
By which he did aſcend. *Julius Cæſar*, A. 2. S. 1.

Ah! gracious lord, theſe days are dangerous!
Virtue is choak'd with foul ambition,
And charity chas'd hence by rancour's hand;
Foul ſubornation is predominant,
And equity exil'd your highneſs' land.

Henry VI. P. 2. A. 3, S. 1.

—— Fare thee well, great heart!
Ill weav'd ambition, how much art thou ſhrunk!
When that this body did contain a ſpirit,
A kingdom for it was too ſmall a bound;
But now, two paces of the vileſt earth
Is room enough. *Henry IV.* P. 1. A. 5, S. 4.

You all did ſee, that, on the lupercal,
I thrice preſented him a kingly crown,
Which he did thrice refuſe. Was this ambition?
Yet Brutus ſays, he was ambitious;
And, ſure he is an honourable man.
I ſpeak not to diſprove what Brutus ſpoke,
But here I am to ſpeak what I do know.

Julius Cæſar, A. 3, S. 2.

[1] *Common proof.*] Common experiment. JOHNSON.
Rather, continually *ſeen* or *found*. The ſubſtantive for the verb.
A. B.

—— Urge

—— Urge them, while their ſouls
Are capable of this ambition;
Leſt zeal, now melted, by the windy breath
Of ſoft petitions, pity, and remorſe,
Cool and congeal again to what it was.
King John, A. 2, S. 2.

—— Love, and meekneſs, lord,
Become a churchman better than ambition;
I could ſay more,
But reverence to your calling makes me modeſt.
Henry VIII. A. 5, S. 2.

Cromwell, I charge thee, fling away ambition;
By that ſin fell the angels, how can man then,
The image of his Maker, hope to win by't?
Love thyſelf laſt: cheriſh thoſe hearts that hate thee;
Corruption wins not more than honeſty.
Henry VIII. A. 3, S. 2.

AMITY.

Madam, although I ſpeak it in your preſence,
You have a noble and a true conceit
Of god-like amity. *Merchant of Venice, A.* 3, *S.* 4.

ANGER.

—— To climb ſteep hills,
Requires ſlow pace at firſt: Anger is like
A full-hot horſe; who being allow'd his way,
Self-mettle tires him. *Henry VIII.* A. 1, S. 1.

Anger's my meat; I ſup upon myſelf,
And ſo ſhall ſtarve with feeding—Come, let's go:
Leave this faint puling, and lament as I do,
In anger, Juno-like. *Coriolanus*, A. 4, S. 2.

—— It engenders choler, planteth anger;
And better 'twere, that both of us did faſt,—
Since, of ourſelves, ourſelves are cholerick,—

Than feed it with ſuch over-roaſted fleſh.
Taming of the Shrew, A. 4, S. 2.

—— Touch me with noble anger!
O, let not women's weapons, water-drops,
Stain my man's cheeks! *Lear*, A. 2, S. 4.

ANGLING.

The pleaſant'ſt angling is to ſee the fiſh
Cut with her golden oars the ſilver ſtream,
And greedily devour the treacherous bait.
Much ado about nothing, A. 3, S. 1.

ANSWER.

The anſwer is as ready as a borrow'd cap[1].
Henry IV. P. 2, A. 2, S. 2.

APPLAUSE.

O, thou fond many! with what loud applauſe
Did'ſt thou beat heaven with bleſſing Bolingbroke,
Before he was what thou would'ſt have him be!
And being now trimm'd in thine own deſires,
Thou beaſtly feeder, art ſo full of him,
That thou provok'ſt thyſelf to caſt him up.
Henry IV. P. 2, A. 1, S. 3.

[1] *The anſwer is as ready as a borrow'd cap.*] But how is a borrow'd cap ſo ready? read a *borrower's cap*, and then there is ſome humour in it; for a man that goes to borrow money is of all others the moſt complaiſant; his cap is always at hand. WARBURTON.

Perhaps the old reading, *a borrow'd cap*, might be right. Falſtaff's followers, when they ſtole any thing, called it a *purchaſe*. A *borrowed cap* might be a *ſtolen* one; which is ſufficiently ready, being, as Falſtaff ſays, *to be found on every hedge*. MALONE.

Perhaps we ſhould read, *as ready as borrow'd crap*. *Crap*, in vulgar language, is *money*. The expreſſion is ſuch as may well be expected from Poins.

The meaning will be, that borrowed money, as it is eaſily gotten, ſo it is frequently ſquandered with little thought; or, according to the proverb, "lightly come, lightly go." A. B.

—— No

—— No man is the lord of any thing,
(Though in and of him there is much consisting)
Till he communicate his parts to others:
Nor doth he of himself know them for aught,
Till he behold them form'd in the applause
Where they are extended.
Troilus and Cressida, A. 3, S. 3

ARROW.

I go, I go; look, how I go;
Swifter than arrow from the Tartar's bow.
Midsummer Night's Dream, A. 3, S. 2.

In my school days, when I had lost one shaft,
I shot his fellow of the self-same flight
The self-same way, with more advised watch,
To find the other forth; and by advent'ring both,
I oft found both. *Merchant of Venice*, A. 1. S. 1.

That which I owe is lost: but if you please
To shoot another arrow that self way
Which you did shoot the first, I do not doubt,
As I will watch the aim, or to find both,
Or bring your latter hazard back again.
Merchant of Venice, A. 1, S. 1.

ART.

—— Graves, at my command,
Have wak'd their sleepers; op'd and let them forth
By my so potent art. *Tempest*, A. 5, S. 1.

—— I must
Bestow upon the eyes of this young couple
Some vanity of mine art *Tempest*, A. 4, S. 1.

I would I had bestow'd that time in the tongues, that I have in fencing, dancing, and bear-bating; O, had I but followed the arts!
Twelfth Night, A. 1. S. 3.

Navarre

Navarre ſhall be the wonder of the world;
Our court ſhall be a little academe,
Still and contemplative in living art.
Love's Labour Loſt, A. 1, S. 1.

ATTEMPT.

The quality and hair of our attempt [1]
Brooks no diviſion. *Henry IV.* P. 1, A. 4, S. 1.

AUTHORITY.

——— So pleaſe thee to return with us,
And of our Athens (thine and ours) to take
The captainſhip, thou ſhalt be met with thanks,
Allow'd with abſolute power [2], and thy good name
Live with authority. *Timon of Athens*, A. 5, S. 2.

I muſt be patient; there is no fettering of authority. I'll beat him, by my life, if I can meet him

[1] *The quality and hair of our attempt.*] The *hair* ſeems to be the *complexion*, the *character*. The metaphor appears harſh to us, but perhaps was familiar in our author's time. We ſtill ſay ſomething is *againſt the hair*, or *againſt the grain*, that is, againſt the natural tendency. JOHNSON.

I am not ſatisfied with this interpretation, and therefore read,
"The quality and *aire* of our attempt."
An *aire*, or *airy*, is the neſt of a bird of prey: which neſts are always built on the tops of the loftieſt trees. The ſenſe of the paſſage is,—our attempt being great and *towering*, &c. A. B.

[2] *Allow'd with abſolute power.*] This is neither Engliſh nor ſenſe. We ſhould read,
"Hallow'd with abſolute power."
i. e. thy power ſhall be held *ſacred*. For abſolute power being an attribute of the gods, the ancients thought that he, who held it in ſociety, was become ſacred, and his perſon inviolable. On this account the Romans called the tribunitial power of the Emperors, *ſacroſancta poteſtas*. WARBURTON.

Allowed is *licenſed*, *privileged*, *uncontrolled*. So of a buffoon, in Love's Labour Loſt, it is ſaid, that he is *allowed*, that is, at liberty to ſay what he will, a privileged ſcoffer. JOHNSON.

"Allow'd with abſolute power," is, *abſolute power ſhall be allowed or granted thee.* What can poſſibly be clearer? A. B.

with any convenience, an he were double and double a lord. *All's well that ends well*, A. 2, S. 3.

——— My authority bears a credent bulk,
That no particular ſcandal once can touch,
But it confounds the breather.
Meaſure for Meaſure, A. 4, S. 4.

——— Authority, though it err like others,
Hath yet a kind of medicine in itſelf,
That ſkins the vice o' the top.
Meaſure for Meaſure, A. 2, S. 2.

B.

BABES.

AS looks the mother on her lovely babe,
When death doth cloſe his tender dying eyes,
See, ſee, the pining malady of France;
Behold the wounds, the moſt unnatural wounds,
Which thou thyſelf haſt given her woful breaſt!
Henry VI. P. 1, A. 3, S. 3.

Is this the ſcourge of France?
Is this the Talbot, ſo much fear'd abroad,
That with his name the mothers ſtill their babes?
Henry VI. P. 1, A. 2, S. 3.

—— In thy ſight to die, what were it elſe,
But like a pleaſant ſlumber in thy lap?
Here could I breathe my ſoul into the air,
As mild and gentle as the cradle babe,
Dying with mother's dug between its lips.
Henry VI. P. 2, A. 3, S. 2.

——— Spare not the babe,
Whoſe dimpled ſmiles from fools exhauſt their mercy;
Think it a baſtard, whom the oracle

Hath

Hath doubtfully pronounc'd thy throat ſhall cut,
And mince it ſans remorſe. *Timon*, A. 4, S. 3.

Ah, my poor princes! ah, my tender babes!
My unblown flowers, new-appearing ſweets!
If yet your gentle ſouls fly in the air,
Hover about me with your airy wings.
Richard III. A. 4, S. 4.

Thus lay the gentle babes, girdling each other
Within their alabaſter innocent arms:
Their lips were four red roſes on a ſtalk,
Which, in their ſummer beauty, kiſs'd each other,
The moſt repleniſhed ſweet work of nature,
That, from the prime creation, e'er ſhe fram'd.
Richard III. A. 4, S. 3.

BACCHUS.

Come thou monarch of the vine,
Plumpy Bacchus, with pink eyne.[1]
Antony and Cleopatra, A, 2, S. 7.

BACHELOR.

When I ſaid I would die a bachelor, I did not think I ſhould live till I were marry'd.
Much ado about nothing, A. 2, S. 3.

Shall I never ſee a bachelor of threeſcore again? Go to, i' faith; an thou wilt needs thruſt thy neck into a yoke, wear the print of it, and ſigh away Sundays. *Much ado about nothing*, A. 1, S. 1.

[1] ——— *with pink eyne.*] Dr. Johnſon, in his Dictionary, ſays a *pink eye* is a ſmall eye, and quotes this paſſage for his authority. *Pink eyne*, however, may be *red eyes*. Eyes inflamed with drinking are very well appropriated to Bacchus. STEEVENS.

"*Pink eyne*," in this place, I believe, are neither *ſmall eyes* nor *red eyes*, but *twinkling* eyes; and ſuch as are uſually obſerved in drunken perſons. *To pink*, is to wink with the eyes. "He is "quite *pinky*," for "he is quite *fuddled*," is now made uſe of in ordinary converſation. A. B.

—— [1] Thy broom groves,
Whose shadow the dismissed bachelor loves.
Tempest, A. 4, S. 1.

BANISHMENT.

When thou dost hear I am as I have been,
Approach me: and thou shalt be as thou wast,
The tutor and the feeder of my riots:
'Till then I banish thee. *Henry IV.* P. 2, A. 5, S. 5.
—— Ha! banishment?
It comes not ill; I hate not to be banish'd;
It is a cause worthy my spleen and fury,
That I may strike at Athens. I'll cheer up
My discontented troops, and lay for hearts.
Timon of Athens, A. 3, S. 5.

BANKRUPT.

Sweep on, you fat and greasy citizens;
'Tis just the fashion: wherefore do you look
Upon that poor and broken bankrupt there?
As you like it, A. 2, S. 1.

BARBARISM.

Whereupon the Grecians begin to proclaim barbarism [2], and policy grows into an ill opinion.
Troilus and Cressida, A. 5, S. 4.

BASE-

[1] —— *and thy broom groves.*] A grove of *broom*, I believe, was never heard of, as it is a low shrub, and not a tree. Hanmer reads *brown* groves. STEEVENS.

Broom is here used adjectively, I believe, for *thick*, *close*. The broom shrub is remarkably close knit, and almost impervious. A. B.

[2] —— *to proclaim barbarism.*] To set up the authority of ignorance, to declare that they will be governed by policy no longer. JOHNSON.

To *proclaim*, means in this place, I think, to *shew*, and not to

BASENESS.

——— Thou art not noble;
For all the accommodations, that thou bear'ſt,
Are nurs'd by baſeneſs. *Meaſ. for Meaſ.* A. 3, S. 1.

BASILISK.

Yet do not go away;—Come, baſiliſk,
And kill the innocent gazer with thy ſight;
For in the ſhade of death I ſhall find joy;
In life, but double death, now Gloſter's dead.
Henry VI. P. 2, A. 3, S. 2.

Make me not ſighted like the baſiliſk:
I have look'd on thouſands, who have ſped the better
By my regard, but kill'd none ſo.
Winter's Tale, A. 1, S. 2.

BATTLE.

Liſt his diſcourſe of war, and you ſhall hear
A fearful battle render'd you in muſic:
Turn him to any cauſe of policy,
The gordian knot of it he will unlooſe,
Familiar as his garter. *Henry V.* A. 1, S. 1.

—— I call you ſervile miniſters,
That have with two pernicious daughters join'd
Your high engender'd battles, 'gainſt a head
So old and white as this. *Lear*, A. 3, S. 2.

Never did captive with a freer heart
Caſt off his chains of bondage, and embrace
His golden uncontrol'd enfranchiſement,
More than my dancing ſoul doth celebrate
This feaſt of battle with mine adverſary.
Richard II. A. 1, S. 3.

to *declare. The Greeks, by their actions, ſeem degenerating into barbariſm—They ſhew an inclination to barbariſm.* This, I believe, is the meaning, and not, as Dr. Johnſon ſuppoſes, that they openly declare they will not any longer be governed by policy. A. B.

Little of this great world can I ſpeak,
More than pertains to feats of broil and battle;
And therefore little ſhall I grace my cauſe,
In ſpeaking for myſelf. *Othello*, A. 1, S. 3.

—— Of no right, nor colour like to right,
He doth fill fields with harneſs in the realm;
Turns head againſt the lion's armed jaws;
And being no more in debt to years than thou,
Leads ancient lords and reverend biſhops on,
To bloody battles, and to bruiſing arms.
Henry IV. P. 1, A. 3, S. 2.

The noiſe of battle hurtled in the air,
Horſes did neigh, and dying men did groan;
And ghoſts did ſhriek, and ſqueal about the ſtreets.
O Cæſar! theſe things are beyond all uſe,
And I do fear them. *Julius Cæſar*, A. 2, S. 2.

'Tis poſitive 'gainſt all exception, lords,
That our ſuperfluous lacqueys, and our peaſants,
Who, in unneceſſary action, ſwarm
About our ſquares of battle,—were enough
To purge this field of ſuch a hilding foe.
Henry V. A. 4, S. 2.

—— Their executors the knaviſh crows,
Fly o'er them all, impatient for their hour.
Deſcription cannot ſuit itſelf in words,
To demonſtrate the life of ſuch a battle
In life ſo lifeleſs as it ſhews itſelf.
Henry V. A. 4, S. 2.

BAWCOCK.

Why, that's my bawcock [1].
Winter's Tale, A. 1, S. 2.

BEAUTY.

[1] *Why, that's my bawcock.*] Perhaps from *beau* and *coq*. It is ſtill ſaid, in vulgar language, that ſuch a one is a *jolly cock*, a *cock of the game*. STEEVENS.

Mr.

BEAUTY.

——— Look on beauty,
And you ſhall ſee 'tis purchas'd by the weight;
Which therein works a miracle in nature,
Making them lighteſt that wear moſt of it.
Merchant of Venice, A. 3, S. 2.

Beauty provoketh thieves ſooner than gold.
As you like it, *A.* 1, S. 3.

——— My beauty, though but mean,
Needs not the painted flouriſh of your praiſe;
Beauty is bought by judgment of the eye,
Nor utter'd by baſe ſale of chapmen's tongues.
Love's Labour Loſt, A. 2, S. 1.

As plays the ſun upon the glaſſy ſtreams,
Twinkling another counterfeited beam,
So ſeems this gorgeous beauty to mine eyes.
Fain would I woo her, yet I dare not ſpeak.
Henry VI. P. 1, A. 5, S. 4.

Oh faireſt beauty, do not fear, nor fly;
For I will touch thee but with reverent hands.
I kiſs theſe fingers for eternal peace,
And lay them gently on thy tender ſide.
Henry VI. P. 1, A. 5, S. 4.

'Tis beauty that doth oft make women proud;
But, God he knows, thy ſhare thereof is ſmall:
'Tis virtue, that doth make them moſt admir'd;
The contrary doth make thee wonder'd at.
Henry VI. P. 3, A. 1, S. 4.

She will not ſtay the ſiege of loving terms,
Nor bide the encounter of aſſailing eyes,
Nor ope her lap to ſaint-ſeducing gold:

Mr. Steevens is right, I believe, in ſaying that "bawcock" comes from *beau* and *coq*; but it can hardly be ſuppoſed that Leontes, a king, ſhould call his ſon a *jolly cock*, or a *cock of the game*.
"That's my bawcock," *i. e.* that's my fine fellow.
The Scots ſay, "Bra Cock." *Bra* is contracted of *brave*. A. B.

O, ſhe is rich in beauty!
Romeo and Juliet, A. 1, S. 1.

——— He loſt a wife,
Whoſe beauty did aſtoniſh the ſurvey
Of richeſt eyes; whoſe words all ears took captive;
Whoſe dear perfection, hearts that ſcorn'd to ſerve,
Humbly call'd miſtreſs.
All's well that ends well, A. 5, S. 3.

Your beauty was the cauſe of that effect;
Your beauty which did haunt me in my ſleep,
To undertake the death of all the world,
So I might live one hour in your ſweet boſom.
Richard III. A. 1, S. 2.

I never ſu'd to friend, nor enemy;
My tongue could never learn ſweet ſoothing word;
But now thy beauty is propos'd my fee,
My proud heart ſues, and prompts my tongue to ſpeak.
Richard III. A. 1, S. 2.

You nimble lightnings, dart your blinding flames
Into her ſcornful eyes! Infect her beauty,
You fen-ſuck'd fogs, drawn by the powerful ſun,
To fall and blaſt her pride! *Lear*, A. 2, S. 4.

My lord and maſter loves you; O, ſuch love
Could be but recompens'd, though you were crown'd
The nonpareil of beauty! *Twelfth Night*, A. 1, S. 5.

'Tis beauty truly blent, whoſe red and white
Nature's own ſweet and cunning hand laid on.
Twelfth Night, A. 1, S. 5.

O, ſhe doth teach the torches to burn bright!
Her beauty hangs upon the cheek of night,
Like a rich jewel in an Æthiope's ear;
Beauty too rich for uſe, for earth too dear!
Romeo and Juliet, A. 1, S. 5.

——— Black maſks
Proclaim an enſhield beauty ten times louder

Than

Than beauty could difplay'd.

Meafure for Meafure, A. 2, S. 4.

The hand that hath made you fair, hath made you good: the goodnefs, that is cheap in beauty, makes beauty brief in goodnefs; but grace, being the foul of your complexion, fhould keep the body of it ever fair. *Meafure for Meafure*, A. 3, S. 1.

—— Beauty is a witch,
Againft whofe charms faith melteth into blood.

Much ado about nothing, A. 2, S. 1.

BEGGAR.

I fee, Sir, you are liberal in offers:
You taught me firft to beg; and now, methinks,
You teach me how a beggar fhould be anfwer'd.

Merchant of Venice, A. 4, S. 1.

BLOOD.

O, what authority and fhew of truth
Can cunning fin cover itfelf withal!
Comes not that blood, as modeft evidence,
To witnefs fimple virtue?

Much ado about nothing, A. 4, S. 1.

Wifdom and blood combating in fo tender a body, we have ten proofs to one, that blood hath the victory. *Much ado about nothing*, A. 2, S. 3.

—— Why, how now, gentlemen?
What fee you in thofe papers, that you lofe
So much complexion? look ye, how they change!
Their cheeks are paper.—Why, what read you there,
That hath fo cowarded and chas'd your blood
Out of appearance? *Henry V.* A. 2, S. 2.

—— He, to day that fheds his blood with me,
Shall be my brother; be he ne'er fo vile,
This day fhall gentle his condition;
And gentlemen in England, now a bed,

Shall

Shall think themſelves accurs'd, they were not here.
Henry V. A. 4, S. 3.

——— Tell him, we will come on,
Though France himſelf, and ſuch another neighbour
Stand in our way. If we be hinder'd,
We ſhall your tawny ground with your red blood
Diſcolour. *Henry V.* A. 3, S. 6.

—— Thoſe that could ſpeak low, and tardily,
Would turn their own perfection to abuſe,
To ſeem like him: ſo that, in ſpeech, in gait,
In diet, in affections of delight,
In military rules, humours of blood,
He was the mark and glaſs, copy and book,
That faſhion'd others. *Henry IV.* P. 2, A. 2, S. 3.

Prince Harry is valiant: the cold blood he did naturally inherit of his father, he hath, like lean, ſteril, and bare land, manured, huſbanded, and tilled, with excellent endeavour of drinking good, and good ſtore of fertile ſherris, that he is become very hot, and valiant. If I had a thouſand ſons, the firſt human principle I would teach them, ſhould be,—to forſwear thin potations, and to addict themſelves to ſack. *Henry IV.* P. 2, A. 4, S. 3.

——— The tide of blood in me
Hath proudly flow'd in vanity, till now:
Now doth it turn, and ebb back to the ſea;
Where it ſhall mingle with the ſtate of floods,
And flow henceforth in formal majeſty.
Henry IV. P. 2, A. 5, S. 2.

O, pardon me, thou bleeding piece of earth,
That I am meek and gentle with theſe butchers!
Thou art the ruins of the nobleſt man,
That ever lived in the tide of times.
Woe to the hand that ſhed this coſtly blood!
Julius Cæſar, A. 3, S. 1.

I know not, gentlemen, what you intend,

Who

Who elſe muſt be let blood, who elſe is rank:
If I myſelf, there is no hour ſo fit
As Cæſar's death's hour, nor no inſtrument
Of half that worth, as thoſe your ſwords, made rich
With the moſt noble blood of all this world.

Julius Cæſar, A. 3, S. 1.

Had I as many eyes as thou haſt wounds,
Weeping as faſt as they ſtream forth thy blood,
It would become me better than to cloſe
In terms of friendſhip with thine enemies.
Pardon me, Julius! *Julius Cæſar*, A. 3, S. 1.

[1] She dreamt to-night ſhe ſaw my ſtatue,
Which, like a fountain, with a hundred ſpouts,
Did run pure blood; and many luſty Romans
Came ſmiling, and did bathe their hands in it.
And theſe does ſhe apply for warnings, and portents
And evils imminent. *Julius Cæſar*, A. 2, S. 2.

I will fetch thy rim out at thy throat,
In drops of crimſon blood[2]. *Henry V*. A. 4, S. 4.

—— Be

[1] *She dreamt to-night ſhe ſaw my ſtatue.*] The defect of the metre in this line, and a redundant ſyllable in another a little lower, ſhow, that this paſſage, like many others, has ſuffered by the careleſſneſs of the tranſcriber. It ought, perhaps, to be regulated thus:

She dreamt to-night ſhe ſaw my ſtatue, which,
Like a fountain with a hundred ſpouts, did run
Pure blood; and many luſty Romans came
Smiling, and did bathe their hands in't; and theſe
Does ſhe apply for warnings, and portents
Of evils imminent. MALONE.

It will read better thus:—

She dreamt to-night ſhe ſaw my ſtatue, which,
Like to a fountain with a hundred ſpouts,
Did run pure blood; and many luſty Romans
Came ſmiling, and did bathe their hands in it.
Theſe ſhe applies for warnings, and portents
Of evils imminent. A. B.

[2] For, *I will fetch thy rym out at thy throat,*
In drops of crimſon blood.] We ſhould read,

I will

—— Be not fond,
To think that Cæſar bears ſuch rebel blood,
That will be thaw'd from the true quality
With that which melteth fools; I mean, ſweet words,
Low crooked curtſies, and baſe ſpaniel fawning.
Julius Cæſar, A. 3, S. 1.

—— Age, thou art aſham'd:
Rome, thou haſt loſt the breed of noble bloods!
When went there by an age, ſince the great flood,
But it was fam'd with more than with one man?
When could they ſay, 'till now, that talk'd of Rome,
That her wide walls incompaſs'd but one man?
Julius Cæſar, A. 1, S. 2.

I can raiſe no money by vile means:
By heaven, I had rather coin my heart,
And drop my blood for drachmas, than to wring
From the hard hands of peaſants their vile traſh,
By any indirection. *Julius Cæſar*, A. 4, S. 3.

Here's a parchment, with the ſeal of Cæſar,

I will fetch thy ranſom out of thy throat.
WARBURTON.

I know not what to do with *rym*. The meaſure gives reaſon to ſuppoſe that it ſtands for ſome monoſyllable, and beſide, *ranſom* is a word not likely to have been corrupted. JOHNSON.

It appears from Sir A. Gorges' tranſlation of Lucan, that ſome part of the inteſtines was anciently called the *rimme*.

" The ſlender rimme, too weak to part
" The boyling liver from the heart."
—— *parvuſque ſecat vitalia limes.* L. 623.

I believe it is now called the *diaphragm* in human creatures, and the ſkirt, or midriff, in beaſts. STEEVENS.

In the paſſage quoted from Gorges' tranſlation of Lucan, *rimme* has certainly the ſame meaning as the Latin word *limes*; and may ſtand for the diaphragm, or that membrane which divides the upper cavity of the body from the lower. But the *rym* is properly the peritoneum, or caul, which covers the bowels.

Piſtol's expreſſion ſeems equivalent to the one now uſed. " I " will not be ſo eaſily ſatisfied—I will have your *heart's blood*." Such, I believe, is the meaning. A. B.

I found

I found it in his closet, 'tis his will:
Let but the commons hear this testament,
(Which, pardon me, I do not mean to read)
And they would go and kiss dead Cæsar's wounds,
And dip their napkins in his sacred blood!

Julius Cæsar, A. 3, S. 2.

Look! in this place, ran Cassius' dagger through:
See, what a rent the envious Casca made:
Through this, the well-beloved Brutus stabb'd;
And, as he pluck'd his cursed steel away,
Mark how the blood of Cæsar follow'd it.

Julius Cæsar, A. 3, S. 2.

I have neither wit, nor words, nor worth,
Action, nor utterance, nor the power of speech,
To stir men's blood: I only speak right on;
I tell you what, which you yourselves do know;
Shew you sweet Cæsar's wounds, poor, poor, dumb mouths!
And bid them speak for me.

Julius Cæsar, A. 3, S. 2.

Why should a man, whose blood is warm within,
Sit like his grandsire cut in alabaster?
Sleep when he wakes? and creep into the jaundice
By beeing peevish? *Merchant of Venice*, A. 1, S. 1.

The brain may devise laws for the blood; but a hot temper leaps o'er a cold decree.

Merchant of Venice, A. 1, S. 2.

Madam, you have bereft me of all words,
Only my blood speaks to you in my veins.

Merchant of Venice, A. 3, S. 2.

—— Lord Angelo is precise;
Stands at a guard with envy; scarce confesses
That his blood flows, or that his appetite
Is more to bread than stone.

Measure for Measure, A. 1, S. 4.

—— A man

——— A man whose blood
Is very snow-broth. *Meas. for Meas.* A. 1, S. 5.

Why does my blood thus muster to my heart,
Making both it unable for itself,
And dispossessing all my other parts
Of necessary fitness? *Meas. for Meas.* A. 2, S. 4.

——— Joan of Arc hath been
A virgin from her tender infancy,
Chaste and immaculate in every thought;
Whose maiden blood, thus rigorously effus'd,
Will cry for vengeance at the gates of heaven.
Henry VI. P. 1, A. 5, S. 5.

——— King Henry's blood,
The honourable blood of Lancaster,
Must not be shed by such a jaded groom [1].
Henry IV. P. 2, A. 4, S. 1.

Though now this grained face of mine be hid
In sap-consuming winter's drizzled snow,
And all the conduits of my blood froze up;
Yet hath my night of life some memory,
My wasting lamps some fading glimmer left.
Comedy of Errors, A. 5, S. 1.

What, will the aspiring blood of Lancaster
Sink in the ground? I thought it would have mounted.
See, how my sword weeps for the poor king's death:
O, may such purple tears be always shed
From those that wish the downfal of our house!
Henry VI. P. 3, A. 5, S. 6.

The wrinkles on my brows, now fill'd with blood,
Were liken'd oft to kingly sepulchres;

[1] *Such a jaded groom.*] This epithet appears to me so strange, that I suspect some corruption. The quarto reads either *lady* groom, or *jady* groom, it is difficult to say which. MALONE.

"Jady groom" is the right reading (*jadis*, Fr.) "heretofore." The sense of the passage is—Thou who wert heretofore a groom, and held my stirrup. A. B.

For who liv'd king but I could dig his grave?
And who durst smile, when Warwick bent his brow?
Henry VI. P. 3, A. 5, S. 2.

——— His sword (death's stamp)
Where it did mark, it took; from face to foot
He was a thing of blood, whose every motion
Was tim'd with dying cries [1]. *Coriolanus*, A. 2, S. 2.

——— The breasts of Hecuba,
When she did suckle Hector, look'd not lovelier
Than Hector's forehead, when it spit forth blood
At Grecian swords contending. *Coriolanus*, A. 1, S. 3.

He was not taken well; he had not din'd:
The veins unfill'd, our blood is cold, and then
We pout upon the morning, are unapt
To give or to forgive; but when we have stuff'd
These pipes, and these conveyances of our blood
With wine and feeding, we have suppler souls
Than in our priest-like fasts. *Coriolanus*, A. 5, S. 1.

——— Succeed thy father
In manners, as in shape! thy blood, and virtue,
Contend for empire in thee; and thy goodness
Share with thy birth-right!
All's well that ends well, A. 1, S. 1.

See, his face is black, and full of blood;
His eye-balls further out than when he liv'd,
Staring full ghastly like a strangled man:
His hair up-rear'd, his nostrils stretch'd with strug-
gling,
His hands abroad display'd, as one that grasp'd

[1] ——— *every motion*
Was tim'd with dying cries.] The cries of the slaughtered regularly followed his motions, as music and a dancer accompany each other. JOHNSON.

There is no necessity for this ludicrous explanation. The sense is easy. Wherever he shewed himself the cries of dying men were heard. A. B.

And

And tugg'd for life, and was by ſtrength ſubdu'd.
Henry VI. P. 2, A. 3, S. 2.

Poor honeſt lord, brought low by his own heart,
Undone by goodneſs! Strange, unuſual blood,
When man's worſt ſin is, he does too much good
Timon of Athens, A. 4, S. 2.

Pale aſhes of the houſe of Lancaſter!
Thou bloodleſs remnant of that royal blood!
Be it lawful that I invocate thy ghoſt,
To hear the lamentations of poor Anne,
Wife to thy Edward, to thy ſlaughter'd ſon.
Richard III. A. 1, S. 2.

Curſed the blood, that let this blood from hence!
More direful hap betide that hated wretch,
That makes us wretched by the death of thee,
Than I can wiſh to adders, ſpiders, toads,
Or any creeping venom'd thing that lives!
Richard III. A. 1, S. 2.

Murder her brothers, and then marry her!
Uncertain way of gain! but I am in
So far in blood, that ſin will pluck on ſin;
Tear-falling pity dwells not in this eye.
Richard III. A. 4, S. 2.

——— I'll empty all theſe veins,
And ſhed my dear blood drop by drop i' the duſt,
But I will lift the down-trod Mortimer
As high i' the air as this unthankful king,
As this ingrate and canker'd Bolingbroke.
Henry IV. P. 1, A. 1, S. 3.

——— She bids you
Upon the wanton ruſhes lay you down,
And reſt your gentle head upon her lap,
And ſhe will ſing the ſong that pleaſeth you,
And on your eye-lids crown the god of ſleep,
Charming your blood with pleaſing heavineſs.
Henry IV. P. 1, A. 3, S. 1.

He

He presently,—as greatneſs knows itſelf—
Steps me a little higher than his vow
Made to my father, while his blood was poor,
And now, forſooth, takes on him to reform
Some certain edicts, and ſome ſtrait decrees,
That lie too heavy on the commonwealth.
Henry IV. P. 1, A. 4, S. 3.

By all the operations of the orbs,
From whom we do exiſt, and ceaſe to be;
Here I diſclaim all my paternal care,
Propinquity and property of blood,
And as a ſtranger to my heart and me
Hold thee, from this, for ever. *Lear*, A. 1, S. 1.

For Andrew, if he were opened, and you find ſo much blood in his liver as will clog the foot of a flea, I'll eat the reſt of the anatomy.
Twelfth Night, A. 3, S. 2.

Here is your huſband, like a mildew'd ear,
Blaſting his wholeſome brother. Have you eyes?
Could you on this fair mountain leave to feed,
And batten on this moor? Ha! have you eyes?
You cannot call it love: for, at your age,
The hey-day in the blood is tame, 'tis humble,
And waits upon the judgment; and what judgment
Would ſtep from this to this? *Hamlet*, A. 3, S. 4.

For Hamlet, and the trifling of his favour,
Hold it a faſhion, and a toy in blood;
A violet in the youth of primy nature,
Forward, not permanent, ſweet, not laſting,
The perfume and ſuppliance of a minute.
Hamlet, A. 1, S. 3.

——— What if this curſed hand
Were thicker than itſelf with brother's blood?
Is there not rain enough in the ſweet heavens,
To waſh it white as ſnow? *Hamlet*, A. 3, S. 3.

D ——Can

——— Can ſodden water,
[1] A drench for ſur-reyn'd jades, their barley broth,
Decoct their cold blood to ſuch valiant heat?
Henry V. A. 3, S. 5.

BODY.

——— This common body,
Like to a vagabond flag upon the ſtream,
Goes to, and back, lackying the varying tide,
To rot itſelf with motion.
Antony and Cleopatra, A. 1, S. 4.

——— The publick body,—which doth ſeldom
Play the recanter,—feeling in itſelf
A lack of Timon's aid, hath ſenſe withal
Of its own fall, reſtraining aid to Timon [2];
And ſends forth us to make their ſorrow'd render.
Timon, A. 5, S. 2.

I once did lend my body for his wealth [3].
Merchant of Venice, A. 5, S. 1.

[1] *A drench for ſur-reyn'd jades.*] The exact meaning of *ſur-reyn'd* I do not know. It is common to give horſes over-ridden, or feveriſh, ground malt and hot water mixed, which is called a *maſh*. To this he alludes. JOHNSON.

"Sur-reyn'd" is *old*, *worn-out*. The French word *ſurannè* Anglicised, and then corrupted. It ſhould be printed *ſuran'd*. A. B.

[2] ——— *reſtraining aid to Timon.*] I think it ſhould be *refraining aid*, that is, with-holding aid that ſhould have been given to Timon. JOHNSON.

I believe we ſhould read the paſſage thus:

——— feeling in itſelf
A lack of Timon's aid: *and* ſenſe withal,
Of its own fall---reſtraining aid *for* Timon,
Now ſends us forth, &c.

Reſtraining ſeems to be uſed in the ſenſe of *keeping*, *reſerving*. A. B.

[3] ——— *for his wealth.*] For his advantage; to obtain his happineſs. JOHNSON.

It would perhaps be better to read "for his health," *i. e.* for his *good*, for his *welfare*. A. B.

BOND.

BOND.

If every ducat in ſix thouſand ducats
Were in ſix parts, and every part a ducat,
I would not draw them, I would have my bond.

Merchant of Venice, A. 4, S. 1.

Till thou can'ſt rail the ſeal from off my bond,
Thou but offend'ſt thy lungs to ſpeak ſo loud:
Repair thy wit, good youth, or it will fall
To cureleſs ruin. *Merchant of Venice*, A. 4, S. 1.

I'll have my bond; I will not hear thee ſpeak:
I'll have my bond; and therefore ſpeak no more.
I'll not be made a ſoft and dull-ey'd fool,
To ſhake the head, relent, and ſigh, and yield
To Chriſtian interceſſors.

Merchant of Venice, A. 3, S. 3.

—— Speak not againſt my bond;
I have ſworn an oath, that I will have my bond:
Thou call'dſt me dog, before thou hadſt a cauſe;
But, ſince I am a dog, beware my fangs.

Merchant of Venice, A. 3, S. 3.

—— By our holy ſabbath have I ſworn,
To have the due and forfeit of my bond:
If you deny it, let the danger light
Upon your charter, and your city's freedom.

Merchant of Venice, A. 4, S. 1.

A bankrupt, a prodigal, who dare ſcarce ſhow his head on the Rialto;—a beggar that uſed to come ſo ſmug upon the mart; let him look to his bond: he was wont to call me uſurer; let him look to his bond: he was wont to lend money for a Chriſtian courteſy;—let him look to his bond.

Merchant of Venice, A. 3, S. 1.

BOSOM.

—— I have truſted thee,
And prieſt-like, thou

Haſt cleans'd my boſom; I from thee departed
Thy penitent reform'd. *Winter's Tale*, A. 1, S. 2.

But, howſoever thou purſu'ſt this act,
Taint not thy mind, nor let thy ſoul contrive
Againſt thy mother aught; leave her to heaven,
And to thoſe thorns that in her boſom lodge,
To prick and ſting her. *Hamlet*, A. 1, S. 5.

Time was, I did him a deſired office,
Dear almoſt as his life; which gratitude
Through flinty Tartar's boſom would peep forth,
And anſwer thanks.
All's well that ends well, A. 4, S. 4.

BOUNTY.

Evermore thanks, the exchequer of the poor;
Which, till my infant fortune comes to years,
Stands for my bounty. *Richard II.* A. 2, S. 3.

—— For his bounty,
There was no winter in't; an autumn 'twas,
That grew the more by reaping: his delights
Were dolphin-like; they ſhew'd his back above
The element they liv'd in: in his livery
Walk'd crowns, and crownets.
Antony and Cleopatra, A. 5, S. 2.

—— Tell me, my daughters,
(Since now we will diveſt us, both of rule,
Intereſt of territory, cares of ſtate),
Which of you, ſhall we ſay, doth love us moſt?
That we our largeſt bounty may extend
Where nature doth with merit challenge [1].
Lear, A. 1, S. 1.

[1] *Where nature doth with merit challenge.*] Where the claim of *merit* is ſuperadded to that of *nature*, or where a ſuperior degree of natural affection is joined to the claim of other merits. STEEVENS.

"Challenge," in this place, ſeems to be *rivalry, competition*. "Where nature doth with merit challenge"---*where* nature and merit are contending for ſuperiority. A. B.

—— I thank

——I thank thee, king,
For thy great bounty, that not only giv'ſt
Me cauſe to wail, but teacheſt me the way
How to lament the cauſe. *Richard II.* A. 4, S. 1.

Uſe every man after his deſert, and who ſhall 'ſcape whipping? Uſe them after your own honour and dignity: the leſs they deſerve, the more merit is in your bounty. *Hamlet*, A. 2, S. 2.

——I preſume,
That, as my hand has open'd bounty to you,
My heart dropp'd love, my power rain'd honour more
On you, than any; ſo your hand, and heart,
Your brain, and every function of your power,
Should, notwithſtanding that your bond of duty,
As 'twere in love's particular, be more
To me, your friend, than any.
Henry VIII. A. 3, S. 2.

BOURN.

From the dread ſummit of this chalky bourn[1]:
Look up a height;—the ſhrill gorg'd lark ſo far
Cannot be ſeen or heard: do but look up.
Lear, A. 4, S. 6.

[1] *Chalky bourn.*] *Bourn* ſeems here to ſignify a *hill.* Its common ſignification is a *brook.* Milton, in Comus, uſes *boſky bourn*, in the ſame ſenſe, perhaps, with Shakeſpeare. But in both authors it may mean only a boundary. JOHNSON.

"Chalky bourn"---we ſhould read "*borne*," a *boundary*, to diſtinguiſh it from *bourn*, a *brook* or *river*. *Bourn*, as Dr. Johnſon obſerves, is in this place a *hill.*

Hills, it is well known, ſerve in ſeveral parts of the world as boundaries of particular countries, ſuch are the Alps, the Pyrenees, &c. &c. The term *borne*, therefore, which originally ſignified nothing more than *boundary*, was at length corruptedly employed to ſignify the hill itſelf---and thence "chalky borne," "boſky "borne," &c. A. B.

BOWELS.

I do retort the ſolus in thy bowels:
For I can take.[1] *Henry V.* A. 2, S. 1.

BOY.

There's nothing here that is too good for him,
But only ſhe; and ſhe deſerves a lord,
That twenty ſuch rude boys might tend upon,
And call her hourly, miſtreſs.
All's well that ends well, A. 3, S. 2.

—— I know them, yea,
And what they weigh, even to the utmoſt ſcruple:
Scambling, out-facing, faſhion-mong'ring boys.
Much ado about nothing, A. 5, S. 1.

Good faith, this ſame young ſober blooded boy doth not love me; nor a man cannot make him laugh;—but that's no marvel, he drinks no wine. There's never any of theſe demure boys come to any proof. *Henry IV.* P. 2, A. 4, S. 3.

—— Shall a beardleſs boy,
A cocker'd ſilken wanton brave our fields,
And fleſh his ſpirit in a warlike ſoil,
Mocking the air with colours idly ſpread,
And find no check? *King John*, A. 5, S. 1.

—— Hubert, throw thine eye
On yon young boy: I'll tell thee what, my friend,
He is a very ſerpent in my way;
And, whereſoe'er this foot of mine doth tread,
He lies before me. *King John*, A. 3, S. 3.

—— Father Cardinal, I have heard you ſay,

[1] *For I can take.*] I know not well what he can *take*. The quarto reads *talk*. In our author to *take* is ſometimes to *blaſt*, which ſenſe may ſerve in this place. JOHNSON.

"Take" is undoubtedly the true reading. The meaning is, I am not to be *bullied*, I am not to be affronted with impunity. A. B.

That

That we ſhall ſee and know our friends in heaven;
If that be true, I ſhall ſee my boy again.
King John, A. 3, S. 4.

—— Where is your darling Rutland?
Look, York; I ſtain'd this napkin with the blood
That valiant Clifford, with his rapier's point,
Made iſſue from the boſom of the boy:
And, if thine eyes can water for his death,
I give thee this to dry thy cheeks withal.
Henry VI. P. 3, A. 1, S. 4.

—— My mother bows;
As if Olympus to a mole-hill ſhould
In ſupplication nod: and my young boy
Hath an aſpect of interceſſion, which
Great nature cries, Deny not.
Coriolanus, A. 5, S. 3.

—— Why doſt not ſpeak?
Think'ſt thou it honourable for a noble man
Still to remember wrongs?—Daughter, ſpeak you;
He cares not for your weeping.—Speak thou, boy;
Perhaps, thy childiſhneſs will move him more
Than can our reaſons. *Coriolanus*, A. 5, S. 3.

We were, fair queen,
Two lads, that thought there was no more behind,
But ſuch a day to-morrow as to day,
And to be boy eternal. *Winter's Tale*, A. 1, S. 2.

That moſt ungrateful boy there, by your ſide,
From the rude ſea's enrag'd and foamy mouth
Did I redeem; a wreck paſt hope he was:
His life I gave him, and did thereto add
My love. *Twelfth Night*, A. 5. S. 1.

B R E A T H.

The deep-revolving witty Buckingham
No more ſhall be the neighbour to my counſels:

Hath he ſo long held out with me untir'd,
And ſtops he now for breath?

Richard III. A. 4, S. 2.

—— Hinge thy knee,
And let his very breath, whom thoul't obſerve,
Blow off thy cap; praiſe his moſt vicious ſtrain,
And call it excellent. *Timon*, A. 4, S. 3.

She ſpeaks poniards, and every word ſtabs: if her breath were as terrible as her terminations, there were no living near her, ſhe would infect to the North ſtar.

Much ado about nothing, A. 2, S. 1.

—— Here are ſever'd lips,
Parted with ſugar breath; ſo ſweet a bar
Should ſunder ſuch ſweet friends: here in her hairs
The painter plays the ſpider, and hath woven
A golden meſh to entrap the hearts of men,
Faſter than gnats in cobwebs.

Merchant of Venice, A. 3, S. 2.

—— Give him no breath, but now
Make boot of his diſtraction: never anger
Made good guard for itſelf.

Antony and Cleopatra, A. 4, S. 1.

—— Still, methinks,
There is an air comes from her; what fine chiſel
Could ever yet cut breath? Let no man mock me,
For I will kiſs her. *Winter's Tale*, A. 5, S. 3.

O balmy breath, that doſt almoſt perſuade
Juſtice herſelf to break her ſword! Once more.—
Be thus when thou art dead, and I will kill thee,
And love thee after. *Othello*, A. 5, S. 2.

A love that makes breath poor, and ſpeech unable;
Beyond all manner of ſo much I love you[1].

Lear, A. 1, S. 1.

BUSI-

[1] *Beyond all manner of ſo much.*] Beyond all aſſignable quantity.

BUSINESS.

—— But this ſwift buſineſs
I muſt uneaſy make, leſt too light winning
Make the prize light. *Tempeſt*, A. 1, S. 2.

This is no mortal buſineſs, nor no ſound
That the earth owes. *Tempeſt*, A. 1, S. 2.

I will ſeek him, ſir, preſently;[1] convey the buſineſs as I ſhall find means, and acquaint you withal.
Lear, A. 1, S. 2.

—— My buſineſs in this ſtate
Made me a looker on here in Vienna,
Where I have ſeen corruption boil and bubble,
Till it o'er-run the ſtew.
Meaſure for Meaſure, A. 5, S. 1.

Our hands are full of buſineſs: let's away;
Advantage feeds him fat, while men delay.
Henry IV. P. 1, A. 3, S. 2.

tity. I love you beyond limits, and cannot ſay it is *ſo much*, for how much ſoever I ſhould name, it would be yet more.
JOHNSON.

The preſent reading is harſh. I would ſtrike out the prepoſition *of*, and read and point thus:
"A love that makes breath poor, and ſpeech unable
"Beyond all manner. So much I love you."
i. e. *A love which cannot be expreſſed in words---a love of which you can have no conception*. A. B.

[1] *Convey the buſineſs*.] *Convey*, for *introduce*. But *convey* is a fine word, as alluding to the practice of clandeſtine conveying goods, ſo as not to be found upon the felon. WARBURTON.

To *convey*, is rather to *carry through*, than to introduce; in this place it is to *manage artfully*. We ſay of a juggler, that he has a clean *conveyance*. JOHNSON.

"Convey the buſineſs" can mean nothing more than *make him acquainted with the buſineſs*, or *break the buſineſs to him*. Edmund, though he really means to manage artfully, would never intimate ſo much to his father; but on the contrary, appear open and plain in his dealing. A. B.

I am

I am ſorry
To ſee you ta'en from liberty, to look on
The buſineſs preſent.[a] *Henry VIII.* A. 1, S. 1.

C.

CALUMNY.

PRAISE her but for this her without-door form,
(Which on my faith deſerves high ſpeech) and ſtraight
The ſhrug, the hum, or ha; theſe petty brands,
That calumny doth uſe:—Oh, I am out,
That mercy does; for calumny will fear
Virtue itſelf;—theſe ſhrugs, theſe hums, and ha's,
When you have ſaid, ſhe's goodly, come between,
Ere you can ſay ſhe's honeſt.
Winter's Tale, A. 2, S. 1.

Be thou as chaſte as ice, as pure as ſnow, thou ſhalt not eſcape calumny. *Hamlet,* A. 3, S. 1.

—— My place i' the ſtate,
Will ſo your accuſation over-weigh,
That you ſhall ſtifle in your own report,
And ſmell of calumny.
Meaſure for Meaſure, A. 2, S. 4.

I am right glad to catch this good occaſion
Moſt thoroughly to be winnow'd, where my chaff
And corn ſhall fly aſunder: for, I know,

[a] *I am ſorry*
To ſee you ta'en from liberty, to look on
The buſineſs preſent.] I am ſorry that I am obliged to be preſent, and an eye-witneſs of your loſs of liberty. JOHNSON.
Does it not rather mean, I am ſorry you are deprived of liberty, by which you will ſee, or diſcover, what buſineſs is now in hand or going forward? A. B.

There's none ſtands under more calumnious tongues,
Than I myſelf. *Henry VIII.* A. 5, S. 1.

No might nor greatneſs in mortality
Can cenſure 'ſcape; back-wounding calumny
The whiteſt virtues ſtrikes.
Meaſure for Meaſure, A. 3, S. 2.

CANNON.

—— Depart in peace:
Be thou as lightning in the eyes of France;
For ere thou canſt report I will be there,
The thunder of my cannon ſhall be heard:
So, hence! *King John*, A. 1, S. 1.

The cannons have their bowels full of wrath;
And ready mounted are they, to ſpit forth
Their iron indignation 'gainſt your walls.
King John, A. 2, S. 1.

CAPACITY.

—— Your capacity
Is of that nature, that to your huge ſtore
Wiſe things ſeem fooliſh, and rich things but poor.
Love's Labour Loſt, A. 5. S. 2.

CELERITY.

Celerity is never more admir'd,
That by the negligent.
Antony and Cleopatra, A. 3, S. 7.

CEREMONY.

And what art thou, thou idol ceremony?
What kind of god art thou, that ſuffer'ſt more
Of mortal griefs, than do thy worſhippers?
What are thy rents? what are thy comings-in?
Art thou aught elſe but place, degree, and form,
Creating awe and fear in other men?

Wherein

Wherein thou art leſs happy being fear'd,
Than they in fearing. *Henry V.* A. 4, S. 1.

CHALLENGE.

——I never in my life
Did hear a challenge urg'd more modeſtly,
Unleſs a brother ſhould a brother dare
To gentle exerciſe and proof of arms.
Henry IV. P. 1, A. 5. S. 2.

CHARITY.

——O father abbot,
An old man broken with the ſtorms of ſtate,
Is come to lay his weary bones among ye;
Give him a little earth for charity!
Henry VIII. A. 4, S. 2.

You ſpeak not like yourſelf; who ever yet
Have ſtood to charity, and diſplay'd the effects
Of diſpoſition gentle, and of wiſdom
O'er-topping woman's power.
I have no ſpleen againſt you; nor injuſtice
For your, or any. *Henry VIII.* A. 2, S. 4.

He hath a tear for pity, and a hand,
Open as day for melting charity;
Yet notwithſtanding, being incens'd he's flint:
As humorous as winter,[1] and as ſudden

[1] —— *humorous as winter.*] That is, changeable as the weather of a winter's day. JOHNSON.

A *winter*'s day has generally too decided a character to admit Dr. Johnſon's interpretation without ſome licence: a licence, however, which our author has perhaps taken. MALONE.

The meaning of the word "humorous," in this place, has not been properly explained. It does not here ſignify *changeable*, but on the contrary *fixed*, *obſtinate*. A *humorous man*, may mean a man wedded to his opinion; or whoſe opinions or notions are rigid and ſevere. When we now ſay, *he will have his humour*, we mean, *he is an obſtinate man*. A. B.

As

As flaws congealed in the ſpring of day.
Henry IV. P. 2, A. 4, S. 4.

—— From low farms,
[1] Poor pelting villages, ſheep-cotes and mills,
Sometime with lunatic bans, ſometime with prayers,
Inforce their charity. *Lear*, A. 2. S. 3.

CHARM.

—— Your charm ſo ſtrongly works 'em,

[1] *Poor pelting villages.*] *Pelting* is uſed by Shakeſpeare in the ſenſe of *beggarly:* I ſuppoſe from *pelt*, a ſkin. WARBURTON.

Pelting is, I believe, only an accidental depravation of *petty*. Skakeſpeare uſes it in the Midſummer Night's Dream, of *ſmall brooks*. JOHNSON.

Beaumont and Fletcher often uſe the word in the ſame ſenſe as Shakeſpeare. So in King and no King:

"This pelting, prating peace is good for nothing."

Spaniſh Curate, "To learn the pelting law."
Midſummer Night's Dream, "Every pelting river."
Meaſure for Meaſure, "Every pelting petty officer."
Troilus and Creſſida, "We have had pelting wars ſince "you refus'd "The Grecian cauſe."

From the firſt of the two laſt inſtances, it appears not to be a *corruption of petty*, which is uſed the next word to it, but ſeems to be the ſame as *paltry*; and if it comes from *pelt*, a ſkin, as Dr. Warburton ſays, the poets have furniſhed *villages*, *peace*, *law*, *rivers*, *officers of juſtice* and *war*, out of one wardrobe. STEEVENS.

"Pelting" ſhould in this place be "palting," which ſignifies *paltry*, *trifling*: "Pelting" is *fuming*, *fretful*. *Pelting* and *palting*, or *paltring*, are frequently confounded and miſtaken for each other. But I will endeavour to ſhew, from the above quoted paſſages, the different ſignifications of the words.

"This *pelting*, prating peace." It ſhould be *palting*, meaning, this *trifling*, prating peace, &c.

"To learn the *pelting* law." Here too it ſhould be *palting*, or *paltring*. To *palter*, is ſometimes to *ſhift*, to *dodge*. The propriety of the epithet, therefore, when applied to *law*, is eaſily ſeen.

"Every *pelting* river." Palting, *i. e.* paltry.

"Every *pelting* petty officer, i. e. *noiſy*, *turbulent*.

"We have had *pelting* wars," &c. i. e. *fuming*, angry wars. &c. A. B.

That

That if you now beheld them, your affections
Would become tender. *Tempest*, A. 5, S. 1.

—— All the charms
Of Sycorax, toads, beetles, bats, light on you!
Tempest, A. 1, S. 2.

—— The charm dissolves apace;
And as the morning steals upon the night,
Melting the darkness, so their rising senses
Begin to chase the ignorant fumes that mantle
Their clearer reason. *Tempest*, A. 5, S. 1.

—— My high charms work,
And these, mine enemies, are all knit up
In their distractions. *Tempest*, A. 3, S. 3.

I pray you all, tell me what they deserve,
That do conspire my death with devilish plots
Of damned witchcraft; and that have prevail'd
Upon my body with their hellish charms?
Richard III. A. 3, S. 4.

CHASTITY.

He hath bought a pair of cast lips of Diana: a nun of winter's sisterhood kisses not more religiously; the very ice of chastity is in them.
As you like it, A. 3, S. 4.

—— She's not forward, but modest as the dove;
She is not hot, but temperate as the morn;
For patience she will prove a second Grissel;
And Roman Lucrece for her chastity.
Taming of the Shrew, A. 2, S. 1.

My chastity's the jewel of our house,
Bequeathed down from many ancestors;
Which were the greatest obloquy i' the world
In me to lose. *All's well that ends well*, A. 4, S. 2.

Out on thy seeming! I will write against it:

You

You ſeem to me as Dian in her orb;
As chaſte as is the bud ere it be blown.
Much ado about nothing, A. 4, S. 1.

——— O ill-ſtarr'd wench!
Pale as thy ſmock! when we ſhall meet at compt,
This look of thine will hurl my ſoul from heaven,
And fiends will ſnatch at it. Cold, cold, my girl,
Even like thy chaſtity. *Othello*, A. 5, S. 2.

CHILD, CHILDREN.

He hath play'd on this prologue, like a child on a recorder; a ſound, but not in government.
Midſummer Night's Dream, A. 5, S. 1.

It is a gallant child; one that, indeed, phyſicks the ſubject, makes old hearts freſh; they, that went on crutches ere he was born, deſire yet their life to ſee him a man. *Winter's Tale*, A. 1, S. 1.

He makes a July's day ſhort as December;
And, with his varying childneſs, cures in me
Thoughts that would thick my blood.
Winter's Tale, A. 1, S. 2.

If ever he have child, abortive be it,
Prodigious, and untimely brought to light,
Whoſe ugly and unnatural aſpect
May fright the hopeful mother at the view;
And that be heir to his unhappineſs!
Richard III. A. 1, S. 2.

You have no children, butchers! if you had,
The thought of them would have ſtirr'd up remorſe;
But, if you ever chance to have a child,
Look in his youth to have him ſo cut off,
As, deathſmen! you have rid this ſweet young prince.
Henry VI. P. 3, A. 5, S. 5.

Some ſay, that ravens foſter forlorn children,
The whilſt their own birds famiſh in their neſts:
O, be to me, though thy hard heart ſay no,

Nothing fo kind, but fomething pitiful!
Titus, A. 2, S. 3.

By being feldom feen, I could not ftir,
But, like a comet, I was wonder'd at:
That men could tell their children, This is he;
Others would fay, where? which is Bolingbroke?
Henry IV. P. 1, A. 3, S. 2.

And as our vineyards, fallows, meads, and hedges,
Defective in their natures, grow to wildnefs;
Even fo our houfes, and ourfelves, and children,
Have loft, or do not learn, for want of time,
The fciences that fhould become our country.
Henry V. A. 5, S. 2.

Bring me a father, that fo lov'd his child,
Whofe joy of her is overwhelm'd like mine,
And bid him fpeak of patience.
Much ado about nothing, A. 5, S. 1.

—— Glofter's fhew
Beguiles him, as the mournful crocodile
With forrow fnares relenting paffengers;
Or as the fnake, roll'd on a flowering bank,
With fhining checker'd flough, doth fting a child,
That, for the beauty, thinks it excellent.
Henry VI. P. 2, A. 3, S. 1.

Offer'd by a child to an old man; which is wit-old[1].
Love's Labour Loft, A. 5, S. 1.

CHOICE.

—— If there were a fympathy in choice,
War, death, or ficknefs did lay fiege to it;
Making it momentary as a found,
Swift as a fhadow, fhort as any dream.
Midfummer Night's Dream, A. 1, S. 1.

[1] *Offer'd by a child to an old man, which is wit-old.*] An equivoque. "Wit-old" may mean, either *old in wit*, or according to the found, *wittol*, a contented cuckold. A. B.

CLOUD.

CLOUD.

Thoſe things ſeem ſmall, and undiſtinguiſhable,
Like far-off mountains turned into clouds.
Midſummer Night's Dream, A. 4, S. 1.

Sometime, we ſee a cloud that's dragoniſh;
A vapour, ſometime, like a bear, or lion,
A tower'd citadel, a pendent rock,
A forked mountain, or blue promontory
With trees upon't, that nod unto the world,
And mock our eyes with air. *Ant. and Cle.* A. 4, S. 12.

CLOWN.

—— [1] The royniſh clown, at whom ſo oft
Your grace was wont to laugh, is alſo miſſing.
As you like it, A. 2, S. 2.

COMFORT.

—— If it were now to die,
'Twere now to be moſt happy; for, I fear,
My ſoul hath her content ſo abſolute,
That not another comfort like to this
Succeeds in unknown fate. *Othello*, A. 2, S. 1.

—— Every wretch, pining and pale before,
Beholding him, plucks comfort from his looks:
A largeſs univerſal, like the ſun,
His liberal eye doth give to every one,
Thawing cold fear. *Henry V.* A. 4, Chorus.

—— Brother, men
Can counſel, and give comfort to that grief
Which they themſelves not feel.
Much ado about nothing, A. 5, S. 1.

[1] *The royniſh clown.*] *Royniſh*, from *rogneux*, Fr. mangy, ſcurvy. STEEVENS.

Mr. Steevens has miſtaken the ſenſe. *To royne*, is *to bite.* "Royniſh," in this place, is conſequently *ſatirical carping*. RONGER, MORDRE (Medire, *reprendre*, cenſurer avec malignité.) *Dict.* A. B.

——— Give not me counſel;
Nor let no comforter delight mine ear,
But ſuch a one whoſe wrongs do ſuit with mine.
Much ado about nothing, A. 5, S. 1.

What ſay you now? What comfort have we now?
By heaven, I'll hate him everlaſtingly,
That bids me be of comfort any more.
Richard II. A. 3, S. 2.

—— None of you will bid the winter come,
To thruſt his icy fingers in my maw;
Nor let my kingdom's rivers take their courſe
Through my burn'd boſom; nor intreat the north,
To make his bleak winds kiſs my parched lips,
And comfort me with cold. *King John*, A. 5, S. 7.

——— Is this your comfort?
The cordial that ye bring a wretched lady?
A woman loſt among ye, laugh'd at, ſcorn'd?
I will not wiſh ye half my miſeries,
I have more charity. *Henry VIII.* A. 3, S. 1.

O prince, I conjure thee, as thou believ'ſt
There is another comfort than this world,
That thou neglect me not, with that opinion
That I am touch'd with madneſs.
Meaſure for Meaſure, A. 5, S. 1.

——— Think with thyſelf,
How more unfortunate than all living women
Are we come hither: ſince that thy ſight, which ſhould
Make our eyes flow with joy, hearts dance with comforts,
Conſtrains them weep, and ſhake with fear and ſorrow,
Making the mother, wife, and child, to ſee
The ſon, the huſband, and the father tearing
His country's bowels out. *Coriolanus*, A. 5, S. 3.

—— To apprehend thus,
Draws us a profit from all things we ſee:

And

And often, to our comfort, ſhall we find
The ſharded beetle in a ſafer hold
Than is the full-wing'd eagle. *Cymbeline*, A. 3, S. 3.

—— Moſt miſerable
Is the deſire that's glorious: bleſſed be thoſe,
How mean ſoe'er, that have their honeſt wills,
Which ſeaſons comfort. *Cymbeline*, A. 1, S. 7.

COMMENDATION.

This commendation I can afford her; that were ſhe other than ſhe is, ſhe were unhandſome; and being no other but as ſhe is, I do not like her.
Much ado about nothing, A. 1, S. 1.

COMPANY, COMPANIONS.

He draweth out the thread of his verboſity finer than the ſtaple of his argument. I abhor ſuch phanatical phantaſms, ſuch unſociable and point-deviſe companions. *Love's Labour Loſt*, A. 5, S. 1.

— Proclaim it, Weſtmoreland, through my hoſt,
That he, which hath no ſtomach to this fight,
Let him depart; his paſſport ſhall be made,
And crowns for convoy put into his purſe:
We would not die in that man's company,
That fears his fellowſhip to die with us.
Henry V. A. 4, S. 3.

Reply not to me with a fool-born jeſt;
Preſume not, that I am the thing I was;
For heaven doth know, ſo ſhall the world perceive,
That I have turned away my former ſelf;
So will I thoſe that kept me company.
Henry IV. P. 2, A. 5, S. 5.

I have forſworn his company hourly, any time this two and twenty years, and yet I am bewitch'd with the rogue's company. If the raſcal have not given me medicines to make me love him, I'll be hang'd; it could not be elſe. *Henry IV.* P. 1, A. 2, S. 2.

There's but a ſhirt and a half in all my company; and the half-ſhirt is two napkins, tack'd together, and thrown over the ſhoulders like a herald's coat without ſleeves; and the ſhirt, to ſay the truth, ſtolen from my hoſt of Saint Alban's, or the red-noſe inn-keeper of Daintry. But that's all one; they'll find linen enough on every hedge.

Henry IV. P. 1, A. 4, S. 2.

—— Some four or five attend him;
All, if you will; for I myſelf am beſt,
When leaſt in company [1]. *Twelfth Night*, A. 1, S. 4.

COMPETENCY.

For aught I ſee, they are as ſick, that ſurfeit with too much, as they that ſtarve with nothing: it is no mean happineſs, therefore, to be ſeated in the mean; ſuperfluity comes ſooner by white hairs, but competency lives longer.

Merchant of Venice, A. 1, S. 2.

COMPLEXION.

——— Call us ten times frail;
For we are as ſoft as our complexions are,
And credulous to falſe prints.

Meaſure for Meaſure, A. 2, S. 4.

CONFERENCE.

I will fetch you a tooth-picker now from the fartheſt inch of Aſia; bring you the length of Preſter John's foot; fetch you a hair of the great Cham's

[1] —— *for I myſelf am beſt,*
When leaſt in company.]
" *Nunquam minus ſolus quam cum ſolus.*" A. B.

beard;

beard; do you any embassage to the Pigmies, rather than hold three words conference with this harpy.

Much ado about nothing, A. 2, S. 1.

CONSCIENCE, CONSCIENCES.

—— Twenty consciences,
That stand 'twixt me and Milan, candy'd be they,
And melt, ere they molest. *Tempest*, A. 2, S. 1.

Thus conscience does make cowards of us all;
And thus the native hue of resolution
Is sickly'd o'er with the pale cast of thought;
And enterprizes of great pith and moment [1],
With this regard, their currents turn awry,
And lose the name of action. *Hamlet*, A. 3, S. 1.

— Conscience is but a word that cowards use,
Devis'd at first to keep the strong in awe;
Our strong arms be our conscience, swords our law.

Richard III. A. 5, S. 3.

My conscience hath a thousand several tongues,
And every tongue brings in a several tale,
And every tale condemns me for a villain.

Richard III. A. 5, S. 3.

What stronger breast-plate than a heart untainted?
Thrice is he arm'd, that hath his quarrel just;
And he but naked, though lock'd up in steel,
Whose conscience with injustice is corrupted.

Henry VI. P. 2, A. 3, S. 2.

Certainly the Jew is the very devil incarnation; and in my conscience, my conscience is but a kind

[1] —— *great pith and moment.*] Thus the folio. The quartos read, of great *pitch*. STEEVENS.

Pitch seems to be the better reading. The allusion is to the *pitching*, or throwing the bar; a manly exercise, usual in country villages. REMARKS.

"Enterprizes of great pith and moment," is, enterprizes of great *matter* and *moment*. Pith is unquestionably the true reading. A. B.

of hard conſcience, to offer to counſel me to ſtay with the Jew. *Merchant of Venice*, A. 2, S. 2.

CONSIDERATION.

—— At that very moment,
Conſideration like an angel came,
And whipp'd the offending Adam out of him;
Leaving his body as a paradiſe,
To envelop and contain celeſtial ſpirits.
Henry V. A. 1, S. 1.

CONSPIRACY.

—— O conſpiracy!
Sham'ſt thou to ſhew thy dangerous brow by night,
When evils are moſt free? O, then, by day,
Where wilt thou find a cavern dark enough,
To maſk thy monſtrous viſage? Seek none conſpiracy;
Hide it in ſmiles, and affability;
For if thou path, thy native ſemblance on,
Not Erebus itſelf were dim enough
To hide thee from prevention.
Julius Cæſar, A. 2, S. 1.

CONTEMPLATION.

—— When would you, my liege,
In leaden contemplation, have found out
Such fiery numbers, as the prompting eyes
Of beauteous tutors have enrich'd you with?
Love's Labour Loſt, A. 4, S. 3.

When holy and devout religious men
Are at their beads, 'tis hard to draw them thence;
So ſweet is zealous contemplation.
Richard III. A. 3, S. 7.

CONTENT.

—— O now, for ever,
Farewel the tranquil mind! farewel content;
Farewel the plumed troop, and the big wars,
That make ambition virtue! *Othello*, A. 3, S. 3.

Where zeal strives to content, and the contents
Dies in the zeal of that which it presents,
There form confounded makes most form in mirth;
When great things labouring perish in their birth.
Love's Labour Lost, A. 5, S. 2.

If thou, that bidst me be content, wert grim,
Lame, foolish, crooked, swart, prodigious,
Patch'd with foul moles, and eye-offending marks,
I would not care, I then would be content.
King John, A. 3, S. 1.

—— Best state, contentless,
Hath a distracted and most wretched being,
Worse than the worst, content.
Timon of Athens, A, 4, S. 3.

This diamond he greets your wife withal,
By the name of most kind hostess; and shut up
In measureless content.[1] *Macbeth*, A. S. 1.

CONTENTION.

—— Let this world no longer be a stage,
To feed contention in a lingering act;
But let one spirit of the first-born Cain
Reign in all bosoms, that, each heart being set
On bloody courses, the rude scene may end,
And darkness be the burier of the dead!
Henry IV. P. 2. A. 1, S. 1.

[1] —— *Shut up*
In measureless content.] Mr. Steevens says, that to *shut up* is to conclude; and then quotes three or four passages to prove, that such is its meaning. *Shut up in*, however, is *given up to—enjoying*.
"My soul hath her content so absolute," &c. *Othello*.
A. B.

—— Every minute now,
Should be the father of ſome ſtratagem :
The times are wild, contention, like a horſe
Full of high ſeeding, madly hath broke looſe,
And bears down all before him.

Henry IV. P. 2, A. 1, S. 1.

COUNTENANCE.

—— Thou ſhalt not ſee me bluſh,
Nor change my countenance for this arreſt;
A heart unſpotted is not eaſily daunted.
The pureſt ſpring is not ſo free from mud,
As I am clear from treaſon to my ſovereign :

Henry VI. P. 2, A. 3, S. 1.

Stand here by me, Maſter Robert Shallow, ; I will make the king do you grace : I will leer upon him, as a' comes by ; and do but mark the countenance that he will give me. *Henry IV.* P. 2, A. 5, S. 5.

—— Pardon me, I pray you ;
I thought, that all things had been ſavage here,
And therefore put I on the countenance
Of ſtern commandment. *As you like it*, A. 2, S. 7.

—— Heaven witneſs ;
I have been to you a true and humble wife,
At all times to your will conformable :
Ever in fear to kindle your diſlike,
Yea, ſubject to your countenance ; glad, or ſorry,
As I ſaw it inclin'd. *Henry VIII.* A. 2, S. 4.

O, he ſits high in all the people's hearts :
And that, which would appear offence in us,
His countenance, like richeſt alchemy,
Will change to virtue, and to worthineſs.

Julius Cæſar, A. 1, S. 3.

Turn from me then that noble countenance,
Wherein the worſhip of the whole world lies.[1]

Antony and Cleopatra, A. 4, S. 12.

COUNTERFEIT.

'Sblood, 'twas time to counterfeit, or that hot termagant Scot had paid me ſcot and lot too. Counterfeit? I lie, I am no counterfeit: to die, is to be a counterfeit; for he is but the counterfeit of a man, who hath not the life of a man; but to counterfeit dying, when a man thereby liveth, is to be no counterfeit, but the true and perfect image of life indeed.

Henry IV. P. 1, A. 5, S. 4.

COURAGE.

By how much unexpected, by ſo much
We muſt awake endeavour for defence;
For courage mounteth with occaſion.

King John, A. 2, S. 1.

COURT.

If thou never waſt at court, thou never ſaw'ſt good manners; if thou never ſaw'ſt good manners, then thy manners muſt be wicked; and wickedneſs is ſin, and ſin is damnation. *As you like it*, A. 3, S. 2.

We two alone will ſing like birds i'the cage:
When thou doſt aſk my bleſſing, I'll kneel down
And aſk of thee forgiveneſs: ſo we'll live,
And pray, and ſing, and tell old tales, and laugh
At gilded butterflies, and hear poor rogues
Talk of court news. *Lear*, A. 5, S. 3.

Theſe are kind creatures. Gods, what lies I have heard!

[1] *The worſhip of the whole world.*] The *worſhip* is the dignity, the *authority*. JOHNSON.

This can hardly be ſaid of Antony, who has entirely loſt his dignity and authority. Eros rather means to ſay, *whom the whole world ſhould, or ought to worſhip and obey.* A. B.

Our

Our courtiers say, all's savage, but at court:
Experience, O, thou disprov'st report![1]

Cymbeline, A. 4, S. 2.

—— Up to yon hill,
Your legs are young; I'll tread these flats. Consider,
When you above perceive me like a crow,
That it is place, which lessens, and sets off.
And you may then revolve what tales I have told you,
Of courts, of princes, of the tricks in war.

Cymbeline, A. 3, S. 3.

—— This mortal house I'll ruin,
Do Cæsar what he can. Know, sir, that I
Will not wait pinion'd at your master's court;
Nor once be chastiz'd with the sober eye
Of dull Octavia. *Antony and Cleopatra*, A. 5, S. 2.

I knew him once a servant of the prince; I cannot tell, good sir, for which of his virtues it was, but he was certainly whipp'd out of the court.

Winter's Tale, A. 4, S. 2.

Seest thou not the air of the court, in these enfoldings? hath not my gait in it, the measure of the court? receives not thy nose court-odour from me? reflect I not on thy baseness, court contempt?

Winter's Tale, A. 4, S. 3.

COURTESY.

—— He did seem to dive into their hearts,
With humble and familiar courtesy;
Off goes his bonnet to an oyster-wench;
A brace of draymen bid—God speed him well,
And had the tribute of his supple knee,
With—Thanks, my country-men, my loving friends.

Richard II. A. 1, S. 4.

[1] *Experience, O, thou disprov'st report.*] We should read, "Experience, O, *how* thou disprov'st report." A. B.

The

The elephant hath joints, but none for courtesy;
His legs are for necessity, not for flexure.
Troilus and Cressida, A. S. 3.

—— This is he,
That kiss'd away his hand in courtesy;
This is the ape of form, Monsieur the nice,
That, when he plays at tables, chides the dice
In honourable terms. *Love's Labour Lost*, A. 5, S. 2.

—— Thou hast never in thy life
Shew'd thy dear mother any courtesy;
When she (poor hen) fond of no second brood,
Has cluck'd thee to the wars, and safely home,
Loaden with honour. *Coriolanus*, A. 5, S. 3.

The courtesy of nations allows you my better, in that you are the first-born; but the same tradition takes not away my blood, were there twenty brothers betwixt us. *As you like it*, A. 1, S. 1.

—— Pluck commiseration of his state
From brassy bosoms, and rough hearts of flint,
From stubborn Turks, and Tartars, never train'd
To offices of tender courtesy.
Merchant of Venice, A. 4, S. 1.

Is it possible, disdain should die, while she hath such meet food to feed it, as Signior Benedick? Courtesy itself must convert to disdain, if you come in her presence. *Much ado about nothing*, A. 1, S, 1.

These couchings and these lowly courtesies,
Might fire the blood of ordinary men;
And turn pre-ordinance, and first decree,
Into the lane of children.[1]
Julius Cæsar, A. 3, S. 1.

COW-

[1] *Into the lane of children.*] I do not well understand what is meant by the *lane* of children. I should read, the *law* of children. That is, change pre-ordinance and decree into the law of children; into such slight determinations as every start of will would alter. *Lane* and *law*, in some manuscripts, are not easily distinguished. JOHNSON.

If

COWARDICE.

I do defy him,
Call him—a ſlanderous coward, and a villain:
Which to maintain, I would allow him odds;
And meet him, were I ty'd to run a-foot,
Even to the frozen ridges of the Alps.

Richard II. A. 1, S. 1.

Young as I am, I have obſerv'd theſe three ſwaſhers. I am boy to them all three: but all they three, though they would ſerve me, could not be man to me; for, indeed, three ſuch anticks do not amount to a man. For Bardolph,—he is white-liver'd, and red-faced; by the means whereof, a' faces it out; but fights not. For Piſtol—he hath a killing tongue, and a quiet ſword; by the means whereof a' breaks words, and keeps whole weapons. For Nym,—he hath heard, that men of few words are the beſt of men; and therefore he ſcorns to ſay his prayers, leſt a' ſhould be thought a coward. *Henry V.* A. 3, S. 2.

The ſecond property of your excellent ſherris is—the warming of the blood; which, before cold and ſettled, left the liver white and pale, which is the badge of puſillanimity and cowardice; but the ſherris warms it, and makes it courſe from the inwards to the parts extreme. It illumineth the face;

If the *lane of children* be the true reading, it may poſſibly receive illuſtration from the following paſſage in Ben Jonſon's Staple of News:

"A narrow minded man! my thoughts do dwell all in a lane."

The *lane of children* will then mean the narrow conceits of children, which muſt change as their minds grow more enlarged.

STEEVENS.

I believe we ſhould read *bane*—*Bane* in its ordinary acceptation is *hurt*, *injury*; and by a licence common with our author, it may poſſibly be uſed for *puniſhment*. "*You behave, by theſe low* "*courteſies, and crouchings, like children, and many men might be* "*tempted to puniſh you as ſuch.*" A. B.

which,

which, as a beacon, gives warning to all the reſt of this little kingdom, man, to arm.

Henry IV. P. 2, A. 4, S. 3.

Cowards die many times before their deaths;
The valiant never taſte of death but once.
Of all the wonders that I yet have heard,
It ſeems to me moſt ſtrange that men ſhould fear,
Seeing that death a neceſſary end,
Will come, when it will come.

Julius Cæſar, A. 2, S. 2.

How many cowards, whoſe hearts are all as falſe as ſtairs of ſand, wear yet upon their chins the beards of Hercules, and frowning Mars; who, inward ſearch'd, have livers white as milk?

Merchant of Venice, A. 3, S. 2.

—— Thou ſlave, thou wretch, thou coward;
Thou little valiant, great in villainy!
Thou ever ſtrong upon the ſtronger ſide!
Thou fortune's champion, that doſt never fight,
But when her humorous ladyſhip is by
To teach thee ſafety! *King John*, A. 3, S. 1.

—— (In my heart
Lie there what hidden woman's fear there will)
We'll have a ſwaſhing and a martial outſide;
As many other manniſh cowards have,
That do outface it with their ſemblances.

As you like it, A. 1, S. 3.

He's a coward, and a coyſtril,[1] and will not drink to my niece, till his brains turn o'the toe like a pariſh-top. *Twelfth Night*, A. 1, S. 3.

[1] *A coyſtril.*] *i. e.* a coward cock. It may, however, be a keſtril, or baſtard hawk. STEEVENS.

A "coiſtril," is likewiſe a *lad*, a ſtripling. It ſeems here to be uſed for a milk-ſop. "A coward and a coyſtril an he will "not drink."—*i. e.* A coward and a milk-ſop if he will not drink, &c. A. B.

—He

—— He ſtopt the fliers;
And, by his rare example, made the coward
Turn terror into ſport: as waves before
A veſſel under ſail, ſo men obey'd,
And fell below his ſtern.[1] *Coriolanus*, A. 2, S. 2.

He excels his brother for a coward, yet his brother is reputed one of the beſt that is: In a retreat he outruns any lacquey.

All's well that ends well, A. 4, S. 3.

—— I know him a notorious liar,
Think him a great way fool, ſolely a coward;
Yet theſe fix'd evils ſit ſo fit in him,
That they take place, when virtue's ſteelly bones
Look bleak in the cold wind.

All's well that ends well, A. 1, S. 1.

I never dealt better ſince I was a man; all would not do. A plague of all cowards!—Let them ſpeak: if they ſpeak more or leſs than truth, they are villains, and the ſons of darkneſs.

Henry IV. P. 1, A. 2, S. 4.

A plague of all cowards, I ſay, and a vengeance too! marry, and amen!—Give me a cup of ſack, boy. A plague of all cowards!—Is there no virtue extant? *Henry IV.* P, 1, A. 2, S. 4.

—— I was never curſt;
I have no gift at all in ſhrewiſhneſs;
I am a right maid for my cowardice.

Midſummer Night's Dream, A. 3, S. 2.

—— I hold it cowardice,
To reſt miſtruſtful where a noble heart
Hath pawn'd an open hand in ſign of love.

Henry VI. P. 3, A. 4, S. 2.

CREA-

[1] *And fell below his ſtern.*] We ſhould read, according to the old copy,

—— *his ſtem* ——

The *ſtem* is that end of the ſhip which leads. STEEVENS.

W-

CREATURE.

——— This is a creature,
Would ſhe begin a ſect, might quench the zeal
Of all profeſſors elſe; make proſelytes
Of who ſhe but bid follow.

Winter's Tale, A. 5, S. 1

——— O thou thing,
Which I'll not call a creature of thy place,
Leſt barbariſm, making me the precedent,
Should a like language uſe to all degrees,
And mannerly diſtinguiſhment leave out
Betwixt the prince and beggar!—

Winter's Tale, A. 2, S. 1.

——— Call the creatures—
Whoſe naked natures live in all the ſpight
Of wreakful heaven; whoſe bare unhouſed trunks
To the conflicting elements expoſed,
Anſwer mere nature—bid them flatter thee;

Timon of Athens, A. 4, S. 3.

Divineſt creature, bright Aſtræa's daughter,
How ſhall I honour thee for this ſucceſs?
Thy promiſes are like Adonis' gardens,
That one day bloom'd, and fruitful were the next.

Henry VI. P. 1. A. 1, S. 6.

CRIME.

If little faults, proceeding on diſtemper,
Shall not be wink'd at, how ſhall we ſtretch our eye
When capital crimes, chew'd, ſwallow'd, and digeſted,
Appear before us?— *Henry V.* A. 2, S. 2.

We ſhould read ———
Fell *before* his *ſtem.*
Stem does not here mean any part of a ſhip.—*Stem* is uſed for *proweſs, valour.* "Fell before his ſtem," *yielded to his proweſs.*
A. B.

All

All have not offended;
For those that were, it is not square, to take,
On those that are, revenges: crimes, like lands,
Are not inherited. *Timon of Athens*, A. 5. S. 5.

CROWN.

—— Look down, you gods,
And on this couple drop a blessed crown.
Tempest, A. 5, S. 1.

Say to great Cæsar this, in disputation,[1]
I kiss his conquering hand: tell him, I am prompt
To lay my crown at his feet, and there to kneel:
Tell him, from his all-obeying breath I hear
The doom of Egypt.
Antony and Cleopatra, A. 3, S. 11.

Thus was I, sleeping, by a brother's hand,
Of life, of crown, of queen at once dispatch'd,
Cut off even in the blossoms of my sin,
Unhousell'd, disappointed, unaneal'd;
No reckoning made, but sent to my account
With all my imperfections on my head.
Hamlet, A. 1, S. 5.

Had I so lavish of my presence been,
So common-hackney'd in the eyes of men,
So stale and cheap to vulgar company;

[1] *Say to great Cæsar this, in disputation,*
I kiss his conquering hand.] The poet certainly wrote:
Say to great Cæsar this; in *deputation*
I kiss his conquering hand.
i. e. by *proxy*. I depute you to pay him that duty in my name.
WARBURTON.

I am not certain that this change is necessary. *I kiss his hand in disputation*, may mean, I own he has the better in the controversy—I confess my inability to *dispute* or *contend* with him.
STEEVENS.

I would read thus:
Say to great Cæsar,—in *disreputation*
I kiss his conquering hand.
i. e. I am disgraced; and I submit to him. A. B.

Opinion, that did help me to the crown,
Had ſtill kept loyal to poſſeſſion.

Henry IV. P. 1, A. 3, S. 2.

——— Do but think,
How ſweet a thing it is to wear a crown;
Within whoſe circuit is Elyſium,
And all that poets feign of bliſs and joy.

Henry VI. P. 3, A. 1, S. 2.

The ſons of Edward ſleep in Abraham's boſom,
And Anne my wife hath bid the world good night.
Now, for I know the Bretagne Richmond aims
At young Elizabeth, my brother's daughter,
And, by that knot, looks proudly on the crown,
To her go I, a jolly thriving wooer.

Richard III. A. 4, S. 3.

Since this earth affords no joy to me,
But to command, to check, to o'erbear ſuch,
As are of better perſon than myſelf,
I'll make my heaven—to dream upon the crown.

Henry VI. P. 3, A. 3, S. 2.

My crown is in my heart, not on my head;
Not deck'd with diamonds, and Indian ſtones,
Nor to be ſeen: my crown is call'd, content;
A crown it is, that ſeldom kings enjoy.

Henry VI. P. 3, A. 3, S. 1.

—— Now, for thee thine uncles and myſelf,
Have in our armours watch'd the winter's night;
Went all a-foot in Summer's ſcalding heat,
That thou might'ſt repoſſeſs the crown in peace;
And of our labours thou ſhalt reap the gain.

Henry VI. P. 3, A. 5, S. 7.

Oh, what a ſcandal is it to our crown,
That two ſuch noble peers as ye, ſhould jar!
Believe me, lords, my tender years can tell,
Civil diſſention is a viperous worm,
That gnaws the bowels of the common-wealth.

Henry VI. P. 1. A. 3, S. 1.

—— Heaven knows, my ſon,
By what by-paths, and indirect crook'd ways,
I met this crown; and I myſelf know well,
How troubleſome it ſat upon my head;
To thee it ſhall deſcend with better quiet,
Better opinion, better confirmation.

Henry IV. P. 2, A. 4, S. 1.

—— There is your crown;
And he that wears the crown immortally,
Long guard it yours! If I affect it more,
Than as your honour, and as your renown,
Let me no more from this obedience riſe,
Which my moſt true, and inward-duteous ſpirit
Teacheth, this proſtrate and exterior bending!

Henry IV. P. 2, A. 4, S. 4.

White beards have arm'd their thin and hairleſs ſcalps
Againſt thy Majeſty; boys, with women's voices,
Strive to ſpeak big, and claſp their female joints
In ſtiff unwieldy arms againſt thy crown.

Richard II. A. 3, S. 2.

—— If you hide the crown
Even in your hearts, there will he rake for it:
And therefore in fierce tempeſt is he coming,
In thunder, and in earthquake, like a Jove,
That, if requiring fail, he will compel.

Henry V. A. 2, S. 4.

Many years of happy days befal
My gracious ſovereign, my moſt loving liege!
Each day ſtill better other's happineſs;
Until the heav'ens, envying earth's good hap,
Add an immortal title to your crown.

Richard II. A. 1, S. 1.

He bids you, in the bowels of the Lord,
Deliver up the crown; and to take mercy
On the poor ſouls, for whom this hungry war

Opens his vafty jaws: and on your head
Turns he the widows' tears, the orphans' cries,
The dead men's blood, the pining maidens' groans.
Henry V. A. 2, S. 4.

His looks are full of peaceful majefty;
His head by nature fram'd to wear a crown,
His hand to wield a fceptre, and himfelf
Likely, in time, to blefs a regal throne.
Henry VI. P. 3, A. 4, S. 6.

——— Within the hollow crown,
That rounds the mortal temples of a king,
Keeps Death his court; and there the antic fits,
Scoffing his ftate, and grinning at his pomp;
Allowing him a breath, a little fcene,
To monarchize, be fear'd, and kill with looks;
Infufing him with felf and vain conceit;
As if this flefh, which walls about our life,
Were brafs impregnable; and humour'd thus,
Comes at the laft, and with a little pin,
Bores through his caftle wall, and farewell king!
Richard II. A. 3, S. 2.

A wifp of ftraw were worth a thoufand crowns,
To make this fhamelefs callat know herfelf.[1]
Henry VI. P. 3, A. 2, S. 2.

Fearlefs minds climb fooneft unto crowns.
Brother, we will proclaim you out of hand;
[2]The bruit thereof will bring you many friends.
Henry VI. P. 3. A. 4, S. 7.

[1] *To make this fhamelefs callat know herfelf.*] *Callat*, a lewd woman, a drab, perhaps fo called from the French calote, which was a fort of head-drefs, worn by country girls. STEEVENS.

"A callat," is likewife a *fcold*, a *railer*.

Edward foon after fays, "No wrangling, woman:" and when he ftabs the prince, her fon, he ufes the fame language, "take that, thou likenefs of this railer here!" A. B.

[2] *The bruit*] i. e. Noife. STEEVENS.

"*Bruit*," French, is rather *rumour* than *noife*. A. B.

 CUPID.

CUPID.

Yet mark'd I where the bolt of Cupid fell:
It fell upon a little weſtern flower——
Before, milk-white; now purple with love's wound—
And maidens call it, love-in-idleneſs.
Midſummer Night's Dream, A. 2, S. 2.

I might ſee young Cupid's fiery ſhaft
Quench'd in the chaſte beams of the wat'ry moon;
And the imperial votreſs paſſed on,
In maiden meditation, fancy-free.
Midſummer Night's Dream, A. 2, S 2.

——— I ſaw,
Flying between the cold moon and the earth,
Cupid all arm'd: a certain aim he took
At a fair veſtal, throned by the weſt,
And loos'd his love-ſhaft ſmartly from his bow,
As it ſhould pierce a hundred thouſand hearts.
Midſummer Night's Dream, A. 2, S. 2.

Rouſe yourſelf, and the weak wanton, Cupid,
Shall from your neck unlooſe his amorous fold,
And, like a dew-drop from the lion's mane,
Be ſhook to air. *Troilus and Creſſida*, A. 3, S. 3.

I ſwear to thee by Cupid's ſtrongeſt bow,
By his beſt arrow with the golden head;
In that ſame place thou haſt appointed me,
To-morrow, truly, will I meet with thee.
Midſummer Night's Dream, A. 1, S. 1.

When light wing'd toys
Of feather'd Cupid, ſeal with wanton dulneſs
My ſpeculative and active inſtruments,
That my diſports corrupt and taint by buſineſs,
Let houſewives make a ſkillet of my helm,

And

And all indign and baſe adverſities
Make head againſt my eſtimation.

Othello, A. 1, S. 3.

The barge ſhe ſat in, like a burniſh'd throne,
Burnt on the water; the poop was beaten gold;
Purple the ſails, and ſo perfum'd, that
The winds were love-ſick with them: the oars were
ſilver,
Which to the tune of flutes kept ſtroke, and made
The water which they beat, to follow faſter,
As amorous of their ſtrokes. For her own perſon,
It beggar'd all deſcription: ſhe did lie
In her pavilion (cloth of gold, of tiſſue),
O'er-picturing that Venus, where we ſee
The fancy out-work nature: on each ſide her,
Stood pretty dimpled boys, like ſmiling cupids,
With divers-colour'd fans, whoſe wind did ſeem
To glow the delicate cheeks which they did cool,
And what they undid, did.

Antony and Cleopatra, A. 2, S. 2.

This Signior Junio's giant-dwarf, Dan Cupid;
Regent of love rhimes, lord of folded arms,
The anointed ſovereign of ſighs and groans,
Liege of all loiterers and malcontents,
And I to be a corporal of his field.

Love's Labour Loſt, A. 3, S. 1.

CUR.

Huntſman, I charge thee, tender well my hounds:
Brach Merriman,—the poor cur is imboſt[1].

Tam. Shrew. Induct. S. I.

Braſs,

[1] —*Tender well my hounds:*
Brach Merriman,—the poor cur is imboſt.
Sir J. Hanmer reads, "leach Merriman;" that is, *apply ſome remedies* to Merriman, the poor cur has his *joints ſwell'd*. Perhaps

Brafs, cur[2]!
Thou damned and luxurious mountain goat,
Offer'ſt me brafs? *Henry V.* A. 4, S. 4.

CURRENT.

I'll read you matter, deep, and dangerous;
As full of peril, and advent'rous ſpirit,
As to o'er-walk a current, roaring loud,
On the unſteadfaſt footing of a ſpear.
Hen. IV. P. 1. A. 1, S. 3.

The current, that with gentle murmur glides,
Thou know'ſt, being ſtopp'd, impatiently doth rage.
Two Gent. of Verona, A. 2. S. 7.

CURSE.

Over thy wounds now do I propheſy——
Which, like dumb mouths, do ope their ruby lips,

haps we might read—*bathe* Merriman, which is, I believe, the common practice of huntſmen. JOHNSON.

If for "*hounds,*" we read *hound,* and point the paſſage differently, the whole will be ſufficiently clear.

" Huntſman, I charge thee, tender well my hound
" Brach Merriman:—the poor cur is imboſt." A. B.

[2] *Braſs, cur!*] Either Shakeſpeare had very little knowledge of the French language, or his over-fondneſs for punning led him in this place, contrary to his own judgment, into an error. Almoſt every one knows that the French word *bras,* is pronounced *braw;* and what reſemblance of ſound does this bear to *braſs,* that Piſtol ſhould reply, *braſs, cur?* RAWLINSON.

If the pronunciation of the French language be not changed ſince Shakeſpeare's time, which is not unlikely, it may be ſuſpected ſome other man wrote the French lines. JOHNSON.

The editors are miſtaken. *Bras* is not pronounced *braw,* unleſs it be by the Engliſh. The *s* is always ſounded by a Frenchman. A. B.

To

To beg the voice and utterance of my tongue:
A curſe ſhall light upon the limbs of men;
Domeſtic fury, and fierce civil ſtrife,
Shall cumber all the parts of Italy.

J. Cæſar, A. 3, S. 1.

Good father cardinal, cry thou, amen,
To my keen curſes; for without my wrong,
There is no tongue hath power to curſe him right.

King John, A. 3, S. 1.

— To arms! be champion of our church!
Or let the church, our mother, breathe her curſe,
A mother's curſe, on her revolting ſon.

King John, A. 3, S. 1.

—— Thou know'ſt, great ſon,
The end of war's uncertain; but this certain,
That if thou conquer Rome, the benefit
Which thou ſhalt thereby reap, is ſuch a name,
Whoſe repetition will be dogg'd with curſes.

Coriolanus, A. 5, S. 3.

—— Wherefore ſhould I curſe them?
Would curſes kill, as doth the mandrake's groan,
I would invent as bitter ſearching terms,
As curſt, as harſh, and horrible to hear,
Deliver'd ſtrongly through my fixed teeth,
With full as many ſigns of deadly hate,
As lean-fac'd envy in her loathſome cave.

Hen. VI. P. 2. A. 3, S. 2.

Can curſes pierce the clouds, and enter heaven?—
Why, then give way, dull clouds, to my quick curſes!
Though not by war, by ſurfeit die your king,
As ours by murder, to make him a king!

Rich. III. A. 1, S. 3.

What! I that kill'd her huſband, and his father,
To take her in her heart's extremeſt hate;

With curſes in her mouth, tears in her eyes,
The bleeding witneſs of her hatred by:
With God, her conſcience, and theſe bars againſt
me!
And I no friends to back my ſuit withal,
But the plain devil, and diſſembling looks,
And yet to win her—all the world to nothing!
Rich. III. A. 1, S. 2.

Sir, will you, with thoſe infirmities ſhe owes,[1]
Unfriended, new-adopted to our hate,
Dower'd with our curſe, and ſtranger'd with our
oath,
Take her, or leave her? *Lear,* A. 1, S. 1.

—— Blaſts and fogs upon thee!
The[2] untented woundings of a father's curſe,
Pierce every ſenſe about thee!—Old fond eyes,
Beweep this cauſe again, I'll pluck you out,
And caſt you, with the waters that you loſe,
To temper clay.——— *Lear,* A. 1, S. 4.

[1] —*Owes.*] *i. e.* is poſſeſſed of. STEEVENS.

"Owes," for *owns.* "Infirmities ſhe owes," *Infirmities which ſhe cannot but acknowledge.* We do not ſay that a perſon is *poſſeſſed* of infirmities. A. B.

[2] *The untented woundings.*] Untented wounds, means wounds in their worſt ſtate, not having a *tent* in them to digeſt them; and may poſſibly ſignify here ſuch as will not admit of having a tent put into them for that purpoſe. STEEVENS.

"Untented wounds" may perhaps be underſtood; but "untented woundings" is, in my opinion, without a meaning. I think we may read *unſhented* or *unſhended woundings.* To *ſhend,* in Chaucer and Spenſer, is to *blame.* "*Unſhented woundings of a father's curſe,*" may therefore mean the unblamed or unblameable curſes of a father, &c.—Curſes, which conſidering your conduct, no one will cenſure me for.

A. B.

CUSTOM,

CUSTOM.

The tyrant cuſtom, moſt grave ſenators,
Hath made the flinty and ſteel couch of war,
My thrice-driven bed of down.

Othello, A. 1, S. 3.

New cuſtoms,
Though they be never ſo ridiculous,
Nay, let 'em be unmanly, yet are follow'd.

Henry VIII. A. 1. S. 3.

D.

DANCE, DANCER.

WHEN you do dance, I wiſh you
A wave o'the ſea, that you might ever do
Nothing but that; move ſtill, ſtill ſo,
And own no other function.

Winter's Tale, A. 4, S. 3.

——— He, at Philippi, kept
His ſword even like a dancer, while I ſtruck
The lean and wrinkled Caſſius; and 'twas I,
That the mad Brutus ended. *Ant. & Cleop.* A. 3, S. 9.

Suppoſe the ſinging birds, muſicians;
The graſs whereon thou tread'ſt, the preſence ſtrow'd;
The flowers, fair ladies; and thy ſteps, no more,
Than a delightful meaſure or a dance.

Richard II. A. 1, S. 3.

DANGER.

——— In thy danger;
If ever danger do environ thee,
Commend thy grievance to my holy prayers,
For I will be thy bead's-man.

Two Gent. of Verona, A. 1, S. 1.

Omiſſion to do what is neceſſary
Seals a commiſſion to a blank of danger;
And danger, like an ague, ſubtly taints
Even then when we ſit idly in the ſun.

Troilus and Creſſida. A. 3, S. 3.

The ſpinſters, carders, fullers, weavers, who,
Unfit for other life, compell'd by hunger
And lack of other means, in deſperate manner
Daring the event to the teeth, are all in uproar,
And danger ſerves among them.

Henry VIII. A. 1, S. 2.

It was your pre-ſurmiſe, your ſon might drop:
You were adviſ'd his fleſh was capable
Of wounds, and ſcars, and that his forward ſpirit
Would lift him where moſt trade of danger rang'd:
Yet did you ſay,—Go forth.

Henry IV. P. 2, A. 1, S. 1.

——— The poor condemned Engliſh,
Like ſacrifices, by their watchful fires
Sit patiently, and inly ruminate
The morning's danger; and their geſture ſad,
Inveſting lank-lean cheeks, and war-worn coats,
Preſenteth them unto the gazing moon
So many horrid ghoſts. *Henry V.* A. 4, *Chorus.*

—— Danger knows full well,
That Cæſar is more dangerous than he.
We are two lions, litter'd in one day,
And I the elder and more terrible.

J. Cæſar, A. 2, S. 2.

We muſt not think, the Turk is ſo unſkilful,
To leave that lateſt, which concerns him firſt;
Neglecting an attempt of eaſe, and gain,
To wake, and wage, a danger profitleſs.[1]

Othello, A. 1, S. 3.

[1] *To wake, and wage, a danger profitleſs.*] To *wage* here, as in many other places of Shakeſpeare, ſignifies to fight, to combat.
STEEVENS.

This

Now 'tis the ſpring, and weeds are ſhallow-rooted;
Suffer them now, and they'll o'ergrow the garden,
And choak the herbs for want of huſbandry.
The reverent care, I bear unto my lord,
Made me collect theſe dangers in the duke.
Henry VI. P. 2, A. 3, S. 1.

DARKNESS.

——— If I muſt die,
I will encounter darkneſs as a bride,
And hug it in my arms. *Meaſ. for Meaſ.* A. 3. S. 1.

DAY.

This day is call'd—the feaſt of Criſpian:
He that out-lives this day, and comes ſafe home,
Will ſtand a tip-toe when this day is nam'd,
And rouſe him at the name of Criſpian.
He, that ſhall live this day, and ſee old age,
Will yearly on the vigil feaſt his friends,
And ſay—to morrow is Saint Criſpian.
Hen. V. A. 4, S. 3.

——— Look, the gentle day,
Before the wheels of Phœbus, round about
Dapples the drowſy eaſt with ſpots of grey.
Much ado about nothing, A. 5, S. 3.

Like an unſeaſonable ſtormy day,
Which makes the ſilver rivers drown their ſhores,
As if the world were all diſſolv'd to tears!
So high above his limits ſwells the rage
Of Bolingbroke. *Richard II.* A. 3, S. 2.

This line, I think, ſhould be pointed thus:
"To wake, and wage a danger profitleſs."
To "wage war" is to *engage in war.* To "wage danger" will therefore ſignify to *engage in an hazardous exploit.* A. B.

The

The gaudy, blabbing, and remorseful day
Is crept into the bosom of the sea;
And now loud howling wolves arouse the jades
That drag the tragic melancholy night;
Who with their drowsy, slow, and flagging wings
Clip dead men's graves, and from their misty jaws
Breathe foul contagious darkness in the air.
Henry VI. P. 2, A. 4, S. 1.

——— O, such a day,
So fought, so follow'd, and so fairly won,
Came not, till now, to dignify the times,
Since Cæsar's fortunes! *Henry IV.* P. 2, A. 1, S. 1.

———O, that a man might know
The end of this day's business, ere it come!
But it sufficeth, that the day will end,
And then the end is known.— *J. Cæsar,* A. 5, S. 1.

So I were out of prison, and kept sheep,
I should be merry as the day is long;
And so I would be here, but that I doubt
My uncle practises more harm to me.
K. John, A. 4, S. 1.

No scape of nature, no distemper'd day,
No common wind, no customed event,
But they will pluck away his natural cause,
And call them meteors, prodigies, and signs,
Abortives, presages, and tongues of heaven.
K. John, A. 3, S. 4.

The sun is in the heaven; and the proud day,
Attended with the pleasures of the world,
Is all too wanton, and too full of gawds,
To give me audience.— *K. John,* A. 3, S. 3.

On this day, let seamen fear no wreck,
No bargains break, that are not this day made.
This day, all things begun come to ill end;
Yea, faith itself to hollow falsehood change.
K. John, A. 3. S. 1.

Oh,

Oh,[1] how this ſpring of love reſembleth
The uncertain glory of an April day;
Which now ſhews all the beauty of the ſun,
And by and by a cloud takes all away!

Two Gent. of Verona, A. 1, S. 3.

If it be a hot day, and I brandiſh any thing but my bottle, I would I might never ſpit white again.[2]

Henry IV. P. 2, A. 1, S. 2.

DEATH.

Now boaſt thee, death! in thy poſſeſſion lies
A laſs unparallel'd.—Downy windows, cloſe;
And golden Phœbus never be beheld
Of eyes again ſo royal! *Ant. & Cleop.* A. 5, S. 2.

——— If he be ſlain, ſay ſo:
The tongue offends not, that reports his death.

[1] *Oh, how this ſpring of love reſembleth.*] At the end of this verſe there is wanting a ſyllable, for the ſpeech apparently ends in a quatrain. I find nothing that will rhyme to *ſun*, and therefore I ſhall leave it to ſome happier critic. I ſuſpect that the author might write thus:

"O, how this ſpring of love reſembleth right,
The uncertain glory of an April day;
Which now ſhews all the glory of the light,
And by and by a cloud takes all away!"

Light was either by negligence or affectation changed to *ſun*, which, conſidered without the rhyme, is indeed better. The next tranſcriber, finding that the word *right* did not rhyme to *ſun*, ſuppoſed it incorrectly written, and left it out. JOHNSON.

I think we may read——

"Oh, how love's ſpring reſembleth in its run,
The uncertain glory of an April day;
Which now ſhews all the beauty of the ſun,
And by and by a cloud takes all away!" A. B.

[2] *Would I might never ſpit white again.*] *i. e.* May I never have my ſtomach inflamed with liquor, for to *ſpit white* is the conſequence of inward heat. STEEVENS.

"May I never *ſpit white* again" is a vulgariſm. The meaning ſimply is, *may I never ſpit again—may I die.* For it ſhould be remembered, that if a man ſpits at all, he muſt *ſpit white*. A. B.

And

And he doth ſin, that doth belie the dead;
Not he, which ſays the dead is not alive.

Henry IV. P. 2, A. 1, S. 1.

In few, his death (whoſe ſpirit lent a fire
Even to the dulleſt peaſant in his camp)
Being bruited once, took fire and heat away
From the beſt temper'd courage in his troops.

Henry IV. P. 2, A. 1, S. 1.

I am a tainted wether of the flock,
Meeteſt for death; the weakeſt kind of fruit
Drops earlieſt to the ground, and ſo let me.

Merch. of Venice, A. 4, S. 1.

Your father was ever virtuous; and holy men,
At their death, have good inſpirations.

Merch. of Venice, A. 1, S. 2.

Young Arthur's death is common in their mouths,
And when they talk of him, they ſhake their heads,
And whiſper one another in the ear;
And he, that ſpeaks, doth gripe the hearer's wriſt;
Whilſt he, that hears, makes fearful action
With wrinkled brows, with nods, with rolling eyes.

King John, A. 4, S. 2.

—— Without this match,
The ſea enraged is not half ſo deaf,
Lions more confident, mountains and rocks
More free from motion; no, not Death himſelf
In mortal fury half ſo peremptory,
As we to keep this city. *King John*, A. 2, S. 2.

——— Oh amiable lovely death!
Thou odoriferous ſtench! ſound rottenneſs!
Ariſe forth from the couch of laſting night,
Thou hate and terror to proſperity,
And I will kiſs thy deteſtable bones.

King John, A. 3, S. 4.

—— If

—— If thou art rich, thou art poor;
For like an aſs whoſe back with ingots bows,
Thou bear'ſt thy heavy riches but a journey,
And death unloads thee. *Meaſ. for Meaſ.* A. 3, S. 1.

To ſue to live, I find, I ſeek to die;
And, ſeeking death, find life.
Meaſure for Meaſure, A. 3, S. 1.

—— Thy beſt of reſt is ſleep,
And that thou oft provok'ſt, yet groſſly fear'ſt
Thy death, which is no more.
Meaſure for Meaſure, A. 3, S. 1.

O Warwick! Warwick! that Plantagenet,
Which held thee dearly as his ſoul's redemption,
Is by the ſtern Lord Clifford done to death.[1]
Henry VI. P. 3, A. 2, S. 1.

The weарieſt and moſt loathed worldly life,
That age, ach, penury, and impriſonment,
Can lay on nature, is a paradiſe
To what we fear of death.
Meaſure for Meaſure, A. 3, S. 1.

When firſt this order was ordain'd,
Knights of the garter were of noble birth;
Valiant, and virtuous, full of haughty courage,
Such as were grown to credit by the wars;
Not fearing death, nor ſhrinking for diſtreſs,
But always reſolute in moſt extremes.
Henry VI. P. 1, A. 4, S. 1.

Why ſtand we like ſoft-hearted women here,
Wailing our loſſes, whiles the foe doth rage:

[1] *Is by the ſtern Lord Clifford done to death.*] *Done to death* for *killed*, was a common expreſſion long before Shakeſpeare's time. Thus Chaucer:—

And ſaid, that if ye *done* us both *to die*.

And Spencer mentions a plague which many *did to dye*.

JOHNSON.

The expreſſion is according to the French idiom—*faire mourir*. A. B.

Here

Here on my knee I vow to God above,
I'll never pauſe again; never ſtand ſtill,
Till either death hath clos'd theſe eyes of mine,
Or fortune given me meaſure of revenge.

Henry VI. P. 3, A. 2, S. 3.

Her blood is ſettled, and her joints are ſtiff,
Life and theſe lips have long been ſeparated;
Death lies on her, like an untimely froſt
Upon the ſweeteſt flower of all the field.

Romeo and Juliet, A. 4, S. 5.

Let them pull all about mine ears; preſent me
Death on the wheel, or at wild horſes heels;
Or pile ten hills on the Tarpeian rock,
That the precipitation might down ſtretch
Below the beam of ſight, yet will I ſtill
Be thus to them. *Coriolanus*, A. 3, S. 2.

If I ſay, fine, cry fine; if death, cry death;
Inſiſting on the old prerogative
And power i'the truth o'the cauſe.[1]

Coriolanus, A. 3. S. 3.

Let them pronounce the ſteep Tarpeian death,
Vagabond exile, fleaing: pent to linger
But with a grain a day, I would not buy
Their mercy at the price of one fair word.

Coriolanus, A. 3, S. 3.

[1] *Inſiſting on the old prerogative,*
And power i'the truth o'the cauſe.] This is not eaſily underſtood; we might read,

O'er the truth of the cauſe. JOHNSON.

Very eaſily underſtood ſurely. *Truth* is, in this place, ſupport. *Inſiſting on your old prerogative and power in ſupport of the cauſe*; i. e. the cauſe of the people. A. B.

Though

Though I kill him not, I am the cauſe
His death was ſo effected: better 'twere,
I met the ravin lion when he roar'd,
With ſharp conſtraint of hunger.
All's well that ends well, A. 3, S. 2.

Call me their traitor!—thou injurious tribune!
Within thine eyes ſat twenty thouſand deaths,
In thy hands clutch'd as many millions, in
Thy lying tongue both numbers, I would ſay,
Thou lieſt unto thee, with a voice as free
As I do pray the gods. *Coriolanus*, A. 3, S. 3.

All comfort go with thee!
For none abides with me: my joy is—death!
Death, at whoſe name I oft have been afraid,
Becauſe I wiſh'd this world's eternity.——
Henry VI. P. 2, A. 2, S. 4.

Oft have I ſeen a timely-parted ghoſt,
Of aſhy ſemblance, meagre, pale, and bloodleſs
Being all deſcended to the labouring heart;
Who in the conflict that it holds with death,
Attracts the ſame for aidance 'gainſt the enemy,
Which with the heart there cools, and ne'er returns,
To bluſh and beautify the cheek again.
Henry VI. P. 2, A. 3, S. 2.

Beware of yonder dog;
Look, when he fawns, he bites; and when he bites,
His venom tooth will rankle to the death:
Have not to do with him, beware of him;
Sin, death, and hell, have ſet their marks upon him,
And all their miniſters attend on him.
Rich. III. A. 1, S. 3.

Have I a tongue to doom my brother's death,
And ſhall that tongue give pardon to a ſlave?
My brother kill'd no man, his fault was thought,
And yet his puniſhment was bitter death.

Who ſu'd to me for him? who, in my wrath,
Kneel'd at my feet, and bid me be adviſ'd?
Rich. III. A. 2, S. 1.

I have bewept a worthy huſband's death,
And liv'd by looking on his images:
But now, two mirrors of his princely ſemblance
Are crack'd in pieces by malignant death;
And I for comfort have but one falſe glaſs,
That grieves me when I ſee my ſhame in him.
Rich. III. A. 2, S. 2.

The bloody proclamation to eſcape,
That follow'd me ſo near (O our lives' ſweetneſs!
That we the pain of death would hourly bear,
Rather than die at once!) taught me to ſhift
Into a mad man's rags. *Lear*, A. 5, S. 3.

O wretched ſtate! O boſom black as death!
O limed ſoul, that ſtruggling to be free,
Art more engag'd! Help, angels, make aſſay!
Bow, ſtubborn knees! and, heart, with ſtrings of ſteel,
Be ſoft as ſinews of the new-born babe.
Hamlet, A. 3, S. 3.

Who would fardles bear,
To groan and ſweat under a weary life;
But that the dread of ſomething after death—
The undiſcover'd country, from whoſe bourn
No traveller returns—puzzles the will,
And makes us rather bear thoſe ills we have,
Than fly to others that we know not of.
Hamlet, A. 3, S. 1.

Young Fortinbras—
Holding a weak ſuppoſal of our worth,
Or thinking by our late dear brother's death,
Our ſtate to be disjoint and out of frame—

Col-

Colleagued[1] with this dream of his advantage,
He hath not fail'd to pester us with message,
Importing the surrender of those lands
Lost by his father. *Hamlet*, A. 1, S. 2.

I'll call thee Hamlet,
King, father, royal Dane: O, answer me!
Let me not burst in ignorance! but tell,
Why thy canoniz'd bones, hearsed in death,
Have burst their cearments? Why the sepulchre,
Wherein we saw thee quietly in-urn'd,
Hath op'd his ponderous and marble jaws,
To cast thee up again? *Hamlet*, A. 1, S. 4.

He is a devil in private brawl: souls and bodies, hath he divorced three; and his incensement at this moment is so implacable, that satisfaction can be none but by pangs of death and sepulchre.

Twelfth Night, A. 3, S. 4.

You gentle gods, give me but this I have,
And sear up my embracements from a next
With bonds of death!—Remain, remain thou here,
While sense can keep it on![2]

Cymbeline, A. 1, S. 2.

—— The next time I do fight,
I'll make death love me; for I will contend
Even with his pestilent scythe.

Ant. and Cleop. A. 3, S. 11.

[1] *Colleagued with this dream of his advantage.*] The meaning is, he goes to war so indiscreetly and unprepared, that he has no allies to support him but a *dream* with which he is colleagued or confederated. WARBURTON.

"Colleagued with this dream of his advantage," is merely, *thinking it might turn out to his advantage or benefit.* A. B.

[2] *While sense can keep it on.*] The expression means, while sense can maintain its operations; while sense continues to have power. STEEVENS.

"While sense can keep it on." *Sense* in this place is *life, motion,* and not the intellectual faculty. Posthumus would say, that while he has life the ring shall remain on his finger.

A. B.

—— I, in mine woe charm'd,
Could not find death, where I did hear him groan,
Nor feel him where he ſtruck: being an ugly monſter,
'Tis ſtrange he hides him in freſh cups, ſoft beds,
Sweet words; or hath more miniſters than we
That draw his knives i'the war.

Cymbeline, A. 5, S. 3.

——— Death!
Come grin on me, and I will think thou ſmil'ſt,
And buſs thee as thy wife! Miſery's love;
Oh, come to me! *King John*, A. 3, S. 4.

Better it were a brother dy'd at once,
Than that a ſiſter, by redeeming him,
Should die forever.

Meaſure for Meaſure, A. 2, S. 4.

Madam, I'll follow you unto the death.[1]

King John, A. 1, S. 1.

Here's a ſtay,[2]
That ſhakes the rotten carcaſe of old Death
Out of his rags! here's a large mouth, indeed,
That ſpits forth death, and mountains, rocks, and ſea.

King John, A. 2, S. 2.

DEED,

[1] *Unto the death.*] This expreſſion is common among our ancient writers. STEEVENS.

"Unto the death" is according to the French idiom—*juſqu'a la mort.* A. B.

[2] *Here's a ſtay,*
That ſhakes the rotten carcaſe of old Death
Out of his rags.

I cannot but think every reader wiſhes for ſome other word in the place of *ſtay*, which, though it may ſignify an hindrance, or *man* that *binders*, is yet very improper to introduce the next line. I read

"Here's a flaw
"That ſhakes, &c."

that is, here is a *guſt* of bravery, a *blaſt* of menace. JOHNSON.

I cannot

DEED, DEEDS.

——— To do this deed,
Promotion follows: If I could find example
Of thouſands, that had ſtruck anointed kings,
And flouriſh'd after, I'd not do't.
Winter's Tale, A. 1, S. 2.

——— It is great
To do that thing that ends all other deeds;
Which ſhackles accidents, and bolts up change;
Which ſleeps, and never palates more the dung,
The beggar's nurſe and Cæſar's.
Antony and Cleopatra, A. 5, S. 2.

——— How he gliſters
Through my dark ruſt! and how his piety
Does my deeds make the blacker!
Winter's Tale, A. 3, S. 2.

——— O, ſuch a deed,
As from the body of contraction plucks
The very ſoul; and ſweet religion makes
A rhapſody of words. *Hamlet*, A. 3, S. 4.

——— What! gone without a word?
Ay, ſo true love ſhould do: it cannot ſpeak;
For truth hath better deeds, than words, to grace it.
Two Gentlemen of Verona, A. 2, S. 2.

——— By my hopes,—
This preſent enterprize ſet off his head,—
I do not think, a braver gentleman,
More active-valiant, or more valiant-young,—

I cannot diſcover any meaning in the preſent reading, "Here's "a ſtay, &c." and am firmly perſuaded that the poet muſt have written, *Here's a ſay*, i. e. here's a ſpeech, &c. That this is the true reading, the whole tenour of Falconbridge's reply will ſhew: —"Here's a mouth, indeed"—"Zounds! I was never ſo be-"thump'd with words," &c.

"Here's a ſay," is not, indeed, a very elegant expreſſion; but it accords ſufficiently well with the character of Falconbridge.

A. B.

More daring, or more bold, is now alive,
To grace this latter age with noble deeds.
Henry IV. P. 1, A. 5, S. 1.

If thou delight to view thy heinous deeds,
Behold this pattern of thy butcheries:—
Oh, gentlemen, ſee, ſee! dead Henry's wounds
Open their congeal'd mouths, and bleed afreſh!
Richard III. A. 1, S. 2.

——— The time will come,
That I ſhall make this northern youth exchange
His glorious deeds for my indignities.
Percy is but my factor, good my lord,
To ingroſs up glorious deeds on my behalf.
Henry IV. P. 1, A. 3, S. 2.

How oft the ſight of means to do ill deeds,
Makes deeds ill done? Hadeſt not thou been by,
A fellow by the hand of nature mark'd,
Quoted, and ſign'd, to do a deed of ſhame,
This murder had not come into my mind.
King John, A. 4, S. 2.

This is the man ſhould do the bloody deed;
The image of a wicked heinous fault
Lives in his eye; that cloſe aſpect of his
Does ſhew the mood of a much-troubled breaſt.
King John, A. 4, S. 2.

Good friends, ſweet friends, let me not ſtir you up
To ſuch a ſudden flood of mutiny.
They, that have done this deed, are honourable;
What private griefs they have, alas, I know not,
That made them do it. *Julius Cæſar,* A. 3, S. 2.

How far that little candle throws his beams!
So ſhines a good deed in a naughty world.
Merchant of Venice, A. 5, S. 1.

——— Who ſhall believe,
But you miſuſe the reverence of your place;
Employ the countenance and grace of heaven,

As a falſe favourite doth his prince's name,
In deeds diſhonourable? *Henry IV.* P. 2, A. 4, S. 2.

I thank you, princes, for my daughter's death;
Record it with your high and worthy deeds;
'Twas bravely done, if you bethink you of it.
Much ado about nothing, A. 5, S. 1.

This would'ſt thou ſay,—Your ſon did thus and thus;
Your brother, thus; ſo fought the noble Douglas;
Stopping my greedy ear with their bold deeds:
But in the end, to ſtop mine ear indeed,
Thou haſt a ſigh to blow away this praiſe,
Ending with—brother, ſon, and all are dead.
Henry IV. P. 2, A. 1, S. 1.

If thou doſt ſlander her, and torture me,
Never pray more: abandon all remorſe;
On horror's head, horrors accumulate;
Do deeds to make heaven weep, all earth amaz'd;
For nothing canſt thou to damnation add,
Greater than that. *Othello*, A. 3, S. 3.

——— I pray you, in your letters,
When you ſhall theſe unlucky deeds relate,
Speak of me as I am; nothing extenuate,
Nor ſet down aught in malice. *Othello*, A. 5, S. 2.

DEER.

——For his weeping in the needleſs ſtream;
Poor deer, quoth he, thou mak'ſt a teſtament
As worldlings do, giving the ſum of more
To that which had too much.
As you like it, A. 2, S. 1.

DESIGN.

[1] He hath diſcover'd my deſign, and I
G 4 Remain

[1] *He hath diſcover'd my deſign, and I Remain a pinch'd thing.*] Alluding to the ſuperſtition of

Remain a pinch'd thing; yea, a very trick
For them to play at will. *Winter's Tale*, A. 2, S. 1.

DESIRES.

——— Thy defires
Are wolfifh, bloody, ftarv'd and ravenous.
Merchant of Venice, A. 4, S. 1.

But now I am return'd, and that war-thoughts
Have left their places vacant, in their rooms
Come thronging foft and delicate defires,
All prompting me how fair young Hero is.
Much ado about nothing, A. 1, S. 1.

DESPAIR.

You common cry of curs!
Let every feeble rumour fhake your hearts!
Your enemies with nodding of their plumes,
Fan you into defpair! Have the power ftill
To banifh your defenders. *Coriolanus*, A. 3, S. 3.

Oft expectation fails, and moft oft there
Where moft it promifes; and oft it hits,
Where hope is coldeft, and defpair moft fits.
All's well that ends well, A. 2, S. 1.

O thou eternal Mover of the heavens,
Look with a gentle eye upon this wretch!
Oh, beat away the bufy meddling fiend,
And from his bofom purge this black defpair.
Henry VI. P. 2, A. 3, S. 3.

of the vulgar, concerning thofe that were enchanted, and faftened to the fpot, by charms fuperior to their own.

WARBURTON.

The fenfe, I think, is, he hath now difcovered my defign, and I am treated as a mere baby, a thing pinched out of clouts, a puppet for them to move and actuate as they pleafe. Dr. Warburton's fuppofed allufion to enchantments is quite befide the purpofe.

REVISAL.

"Pinch'd thing" fhould certainly be *pinch'n*, i. e. *one who is to be played upon*. The word is ufed by Chaucer. *Pincer*, Fr. to jeer, to banter.

A. B.

DETRAC-

DETRACTION.

Happy are they that hear their detractions, and can put them to mending.

Much ado about nothing, A. 2, S. 3.

DEVIL.

——— Divinity of hell!
When devils will their blackest sins put on,
They do suggest at first with heavenly shews,
As I do now. *Othello*, A. 2, S. 3.

Whatsoever cunning fiend it was,
That wrought upon thee so preposterously,
He hath got the voice in hell for excellence:
And other devils, that suggest by treasons,
Do botch and bungle up damnation
With patches, colours, and with forms being fetch'd
From glistering semblances of piety.

Henry V. A. 2, S. 2.

I press me none but good housholders, yeomen's sons; inquire me out contracted bachelors, such as had been ask'd twice on the bans: such a commodity of warm slaves, as had as lief hear the devil as a drum; such as fear the report of a caliver, worse than a struck fowl, or a hurt wild-duck.

Henry IV. P. 1, A. 4, S. 2.

Something may be done, that we will not:
And sometimes we are devils to ourselves,
When we will tempt the frailty of our powers,
Presuming on their changeful potency.

Troilus and Cressida, A. 4, S. 4.

——— Worthy duke,
You bid me seek redemption of the devil:
Hear me yourself. *Measure for Measure*, A. 5, S. 1.

——— Let the devil
Be sometimes honour'd for his burning throne.

Measure for Measure, A. 5, S. 1.

The

The devil can cite ſcripture for his purpoſe.
Merchant of Venice, A. 1, S. 3.

Come, ſwear it, damn thyſelf;
Leſt, being like one of heaven, the devils themſelves
Should fear to ſeize thee: therefore be double damn'd,
Swear—thou art honeſt. *Othello*, A. 4, S. 2.

——— Whip me, ye devils,
From the poſſeſſion of this heavenly ſight!
Blow me about in winds! roaſt me in ſulphur!
Waſh me in ſteep-down gulfs of liquid fire!—
O Deſdemona! Deſdemona! dead?
Othello, A. 5, S. 2.

DEW.

Let me wipe off this honourable dew,
That ſilverly doth progreſs on thy cheeks:
This ſhower, blown up by tempeſt of the ſoul,
Startles mine eyes, and makes me more amaz'd
Than had I ſeen the vaulty top of heaven
Figur'd quite o'er with burning meteors.
King John, A. 5, S. 2.

As wicked dew, as e'er my mother bruſh'd
With raven's feather from unwholeſome fen,
Drop on you both! *Tempeſt*, A. 1, S. 2.

O, that this too too ſolid fleſh would melt,
Thaw, and reſolve itſelf into a dew!
Or that the Everlaſting had not fix'd
His canon 'gainſt ſelf-ſlaughter! *Hamlet*, A. 1, S. 2.

My hounds are bred out of the Spartan kind,
So flew'd, ſo ſanded, and their heads are hung
With ears that ſweep away the morning dew;
Crook-knee'd, and dew-lap'd, like Theſſalian bulls:
Slow in purſuit, but match'd in mouth like bells,
Each under each.
Midſummer Night's Dream, A. 4, S. 1.

DIS-

DISCOURSE.

These high wild hills, and rough uneven ways,
Draw out our miles, and make them wearisome:
And yet your fair discourse hath been as sugar,
Making the hard way sweet and delectable.
Richard II. A. 2, S. 3.

What should we speak of,
When we are as old as you? When we shall hear
The rain and wind beat dark December, how,
In this our pinching cave, shall we discourse
The freezing hours away? *Cymbeline*, A. 3, S. 3.

—— These things to hear,
Would Desdemona seriously incline:
But still the house affairs would draw her thence;
Which ever as she could with haste dispatch,
She'd come again, and with a greedy ear
Devour up my discourse. *Othello*, A. 1, S. 3.

Of government the properties to unfold,
Would seem in me to affect speech and discourse.
Measure for Measure, A. 1, S. 1.

DISCRETION.

Good Michael, look you to the guard to-night:
Let's teach ourselves that honourable stop,
Not to out-sport discretion. *Othello*, A. 2, S. 3.

DISEASE.

—— We are all diseas'd;
And, with our surfeiting, and wanton hours,
Have brought ourselves into a burning fever,
And we must bleed for it: of which disease
Our late king, Richard, being infected, dy'd.
Henry IV. P. 2, A. 4, S. 1.

I can get no remedy against this consumption of the purse; borrowing only lingers and lingers it out, but the disease is incurable. *Henry IV.* P. 2, A. 1, S. 2.

Before

Before the curing of a ſtrong diſeaſe,
Even in the inſtant of repair and health,
The fit is ſtrongeſt; evils, that take leave,
On their departure moſt of all ſhew evil.
King John, A. 3, S. 4.

He will hang upon him like a diſeaſe: he is ſooner caught than the peſtilence, and the taker runs preſently mad. *Much ado about nothing*, A. 1, S. 1.

DISTRESS.

—— The thorny point
Of bare diſtreſs hath ta'en from me the ſhew
Of ſmooth civility. *As you like it*, A. 2, S. 7.

DIVINE.

It is a good divine that follows his own inſtructions. *Merchant of Venice*, A. 1, S. 2.

DOVE.

The dove purſues the griffin; the mild hind
Makes ſpeed to catch the tyger.
Midſummer Night's Dream, A. 2, S. 2.

DREAM.

My ſpirits, as in a dream, are all bound up.
Tempeſt, A. 1, S. 2.

—— We are ſuch ſtuff
As dreams are made on, and our little life
Is rounded with a ſleep. *Tempeſt*, A. 4, S. 1.

—— Dreams are toys:
Yet, for this once, yea, ſuperſtitiouſly,
I will be ſquar'd by this. *Winter's Tale*, A. 3, S. 3.

I have heard, (but not believ'd) the ſpirits of the dead
May walk again; if ſuch things be, thy mother
Appear'd to me laſt night; for ne'er was dream
So like a waking. *Winter's Tale*, A. 3, S. 3.

—— Poor

——— Poor wretches, that depend
On greatneſs' favour, dream as I have done;
Wake, and find nothing. But, alas, I ſwerve:
Many dream not to find, neither deſerve,
And yet are ſteep'd in favours. *Cymbeline*, A. 5, S. 4.

——— To die;—to ſleep;—
To ſleep! perchance, to dream;—Ay, there's the rub;
For in that ſleep of death what dreams may come,
When we have ſhuffled off this mortal coil [1],
Muſt give us pauſe: there's the reſpect,
That makes calamity of ſo long life.
Hamlet, A. 3, S. 1.

I dreamt, my lady came and found me dead;
(Strange dream! that gives a dead man leave to think)
And breath'd ſuch life with kiſſes in my lips,
That I reviv'd, and was an emperor.
Romeo and Juliet, A. 5, S. 1.

[2] If I may truſt the flattering truth of ſleep,
My dreams preſage ſome joyful news at hand:
My boſom's lord ſits lightly on his throne;
And, all this day, an unaccuſtom'd ſpirit
Lifts me above the ground with cheerful thoughts.
Romeo and Juliet, A. 5, S. 1.

[1] ——— *mortal coil.*] *i. e.* Turmoil; buſtle. WARBURTON.

"When we have ſhuffled off this mortal coil," *i. e.* When we have ſhaken off the ſhackles which at preſent bind, or hold us.

Coil is uſed in alluſion to the coiling or ſtrengthening of a rope by winding it in the form of a ring, whence *coil* is fetter. A. B.

[2] *If I may truſt the flattering truth of ſleep.*] The ſenſe is, if I may only truſt the honeſty of ſleep, which I know, however, not to be ſo nice as not often to practiſe flattery. JOHNSON.

The oldeſt copy reads, "the flattering *eye* of ſleep." Whether this reading ought to ſuperſede the more modern one, I ſhall not pretend to determine; it appears to me, however, the moſt eaſily intelligible of the two. STEEVENS.

The ſenſe, I think, is,—"If I may give any credit to the viſions of the night, which have been flattering to me, ſome joyful news is at hand." A. B.

——— I talk

——— I talk of dreams;
Which are the children of an idle brain,
Begot of nothing but vain phantafy;
Which is as thin of fubftance as the air;
And more inconftant than the wind, who wooes
Even now the frozen bofom of the north,
And, being anger'd, puffs away from thence,
Turning his face to the dew-dropping fouth.
Romeo and Juliet, A. 1, S. 4.

I know thee not, old man: fall to thy prayers:
How ill white hairs become a fool, and jefter!
I have long dream'd of fuch a kind of man,
So furfeit-fwell'd, fo old, and fo profane;
But, being awake, I do defpife my dream.
Henry IV. P. 2, A. 5, S. 5.

Between the acting of a dreadful thing,
And the firft motion, all the interim is
Like a phantafma, or a hideous dream;
The genius, and the mortal inftruments,
Are then in council, and the ftate of man,
Like to a little kingdom, fuffers then
The nature of an infurrection.
Julius Cæfar, A. 2, S. 1.

Think our former ftate a happy dream;
From which awak'd, the truth of what we are
Shews us but this: I am fworn brother, fweet,
To grim neceffity; and he and I
Will keep a league till death. *Richard II.* A. 5, S. 1.

——— Thou proud dream,
That play'ft fo fubtly with a king's repofe,
I am a king, that find thee: and I know,
'Tis not the balm, the fcepter, and the ball,
The fword, the mace, the crown imperial,
The enter-tiffued robe of gold and pearl,
The farfed title running 'fore the king,
The throne he fits on, nor the tide of pomp
That beats upon the high fhore of the world,

No,

No, not all these, laid in bed majestical,
Can sleep so soundly as the wretched slave;
Who, with a body fill'd, and vacant mind,
Gets him to rest, cramm'd with distressful bread,
Never sees horrid night, the child of hell;
But, like a lacquey, from the rise to set,
Sweats in the eye of Phœbus, and all night
Sleeps in elysium. *Henry V.* A. 4, S. 1.

There is some ill a brewing towards my rest,
For I did dream of money-bags to-night.
Merchant of Venice, A. 2, S. 5.

DUTY.

——— Others there are,
Who, trimm'd in forms and visages of duty,
Keep yet their hearts attending on themselves;
And throwing but shows of service on their lords,
Do well thrive by them, and, when they have lin'd their coats,
Do themselves homage: these fellows have some soul,
And such a one do I profess myself.
Othello, A. 1, S. 1.

——— Throw away respect,
Tradition, form, and ceremonious duty,
For you have but mistook me all this while:
I live on bread like you, feel want, taste grief,
Need friends;—subjected thus,
How can you say to me—I am a king?
Richard II. A. 3, S. 2.

Every subject's duty is the king's: but every subject's soul is his own. Therefore should every soldier in the wars do as every sick man in his bed, wash every moth out of his conscience: and doing so, death is to him advantage; or not dying, the time was blessedly lost, wherein such preparation was gained: and, in him that escapes, it were not sin to think, that, making God so free an offer, he let him out-

out-live that day to ſee his greatneſs, and to teach others how they ſhould prepare. *Henry V.* A. 4, S. 1.

—— We thought ourſelf thy lawful king:
And if we be, how dare thy joints forget
To pay their awful duty to our preſence?
If we be not, ſhew us the hand of God
That hath diſmiſs'd us from our ſtewardſhip.

Richard II. A. 3, S. 3.

——— Be pleaſed then
To pay that duty, which you truly owe,
To him that owes it, namely, this young prince:
And then our arms, like to a muzzled bear,
Save in aſpect, have all offence ſeal'd up.

King John, A. 2, S. 1.

Though all the world ſhould crack their duty to you,
And throw it from their ſoul; though perils did
Abound, as thick as thought could make 'em, and
Appear in forms more horrid; yet my duty,
As doth a rock againſt the chiding flood,
Should the approach of this wild river break,
And ſtand unſhaken yours. *Henry VIII.* A. 3, S. 2.

Such duty as the ſubject owes the prince,
Even ſuch, a woman oweth to her huſband:
And, when ſhe's froward, peeviſh, ſullen, ſour,
And, not obedient to his honeſt will,
What is ſhe but a foul contending rebel,
And graceleſs traitor to her loving lord?

Taming of the Shrew, A. 5, S. 2.

[1] ——— What poor duty cannot do,
Noble reſpect takes it in might, not merit.

Midſummer Night's Dream, A. 5, S. 1.

I love

[1] —— *and what poor duty cannot do,*
Noble reſpect takes it in might, not merit.] The ſenſe of this paſſage, as it now ſtands, if it has any ſenſe, is this: *What the inability of duty cannot perform, regardful generoſity receives as an act of ability, though not of merit.* The contrary is rather true: *What*

I love not to ſee wretchedneſs o'ercharg'd,
And duty in his ſervice periſhing.
Midſummer Night's Dream, A. 5, S. 1.

—— In the modeſty of fearful duty
I read as much, as from the rattling tongue
Of ſaucy and audacious eloquence.
Midſummer Night's Dream, A. 5, S. 1.

——— Never any thing can be amiſs,
When ſimpleneſs and duty tender it.
Midſummer Night's Dream, A. 5, S. 1.

E.

EAR, EARS.

YOU cram theſe words into mine ears againſt
The ſtomach of my ſenſe. *Tempeſt*, A. 2, S. 1.

—— The iſle is full of noiſes,
Sounds, and ſweet airs, that give delight, and hurt not.
Sometimes a thouſand twangling inſtruments
Will hum about mine ears. *Tempeſt*, A. 3, S. 2.

—— Full many a lady
I've ey'd with beſt regard; and many a time

What dutifulneſs tries to perform without ability, regardful generoſity receives as having the merit, though not the power, of complete performance.

We ſhould therefore read,

"And what poor duty cannot do,
"Noble reſpect takes not in might, but merit."

JOHNSON.

"Might," in this place, is not *ability* but *endeavour*.

A. B.

The harmony of their tongues hath into bondage
Brought my too diligent ear. *Tempest*, A. 3, S. 1.

Ah, kill me with thy weapon, not with words!
My breast can better brook thy dagger's point,
Than can my ears that tragic history.——
Henry VI. P. 3, A. 5, S. 6.

Dear Isabel,
I have a motion much imports your good;
Whereto if you'll a willing ear incline,
What's mine is yours, and what is yours is mine.
Measure for Measure, A. 5, S. 1.

Friends, Romans, countrymen, lend me your ears;
I come to bury Cæsar, not to praise him.
The evil that men do lives after them;
The good is oft interred with their bones,
So let it be with Cæsar. *Julius Cæsar*, A. 3, S. 2.

This sleep is sound, indeed; this is a sleep,
That from this golden rigol hath divorc'd
So many English kings. Thy due from me,
Is tears, and heavy sorrows of the blood;
Which nature, love, and filial tenderness,
Shall, O dear father, pay thee plenteously.
Henry IV. P. 2, A. 4, S. 4.

I pray thee, cease thy counsel,
Which falls into mine ears as profitless
As water in a sieve.
Much ado about nothing, A. 5, S. 1.

Ram[1] thou thy fruitful tidings in mine ears,
That long time have been barren.
Antony and Cleopatra, A. 2, S. 5.

EARTH.

[1] *Ram thou thy fruitful tidings.*—] Shakespeare probably wrote (as Sir T. Hanmer observes) *Rain thou*, &c. *Rain* agrees better with the epithets, *fruitful* and *barren*. STEEVENS.

Perhaps.

E A R T H.

Advance your ſtandards, draw your willing ſwords:
For me, the ranſom of my bold attempt,
Shall be this cold corpſe on the earth's cold face;
But if I thrive, the gain of my attempt,
The leaſt of you ſhall ſhare his part thereof.
Richard III. A. 5, S. 3.

Feed not thy ſov'reign's foe, my gentle earth,
Nor with thy ſweets comfort his rav'nous ſenſe;
But let thy ſpiders, that ſuck up thy venom,
And heavy-gaited toads, lie in their way.
Richard II. A. 3, S. 2.

The bay-trees in our country are all wither'd,
And meteors fright the fixed ſtars of heaven;
The pale-fac'd moon looks bloody on the earth,
And lean-look'd prophets whiſper fearful change.
Richard II. A. 2, S. 4.

As a long-parted mother with her child
Plays fondly, with tears and ſmiles, in meeting;
So, weeping, ſmiling, greet I thee, my earth,
And do thee favour with my royal hand.
Richard II. A. 3, S. 2.

I am ſorry I ſhould force you to believe
That, which I would to heaven I had not ſeen;
But theſe, mine eyes, ſaw him in bloody ſtate,
Rend'ring faint quittance, wearied and out-breath'd,
To Harry Monmouth; whoſe ſwift wrath beat down
The never-daunted Percy to the earth.
Henry IV. P. 2, A. 1, S. 1.

Perhaps we ſhould read, *Cram thou*, &c. Shakeſpeare writes in another place;
"You cram theſe news into mine ear againſt
"The ſtomach of my ſenſe."
Hanmer's emendation, however, is certainly deſerving of notice. A. B.

—Seek through the regions of the earth
For one his like, there would be ſomething failing
In him that ſhould compare. I do not think,
So fair an outward, and ſuch ſtuff within,
Endows a man but he. *Cymbeline*, A. 1, S. 1.

All you unpubliſh'd virtues of the earth,
Spring with my tears! be aidant, and remediate,
In the good man's diſtreſs!—Seek, ſeek, for him;
Leſt his ungovern'd rage diſſolve the life
That wants the means to lead it.

Lear, A. 4, S. 4.

I have of late (but wherefore, I know not) loſt all my mirth; foregone all cuſtom of exerciſes: and indeed, it goes ſo heavily with my diſpoſition, that this goodly frame, the earth, ſeems to me a ſteril promontory: this moſt excellent canopy, the air, look you, this brave o'er-hanging firmament, this majeſtical roof, fretted with golden fire, why it appears no other thing to me, than a foul and peſtilent congregation of vapours.

Hamlet, A. 2, S. 2.

My[1] boſky acres, and my unſhrubb'd down,
Rich ſcarf to my proud earth.

Tempeſt, A. 4, S. 1.

EAST.

—— Who ſees the heavenly Roſaline,
That like a rude and ſavage man of Inde,
At the firſt opening of the gorgeous Eaſt,
Bows not his vaſſal head.

Love's Labour Loſt, A. 4, S. 3.

[1] *My boſky acres.*] *Boſky* is *woody*. *Boſquet*, French.
STEEVENS.

"Boſky acres," muſt mean *fat*, *fertile* acres. *Boſky* is frequently uſed in that ſenſe. A. B.

ECHO.

——Wilt thou hunt?
Thy hounds ſhall make the welkin anſwer them,
And fetch ſhrill echoes from the hollow earth.
Taming of the Shrew, Induct.

——Let us ſit,
And—whilſt the babbling echo mocks the hounds,
Replying ſhrilly to the well-tun'd horns,
As if a double hunt were heard at once——
Let us ſit down and mark their yelling noiſe.
Titus Andronicus, A. 2, S. 3.

——Do but ſtart
An echo with the clamour of thy drum,
And even at hand a drum is ready brac'd,
That ſhall reverberate all as loud as thine;
Sound but another, and another ſhall,
As loud as thine, rattle the welkin's ear,
And mock the deep-mouth'd thunder.
King John, A. 5, S. 2.

ENEMY, ENEMIES.

I thought I ſhould have ſeen ſome Hercules,
A ſecond Hector, for his grim aſpect,
And large proportion of his ſtrong-knit limb.
Alas! this is a child, a ſilly dwarf;
It cannot be, this weak and wrizzl'd ſhrimp
Should ſtrike ſuch terror to his enemies.
Henry VI. P. 1, A. 2, S. 3,

I would to God, my name were not ſo terrible to the enemy as it is. 'Twere better to be eaten to death with ruſt, than to be ſcour'd to nothing with perpetual motion.
Henry IV. P. 2, A. 1, S. 2.

'Tis but thy name, that is my enemy;
Thou art thyſelf, though not a Montague.[1]
What's Montague? It is not hand, nor foot,
Nor arm, nor face, nor any other part:
What's in a name? that which we call a roſe,
By any other name would ſmell as ſweet.

Romeo and Juliet, A. 2, S. 2.

My lord cardinal, you are not to be taught,
That you have many enemies, that know not
Why they are ſo, but, like to village curs,
Bark when their fellows do.

Henry VIII. A. 2, S. 4.

Diſguiſe, I ſee, thou art a wickedneſs,
Wherein the pregnant enemy[2] does much.

Twelfth Night, A. 2, S. 2.

[1] *Thou art thyſelf, though not a Montague.*] I think the true reading is,

"Thou art thyſelf, *then* not a Montague." Thou art a being of peculiar excellence, and haſt none of the malignity of the family from which thou haſt thy name. JOHNSON.

There is certainly ſome obſcurity in this paſſage, which might poſſibly be removed by reading,

"Thou art thyſelf, though *yet* a Montague." Or thus;

"Thou art thyſelf, *although* a Montague."

At beſt Juliet's meaning ſeems to be, that though he was a Montague by name, and therefore her enemy, yet for his perſon and mind, ſhe might ſtill be allowed to love him.

REMARKS.

I think the commentators have miſtaken the poet's meaning. I would read thus:

"'Tis but thy name that is mine enemy,
"Not thou thyſelf, though thou'rt a Montague." A. B.

[2] *The pregnant enemy.*] Is, I believe, the dexterous fiend, or enemy of mankind. JOHNSON.

I do not think that "pregnant" in this place ſignifies *dexterous*, but *great*, *powerful*, *full of conſequence*. A. B.

ENGLAND,

ENGLAND.

We never valu'd this poor ſeat of England;
And therefore living hence, did give ourſelf
To barbarous licence; as 'tis ever common,
That men are merrieſt when they are from home.
But tell the Dauphin, I will keep my ſtate;
Be like a king, and ſhew my ſail of greatneſs,
When I do rouſe me in my throne of France.

Henry V. A. 1, S. 2.

O England!—model to thy inward greatneſs,
Like little body with a mighty heart——
What might'ſt thou do, that honour would thee do,
Were all thy children kind and natural!

Henry V. Chorus, A. 2.

England, bound in with the triumphant ſea,
Whoſe rocky ſhore beats back the envious ſiege
Of wat'ry Neptune, is now bound in with ſhame,
With inky blots, and rotten parchment bonds.[1]
That England, that was wont to conquer others,
Hath made a ſhameful conqueſt of itſelf.

Richard II. A. 2, S. 1.

Have you a ruffian, that will ſwear, drink, dance,
Revel the night; rob, murder, and commit
The oldeſt ſins, the neweſt kind of ways?
England ſhall give him office, honour, might:
For the Fifth Harry from curb'd licence plucks
The muzzle of reſtraint, and the wild dog
Shall fleſh his tooth in every innocent.

Henry IV. P. 2, A. 4, S. 4.

[1] *With inky blots, and rotten parchment bonds.*] I ſuſpect that our author wrote, *inky bolts*. How can blots bind in any thing? and do not *bolts* correſpond better with bonds? STEEVENS.

"Inky blots:" *i. e.* the *wording* of the rotten parchments. What are *inky bolts*? or what have inky bolts to do with parchment bonds? A. B

——England never did (nor never ſhall)
Lie at the proud foot of a conqueror,
But when it firſt did help to wound itſelf.

King John, A. 5, S. 7.

—— You degenerate, you ingrate revolts,
You bloody Neroes, ripping up the womb
Of your dear mother England, bluſh for ſhame:
For your own ladies, and pale-viſag'd maids,
Like Amazons, come tripping after drums.

King John, A. 5, S. 2.

By eaſt and weſt let France and England mount
Their battering cannon, charged to the mouths,
'Till their ſoul-fearing clamours have brawl'd down
The flinty ribs of this contemptuous city.

King John, A. 2, S. 2.

Remember whom you are to cope withal;—
A ſort of vagabonds, raſcals, and run-aways,
A ſcum of Brittains, and baſe lackey peaſants,
Whom their o'er-cloy'd country vomits forth,
To deſperate ventures and aſſur'd deſtruction.

Richard III. A. 5, S. 3.

Hath Britain all the ſun that ſhines? Day, night,
Are they not but in Britain? I'the world's volume
Our Britain ſeems as of it, but not in it;
In a great pool, a ſwan's neſt. *Cymbeline*, A. 3, S. 4.

England! if my love thou hold'ſt at aught,
(As my great power thereof may give thee ſenſe;
Since yet the cicatrice looks raw and red
After the Daniſh ſword, and thy free awe
Pays homage to us) thou may'ſt not coldly ſet
Our ſovereign proceſs.[1] *Hamlet*, A. 4, S. 3.

— Were

[1] —— *Set by*
Our ſovereign proceſs.] So Hanmer. The others have only *ſet*. JOHNSON.

—— Set
Our ſovereign proceſs.] I adhere to the reading of the quarto and folio. To *ſet*, is an expreſſion taken from the gaming table. STEEVENS.

We

—— Were I in England, now,
There would this monſter make a man;
Any ſtrange beaſt there makes a man.
Tempeſt, A. 2, S. 2.

England hath long been mad, and ſcarr'd herſelf;
The brother blindly ſhed the brother's blood;
The father raſhly ſlaughter'd his own ſon,
The ſon compell'd, been butcher to the ſire:
Abate the edge of traitors, gracious Lord,
That would reduce theſe bloody days again,
And make poor England weep in ſtreams of blood!
Richard III. A. 5, S. 4.

ERROR.

—— There is no power in Venice,
Can alter a decree eſtabliſhed:
'Twill be recorded for a precedent;
And many an error, by the ſame example,
Will ruſh into the ſtate.
Merchant of Venice, A. 4, S. 1.

—— Indian-like,
Religion in mine error, I adore
The ſun, that looks upon his worſhipper,
But knows of him no more.
All's well that ends well, A. 1, S. 3.

O hateful error, melancholy's child!
Why doſt thou ſhew to the apt thoughts of men,
The things that thou are not? O terror, ſoon conceiv'd,
Thou never com'ſt unto a happy birth,
But kill'ſt the mother that engender'd thee.
Julius Cæſar, A. 5, S. 3.

—— Truſt not my age,
My reverence, calling, or divinity,
If this ſweet lady lie not guiltleſs here,
Under ſome biting error.
Much ado about nothing, A. 4, S. 1.

We ſhould read *jet*, (*jetter*, French) *i. e. reject*, *throw out* my proceſs or ſuit. A. B.

ESTATE.

ESTATE.

— Much I have diſabled mine eſtate,
By ſomething ſhewing a more ſwelling port
Than my faint means would grant continuance.

Merchant of Venice, A. 1, S. 1.

EXPECTATION.

—— Now ſits expectation in the air;
And hides a ſword, from hilts unto the point,
With crowns imperial, crowns, and coronets,
Promis'd to Harry, and his followers.

Henry V. Chorus, A. 2.

He hath borne himſelf beyond the promiſe of his age; doing, in the figure of a lamb, the feats of a lion: he hath, indeed, better'd expectation, than you muſt expect of me to tell you how.

Much ado about nothing, A. 1, S. 1.

O, you hard hearts, you cruel men of Rome,
Knew you not Pompey? Many a time and oft
Have you climb'd up to walls and battlements,
To towers and windows, yea, to chimney tops,
Your infants in your arms, and there have ſat
The live long day, with patient expectation
To ſee great Pompey paſs the ſtreets of Rome.

Julius Cæſar, A. 1, S. 1.

EXPEDITION.

— I have learn'd, that fearful commenting,
Is leaden ſervitor to dull delay;
Delay leads impotent and ſnail-pac'd beggary:
Then fiery expedition be my wing,
Jove's Mercury, and herald for a king!

Richard III. A. 4, S. 3.

EYE, EYES.

Why droops my lord, like over-ripen'd corn,
Hanging the head at Ceres' plenteous load?

Why

Why are thine eyes fix'd to the ſullen earth,
Gazing on that which ſeems to dim thy ſight?
What ſeeſt thou there? king Henry's diadem,
Inchas'd with all the honours of the world?

Henry VI. P. 2, A. 1, S. 2.

What, is the jay more precious than the lark,
Becauſe his feathers are more beautiful?
Or is the adder better than the eel,
Becauſe his painted ſkin contents the eye?
Oh, no. *Taming of the Shrew*, A. 2, S. 3.

Fye! fye! unknit that threat'ning unkind brow;
And dart not ſcornful glances from thoſe eyes,
To wound thy lord, thy king, thy governor.

Taming of the Shrew, A. 5, S. 2.

— There is a credence in my heart,
An eſperance ſo obſtinately ſtrong,
That doth invert the atteſt of eyes and ears;
As if thoſe organs had deceptious functions,
Created only to calumniate.

Troilus and Creſſida, A. 5, S. 2.

His humour is lofty, his diſcourſe peremptory, his tongue filed, his eye ambitious, his gait majeſtical, and his general behaviour vain, ridiculous, and thraſonical. *Love's Labour Loſt*, A. 5. S. 1.

From women's eyes this doctrine I derive:
They ſparkle ſtill the right Promethean fire;
They are the books, the arts, the academies,
That ſhew, contain, and nouriſh all the world.

Love's Labour Loſt, A. 4, S. 3.

Lend me the flouriſh of all gentle tongues.—
Fye, painted rhetorick! O, ſhe needs it not:
A wither'd hermit, five-ſcore winters worn,
Might ſhake off fifty, looking in her eye.

Love's Labour Loſt, A. 4, S. 3.

All tongues ſpeak of him, and the bleared ſights
Are ſpectacled to ſee him: your prattling nurſe
Into a rapture lets her baby cry, While

While ſhe chats him: the kitchen malkin pins
Her richeſt lockram 'bout her reechy neck,
Clambering the walls to eye him.

Coriolanus A. 2, S. 1.

'Tis pretty ſure, and very probable,
That eyes, that are the frail'ſt and ſofteſt things,
Who ſhut their coward gates on atomies,—
Should be call'd tyrants, butchers, murderers.

As you like it, A. 3, S. 5.

Theſe eyes that now are dimm'd with death's black veil,
Have been as piercing as the mid-day ſun,
To ſearch the ſecret treaſons of the world.

Henry VI. P. 3, A. 5, S. 2.

I think, ſhe means to tangle mine eyes too;
No, 'faith, proud miſtreſs, hope not after it;
'Tis not your inky brows, your black-ſilk hair,
Your bugle eye-balls, nor your cheek of cream,
That can entame my ſpirits to your worſhip.

As you like it, A. 3, S. 5.

Where the impreſſion of mine eye enfixing,
Contempt his ſcornful perſpective did lend me,
Which warp'd the line of every other favour;
Scorn'd a fair colour, or expreſs'd it ſtolen;[1]

[1] *Scorn'd a fair colour, or expreſs'd it ſtolen.*] Contempt is brought in lending Bertram her perſpective glaſs, which does its office properly by *warping* the lines of all other faces; or by *expreſſing* or ſhewing native red and white as paint. But with what propriety of ſpeech can this glaſs be ſaid to *ſcorn*, which is an affection of the mind? We ſhould read,

"Scorch'd a fair colour, &c."

i. e. this glaſs repreſented the owner as brown or tanned.

WARBURTON.

The paſſage is corrupt: for, as Dr. Warburton rightly obſerves, a glaſs can hardly be made to *ſcorn*. But why ſhould it be made to *ſcorch?* The poet certainly wrote,

"*Scors'd* a fair colour, &c."

To *ſcoſs* or *ſcorſe*, in old language, is to *change*. A. B.

 Extended

Extended or contracted all proportions,
To a moſt hideous object.
All's well that ends well, A. 5, S. 3.

——— I could well
Beteem them[1] from the tempeſt of mine eyes.
Midſummer Night's Dream, A. 1, S. 1.

What peremptory eagle-ſighted eye
Dares look upon the heaven of her brow,
That is not blinded by her majeſty?
Love's Labour Loſt, A. 4, S. 3.

My aſhes, as the Phœnix, may bring forth
A bird, that will revenge upon you all,
And, in that hope, I throw mine eyes to heaven,
Scorning whate'er you can afflict me with.
Henry VI. P. 3. A. 1, S. 4.

— This town is full of cozenage,
As, nimble jugglers, that deceive the eye,
Dark-working ſorcerers, that change the mind,
Soul-killing witches, that deform the body;
Diſguiſed cheaters, prating mountebanks.
Comedy of Errors, A. 1, S. 2.

Their horſemen ſit like fixed candleſticks,
With torch-ſtaves in their hand; and their poor jades
Lob down their heads, dropping their hides and hips;
The gum down-roping from their pale-dead eyes;
And in their pale dull mouths the gimmal bit
Lies foul with chew'd graſs, ſtill and motionleſs.
Henry V. A. 4, S. 2.

[1] *Beteem them.*] Give them, beſtow upon them. The word is uſed by Spenſer. JOHNSON.

I rather think, that to *beteem* in this place ſignifies, as in the northern counties, to pour out—from *tommer*, Daniſh. STEEVENS.

To "beteem," is to bring forth, to grow. We ſhould read,
—— "*Yet* could I well
"Beteem them from the tempeſt of mine eyes."
i. e. yet could I with my tears cauſe them to grow or flouriſh. A. B.

There

There is none of you so mean and base,
That hath not noble lustre in your eyes,
I see you stand like greyhounds in the slips,
Straining upon the start. *Henry V.* A. 3, S. 1.

Farewell, my lord; securely I espy
Virtue with valour couched in thine eye.
Richard II. A. 1, S. 3.

As in a theatre, the eyes of men,
After a well-grac'd actor leaves the stage,
Are idly bent on him that enters next:
Even so, or with much more contempt, men's eyes
Did scowl on Richard. *Richard II.* A. 5, S. 2.

You would have thought, the very windows spake
So many greedy looks of young and old,
Through casements darted their desiring eyes
Upon his visage. *Richard II.* A. 5, S. 2.

O thou dull God, why ly'st thou with the vile,
In loathsome beds, and leav'st the kingly couch,
A watch-case, or a common larum bell?
Wilt thou upon the high and giddy mast
Seal up the ship-boy's eyes, and rock his brains
In cradle of the rude imperious surge;
And in the visitation of the winds,
Who take the ruffian billows by the top,
Curling their monstrous heads, and hanging them,
With deaf'ning clamours in the slippery clouds,
That, with the hurly, death itself awakes?
Henry IV. P. 2, A. 3, S. 1.

The bird that hath been limed in a bush,
With trembling wings misdoubteth every bush;
And I, the hapless male to one sweet bird,
Have now the fatal object in my eye,
Where my poor young was lim'd, was caught, and kill'd. *Henry VI.* P. 3, A. 5, S. 6.

Edward and Richard, like a brace of greyhounds,
Having the fearful flying hare in sight,

With fiery eyes, ſparkling for very wrath,
And bloody ſteel graſp'd in their ireful hands,
Are at our backs. *Henry VI.* P. 3, A. 2, S. 5.

—— I think him better than I ſay,
And yet, would herein others' eyes were worſe:
Far from her neſt the lapwing cries away;
My heart prays for him, though my tongue do curſe.
Comedy of Errors, A. 4, S. 2.

Alack! there lies more peril in thine eye,
Than twenty of their ſwords.
Romeo and Juliet, A. 2, S. 2.

—— Some ſtrange commotion
Is in his brain: he bites his lip and ſtarts;
Stops on a ſudden, looks upon the ground,
Then lays his finger on his temple; ſtraight,
Springs out into faſt gait; then, ſtops again,
Strikes his breaſt hard, and anon he caſts
His eyes againſt the moon.
Henry VIII. A. 3, S. 2.

What means that hand upon that breaſt of thine?
Why holds thine eye the lamentable rheum,
Like a proud river peering o'er his bounds?
King John, A. 3, S. 1.

Command theſe fretting waters from your eyes
With a light heart.
Meaſure for Meaſure, A. 4, S. 3.

Let me not hold my tongue; let me not, Hubert!
Or, Hubert, if you will, cut out my tongue,
So I may keep mine eyes; O, ſpare mine eyes;
Though to no uſe, but ſtill to look on you!
K. John, A. 4, S. 1.

A fearful eye thou haſt; where is that blood,
That I have ſeen inhabit in thoſe cheeks?
So foul a ſky clears not without a ſtorm;
Pour down thy weather. *King John*, A. 4, S. 2.

—By

—— By this ſcimitar,——
would out-ſtare the ſterneſt eyes that look,
Out-brave the heart moſt daring on the earth,
Pluck the young ſucking cubs from the ſhe-bear,
Yea, mock the lion when he roars for prey,
To win thee, lady.
Merchant of Venice, A. 2, S. 1.

That ſame eye, whoſe bend doth awe the world,
Did loſe his luſtre; I did hear him groan;
Ay, and that tongue of his, that bade the Romans
Mark him, and write his ſpeeches in their books,
Alas! it cry'd, give me ſome drink, Titinius,
As a ſick girl. *Julius Cæſar*, A. 1, S. 2.

A [2] pretty peat! 'tis beſt
Put finger in the eye.——
Taming of the Shrew, A. 1, S. 1.

—— I wiſh mine eyes
Would with themſelves ſhut up my thoughts.
Tempeſt, A. 2, S. 1.

—— Never gaz'd the moon
Upon the water, as he'll ſtand and read,
As 'twere my daughter's eyes.
Winter's Tale, A. 4, S. 3.

The fringed curtains of thine eye advance,
And ſay what thou ſeeſt yond'.
Tempeſt, A. 1, S. 2.

I would have broke mine eye-ſtrings, crack'd them, but
To look upon him, till the diminution
Of ſpace had pointed him ſharp as my needle:
Nay, follow'd him, till he had melted from

[2] *Pretty peat!*] *Peat*, or *pet*, is a word of endearment, from *petit*, little,—as if it meant pretty little thing. JOHNSON.
"Pretty peat," is *pretty lamb*. A *pet lamb* is a lamb brought up in the houſe. A. B.

The

The ſmallneſs of a gnat to air; and then
Have turn'd mine eye, and wept.

Cymbeline, A. 1, S. 4.

Mine eyes
Were not in fault, for ſhe was beautiful;
Mine ears, that heard her flattery; nor my heart,
That thought her like her ſeeming; it had been vicious,
To have miſtruſted her. *Cymbeline*, A. 5. S. 5.

—Like a cloiſtreſs, ſhe will veiled walk,
And water once a day her chamber round
With eye-offending brine.

Twelfth Night, A. 1, S. 1.

O, when my eyes did ſee Olivia firſt,
Methought, ſhe purg'd the air of peſtilence.

Twelfth Night, A. 1, S. 1.

Methinks, I feel this youth's perfections,
With an inviſible and ſubtle ſtealth,
To creep in at my eyes.

Twelfth Night, A. 1, S. 5.

—— Oh, happy fair!
Your eyes are lode-ſtars, and your tongue's ſweet air,
More tuneable than lark to ſhepherd's ear,
When wheat is green, when hawthorn buds appear.

Midſummer Night's Dream, A. 1, S. 1.

Alas! how is't with you?
That you do bend your eye on vacancy,
And with the incorporal air do hold diſcourſe?

Hamlet, A. 3, S. 4.

—— Come, ſir page,
Look on me, with your welkin eye[2]; ſweet villain!

Winter's Tale, A. 1, S. 2.

Why

[2] —— *Welkin eye.*] Blue eye; an eye of the ſame colour with the *welkin*, or ſky. JOHNSON.

" A wel-

—— Why this is not Lear:
Does Lear walk thus? Speak thus? Where are his eyes?
Either his notion weakens, or his difcernings
Are lethargy'd.—Ha! waking?—'tis not fo.—
Who is it that can tell me who I am? Lear's fhadow,
I would learn that; for by the marks
Of fov'reignty, of knowledge, and of reafon,
I fhould be falfe perfuaded I had daughters.—
Your name, fair gentlewoman?

Lear, A. 1, S. 4.

Thefe things, indeed, you have articulated,
Proclaim'd at market-croffes, read in churches;
To face the garment of rebellion
With fome fine colour, that may pleafe the eye
Of fickle changelings, and poor difcontents.

Henry IV. P. 1, A. 5, S. 1.

—— Thofe oppofed eyes,
Which—like the meteors of a troubled heaven,
All of one nature, of one fubftance bred,
Did lately meet in the inteftine fhock,
And furious clofe of civil butchery,
Shall now in mutual well-befeeming ranks,
March all one way. *Henry IV*. P. 1, A. 1. S. 1.

Tell me, fweet lord, what is't that takes from thee
Thy ftomach, pleafure, and thy golden fleep?
Why doft thou bend thine eyes upon the earth,
And ftart fo often when thou fitt'ft alone?

Henry IV. P. 1, A. 2. S. 3.

He was but as the cuckow is in June,
Heard, not regarded; feen, but with fuch eyes,
As fick and blunted with community,
Afford no extraordinary gaze,

" A welkin eye" is a *rolling eye*, or as Leontes would infinuate, a *wanton eye*, and fuch as he fuppofes Hermione's to be. *Welkin* comes from pelcan, Saxon, to *roll about*. A. B.

Such

Such as is bent on ſun-like majeſty,
When it ſhines ſeldom in admiring eyes.

Henry IV. P. 1. A. 3, S. 2.

——— I do ſee
Danger and diſobedience in thine eye;
O, ſir, your preſence is too bold and peremptory,
And majeſty might never yet endure
The moody frontier of a ſervant brow.

Henry IV. P. 1, A. 1, S. 3.

O Thou! whoſe captain I account myſelf,
Look on my forces with a gracious eye;
Put in their hands thy bruiſing irons of wrath,
That they may cruſh down with a heavy fall
The uſurping helmets of our adverſaries!
Make us thy miniſters of chaſtiſement,
That we may praiſe thee in thy victory!

Richard III. A. 5, S. 3.

I will converſe with iron-witted fools,
And unreſpected boys; none are for me,
That look into me with conſiderate eyes.

Richard III. A. 4, S. 2.

We know the time, ſince he was mild and affable;
And, if we did but glance a far-off look,
Immediately he was upon his knee,
That all the court admir'd him for ſubmiſſion;
But meet him now, and be it in the morn,
When every one will give the time of day,
He knits his brow, and ſhews an angry eye.

Henry VI. P. 2. A. 3, S. 1.

A lean cheek; which you have not: a blue[2] eye, and ſunken, which you have not.

As you like it, A. 3, S. 2.

[2] *A blue eye.*] *i. e.* a blueneſs about the eyes. STEEVENS.
"A blue eye." But why a *blue* eye? I believe we ſhould read "a *flu* eye."—*Flu*—*fluiſh*, in the northern counties, is *watery, weak, tender.* "A flu eye" will therefore mean *an eye filled with tears.* Fluer, French, to flow or run. A. B.

F.

FACE.

I HAVE heard of your paintings too well enough; God hath given you one face, and you make yourſelves another: you jig, you amble, and you liſp, and nick-name God's creatures, and make your wantonneſs your ignorance[1]: Go to.

Hamlet, A. 3, S. 1.

I think my wife be honeſt, and think ſhe is not;
I think that thou art juſt, and think thou art not;
I'll have ſome proof: her name that was as freſh
As Dian's viſage, is now begrimm'd and black
As mine own face. *Othello*, A. 3, S. 3.

He falls to ſuch peruſal of my face,
As he would draw it. Long ſtaid he ſo:
At laſt,—a little ſhaking of mine arm,
And thrice his head thus waving up and down,—
He rais'd a ſigh ſo piteous and profound,
As it did ſeem to ſhatter all his bulk,
And end his being. *Hamlet*, A. 2, S. 1.

[2] Let no face be kept in mind,
But the fair of Roſalind. *As you like it*, A. 3, S. 2.

[1] *Make your wantonneſs your ignorance.*] You miſtake by *wanton* affectation, and pretend to miſtake by ignorance. JOHNSON.

"Make your wantonneſs your ignorance." The meaning is, when you are guilty of any improper behaviour you would have it attributed to ſimplicity or ignorance, when the fact is, that it is ſtudied. A. B.

[2] *Let no face be kept in mind,*
But the fair of Roſalind.] Thus the old copy. *Fair* is beauty, complexion. The modern editors read—the *face* of Roſalind. STEEVENS.

"The fair of Roſalind" is very harſh. We may ſurely read,
"But of the fair Roſalind."
i. e. but *that of* the fair Roſalind. A. B.

FAIRY.

FAIRY.

[1] Fairies, be gone, and be always away.
Midsummer Night's Dream, A. 4, S. 1.

FAITH.

There are no tricks in plain and simple faith:
But hollow men, like horses hot at hand,
Make gallant shew and promise of their mettle,
But when they should endure the bloody spur,
They fall their crests, and, like deceitful jades,
Sink in the trial. *Julius Cæsar*, A. 4, S. 2.

Thou almost mak'st me waver in my faith,
To hold opinion with Pythagoras,
That souls of animals infuse themselves
Into the trunks of men. *Merchant of Venice*, A. 4, S. 1.

Thou hast no faith left now, unless thou hadst two,
And that's far worse than none.
Two Gentlemen of Verona, A. 5, S. 3.

FALSEHOOD.

O, what a goodly outside falsehood hath!
Merchant of Venice, A. 1, S. 3.

[1] —— *And be always away.*] What! was she giving her attendants an everlasting dismission? No such thing, they were still to be upon duty. I am convinced the poet meant,

And be all ways away.

i. e. disperse yourselves. THEOBALD.

Mr. Upton reads,

And be *away—away.*—

Mr. Heath would read,

And be *always i' th' way.* JOHNSON.

"Always away" is right. It means not that the fairies were never to return, but that they should not presume to disturb Bottom—that during his repose they should keep aloof.

The expression is according to the idiom of the French—Voila mes ordres; restez *toujours* a Paris.—This is by no means to signify that the person so enjoined should never return from Paris, but that he should make it his principal place of residence—that he should remain there until he was recalled. A. B.

If I be falſe, or ſwerve a hair from truth!
Let memory,
From falſe to falſe, among falſe maids in love,
Upbraid my falſehood! when they have ſaid—as falſe
As air, as water, wind, or ſandy earth,
As fox to lamb, as wolf to heifer's calf,
Pard to the hind, or ſtep-dame to her ſon;
Yea, let them ſay, to ſtick the heart of falſehood,
As falſe as Creſſid. *Troilus and Creſſida*, A. 3, S. 2.

FAME.

——— He hath atchiev'd a maid
That paragons deſcription, and wild fame;
One that excels the quirks of blazoning pens,
And, in the eſſential veſture of creation,
Does bear all excellency [1]. *Othello*, A. 2, S. 1.

If you do not all ſhew like gilt two-pences to me; and I, in the clear ſky of fame, o'erſhine you as much as the full moon doth the cinders of the element, which ſhew like pins heads to her; believe not the

[1] *And in the eſſential veſture of creation,*
Does bear all excellency.] It is plain that ſomething very hyperbolical was here intended, But what is there as it ſtands? Why this, that in the eſſence of creation, ſhe bore all excellency. The expreſſion is intolerable, and could never come from one who ſo well underſtood the force of words as our poet. Shakeſpeare certainly wrote,
" And in terreſtrial veſture of creation."
And in this lay the wonder, that all created excellence ſhould be contained within an earthly mortal form. WARBURTON.

I do not think the preſent reading inexplicable. The author ſeems to uſe *eſſential* for *exiſtent*, *real*. She excels the praiſe of invention, ſays he, and in *real* qualities, with which creation has *inveſted* her, bears all excellency. JOHNSON.

I do not find any difficulty in this paſſage. The poet would inſinuate that *woman* is the moſt finiſhed, the moſt perfect work of heaven; and that Deſdemona excels her ſex. A very common thought, but ſomewhat quaintly expreſſed. A. B.

word

word of the noble: therefore let me have right, and let desert mount. *Henry IV.* P. 2, A. 4, S. 3.

I am commanded, with your leave and favour,
Humbly to kiss your hand, and with my tongue
To tell the passion of my sovereign's heart;
Where fame, late entering at his heedful ears,
Hath plac'd thy beauty's image, and thy virtue.
Henry VI. P. 3, A. 3, S. 3.

Let fame, that all hunt after in their lives,
Live registered upon our brazen tombs,
And then grace us in the disgrace of death.
Love's Labour Lost, A. 1, S. 1.

Too much to know, is, to know nought but fame;
And every godfather can give a name.
Love's Labour Lost, A. 1, S. 1.

FAMINE.

——— Yet famine,
Ere clean it o'erthrow nature, makes it valiant.
Plenty, and peace, breeds cowards; hardness ever
Of hardness is mother. *Cymbeline,* A. 3, S. 6.

If you frown upon this proffer'd peace,
To tempt the fury of my three attendants,
Lean famine, quartering steel, and climbing fire;
Who, in a moment, even with the earth
Shall lay your stately and air-braving towers.
Henry VI. P. 1, A. 4, S. 2.

I do remember him at Clement's Inn, like a man made after supper of a cheese-paring: when he was naked, he was for all the world like a fork'd radish, with a head fantastically carv'd upon it with a knife: he was so forlorn, that his dimensions to any thick sight were invisible: he was the very genius of famine. *Henry IV.* P. 2, A, 3, S. 2.

Art thou so bare, and full of wretchedness,
And fear'st to die? famine is in thy cheeks,

Need and oppreſſion ſtarveth in thine eyes,
Upon thy back hangs ragged miſery,
The world is not thy friend, nor the world's law.
Romeo and Juliet, A. 5, S. 1.

FANCY.

Then let us teach our trial patience,
Becauſe it is a cuſtomary croſs;
As due to love, as thoughts, and dreams, and ſighs,
Wiſhes, and tears, poor fancy's followers.
Midſummer Night's Dream, A. 1, S. 1.

—— All the ſtory of the night told over,
And all their minds transfigur'd ſo together,
More witneſſeth than fancy's images,
And grows to ſomething of great conſtancy.
Midſummer Night's Dream, A. 5, S. 1.

—— So full of ſhapes is fancy,
That it alone is high fantaſtical.
Twelfth Night, A. 1, S. 1.

—— Now he's gone, and my idolatrous fancy
Muſt ſanctify his relicks.
All's well that ends well, A. 1, S. 1.

—— All impediments in fancy's courſe
Are motives of more fancy.
All's well that ends well, A. 5, S. 3.

FARM.

[1] I will bring thee where Mrs. Anne Page is at a farm houſe a feaſting; and thou ſhalt woo her: cry'd game, ſaid I well?
Merry Wives of Windſor, A. 2, S. 3.

FATE.

[1] *I will bring thee where Anne Page is; and thou ſhalt woo her; cry'd game, ſaid I well?*] Mr. Theobald alters this nonſenſe to *try'd game*; that is, to nonſenſe of a worſe complexion. Shakeſpeare wrote thus, *cry aim, ſaid I well? i. e.* conſent to it, approve

FATE.

My fate cries out,
And makes each petty artery in this body
As hardy as the Nemean lion's nerve.
Hamlet, A. 1, S. 4.

—— That handkerchief
Did an Egyptian to my mother give:
She, dying, gave it to me;
And bid me, when my fate would have me wive,
To give it her. I did ſo: and take heed on't,
Make it a darling like your precious eye;
To loſe't, give't away, were ſuch perdition,
As nothing elſe could match. *Othello*, A. 3, S. 4.

—— That cuckold lives in bliſs,
Who certain of his fate, loves not his wronger;
But, O, what damned minutes tells he o'er,
Who dotes, yet doubts; ſuſpects, yet ſtrongly loves!
Othello, A. 3, S. 3.

O vain boaſt! Who can control his fate?
Be not afraid, though you do ſee me weapon'd;
Here is my journey's end, here is my butt,
The very ſea-mark of my utmoſt ſail.
Othello, A. 5, S. 2.

—— Take my defiance:

prove it—for to *cry aim*, ſignifies to conſent to, or approve of any thing. The phraſe was taken originally from archery; but the Oxford editor transforms it to *cock* o' th' game; and his improvements of Shakeſpeare's language abound with theſe modern elegancies of ſpeech, ſuch as *mynheers*, bull-baitings, &c.
WARBURTON.

Mr. Steevens would retain "cry'd game," but I cannot think it right. I read,
"Thou ſhalt woo her, and cry *amie*"—
Amie, Fr. a word of endearment. Thou ſhalt woo her, ſays the hoſt, and cry *amie*,—*i. e.* ſalute her with the title of *lovely miſtreſs*, eh, ſaid I well? That this is the true reading the context will clearly ſhew. A. B.

Die;

Die; perish! might but my bending down
Reprieve thee from thy fate, it should proceed.
Measure for Measure, A. 3, S. 1.

FATHER.

To you, your father should be as a god;
One that compos'd your beauties; yea, and one
To whom you are but as a form in wax,
By him imprinted. *Mids Night's Dream*, A. 1, S. 1.

Know of your youth, examine well your blood,
Whether, if you yield not to your father's choice,
You can endure the livery of a nun;
For aye to be in shady cloister mew'd.
Midsummer Night's Dream, A. 1, S. 1.

—— I know not why,
I love this youth; and I have heard you say,
Love's reason's without reason: the bier at door,
And a demand who is't shall die, I'd say,
My father, not this youth. *Cymbeline*, A. 4, S. 2.

I love thee; I have spoke it:
How much the quantity [1], the weight as much,
As I do love my father. *Cymbeline*, A. 4, S. 2.

—— Lift up thy looks:
From my succession wipe me, father! I
Am heir to my affection. *Winter's Tale*, A. 4, S. 3.

—— O, sir,
You have undone a man of fourscore three,

[1] *How much the quantity*] I read,
"As much the quantity." JOHNSON.

I would read and point the passage thus:
"I love thee; I have spoke it:
"How much the *quality*, the weight as much,
"As I do love my father."

I love thee; and in what ("quality") *degree*, I love thee, I have declared, by calling thee brother:—which love is *equal* ("the weight as much") as that I bear to my father. A. B.

That

That thought to fill his grave in quiet; yea,
To die upon the bed my father dy'd.
Winter's Tale, A. 4, S. 3.

Why, look you there! lock, how it ſteals away!
My father, in his habit as he liv'd!
Look, where he goes, even now, out at the portal!
Hamlet, A. 3, S. 4.

So rare a wonder'd father, and a wife,
Make this place paradiſe. *Tempeſt*, A. 4, S. 1.

—— A father
Is, at the nuptial of his ſon, a gueſt
That beſt becomes the table.
Winter's Tale, A. 4, S. 3.

—— Behold, my lords,
Although the print be little, the whole matter
And copy of the father: eye, noſe, lip,
The trick of his frown, his forehead: nay the valley,
The pretty dimples of his chin and cheek.
Winter's Tale, A. 2, S. 3.

If it aſſume my noble father's perſon,
I'll ſpeak to it, though hell itſelf ſhould gape,
And bid me hold my peace. *Hamlet*, A. 1, S. 2.

O, my dear father! Reſtoration, hang
Thy medicine on my lips; and let this kiſs
Repair thoſe violent harms, that my two ſiſters
Have in thy reverence made! *Lear*, A. 4, S. 7.

Had you not been their father, theſe white flakes
Had challeng'd pity of them. Was this a face
To be expos'd againſt the warring winds?
To ſtand againſt the deep dread-bolted thunder?
In the moſt terrible and nimble ſtroke
Of quick, croſs lightning? *Lear*, A. 4, S. 7.

O! your only jig-maker [1]. What ſhould a man do,

[1] *Your only jig-maker.*] There may have been ſome humour in this paſſage, the force of which is now diminiſhed. STEEVENS.

An

do, but be merry? for, look you, how cheerfully my mother looks, and my father died within theſe two hours. *Hamlet*, A. 3, S. 2.

—— This is moſt brave;
That I, the ſon of a dear father murder'd,
Prompted to my revenge by heaven, and hell,
Muſt, like a whore, unpack my heart with words,
And fall a curſing, like a very drab,
A ſcullion! *Hamlet*, A. 2, S. 2.

My father, and my uncle, and myſelf,
Did give him that ſame royalty he wears:
And,—when he was not ſix and twenty ſtrong,
Sick in the world's regard, wretched and low,
A poor unminded out-law ſneaking home,—
My father gave him welcome to the ſhore.
Henry IV. P. 1, A. 4, S. 3.

My father charg'd you in his will to give me good education: you have train'd me up like a peaſant, obſcuring and hiding from me all gentleman-like qualities: the ſpirit of my father grows ſtrong in me, and I will no longer endure it.
As you like it, A. 1, S. 1.

—— Hercules himſelf muſt yield to odds;
And many ſtrokes, though with a little axe,
Hew down and fell the hardeſt timber'd oak.
By many hands your father was ſubdu'd.
Henry VI. P. 3, A. 2, S. 1.

Oh, tyger's heart, wrapp'd in a woman's hide!
How couldſt thou drain the life-blood of the child,
To bid the father wipe his eyes withal,
And yet be ſeen to bear a woman's face?
Henry VI. P. 3, A. 1, S. 4.

An equivoque, I believe, is here intended. Hamlet may mean either jig-maker or gig-maker. *Gigge*, in Chaucer, is an harlot, a ſtrumpet. A. B.

—— I have five hundred crowns,
The thrifty hire I ſav'd under your father,
Which I did ſtore to be my foſter-nurſe,
When ſervice ſhould in my old limbs lie lame,
And unregarded age in corners thrown;
Take that. *As you like it*, A. 2, S. 3.

—— By heaven, I bid you be aſſur'd,
I'll be your father and your brother too!
Let me but bear your love, I'll bear your cares,
Yet weep, that Harry's dead; and ſo will I:
But Harry lives, that ſhall convert thoſe tears,
By number, into hours of happineſs.
Henry IV. P. 2, A. 5, S. 2.

My father is gone wild into his grave,
For in his tomb lie my affections;
And with his ſpirit ſadly I ſurvive,
To mock the expectations of the world;
To fruſtrate prophecies; and to raze out
Rotten opinion, who hath writ me down
After my ſeeming. *Henry IV*. P. 2, A. 5, S. 2.

This [1] young gentlewoman had a father (O, that had! how ſad a paſſage 'tis!) whoſe ſkill was almoſt as great as his honeſty; would for the king's ſake he were living! I think it would be the death of the king's diſeaſe. *All's well that ends well*, A. 1, S. 1.

FAVOUR,

[1] *This young gentlewoman had a father (O, that had! how ſad a paſſage 'tis!)*] Lafeu was ſpeaking of the king's deſperate condition; which makes the Counteſs recall to mind the deceaſed Gerard de Narbon, who, ſhe thinks, would have cured him. But in uſing the word *had*, which implied his death, ſhe ſtops in the middle of her ſentence, and makes a reflection on it, which, according to the preſent reading, is unintelligible. We muſt therefore believe Shakeſpeare wrote, (O that *had!* how ſad a *preſage* 'tis) *i. e.* a preſage that the king muſt now expect no cure, ſince ſo ſkilful a perſon was forced to ſubmit to a malignant diſtemper. WARBURTON.

This emendation is ingenious, perhaps preferable to the preſent reading, yet ſince *paſſage* may be fairly enough explained, I have

FAVOUR, FAVOURITE.

Bid her ſteal into the pleached bower,
Where honey-ſuckles, ripen'd by the ſun,
Forbid the ſun to enter;—like favourites,
Made proud by princes, that advance their pride
Againſt that power that bred it.
Much ado about nothing, A. 3, S. 1.

Nay, but the man that was his bedfellow [1],
Whom he hath cloy'd and grac'd with princely favours.
Henry V. A. 2, S. 2.

FAULT, FAULTS.

Never came reformation in a flood,
With ſuch a heady current, ſcouring faults;
Nor never hydra-headed wilfulneſs
So ſoon did loſe his ſeat, and all at once,
As in this king. *Henry V.* A. 1, S. 1.

His temper, therefore, muſt be well obſerv'd:
Chide him for faults, and do it reverently,
When you perceive his blood inclin'd to mirth:

I have left it in the text. *Paſſage* is *any thing that paſſes*; ſo we now ſay, a *paſſage* of an *author*, and we ſaid about a century ago, the *paſſages of a reign*. When theOunteſs mentions Helena's loſs of a father, ſhe recollects her own loſs of a huſband, and ſtops to obſerve how heavily that word *had* paſſes through her mind. JOHNSON.

Dr. Warburton's reaſoning is falſe and inconcluſive. The *death* of Gerard de Narbon could never be conſidered as a *preſage* that the king muſt now expect no cure, unleſs, indeed, the phyſician had died of the ſame malady as that which the king is ſaid to languiſh under. I think we ſhould read,—

"O that had! how ſad a *paſs* it is."

paſs, for *concluſion*.

We now ſay—Is it come to that paſs? *i. e.* Is that the cloſe of all? A. B.

[1] *That was his bed-fellow.*] The familiar appellation of *bed-fellow*, which appears ſtrange to us, was common to our ancient nobility. STEEVENS.

"Bed-fellow" ſhould, I think, in this place, be printed *bede-fellow*, *i. e.* a *bidden-fellow*, an *intimate*.—Not one who lies in the ſame bed with another. To *bede*, was anciently to *bid*, to *invite*. A. B.

But being moody, give him line and ſcope;
Till that his paſſions, like a whale on ground,
Confound themſelves with working.
Henry IV. P. 2, A. 4, S. 4.

—— The noble Brutus
Hath told you, Cæſar was ambitious:
If it were ſo, it was a grievous fault;
And grievouſly hath Cæſar anſwer'd it.
Here, under leave of Brutus, and the reſt,
(For Brutus is an honourable man;
So are they all, all honourable men)
Come I to ſpeak in Cæſar's funeral.
Julius Cæſar, A. 3, S. 2.

—— Every fault's condemn'd, ere it be done:
Mine were the very cypher of a function,
To find the faults, whoſe fine ſtands in record,
And let go by the actor. *Meaſ. for Meaſ.* A. 2, S. 2.

Preſs not a falling man too far; 'tis virtue;
His faults lie open to the laws; let them,
Not you, correct him. My heart weeps to ſee him
So little of his great ſelf. *Henry VIII.* A. 3, S. 2.

They ſay, beſt men are moulded out of faults;
And, for the moſt, become much more the better,
For being a little bad. *Meaſure for Meaſure*, A. 5, S. 1.

—— Our raſh faults
Make trivial price of ſerious things we have,
Not knowing them, until we know their grave.
All's well that ends well, A. 5, S. 3.

—— Like bright metal on a ſullen ground,
My reformation, glittering o'er my fault,
Shall ſhew more goodly, and attract more eyes,
Than that which hath no foil to ſet it off.
Henry IV. P. 1, A. 1, S. 2.

In the corrupted currents of this world,
Offence's gilded hand may ſhove by juſtice;
And oft 'tis ſeen, the wicked prize itſelf
Buys out the law: But 'tis not ſo above:

There

There is no ſhuffling, there the action lies
In his true nature; and we ourſelves compell'd,
Even to the teeth and forehead of our faults,
To give in evidence. *Hamlet*, A. 3, S. 3.

—— Breathe his faults ſo quaintly,
That they may ſeem the taints of liberty:
The flaſh and out-break of a fiery mind;
A ſavageneſs in unreclaimed blood,
Of general aſſault. *Hamlet*, A. 2, S. 1.

——— Oh heaven! were man
But conſtant, he were perfect; that one error
Fills him with faults.
Two Gentlemen of Verona, A. 5, S. 3.

—— He fiſhes, drinks, and waſtes
The lamps of night in revel: is not more man-like
Than Cleopatra; nor the queen of Ptolemy
More womanly than he: You ſhall find there
A man who is the abſtract of all faults
That all men follow. *Antony and Cleopatra*, A. 1, S. 4.

I muſt not think, there are
Evils enough to darken all his goodneſs:
His faults, in him, ſeem as the ſpots of heaven,
More fiery by night's blackneſs.
Antony and Cleopatra, A. 1, S. 4.

——— Poor wretch,
That, for thy mother's fault, are thus expos'd
To loſs, and what may follow!—Weep I cannot,
But my heart bleeds. *Winter's Tale*, A. 3, S. 3.

——— Taunt my faults
With ſuch full licence, as both truth and malice
Have power to utter. O, then we bring forth weeds,
When our quick winds lie ſtill; and our ills told us,
Is as our earing. *Antony and Cleopatra*, A. 1, S. 2.

F E A R.

I follow'd that I bluſh to look upon:
My very hairs do mutiny; for the white

Reprove

Reprove the brown for raſhneſs, and they them
For fear and doating. *Antony and Cleop.* A. 3, S. 9.

——— We debaſe
The nature of our ſeats, and make the rabble
Call our cares, fears: which will in time break ope
The locks o' the ſenate, and bring in the crows
To peck the eagles. *Coriolanus*, A. 3, S. 1.

The love of wicked friends converts to fear;
That fear, to hate; and hate turns one, or both,
To worthy danger, and deſerved death.
Richard II. A. 5, S. 1.

Thou ſhalt be puniſh'd for thus frighting me,
For I am ſick, and capable of fears;
Oppreſs'd with wrongs, and therefore full of fears;
A woman, naturally born to fears.
King John, A. 3, S. 1.

Things done well,
And with a care, exempt themſelves from fear;
Things done without example, in their iſſue
Are to be fear'd.
We muſt not rend our ſubjects from our laws,
And ſtick them in our will. *Henry VIII.* A. 1, S. 2.

That life is better life, paſt fearing death,
Than that which lives to fear.
Meaſure for Meaſure, A. 5, S. 1.

——— What, pale again?
My fear hath catch'd your fondneſs: Now I ſee
The myſtery of your lonelineſs, and find
Your ſalt tear's head. *All's well that ends well*, A. 1, S. 3.

Now, York, or never, ſteel thy fearful thoughts,
And change miſdoubt to reſolution:
Be that thou hop'ſt to be; or what thou art
Reſign to death, it is not worth the enjoying.
Let pale-fac'd fear keep with the mean-born man,
And find no harbour in a royal heart.
Henry VI. P. 2, A. 3, S. 1.

K Why,

Why, Harry, do I tell thee of my foes,
Which art my near'ſt and deareſt enemy?
Thou that art like enough,—through vaſſal fear,
Baſe inclination, and the ſtart of ſpleen,—
To fight againſt me under Percy's pay.

Henry IV. P. 1, A. 3, S. 2.

Inform her full of my particular fear;
And thereto add ſuch reaſons of your own,
As may compact it more[1]. *Lear*, A. 1, S. 4.

Do you go back diſmay'd? 'tis a loſt fear;
Man but a ruſh againſt Othello's breaſt,
And he retires;—where ſhould Othello go?

Othello, A. 5, S. 2.

Whate'er thou art, for thy good caution, thanks;
Thou haſt harp'd my fear aright[2].

Macbeth, A. 4, S. 1.

—— [3] It harrows me with fear, and wonder.

Hamlet, A. 1, S. 1.

By'r lakin, a parlous fear[4].

Midſummer Night's Dream, A. 3, S. 1.

FEA-

[1] —— *Compact it more.*] Unite one circumſtance with another, ſo as to make a conſiſtent account. JOHNSON.

"Compact" is here uſed in the ſenſe of *ſtrengthen* or *confirm*. "Compact it," is, *ſtrengthen the fear*,—that *fear* which ſhe had juſt before ſpoken of. If we do not read the paſſage thus, *it* has no antecedent. A. B.

[2] *Thou haſt harp'd my fear aright.*] To *harp*, is to touch on a paſſion, as a harper touches a ſtring. STEEVENS.

"Harp'd my fear," ſhould, perhaps, be "happ'd my fear," *i. e.* caught or interpreted my fears aright.

To "happe" is to *catch*. Happer, *Fr.* A. B.

[3] —— *It harrows me, &c.*] To *harrow* is to conquer, to ſubdue. STEEVENS.

"It harrows me with fear and wonder," I am loſt in fear and wonder, I am aſtounded. A. B.

[4] —— *A parlous fear.*] *Parlous*, a word corrupted from *perilous*, i. e. dangerous. STEEVENS.

"Parlous" is frequently uſed for *perilous*, but it is not employed

in

FEATURE.

Thou changed and ſelf-cover'd thing [1], for ſhame,
Be-monſter not thy feature. *Lear*, A. 4, S. 2.

FEEBLE.

Being enfranchis'd, bid him come to me:—
'Tis not enough to help the feeble up,
But to ſupport him after. *Timon of Athens*, A. 1, S. 1.

FIGHT.

—— [2] Yon ribald nag of Egypt,

in that ſenſe here. We cannot well read, a *perilous fear*. *Parlous* is *peerleſs*, as well as *dangerous*, and will therefore ſignify, in this place, *very great*. If, however, we read *parlous feat*, which I think is rather to be preferred, it will mean a *dangerous undertaking*. A. B.

[1] *Thou changed and ſelf-cover'd thing.*] Of theſe lines there is but one copy, and the editors are forced upon conjecture. They have publiſhed this line thus:

"Thou chang'd and *ſelf-converted* thing."

But I cannot but think, that by *ſelf-cover'd* the author meant, thou that haſt *diſguiſed* nature by wickedneſs; thou that haſt *hid* the woman under the fiend. JOHNSON.

I think it not improbable but that the poet might write, "ſelf-convict," alluding to her open and violent abuſe of her father. A. B.

[2] —— *ribald* ——.] A luxurious ſquanderer. POPE.

The word is, in the old edition, *ribaudred*, which I do not underſtand, but mention it, in hopes others may raiſe ſome happy conjecture. JOHNSON.

A *ribald* is a lewd fellow. *Ribaudred*, the old reading, is, I believe, no more than a corruption. Shakeſpeare, who is not always very nice about his verſification, might have written:

"Yon ribald-rid nag of Egypt." STEEVENS.

Ribaudred is, I am perſuaded, the true reading. *Ribaude*, in the French language, is a *whore*, a *ſtrumpet*. I would likewiſe read *hag*. *Ribaudred hag*, i. e. a woman who has been the property of ſeveral men; as was the caſe with Cleopatra. Had our author written *ſtrumpeted hag*, he would, I preſume, have been generally underſtood: *ribaudred hag* is exactly the ſame. The affectation of employing French words was extremely common in Shakeſpeare's time. A. B.

Whom leprosy o'ertake i' the midst o' the fight,
When vantage like a pair of twins appear'd,
Both as the same, or rather ours the elder,—
The brize upon her, like a cow in June,
Hoists sails, and flies. *Antony and Cleopatra*, A. 3, S. 8.

To see thee fight, to see thee foin [1], to see thee traverse, to see thee here, to see thee there; to see thee pass thy punto, thy stock, thy reverse, thy distance, thy montant.

Merry Wives of Windsor, A. 2, S. 3.

——— When he reads
Thy personal venture in the rebels fight,
His wonders and his praises do contend [2],
Which should be thine, or his: silenc'd with that,
In viewing o'er the rest o' the self-same day,
He finds thee in the stout Norweyan ranks.

Macbeth, A. 1, S. 3.

She once being looft [3],

[1] *To see thee foin.*] To *foin*, I believe, was the ancient term for making a thrust in fencing or tilting. STEEVENS.

I rather think that *foil* is the proper word here—*i. e.* to see thee overcome or conquer thine enemy. The *foining*, or *fencing*, of *Caius*, is afterwards spoken of. A. B.

[2] *His wonders and his praises do contend,*
Which should be thine, or his: silenc'd with that.] This is somewhat obscure. We may regulate the passage thus:

——— And when he reads
Thy personal valor in the rebel's fight,
His wonder and his praises do contend.—
Silenced with that which should be thine, not his.

A. B.

[3] ——— *being looft.*] To *loof*, is to bring a ship close to the wind. STEEVENS.

Mr. Steevens observes, that *to loof* is to bring a ship close to the wind—very true; but that is not the poet's particular meaning here. Cleopatra might loof, or luff her vessel, as well for the purpose of meeting the enemy, as for flying from him. To say, therefore, that she *looft*, is saying nothing. *Looft*, in this place, is *aloof*, or at a distance. Cleopatra having run away, says Scarus, Antony quickly followed her. A. B.

The

The noble ruin of her magic, Antony,
Claps on his ſea-wing, and, like a doating mallard,
Leaving the fight in height, flies after her.
Antony and Cleopatra, A. 3, S. 8.

FIGURE.

——— One
[1] To whom you are but as a form in wax,
By him imprinted, and within his power
To leave the figure, or disfigure it.
Midſummer Night's Dream, A. 1, S. 1.

FIRE.

I would not marry her, though ſhe were endowed with all that Adam had left him before he tranſgreſs'd: ſhe would have made Hercules have turn'd ſpit; yea, and have cleft his club to make the fire too.
Much ado about nothing, A. 2, S. 1.

—— Where two raging fires meet together,
They do conſume the thing that feeds their fury:
Though little fire grows great with little wind,
Yet extreme guſts will blow out fire and all.
Taming of the Shrew, A. 2, S. 1.

Thus have I ſhunn'd the fire, for fear of burning;
And drench'd me in the ſea, where I am drown'd.
Two Gentlemen of Verona, A. 1, S. 3.

[1] *To whom you are but as a form in wax,*
By him imprinted, and within his power
To leave the figure, or disfigure it.] We ſhould read,
To 'leve the figure, &c.
i. e. releve, to heighten or to add to the beauty of the figure, which is ſaid to be imprinted by him. 'Tis from the French, *relever*. WARBURTON.

I know not why ſo harſh a word ſhould be admitted with ſo little need; a word that, ſpoken, could not be underſtood, and of which no example can be ſhewn. JOHNSON.

"Lave" is the proper word. *To lave* is a term of art in painting, and ſignifies to *embelliſh*, to *beautify*. A. B.

——Know you not,
The fire, that mounts the liquor 'till it run o'er,
In ſeeming to augment it, waſtes it?
Henry VIII. A. 1, S. 1.

Oh, who can hold a fire in his hand,
By thinking on the froſty Caucaſus?
Or cloy the hungry edge of appetite,
By bare imagination of a feaſt?
Or wallow naked in December ſnow,
By thinking on fantaſtic ſummer's heat?
Richard II. A. 1, S. 3.

FLATTERER.

A thouſand flatterers ſit within thy crown,
Whoſe compaſs is no bigger than thy head;
And yet, incaged in ſo ſmall a verge,
The waſte is no whit leſſer than thy land.
Richard II. A. 2, S. 1.

——He loves to hear,
That unicorns may be betray'd with trees,
And bears with glaſſes, elephants with holes,
Lions with toils, and men with flatterers,
But, when I tell him, he hates flatterers,
He ſays, he does; being then moſt flattered.
Julius Cæſar, A. 2, S. 1.

Here feel we but the icy fang,
And churliſh chiding of the winter's wind;
Which when it bites and blows upon my body,
Even till I ſhrink with cold, I ſmile, and ſay,—
This is no flattery. *As you like it*, A. 2, S. 1.

The people cry, you mock'd them; and, of late,
When corn was given them gratis, you repin'd;
Scandal'd the ſuppliants for the people; call'd them
Time-pleaſers, flatterers, foes to nobleneſs.
Coriolanus, A. 3, S. 1.

——When drums and trumpets ſhall
I' the field prove flatterers, let courts and cities be
Made

Made of all falſe-fac'd ſoothing! When ſteel grows
Soft as the paraſite's ſilk, let him be made
A coverture for the wars! *Coriolanus*, A. 1, S. 9.

—— Why this ſpade? this place?
This ſlave-like habit? and theſe looks of care?
Thy flatterers yet wear ſilk, drink wine, lie ſoft;
Hug their diſeas'd perfumes, and have forgot
That ever Timon was. *Timon of Athens*, A. 4, S. 3.

—— Hence! be gone!—
If thou hadſt not been born the worſt of men,
Thou hadſt been a knave and flatterer.
Timon of Athens, A. 4, S. 3.

—— Shame not theſe woods,
By putting on the cunning of a carper[1].
Be thou a flatterer now, and ſeek to thrive
By that which has undone thee.
Timon of Athens, A. 4, S. 3.

F L E E T.

—— Do but think,
You ſtand upon the rivage, and behold
A city on the inconſtant billows dancing;
For ſo appears this fleet majeſtical,
Holding due courſe to Harfleur.
Henry V. A. 3, Chorus.

[1] —— *the cunning of a carper.*] For the philoſophy of a cynic, of which ſect Apemantus was. WARBURTON.

The *cunning of a carper*, is the inſidious art of a critic. Shame not theſe woods, ſays Apemantus, by coming here to find fault. There is no apparent reaſon why Apemantus (according to Dr. Warburton's explanation) ſhould ridicule his own ſect. STEEVENS.

There is little reaſon to imagine that Apemantus, by calling himſelf a *carper*, had any intention of *ridiculing* his ſect. He is proud of his cynical manners; and had ſaid immediately before to Timon, "thou doſt affect my manners." By *cunning of a carper*, he undoubtedly means, the ſubtilty and ſeverity of a cynic. A. B.

FLESH.

—— Take thou the pound of fleſh;
But, in the cutting it, if thou doſt ſhed
One drop of Chriſtian blood, thy lands and goods
Are by the laws of Venice, confiſcate
Unto the ſtate of Venice.

Merchant of Venice, A. 4, S. 1.

You'll aſk me, why I rather chooſe to have
A weight of carrion fleſh, than to receive
Three thouſand ducats: I'll not anſwer that:
But, ſay, it is my humour; is it anſwer'd?

Merchant of Venice, A. 4, S. 1.

This bond doth give thee here no jot of blood;
The words expreſsly are a pound of fleſh:
Then take thy bond. *Merchant of Venice*, A. 4, S. 1.

——— Here
Will I ſet up my everlaſting reſt;
And ſhake the yoke of inauſpicious ſtars
From this world-wearied fleſh.—Eyes look your laſt!
Arms, take your laſt embrace! and lips, O you
The doors of breath, ſeal with a righteous kiſs.

Romeo and Juliet, A. 5, S. 3.

Hate all, curſe all; ſhew charity to none;
But let the famiſh'd fleſh ſlide from the bone
Ere thou relieve the beggar: give to dogs
What thou deny'ſt to men.

Timon of Athens, A. 4, S. 4.

Lay her i' the earth;——
And from her fair and unpolluted fleſh
May violets ſpring!—I tell thee, churliſh prieſt,
A miniſtring angel ſhall my ſiſter be,
When thou lieſt howling. *Hamlet*, A. 5, S. 1.

—— To die;—to ſleep;—
No more?—and, by a ſleep, to ſay we end
The heart-ach, and the thouſand natural ſhocks

That

That fleſh is heir to,—'tis a conſummation
Devoutly to be wiſh'd. *Hamlet*, A. 3, S. 1.

[1] —— But we all are men,
In our own natures frail; and capable
Of our fleſh, few are angels. *Henry VIII.* A. 5, S. 2.

FLOOD.

—— This man's brow, like to a title leaf,
Foretells the nature of a tragick volume:
So looks the ſtrand, whereon the imperious flood
Hath left a witneſs'd uſurpation.
Henry IV. P. 2, A. 1, S. 1.

FLOWERS.

—— The ruddock would,
With charitable bill (O bill, ſore-ſhaming
Thoſe rich-left heirs, that let their fathers lie
Without a monument!) bring thee all this;
Yea, and furr'd moſs beſides, when flowers are none,
To winter-ground thy corſe. *Cymbeline*, A. 4, S. 2.

With faireſt flowers,
Whilſt ſummer laſts, and I live here, Fidele,
I'll ſweeten thy ſad grave: thou ſhalt not lack
The flower, that's like thy face, pale primroſe; nor
The azur'd hare-bell, like thy veins; no, nor
The leaf of eglantine, whom not to ſlander,
Out-ſweeten'd not thy breath. *Cymbeline*, A. 4, S. 2.

[1] —— *But we all are men,*
In our own natures frail; and capable
Of our fleſh, few are angels.] If this paſſage means any thing, it may mean, *few are perfect while they remain in their mortal capacity.* STEEVENS.

May not Shakeſpeare have written *frail* and *culpable?* The change is eaſy. I would read and point thus:

—— We all are men,
In our own natures frail and culpable;
Of our fleſh few are angels. A. B.

—— O Pro-

——— O Proſerpina,
For the flowers now, that frighted thou let'ſt fall
From Dis's waggon! daffodils,
That come before the ſwallow dares, and take
The winds of March with beauty.
Winter's Tale, A. 4, S. 3.

—— The faireſt flowers o' the ſeaſon
Are our carnations, and ſtreak'd gilly-flowers,
Which ſome call, nature's baſtards: of that kind
Our ruſtick garden's barren.
Winter's Tale, A. 4, S. 3.

— Like the bee tolling from every flower
The virtuous ſweets[1]. *Henry IV.* P. 2, A. 4, S. 4.

FOE, FOES.

Be adviſ'd;
Heat not a furnace for your foe ſo hot
That it do ſinge yourſelf: We may out-run,
By violent ſwiftneſs, that which we run at,
And loſe by over-running. *Henry VIII.* A. 1, S. 1.

—— Like a jolly troop of huntſmen come
Our luſty Engliſh, all with purpled hands,
Dy'd in the dying ſlaughter of their foes.
King John, A, 2, S. 2.

Shall we go throw away our coats of ſteel,
And wrap our bodies in black mourning gowns,
Numb'ring our Ave-Maries with our beads?
Or ſhall we on the helmets of our foes
Tell our devotion with revengeful arms?
Henry VI. P. 3, A. 2, S. 1.

[1] —— *like the bee tolling from every flower The virtuous ſweets.*] The reading of the quarto is *tolling*. The folio reads *culling*. *Tolling* is taking toll. STEEVENS.
"Tolling" is not in this place taking *toll*, or *tribute*, but ſimply *taking away*. The ſenſe is the ſame as *culling*. A. B.

—— Henry,

—— Henry, your ſovereign,
Is priſoner to the foe; his ſtate uſurp'd,
His realm a ſlaughter-houſe, his ſubjects ſlain,
His ſtatutes cancell'd, and his treaſure ſpent;
And yonder is the wolf, that makes this ſpoil.
Henry VI. P. 3, A. 5, S. 4.

—— I ſpake of moſt diſaſtrous chances,
Of moving accidents, by flood, and field;
Of hair-breadth 'ſcapes i' the imminent deadly breach;
Of being taken by the inſolent foe,
And ſold to ſlavery. *Othello*, A. 1, S. 3.

—— I have kept back their foes,
While they have told their money, and let out
Their coin upon large intereſt; I myſelf,
Rich only in large hurts. All thoſe, for this?
Is this the balſam that the uſuring ſenate
Pours into captain's wounds?
Timon of Athens, A. 3, S. 5.

FOOL, FOOLS, FOLLY.

God give them wiſdom, that have it: and thoſe that are fools, let them uſe their talents.
Twelfth Night, A. 1, S. 5.

The lady Olivia has no folly: ſhe will keep no fool, ſir, till ſhe be married; and fools are as like huſbands, as pilchards are to herrings, the huſband's the bigger.
Twelfth Night, A. 3, S. 1.

There is no ſlander in an allow'd fool, though he do nothing but rail: nor no railing in a known diſcreet man, though he do nothing but reprove.
Twelfth Night, A. 1, S. 5.

This fellow is wiſe enough to play the fool;
And, to do that well, craves a kind of wit;
He muſt obſerve their mood on whom he jeſts,
The quality of the perſons, and the time;

And, like the haggard, checks at every feather
That comes before his eye. *Twelfth Night*, A. 3, S. 1,

——— I am a fool,
To weep at what I am glad of. *Tempeſt*, A. 3, S. 1.

The loyalty, well held to fools, does make
Our faith mere folly:—Yet, he that can endure
To follow with allegiance a fallen lord,
Does conquer him that did his maſter conquer,
And earns a place i' the ſtory.
Ant. and Cleop. A. 3, S. 11.

——— You may as well
Forbid the ſea for to obey the moon,
As or, by oath, remove, or counſel, ſhake
The fabrick of his folly. *Winter's Tale*, A. 1, S. 2.

If thou wilt needs marry, marry a fool; for wiſe men know well enough, what monſters you make of them. *Hamlet*, A. 3, S. 1.

——— I muſt have liberty
Withal, as large a charter as the wind,
To blow on whom I pleaſe; for ſo fools have:
And they that are moſt galled with my folly,
They moſt muſt laugh. *As you like it*, A. 2, S. 7.

Thou art a fool: ſhe robs thee of thy name;
And thou wilt ſhow more bright, and ſeem more virtuous
When ſhe is gone. *As you like it*, A. 1, S. 3.

——— When I did hear
The motley fool thus moral on the time,
My lungs began to crow like chanticleer,
That fools ſhould be ſo deep contemplative.
As you like it, A. 2, S. 7.

*And my poor fool is hang'd! No, no, no life.
Lear, A. 5, S. 3.

And

* *And my poor fool is hang'd.*] This is an expreſſion of tenderneſs for his dead Cordelia (not his fool, as ſome have thought), on

And how quote you my folly?[1]

Two Gentlemen of Verona, A. 2, S. 4.

Let thofe, that play your clowns, fpeak no more than is fet down for them: For there be of them, that will themfelves laugh, to fet on fome quantity of barren fpectators to laugh too; though, in the mean time, fome neceffary queftion of the play be then to be confidered: that's villainous; and fhews a moft pitiful ambition in the fool that ufes it.

Hamlet, A. 3, S. 2.

Pity, that fools may not fpeak wifely what wife men do foolifhly. *As you like it*, A. 1, S. 2.

Sirrah, inquire further after me; I had talk of you laft night: though you are a fool and a knave, you fhall eat. *All's well that ends well*, A. 5, S. 2.

—— Never

on whofe lips he is ftill intent, and dies away while he is fearching for life there. That the thoughts of a father, in the bittereft of all moments, while his favourite child lay dead in his arms, fhould recur to the antic who had formerly diverted him, has fomewhat in it that I cannot reconcile to the idea of genuine forrow and defpair.

Befides this, Cordelia was recently hanged; but we know not that the *fool* had fuffered in the fame manner, nor can imagine why he fhould. STEEVENS.

I confefs, I am one of thofe who have thought that Lear means his *fool*, and not *Cordelia*. If he means *Cordelia*, then what I have always confidered as a beauty, is of the fame kind as the accidental ftroke of the pencil that produced the foam. Lear's affectionate remembrance of the *fool* in this place, I ufed to think, was one of thofe ftrokes of genius, or of nature, which are fo often found in Shakefpeare, and in him only. The words *poor fool*, are undoubtedly expreffive of endearment; and Shakefpeare in another place, fpeaking of a dying animal, calls it *poor dappled fool*; but it never is, nor never can be ufed with any degree of propriety, but to commiferate fome very inferior object, which may be loved, without much efteem or refpect. Sir J. REYNOLDS.

If we read, "poor foul," (confidering *foul* like *fool* a word of endearment) all difficulty is at once removed. That the "poor fool," or "poor foul," is meant to be applied to Cordelia, there cannot be the fmalleft doubt; and the words, "no, no, no life," which immediately follow, fufficiently confirm it. A. B.

[1] *How quote you my folly.*] To *quote* is to *obferve*. STEEVENS.

4 "Quote,"

—— Never flee and jeſt at me;
I ſpeak not like a dotard, nor a fool;
As under privilege of age, to brag
What I have done being young, or what would do,
Were I not old. *Much ado about nothing*, A. 5, S. 1.

He is the prince's jeſter: a very dull fool; only his gift is in deviſing impoſſible ſlanders: none but libertines delight in him; and the commendation is not in his wit, but in his villainy.

Much ado about nothing, A. 2, S. 1.

—— Hear you me, Jeſſica:
Lock up my doors; and when you hear the drum,
And the vile ſqueaking of the wry-neck'd fife,
Clamber not you up to the caſements then,
Nor thruſt your head into the public ſtreet,
To gaze on Chriſtian fools with varniſh'd faces.
Merchant of Venice, A. 2, S. 5.

The fool hath planted in his memory
An army of good words: and I do know
A many fools, that ſtand in better place,
Garniſh'd like him, that for a trickſy word
Defy the matter. *Merchant of Venice*, A. 3, S. 5.

—— [1] Carded his ſtate,
Mingled his royalty with carping fools;

Had

" Quote." This word occurs in many of Shakeſpeare's plays—It ſhould be printed *cote*, a French word ſignifying *mark*. *Cote* is thus explained in the Dictionaries, *Marque dont ſe ſervent les gens de pratique*. A. B.

[1] *Carded his ſtate.*] The metaphor ſeems to be taken from mingling *coarſe* wool with *fine*, and carding them together, whereby the value of the latter is diminiſhed. STEEVENS.

By *carding his ſtate*, the king means that his predeceſſor ſet his conſequence to hazard, played it away, as a man loſes his fortune at *cards*. REMARKS.

" Carded his ſtate," is harſh. *To card*, is to mix; and if we acknowledge *carded* to be right, the ſenſe will yet be defective unleſs we are told with what he *mixed his ſtate*. I am therefore inclined to think that Shakeſpeare wrote *gawded his ſtate*, meaning that

Had his great name profaned with their ſcorns;
And gave his countenance, againſt his name,[1]
To laugh at gybing boys. *Henry IV*, P. 1, A. 3. S2.

A fool, a fool!—I met a fool i' the foreſt,
A motley fool,—a miſerable world![2]
As you like it, A. 2. S. 7.

FORTUNE, FORTUNES.

—— 'Tis yet to know,
(Which when I know that boaſting is an honour,
I ſhall promulgate) I fetch my life and being
From men of royal ſiege; and my demerits
May ſpeak, unbonnetted, to as proud a fortune
As this that I have reach'd. *Othello*. A. 1, S. 2.

—— If I do prove her haggard,
Though that her jeſſes were my dear heart-ſtrings,
I'd whiſtle her off, and let her down the wind,
To prey at fortune. *Othello*, A. 3, S. 3.

To be a well-favour'd man is the gift of fortune; but to write and read comes by nature.
Much ado about nothing, A. 3, S. 3.

I count

that he was too fond of *ſhew* and *oſtentation*; and this is the character of Richard. *Gawds*, in old language are *toys*, *trifles*, *ornaments*. A. B.

[1] *And gave his countenance againſt his name.*] Made his preſence injurious to his reputation. JOHNSON.

"Countenance" is *ſupport*. The meaning is, he gave ſupport and protection to what could never do him credit. A. B.

[2] *A motley fool,—a miſerable world!*] What! becauſe he met a motley fool, was it therefore a *miſerable world!* This is ſadly blundered. We ſhould read—a miſerable varlet. WARBURTON.

I ſee no need of change. A *miſerable world* is a parenthetical exclamation frequent among melancholy men, and natural to Jaques at the ſight of a fool, or at the hearing of reflections on the fragility of life. JOHNSON.

Some force may be given to the paſſage, by reading
O miſerable world!

Or

I count myſelf in nothing elſe ſo happy,
As in a ſoul remembering my good friends:
And, as my fortune ripens with thy love,
It ſhall be ſtill thy true-love's recompenſe.
Richard II. A. 2, S. 3.

Will fortune never come with both hands full,
But write her fair words ſtill in fouleſt letters?
She either gives a ſtomach, and no food,—
Such are the poor, in health; or elſe a feaſt,
And takes away the ſtomach,—ſuch are the rich,
That have abundance, and enjoy it not.
Henry IV. P. 2, A. 4, S. 4.

If Brutus will vouchſafe, that Antony
May ſafely come to him, and be reſolv'd
How Cæſar hath deſerv'd to lie in death,
Mark Antony ſhall not love Cæſar dead
So well as Brutus living; but will follow
The fortunes and affairs of noble Brutus,
Thorough the hazards of this untrod ſtate,
With all true faith. *Julius Cæſar*, A. 3, S. 1.

There is a tide in the affairs of men,
Which taken at the flood, leads on to fortune,
Omitted, all the voyage of their life
Is bound in ſhallows, and in miſeries.
Julius Cæſar, A. 4, S. 3.

If Hercules, and Lichas, play at dice
Which is the better man, the greater throw
May turn by fortune from the weaker hand.
Merchant of Venice, A. 2, S. 1.

So may I, blind fortune leading me,
Miſs that which one unworthier may attain,
And die with grieving. *Merchant of Venice*, A. 2, S. 1.

Herein

Or perhaps it will be better to read
O miſerable word!
"A fool! O miſerable word!"—That is, O wretched, that I ſhould be under the neceſſity of calling any man a fool. A. B.

Herein fortune ſhews herſelf more kind
Than is her cuſtom; it is ſtill her uſe,
To let the wretched man out-live his wealth,
To view, with hollow eye and wrinkled brow,
An age of poverty. *Merchant of Venice*, A. 4, S. 1.

[1] Fortune is painted plind, with a muffler before her eyes, to ſignify to you that Fortune is plind.
Henry V. A. 3, S. 6.

With a great heart heave away this ſtorm:
Commend theſe waters to thoſe balmy eyes,
That never ſaw the giant world enrag'd;
Nor met with fortune other than at feaſts,
Full warm of blood, of mirth, of goſſiping.
King John, A. 5, S. 2.

—— All the unſettled humours of the land,—
Raſh, inconſiderate, fiery voluntaries,
With ladies' faces, and fierce dragons' ſpleens,
Have ſold their fortunes at their native homes,
To make a hazard of new fortunes here.
King John, A. 2, S. 1.

You have, by fortune, and his highneſs' favours,
Gone ſlightly o'er low ſteps; and now are mounted,

[1] *Fortune is painted plind, with a muffler before her eyes, to ſignify to you that Fortune is plind.*] Here the fool of a player was for making a joke, as Hamlet ſays, *not ſet down for him, and ſhewing a moſt pitiful ambition* to be witty. For Fluellen, though he ſpeaks with his country accent, yet is all the way repreſented as a man of good plain ſenſe. Therefore, as it appears he knew the meaning of the term *plind*, by his uſe of it, he could never have ſaid that *Fortune was painted plind*, to *ſignify ſhe was plind*. We ſhould, therefore, ſtrike out the firſt *plind*, and read,

"Fortune is painted with a muffler, &c." WARBURTON.

Dr. Warburton is miſtaken. There is here no *ambition to be witty*. Fluellen ſays, "Fortune is painted plind;" but recollecting that Piſtol might not readily comprehend how Fortune could be repreſented or *painted* blind, he goes on—"that is, "with a muffler before her eyes, to ſignify to you that Fortune "is plind." A. B.

Where powers are your retainers: and your words,
Domeſticks to you, ſerve your will, as't pleaſe
Yourſelf pronounce their office. *Henry VIII.* A. 2, S. 4.

——— Deſpight of all miſchance,
Edward will always bear himſelf as king:
Though Fortune's malice overthrow my ſtate,
My mind exceeds the compaſs of her wheel.
Henry VI. P. 3, A. 4, S. 3.

She-wolf of France, but worſe than wolves of France,
Whoſe tongue more poiſons than the adder's tooth!
How ill-beſeeming is it in thy ſex,
To triumph like an Amazonian trull,
Upon their woes, whom fortune captivates!
Henry VI. P. 3, A. 1, S. 4.

As I do live by food, I met a fool;
Who laid him down, and baſk'd him in the ſun,
And rail'd on lady Fortune in good terms.
As you like it, A. 2, S. 7.

Good morrow, fool, quoth I: No, ſir, quoth he,
Call me not fool, till heaven hath ſent me fortune.
As you like it, A. 2, S. 7.

How ſome men creep in ſkittiſh Fortune's hall,
While others play the idiots in her eyes!
How one man eats into another's pride,
While pride is feaſting in his wantonneſs!
Troilus and Creſſida, A. 3, S. 3.

In Fortune's love: the bold and coward,
The wiſe and fool, the artiſt and unread,
The hard and ſoft, ſeem all affin'd and kin:
But in the wind and tempeſt of her frown
Diſtinction with a broad and powerful fan,
Puffing at all, winnows the light away.
Troilus and Creſſida, A. 1, S. 3.

Such wind as ſcatters young men through the world,
To ſeek their fortunes farther than at home,
Where ſmall experience grows.
Taming of the Shrew, A. 1, S. 2.

Wherein have you play'd the knave with Fortune, that ſhe ſhould ſcratch you, who of herſelf is a good lady, and would not have knaves thrive long under her? *All's well that ends well*, A. 5, S. 2.

I have, ere now, ſir, been better known to you, when I have held familiarity with freſher clothes; but I am now, ſir, muddy'd in Fortune's moat, and ſmell ſomewhat ſtrong of her ſtrong diſpleaſure.
All's well that ends well, A. 5, S. 2.

[1] —— One out of ſuits with fortune;
That could give more, but that her hand lacks means. *As you like it*, A. 1, S. 2.

It pleaſes time, and fortune, to lie heavy
Upon a friend of mine; who, in hot blood,
Hath ſtept into the law, which is paſt depth
To thoſe that, without heed, do plunge into it.
Timon of Athens, A. 3, S. 5.

As we do turn our backs
From our companion, thrown into his grave;
So his familiars from his buried fortunes
Slink all away; leave their falſe vows with him,
Like empty purſes pick'd: and his poor ſelf,
A dedicated beggar to the air,
With his diſeaſe of all-ſhunn'd poverty,
Walks, like contempt, alone.
Timon of Athens, A. 4, S. 2.

—— Twinn'd brothers of one womb,—
Whoſe procreation, reſidence, and birth,

[1] —— *One out of ſuits with fortune.*] This ſeems an alluſion to cards, where he that has no more cards to play of any particular ſort is *out of ſuit.* JOHNSON.

Out of ſuit with fortune, I believe, means, turned out of her ſervice, and ſtripped of her livery. STEEVENS.

We ſhould read, "out of fortune's ſuit." *Suite*, Fr. train. *One not in fortune's train*,
That *would* give more, &c. A. B.

Scarce is dividant,—touch them with ſeveral fortunes;
The greater ſcorns the leſſer.
Timon of Athens, A. 4, S. 3.

When Fortune, in her ſhift and change of mood,
Spurns down her late belov'd, all his dependants,
Which labour'd after him to the mountain's top,
Even on their knees and hands, let him ſlip down
Not one accompanying his declining foot.
Timon of Athens, A. 1, S. 1.

—— Every grize of fortune
Is ſmooth'd by that below: the learned pate
Ducks to the golden fool: all is oblique;
There's nothing level in our curſed natures,
But direct villainy. *Timon of Athens*, A. 4, S. 3.

Poor painted queen, vain flouriſh of my fortune!
Fool, fool! thou whett'ſt a knife to kill thyſelf.
The day will come, that thou ſhalt wiſh for me
To help thee curſe this pois'nous bunch-back'd toad.
Richard III. A. 1, S. 3.

Why, what a candy'd deal of courteſy
This fawning greyhound then did proffer me!
Look,—when his infant fortune came to age,
And,—gentle Harry Percy,—and, kind couſin,—
O, the devil take ſuch cozeners!
Henry IV. P. 1, A. 1, S. 3.

To be, or not to be, that is the queſtion:—
Whether 'tis nobler in the mind, to ſuffer
The ſlings and arrows of outrageous fortune;
Or to take arms againſt a ſea of troubles,
And, by oppoſing, end them? *Hamlet*, A. 3, S. 1.

—— Bleſt are thoſe,
Whoſe blood and judgment are ſo well co-mingled,
That they are not a pipe for Fortune's finger
To ſound what ſtop ſhe pleaſe. *Hamlet*, A. 3, S. 2.

—— This accident and flood of fortune
So far exceed all inſtance, all diſcourſe,

That

That I am ready to diſtruſt mine eyes,
And wrangle with my reaſon, that perſuades me
To any other truſt. *Twelfth Night*, A. 4, S. 3.

——— If you could wear a mind
Dark as your fortune is; and but diſguiſe
That, which, to appear itſelf, muſt not yet be,
But by ſelf-danger; you ſhall tread a courſe
Pretty, and full of view [2]. *Cymbeline*, A. 3, S. 4.

Since my dear ſoul was miſtreſs of her choice,
And could of men diſtinguiſh, her election
Hath ſeal'd thee for herſelf: for thou haſt been
As one, in ſuffering all, that ſuffers nothing;
A man, that fortune's buffets and rewards
Haſt ta'en with equal thanks. *Hamlet*, A. 3, S. 2.

——— I ſee, men's judgments are
A parcel of their fortunes; and things outward
Do draw the inward quality after them,
To ſuffer all alike. *Antony and Cleopatra*, A. 3, S. 11.

——— Women are not,
In their beſt fortunes, ſtrong; but want will perjure
The ne'er touch'd veſtal.
Antony and Cleopatra, A. 3, S. 10.

——— Bountiful fortune,
Now my dear lady, hath mine enemies
Brought to this ſhore. *Tempeſt*, A. 1, S. 2.

If I had a mind to be honeſt, I ſee, Fortune would not ſuffer me; ſhe drops booties in my mouth.
Winter's Tale, A. 4, S. 3.

——— Pleaſe your thoughts
In feeding them with thoſe my former fortunes
Wherein I liv'd, the greateſt prince o' the world,

[2] ——— *full of view.*] With opportunities of examining your affairs with your own eyes. JOHNSON.

"Full of view," *promiſing well—likely to ſucceed.* The expreſſion is French—*de pleine vue.* A. B.

The noblest: and do now not basely die,
Nor cowardly. *Antony and Cleopatra*, A. 4, S. 13.

[2] Fortune, she said, was no goddess, that had put such difference betwixt their two estates; Love, no god, that would not extend his might, only where qualities were level; Diana, no queen of virgins, that would suffer her poor knight to be surprised without rescue in the first assault, or ransom afterwards.
All's well that ends well, A. 1, S. 3.

FRIEND.

—— Friends all but now, even now,
In quarter [3], and in terms like bride and groom

[2] *Fortune, she said, was no goddess, &c. Love no god, &c.*] This passage stands thus in the old copies:

Love, no god, that would not extend his might, only where qualities were level; queen of virgins, that would suffer her poor knight, &c.

'Tis evident to every sensible reader, that something must have slipt out here, by which the meaning of the context is rendered defective. The steward is speaking in the very words he overheard of the young lady;—Fortune was no goddess, she said, for one reason; Love, no god, for another; what could she then more properly subjoin, than as I have amended in the text?

Diana, *no queen of virgins, that would suffer her poor knight to be surprised without rescue.*

For in poetical history Diana was well known to preside over *Chastity*, as Cupid over *Love*, or *Fortune* over the *change or regulation* of our *circumstances*. THEOBALD.

This interpolation of Mr. Theobald's is, in my opinion, particularly faulty. To preserve a consistency of character, Helena should rather be made to upbraid *Venus* than *Diana*. The original text is certainly right. We have only to transpose a sentence or two.

"Fortune, she said, was no goddess, that had put such difference betwixt their two estates: Love, no god, that would not extend his might, only where qualities were level. This she delivered in the most bitter touch of sorrow, that e'er I heard a virgin exclaim in.---Queen of virgins! that would suffer her poor knight to be surprised, without rescue, in the first assault, or ransom afterward. This I held my duty, &c." A. B.

[3] *In quarter.*] In their quarters; at their lodgings.
JOHNSON.

"Quarter," I believe, is used for *post* or *station*. A. B.

Divesting

Diveſting them for bed; and then, but now,
(As if ſome planet had unwitted men)
Swords out, and tilting one at other's breaſt,
In oppoſition bloody. *Othello*, A. 2, S. 3.

Whenever Buckingham doth turn his hate
Upon your grace, God puniſh me
With hate in thoſe where I expect moſt love!
When I have moſt need to employ a friend,
And moſt aſſured that he is a friend,
Deep, hollow, treacherous and full of guile,
Be he unto me! *Richard III.* A. 2, S. 1.

—— When he frown'd, it was againſt the French,
And not againſt his friends; his noble hand
Did win what he did ſpend, and ſpent not that
Which his triumphant father's hand had won.
Richard II. A. 2, S. 1.

—— Gentle friends,
Let's kill him boldly, but not wrathfully;
Let's carve him as a diſh fit for the gods,
Not hew him as a carcaſe fit for hounds:
And let our hearts, as ſubtle maſters do,
Stir up their ſervants to an act of rage,
And after ſeem to chide them.
Julius Cæſar, A. 2, S. 1.

Brutus, I do obſerve you now of late:
I have not from your eyes that gentleneſs,
And ſhew of love, as I was wont to have:
You bear too ſtubborn and too ſtrange a hand
Over your friend that loves you.
Julius Cæſar, A. 1, S. 2.

—— Let not my goods friends be griev'd;
(Among which number, Caſſius, be you one)
Nor conſtrue any further my neglect,
Than that poor Brutus, with himſelf at war,
Forgets the ſhews of love to other men.
Julius Cæſar, A. 1, S. 2.

—— Keep this man safe,
Give him all kindness: I had rather have
Such men my friends, than enemies. Go on,
And see whe'r Brutus be alive or dead [3].

Julius Cæsar, A. 5, S. 4.

Thou hast describ'd
A hot friend cooling: Ever note, Lucilius,
When love begins to sicken and decay,
It useth an enforced ceremony.

Julius Cæsar, A. 4, S. 2.

If thou wilt lend this money, lend it not
As to thy friends; for when did friendship take
A breed of barren metal of his friend?
But lend it rather to thine enemy.

Merchant of Venice, A. 1, S. 3.

—— Albeit, I neither lend nor borrow,
By taking, nor by giving of excess,
Yet, to supply the ripe wants of my friend,
I'll break a custom. *Merchant of Venice*, A. 1, S. 3.

The dearest friend to me, the kindest man,
The best condition'd and unweary'd spirit
In doing courtesies; and one in whom
The ancient Roman honour more appears,
Than any that draws breath in Italy.

Merchant of Venice, A. 3, S. 2.

[4] Your worship's friend, and Launcelot, Sir.

Merchant of Venice, A. 2, S. 2.

—— When

[3] —— *Go on,*
And see whe'r Brutus be alive, or dead.
"Whe'r"—Why should we not substitute *if* in lieu of this ugly contraction? A. B.

[4] *Your worship's friend, and Launcelot, Sir.*] Dr. Farmer is of opinion we should read *Gobbo*, instead of *Launcelot*. It may be inferred from the name of *Gobbo*, that Shakespeare designed this character to be represented with a hump-back. STEEVENS.

It is much more likely that Launcelot is called *Gobbo* from his continual

——— When I told you
My ſtate was nothing, I ſhould then have told you
That I was worſe than nothing; for, indeed,
I have engag'd myſelf to a dear friend,
Engag'd my friend to his mere enemy,
I feed my means. *Merchant of Venice*, A. 3, S. 2.

——— Can you think, lords,
That any Engliſhman dare give me counſel?
Or be a known friend, 'gainſt his highneſs' pleaſure,
(Though he be grown ſo deſperate to be honeſt)
And live a ſubject? *Henry VIII.* A. 3, S. 1.

I have trod a meaſure; I have flatter'd a lady; I have been politick with my friend, ſmooth with mine enemy; I have undone three taylors; I have had four quarrels, and like to have fought one.

As you like it, A. 5, S. 4.

I know, the more one ſickens, the worſe at eaſe he is; and that he that wants money, means, and content, is without three good friends;—that the property of rain is to wet, and fire to burn; that good paſture makes fat ſheep; and that a great cauſe of the night, is the lack of the ſun.

As you like it, A. 3, S. 2.

If I be foil'd, there is but one ſham'd that was never gracious; if kill'd, but one dead that is willing to be ſo: I ſhall do my friends no wrong, for I have none to lament me; the world no injury, for in it I have nothing. *As you like it*, A. 1, S. 2.

—— Felleſt foes,
Whoſe paſſions and whoſe plots have broke their ſleep
To take the one the other, by ſome chance,
Some trick not worth an egg, ſhall grow dear friends,
And interjoin their iſſues. *Coriolanus*, A. 4, S. 4.

continual prating, and for which he is reproved by his maſter in a ſubſequent ſcene. A *gob*, in the Northern counties, is a *large open mouth*. A. B.

— To

—— To wail friends loſt,
Is not by much ſo wholeſome, profitable,
As to rejoice at friends but newly found.

Love's Labour Loſt, A. 5, S. 2.

—— Be able for thine enemy
Rather in power, than uſe; and keep thy friend
Under thine own life's key.

All's well that ends well, A. 1, S. 1.

What need we have any friends, if we ſhould never have need of them? they were the moſt needleſs creatures living, ſhould we ne'er have uſe for them: and would moſt reſemble ſweet inſtruments hung up in caſes, that keep their ſounds to themſelves.

Timon of Athens, A. 1, S. 2.

The [1] friends thou haſt, and their adoption try'd,
Grapple them to thy ſoul with hoops of ſteel;
But do not dull thy palm [2] with entertainment
Of each new-hatch'd, unfledg'd comrade.

Hamlet, A. 1, S. 3.

—— Can'ſt thou the conſcience lack,
To think I ſhall lack friends? Secure thy heart;
If I would broach the veſſels of my love,
And try the argument of hearts by borrowing,
Men, and men's fortunes, could I frankly uſe,
As I can bid thee ſpeak. *Timon of Athens*, A. 2, S. 2.

[1] *The friends thou haſt, and their adoption try'd.*] I read, "*adaption* try'd," *i. e.* their ſuitableneſs, their fitneſs to be made your friends being proved, then, &c. A. B.

[2] —— *Do not dull thy palm with entertainment Of each new-hatch'd, unfledg'd comrade.*] The literal ſenſe is, *Do not make thy palm callous, by ſhaking every man by the hand.* The figurative meaning may be, *Do not, by promiſcuous converſation, make thy mind inſenſible to the difference of characters.* JOHNSON.

"Do not dull thy palm," is, I think, *Do not ſully thy honour*, or the honour of thy houſe, by aſſociating with thy inferiors, or with people who are little known to thee. A. B.

What

What viler thing upon the earth, than friends,
Who can bring nobleſt minds to baſeſt ends!
How rarely does it meet with this time's guiſe,
When man was wiſh'd to love his enemies:
Grant, I may ever love, and rather woo
Thoſe that would miſchief me, than thoſe that do!

Timon of Athens, A. 4, S. 4.

Marry, ſir, they praiſe me, and make an aſs of me; now my foes tell me plainly, I am an aſs: ſo that by my foes, ſir, I profit in the knowledge of myſelf; and by my friends I am abuſed.

Twelfth Night, A. 5, S. 1.

Neither a borrower, nor a lender be:
For loan oft loſes both itſelf and friend;
And borrowing dulls the edge of huſbandry.
This above all,—to thine ownſelf be true.

Hamlet, A. 1, S. 3.

Maſter Shallow, my lord Shallow, be what thou wilt, I am fortune's ſteward. Get on thy boots; we'll ride all night:—Oh, ſweet Piſtol!—Away, Bardolph.—Come, Piſtol, utter more to me; and, withal, deviſe ſomething to do thyſelf good.—Boot, boot, maſter Shallow; I know, the young king is ſick for me. Let us take any man's horſes; the laws of England are at my commandment. Happy are they which have been my friends.

Henry IV. P. 2, A. 5, S. 3.

—— Mine honeſt friend,
Will you take eggs for money[1]?

Winter's Tale, A. 1, S. 2.

—— A fel-

[1] *Will you take eggs for money?*] This ſeems to be a proverbial expreſſion, uſed when a man ſees himſelf wronged, and makes no reſiſtance. Its original, or preciſe meaning, I cannot find, but I believe it means, will you be a *cuckold* for hire? The cuckow is reported to lay her eggs in another bird's neſt; he therefore

——— A fellow all in buff;
[2] A back-friend, a ſhoulder-clapper, one that countermands
The paſſages of allies, creeks, and narrow lands.
Comedy of Errors, A. 4, S. 2.

G.

GAWDS.

ALL, with one conſent, praiſe new-born gawds,
Though they are made and moulded of things paſt;
And ſhew to duſt, that is a little gilt,
More land than gilt o'er duſted.
Troilus and Creſſida, A. 3, S. 3.

GENTLEMAN.

Be kind and courteous to this gentleman;
Hop in his walks, and gambol in his eyes;

therefore that has eggs laid in his neſt, is ſaid to be *cucullus*, cuckow'd, or *cuckold*. JOHNSON.

"Will you take eggs for money?" The meaning is, Will you take *ayes* (*i. e.* words) for money? *Aie*, in old language, is uſed both for the affirmative *yes*, and for *egg*. See Chaucer. *Aie*, *Aye*, (Ey, Teut.) an egg. A. B.

[2] *A back-friend, a ſhoulder-clapper, &c. of allies, creeks, and narrow lands.*] It ſhould be written, I think, *narrow lanes*. GREY.

The preceding rhyme forbids us to read *lanes*. A ſhoulder-clapper is a bailiff. STEEVENS.

What is meant by "countermands the paſſages of allies, &c." I cannot poſſibly diſcover. We may ſurely read,
"A back-friend, a ſhoulder-clapper, one who his ſtand maintains,
"I' the paſſages of allies, creeks, and narrow lanes."
This change will make every thing clear and proper. A. B.

Feed him with apricocks and dewberries,
With purple grapes, green figs, and mulberries.
Midſummer Night's Dream, A. 3, S. 1.

If it be ne'er ſo falſe, a true gentleman may ſwear it, in the behalf of his friend:—And I'll ſwear to the prince, thou art a tall fellow of thy hands, and that thou wilt not be drunk; but I know, thou art no tall fellow of thy hands, and that thou wilt be drunk; but I'll ſwear it. *Winter's Tale*, A. 5, S. 2.

You denied to fight with me this other day, becauſe I was no gentleman born: ſee you theſe clothes? ſay you ſee them not, and think me ſtill no gentleman born; you were beſt ſay, theſe robes are not gentleman born. Give me the lie, do; and try whether I am not now a gentleman born.
Winter's Tale, A. 5, S. 2.

I was a gentleman born before my father; for the king's ſon took me by the hand, and call'd me, brother; and then the two kings call'd my father, brother; and then the prince, my brother, and the princeſs, my ſiſter, call'd my father, father; ſo we wept: and there was the firſt gentleman-like tears that ever we ſhed. *Winter's Tale*, A. 5, S. 2.

A ſweeter and a lovelier gentleman,—
Fram'd in the prodigality of nature,
Young, valiant, wiſe, and, no doubt, right royal,
The ſpacious world cannot again afford.
Richard III. A. 1, S. 2.

The gentleman is learn'd, a moſt rare ſpeaker,
To nature none more bound, his training ſuch,
That he may furniſh and inſtruct great teachers,
And never ſeek for aid out of himſelf.
Henry VIII. A. 1, S. 2.

—— You have fed upon my ſignories,
Diſpark'd my parks, and fell'd my foreſt woods;
From mine own windows torn my houſhold coat,
Raz'd out my impreſs, leaving me no ſign,—

Save

Save men's opinions, and my living blood,—
To ſhew the world I am a gentleman.

Richard II. A. 3, S. 1.

A raſcally yea-forſooth knave! to bear a gentleman in hand, and then ſtand upon ſecurity!—I had as lief they would put ratſbane in my mouth, as offer to ſtop it with ſecurity. I look'd he ſhould have ſent me two and twenty yards of ſattin, as I am a true knight, and he ſends me ſecurity.

Henry IV. P. 2, A. 1, S. 2.

GENTLENESS.

What would you have? Your gentleneſs ſhall force,
More than your force move us to gentleneſs.

As you like it, A. 2, S. 7.

GIANT.

—— The poor beetle, that we tread upon,
In corporal ſufferance finds a pang as great
As when a giant dies.

Meaſure for Meaſure, A. 3, S. 1.

GIFTS.

——— At thy birth, dear boy!
Nature and fortune join'd to make thee great:
Of nature's gifts thou may'ſt with lilies boaſt,
And with the half-blown roſe.

King John, A. 3, S. 1.

A gift that I have, a fooliſh extravagant ſpirit, full of forms, figures, ſhapes, objects, ideas, apprehenſions, motions, revolutions: theſe are begot in the ventricle of memory, nouriſhed in the womb of pia-mater, and deliver'd upon the mellowing of occaſion.

Love's Labour Loſt, A. 4, S. 2.

Sit, my preſerver, by thy patient's ſide;
And with this healthful hand, whoſe baniſh'd ſenſe
Thou

Thou haſt repeal'd, a ſecond time receive
The confirmation of my promis'd gift,
Which but attends thy naming.
All's well that ends well, A. 2, S. 3.

She prizes not ſuch trifles as theſe are:
The gifts, ſhe looks from me, are pack'd, and lock'd
Up in my heart; which I have given already,
But not deliver'd. *Winter's Tale*, A. 4, S. 3.

Win her with gifts, if ſhe reſpect not words;
Dumb jewels often, in their ſilent kind,
More than quick words, do move a woman's mind.
Two Gentlemen of Verona, A. 3, S. 1.

GLOBE.

The cloud-capt towers, the gorgeous palaces,
The ſolemn temples, the great globe itſelf,
Yea, all which it inherit, ſhall diſſolve,
And, like this inſubſtantial pageant faded,
Leave not a wreck behind. *Tempeſt*, A. 4, S. 1.

GLORY.

Glory is like a circle in the water,
Which never ceaſeth to enlarge itſelf,
Till by broad ſpreading, it diſperſe to nought.
Henry VI. P. 1, A. 1, S. 2.

I have given here my ſoul's conſent,
To undeck the pompous body of a king;
Make glory baſe; and ſovereignty, a ſlave;
Proud majeſty, a ſubject; ſtate a peaſant.
Richard II. A. 4, S. 1.

O mighty Cæſar! Doſt thou lie ſo low?
Are all thy conqueſts, glories, triumphs, ſpoils,
Shrunk to this little meaſure?—Fare thee well.
Julius Cæſar, A. 3, S. 1.

——— I have ventur'd,
Like little wanton boys that ſwim on bladders,

These

These many ſummers in a ſea of glory;
But far beyond my depth: my high-blown pride
At length broke under me; and now has left me
Weary, and old with ſervice, to the mercy
Of a rude ſtream, that muſt for ever hide me.

Henry VIII. A. 3, S. 2.

— When I am forgotten, as I ſhall be;
And ſleep in dull cold marble, where no mention
Of me more muſt be heard of,—ſay, I taught thee,
Say, Wolſey,—that once trod the ways of glory,
And ſounded all the depths and ſhoals of honour,
Found thee a way, out of his wreck, to riſe in;
A ſure and ſafe one, though thy maſter miſs'd it.

Henry VIII. A. 3, S. 2.

GOD, GODS.

The tartneſs of his face ſours ripe grapes. When he walks, he moves like an engine, and the ground ſhrinks before his treading. He is able to pierce a corſlet with his eye; talks like a knell, and his hum is a battery. He ſits in his ſtate as a thing made for Alexander; what he bids be done, is finiſh'd with his bidding. He wants nothing of a god, but eternity, and a heaven to throne in. *Coriolanus*, A. 5, S. 4.

Rich ſhe ſhall be, that's certain; wiſe, or I'll none; virtuous, or I'll never cheapen her; fair, or I'll never look on her; mild, or come not near me; noble, or not I for an angel; of good diſcourſe, an excellent muſician, and her hair ſhall be of what colour it pleaſe God. *Much ado about nothing*, A. 2, S. 3.

'A made a finer end, and went away, an it had been any Chriſtian child; 'a parted even juſt between twelve and one, e'en at turning o' the tide: for after I ſaw him fumble with the ſheets, and play with flowers, and ſmile upon his fingers ends, I knew there was but one way; for his noſe was as ſharp as a pen, and 'a babbled of green fields. How now, Sir John? quoth

quoth I: what, man! be of good cheer. So 'a cried out—God, God, God! three or four times: now I, to comfort him, bid him 'a ſhould not think of God; I hop'd, there was no need to trouble himſelf with any ſuch thoughts yet. *Henry V.* A. 2, S. 3.

—— There was never yet philoſopher,
That could endure the tooth-ach patiently;
However they have writ the ſtyle of gods,
And made a piſh at chance and ſufferance.
Much ado about nothing, A. 5, S. 1.

Strives Bolingbroke to be as great as we?
Greater he ſhall not be; if he ſerve God,
We'll ſerve him too, and be his fellow ſo.
Richard II. A. 3, S. 2.

—— This man
Is now become a god; and Caſſius is
A wretched creature, and muſt bend his body,
If Cæſar careleſsly but nod on him.
He had a fever when he was in Spain;
And, when the fit was on him, I did mark
How he did ſhake: 'tis true this god did ſhake.
Julius Cæſar, A. 1, S. 2.

—— By the gods,
You ſhall digeſt the venom of your ſpleen,
Though it do ſplit: for, from this day forth,
I'll uſe you for my mirth, yea, for my laughter,
When you are waſpiſh. *Julius Cæſar*, A. 4, S. 3.

If two gods ſhould play ſome heavenly match,
And on the wager lay two earthly women,
And Portia one, there muſt be ſomething elſe
Pawn'd with the other; for the poor rude world
Hath not her fellow. *Merchant of Venice*, A. 3, S. 5.

—— O Cromwell, Cromwell,
Had I but ſerv'd my God with half the zeal

I ſerv'd my king, he would not in mine age
Have left me naked to mine enemies.

Henry VIII. A. 3, S. 2.

By [1] God's ſontics, 'twill be a hard way to hit.

Merchant of Venice, A. 2, S. 2.

O God! methinks it were a happy life,
To be no better than a homely ſwain;
To ſit upon a hill, as I do now,
To carve out dials quaintly, point by point,
Thereby to ſee the minutes how they run:
How many make the hour full complete,
How many hours bring about the day,
How many days will finiſh up the year,
How many years a mortal man may live.

Henry VI. P. 3, A. 2, S. 5.

—— The good gods forbid,
That our renowned Rome, whoſe gratitude
Towards her deſerved children is enroll'd
In Jove's own book, like an unnatural dam
Should now eat up her own!

Coriolanus, A. 3, S. 1.

—— The honour'd gods
Keep Rome in ſafety, and the chairs of juſtice
Supply'd with worthy men! Plant love among us!
Throng our large temples with the ſhews of peace,
And not our ſtreets with war [2]! *Coriolanus*, A. 3, S. 3.

He

[1] *God's ſonties.*] I know not exactly of what oath this is a corruption. I meet with *God's ſanty* in Decker's *Honeſt Whore*; and in another play with *God's ſainte.*

Perhaps it was once cuſtomary to ſwear by the ſanté, *i. e. health* of the Supreme Being, or by his Saints. Oaths of ſuch a form are not unfrequent among our ancient writers. STEEVENS.

"God's ſonties," means, *offenders againſt God---ſinners.* Sontis, *Lat.*

We now ſay, *as I am a ſinner.* A. B.

[2] *Throng our large temples with the ſhews of peace, And not our ſtreets with war.*] I think the tranſcriber's ear

He is their god, he leads them like a thing
Made by ſome other deity than nature,
That ſhapes man better: and they follow him,
Againſt us brats, with no leſs confidence,
Than boys purſuing ſummer butter-flies.

Coriolanus, A. 4, S. 6.

——— So the gods bleſs me,
When all our offices have been oppreſt
With riotous feeders; when our vaults have wept
With drunken ſpilth of wine; when every room
Hath blaz'd with lights, and bray'd with minſtrelſy;
I have retir'd me to a waſteful cock,
And ſet mine eyes at flow. *Timon of Athens*, A. 2, S. 2.

It was ſome friend: therefore, thou happy father,
Think that the cleareſt gods [1], who make them honours
Of men's impoſſibilities, have preſerved thee.

Lear, A. 4, S. 6.

——— He hath fought to-day,
As if a god, in hate of mankind, had
Deſtroy'd in ſuch a ſhape.

Antony and Cleopatra, A. 4, S. 8.

ear deceived him here, as in many other places, and that the poet wrote---"*ſtrew* our large temples, &c." By the "*ſhews* of "peace," I believe, were meant the leaves of the olive; with which the temples might be *ſtrewed*, but could hardly be *thronged*. MALONE.

"Throng our large temples," is without the ſmalleſt queſtion right. The meaning is,---*may our temples, and not our ſtreets, be filled with people.* The former will be tokens or ſhews of *peace*, the latter of *war*. A. B.

[1] ——— *the cleareſt gods.*] The pureſt; the moſt free from evil. JOHNSON.

I ſhould think the poet wrote "deareſt gods." He frequently applies the epithet *dear* to the gods. The *c* and *l*, in cleareſt, when joined, make a perfect *d*. A. B.

GOLD.

He ſeems to be of great authority: cloſe with him; give him gold: and though authority be a ſtubborn bear, yet he is often led by the noſe with gold.

Winter's Tale, A. 4, S. 3.

—— 'Tis gold
Which buys admittance; oft it doth; yea, and makes
Diana's rangers falſe themſelves, yield up
Their deer to the ſtand o' the ſtealer: and 'tis gold
Which makes the true man kill'd, and ſaves the thief.
Cymbeline, A. 2, S. 3.

—— What a god's gold,
'Tis thou that rigg'ſt the bark, and plow'ſt the foam,
Settleſt admired reverence in a ſlave;
To thee be worſhip! and thy ſaints for aye
Be crown'd with plagues, that thee alone obey.
Timon of Athens, A. 5, S. 1.

—— Raſcal thieves,
Here's gold: go ſuck the ſubtle blood o'the grape,
'Till the high fever ſeeth your blood to froth,
And ſo, 'ſcape hanging. *Timon of Athens*, A. 4, S. 3.

—— Go on—here's gold—go on;
Be as a planetary plague, when Jove
Will o'er ſome high-vic'd city hang his poiſon
In the ſick air: let not thy ſword ſkip one:
Pity not honour'd age for his white beard,
He is an uſurer. *Timon of Athens*, A. 4, S. 3.

— Peace; thou know'ſt not gold's effect:
Tell me her father's name, and 'tis enough;
For I will board her, though ſhe chide as loud
As thunder, when the clouds in autumn crack.
Taming of the Shrew, A. 1, S. 2.

The

The providence, that's in a wachful ſtate,
Knows[1] almoſt every grain of Pluto's gold,
Finds bottom in the uncomprehenſive deeps;
Keeps place with thought, and almoſt, like the gods,
Does thoughts unveil in their dumb cradles.
Troilus and Creſſida, A. 3, S. 3.

—— He that doth the ravens feed,
Yea, providently caters for the ſparrow,
Be comfort to my age! Here is the gold;
All this I give you: let me be your ſervant.
As you like it, A. 2, S. 3.

There is thy gold; worſe poiſon to men's ſouls,
Doing more murders in this loathſome world,
Than theſe poor compounds that thou may'ſt not ſell:
I ſell thee poiſon, thou haſt ſold me none.
Romeo and Juliet, A. 5, S. 1.

Gold? yellow, glittering, precious gold? No, gods,
I am no idle votariſt.[1] *Timon of Athens*, A. 4, S. 3.

[1] *Knows almoſt every grain of Pluto's gold.*] I think we ſhould read, of Plutus' gold. It ſhould be remembered, however, that *mines of gold* were anciently ſuppoſed to be *guarded by demons*. STEEVENS.

" Pluto" is right. Pluto is properly the god of riches. Plutus is rather the keeper or diſtributor of thoſe riches. A. B.

[1] —— *no idle votariſt.*] No inſincere or inconſtant ſupplicant. JOHNSON.

Votariſt can ſcarcely ſtand for *ſupplicant*—beſide, Timon was reſigned to his fate, and he had nothing more to aſk. By *votariſt*, he means that he had devoted himſelf to *labour*; and by " no idle one," he would intimate that his reſolution was taken, and that even the ſight of gold has nothing alluring in it, or that can tempt him to break his vows. A. B.

GOOD, GOODNESS.

I never did repent for doing good,
Nor ſhall not now.

Merchant of Venice, A. 3, S. 4.

We, ignorant of ourſelves,
Beg often our own harms, which the wiſe pow'rs
Deny us for our good: ſo find we profit,
By loſing of our prayers.

Antony and Cleopatra, A. 2, S. 1.

O loyal father of a treacherous ſon!
Thou ſheer, immaculate, and ſilver fountain,
From whence this ſtream through muddy paſſages,
Hath held his current, and defil'd himſelf!
Thy overflow of good converts to bad;
And thy abundant goodneſs ſhall excuſe
This deadly blot in thy digreſſing ſon.

Richard II. A. 5, S. 3.

—— I can eaſier teach twenty what were good to be done, than be one of the twenty to follow mine own teaching.

Merchant of Venice, A. 1, S. 2.

——— My vows and prayers
Yet are the king's, and, till my ſoul forſake me,
Shall cry for bleſſings on him; may he live
Longer than I have time to tell his years!
Ever belov'd, and loving, may his rule be!
And, when old time ſhall lead him to his end,
Goodneſs and he fill up one monument.

Henry VIII. A. 2, S. 1.

GRACE, GRACES.

Lady, you are the crueleſt ſhe alive,
If you will lead theſe graces to the grave,
And leave the world no copy.

Twelfth Night, A. 1, S. 5.

Chide

Chide me, dear ſtone; that I may ſay, indeed,
Thou art Hermione: or rather, thou art ſhe,
In thy not chiding; for ſhe was as tender,
As infancy, and grace. *Winter's Tale*, A. 5, S. 3.

—— Take Antony
Octavia to his wife: whoſe beauty claims
No worſe a huſband than the beſt of men;
Whoſe virtue, and whoſe general graces, ſpeak
That which none elſe can utter.
Antony and Cleopatra, A. 2, S. 2.

Make your full reference freely to my lord,
Who is ſo full of grace, that it flows over
On all that need: let me report to him
Your ſweet dependancy; and you ſhall find
A conqueror, that will pray in aid for kindneſs
Where he for grace is kneel'd to.
Antony and Cleopatra, A. 5, S. 2.

See what a grace was ſeated on this brow:
Hyperion's curls; the front of Jove himſelf;
An eye like Mars, to threaten and command;
A ſtation like the herald Mercury [1],
New lighted on a heaven-kiſſing hill;
A combination, and a form, indeed,
Where every god did ſeem to ſet his ſeal,
To give the world aſſurance of a man.
Hamlet, A. 3, S. 4.

—— Alas, ſir,
In what have I offended you? what cauſe
Hath my behaviour given to your diſpleaſure,

[1] *A ſtation.*] *Station*, in this inſtance, does not mean *the ſpot where any one is placed*, but the *act of ſtanding*. STEEVENS.
"A ſtation like the herald mercury,"
is *an elegant, ſtriking figure*. That ſuch is the meaning, the following line will ſhew.
"A combination, and a *form*, indeed." A. B.

That thus you ſhould proceed to put me off,
And take your good grace from me?
Henry VIII. A. 2, S. 4.

Good my lord,
You are full of heavenly ſtuff, and bear the inventory
Of your beſt graces in your mind; the which
You were now running o'er; you have ſcarce time
To ſteal from ſpiritual leiſure a brief ſpan,
To keep your earthly audit. *Henry VIII.* A. 3, S. 2.

Thou ſeeſt, that all the grace that ſhe hath left
Is, that ſhe will not add to her damnation
A ſin of perjury: ſhe not denies it.
Much ado about nothing, A. 4, S. 1.

O Hero! what a Hero hadſt thou been
If half thy outward graces had been plac'd
About the thoughts and counſels of thy heart,
But, fare thee well, moſt foul, moſt fair!
Much ado about nothing, A. 4, S. 1.

GREATNESS.

—— O be ſick, great greatneſs,
And bid thy ceremony give thee cure!
Think'ſt thou, thy fiery fever will go out
With titles blown from adulation?
Will it give place to flexure and low bending?
Canſt thou, when thou command'ſt the beggar's knee,
Command the health of it? *Henry V.* A. 4, S. 1.

O hard condition! twin-born with greatneſs,
Subjected to the breath of every fool,
Whoſe ſenſe no more can feel but his own wringing!
What infinite heart's-eaſe muſt kings neglect,
That private men enjoy? and what have kings,
That private men have not too, ſave ceremony?
Henry V. A. 4, S. 1.

That man, that ſits within a monarch's heart,
And ripens in the ſun-ſhine of his favour,

Would

Would he abuſe the countenance of the king,
Alack, what miſchiefs might he ſet abroach,
In ſhadow of ſuch greatneſs!

Henry IV. P. 2, A. 4, S. 2.

The abuſe of greatneſs is, when it disjoins
Remorſe from power: and, to ſpeak truth of Cæſar,
I have not known when his affections ſway'd
More than his reaſon. *Julius Cæſar*, A. 2, S. 1.

O place and greatneſs, millions of falſe eyes
Are ſtuck upon thee! volumes of report
Run with theſe falſe and moſt contrarious queſts
Upon thy doings! thouſand 'ſcapes of wit
Make thee the father of their idle dream,
And rack thee in their fancies!

Meaſure for Meaſure, A. 4, S. 1.

—— Believe this,
No ceremony that to great ones 'longs,
Not the king's crown, nor the deputed ſword,
The marſhal's truncheon, nor the judge's robe,
Become them with one half ſo good a grace,
As mercy does. *Meaſure for Meaſure*, A. 2, S. 2.

—— Nay then, farewell!
I have touch'd the higheſt point of all my greatneſs;
And, from that full meridian of my glory,
I haſte now to my ſetting: I ſhall fall
Like a bright exhalation in the evening,
And no man ſee me more. *Henry VIII.* A. 3, S. 2.

Farewell, a long farewell, to all my greatneſs!
This is the ſtate of man; to-day he puts forth
The tender leaves of hope, to-morrow bloſſoms,
And bears his bluſhing honours thick upon him:
The third day comes a froſt, a killing froſt,
And, when he thinks, good eaſy man, full ſurely
His greatneſs is a ripening,—nips his root,
And then he falls, as I do. *Henry VIII.* A. 3, S. 2.

—— Who

—— Who deſerves greatneſs,
Deſerves your hate: and your affections are
A ſick man's appetite, who deſires moſt that
Which would increaſe his evil. He that depends
Upon your favours, ſwims with fins of lead,
And hews down oaks with ruſhes.

Coriolanus, A. 1, S. 1.

Things ſmall as nothing, for requeſts ſake only,
He makes important: poſſeſt he is with greatneſs,
And ſpeaks not to himſelf, but with a pride
That quarrels at ſelf breath.

Troilus and Creſſida, A. 2, S. 3.

'Tis certain, greatneſs, once fallen out with fortune,
Muſt fall out with men too: What the declin'd is,
He ſhall as ſoon read in the eyes of others,
As feel in his own fall.

Troilus and Creſſida, A. 3, S. 3.

—— So much is my poverty of ſpirit,
So mighty, and ſo many, my defects,
That I would rather hide me from my greatneſs,
Than in my greatneſs covet to be hid,
And in the vapour of my glory ſmother'd.

Richard III. A. 3, S. 7.

Do you hear how we are ſhent[1] for keeping your greatneſs back? *Coriolanus*, A. 5, S. 2.

GRIEF.

Every one can maſter a grief, but he that has it.

Much ado about nothing, A. 3, S. 2.

1 —— *how we are ſhent.*] *Shent* is brought to deſtruction. JOHNSON.

"*Shent*" does not mean *brought to deſtruction*, but *ſhamed, diſgraced, made aſhamed of himſelf.* PERCY.

"Shent," in this place, is *reproved, blamed.* A, B.

Being

Being that I flow in grief,
The ſmalleſt twine may lead me.
Much ado about nothing, A. 4, S. 1.

——— Grief boundeth where it falls,
Not with the empty hollowneſs, but weight:
I take my leave before I have begun;
For ſorrow ends not, when it ſeemeth done.
Richard II. A. 1, S. 2.

— Perſpectives, which, rightly gaz'd upon,
Shew nothing but confuſion; ey'd awry,
Diſtinguiſh form: ſo your ſweet majeſty,
Looking awry upon your lord's departure,
Find ſhapes of grief, more than himſelf to wail.
Richard II. A. 2, S. 2.

——— Oh, that I were as great
As is my grief, or leſſer than my name!
Or that I could forget what I have been!
Or not remember what I muſt be now!
Richard II. A. 3, S. 3.

——— Still my griefs are mine.
You may my glories and my ſtate depoſe,
But not my griefs; ſtill am I king of thoſe.
Richard II. A. 4, S. 1.

—— My grief lies all within;
And theſe external manners of lament
Are merely ſhadows to the unſeen grief,
That ſwells with ſilence in the tortur'd ſoul.
Richard II. A. 4, S. 1.

— Ere thou bid good night, to quit their grief,
Tell thou the lamentable fall of me,
And ſend the hearers weeping to their beds.
Richard II. A. 5, S. 1.

Thou, the model where old Troy did ſtand;
Thou map of honour; thou moſt beauteous inn,
Why

Why ſhould hard-favour'd grief be lodg'd in thee,
When triumph is become an ale-houſe gueſt?
Richard II. A. 5, S. 1.

——— My grief
Stretches itſelf beyond the hour of death;
The blood weeps from my heart, when I do ſhape,
In forms imaginary, the unguided days,
And rotten times, that you ſhall look upon
When I am ſleeping with my anceſtors.
Henry IV. P. 2, A. 4, S. 4.

As the wretch, whoſe fever-weaken'd joints,
Like ſtrengthleſs hinges, buckle under life,
Impatient of his fit, breaks like a fire
Out of his keeper's arms: even ſo my limbs,
Weaken'd with grief, being now enrag'd with grief,
Are thrice themſelves. *Henry IV.* P. 2, A. 1, S. 1.

I have in equal balance juſtly weigh'd
What wrongs our arms may do, what wrongs we
ſuffer,
And find our griefs heavier than our offences.
We ſee which way the ſtream of time doth run,
And are enforc'd from our moſt quiet ſphere,
By the rough torrent of occaſion.
Henry IV. P. 2, A. 4, S. 1.

——— I ſent your grace
The parcels and particulars of our grief;
The which hath been with ſcorn ſhov'd from the
court,
Whereon this hydra ſon of war is born:
Whoſe dangerous eyes may well be charm'd aſleep,
With grant of our moſt juſt and right deſires.
Henry IV. P. 2, A. 4, S. 2.

——— When your head did but ake,
I knit my handkerchief about your brows,
And with my hand at midnight held your head;
And, like the watchful minutes to the hour,

Still

Still and anon cheer'd up the heavy time;
Saying, what lack you? and, where lies your grief?
King John, A. 4, S. 1.

Grief fills the room up of my abſent child,
Lies in his bed, walks up and down with me;
Puts on his pretty looks, repeats his words,
Remembers me of all his gracious parts,
Stuffs out his vacant garments with his form;
Then, have I reaſon to be fond of grief.
King John, A. 3, S. 4.

Preach ſome philoſophy to make me mad,
And thou ſhalt be canoniz'd cardinal;
For, being not mad, but ſenſible of grief,
My reaſonable part produces reaſon
How I may be deliver'd of theſe woes.
King John, A. 3, S. 4.

I am not mad;—I would to heaven, I were!
For then 'tis like I ſhould forget myſelf:
Oh, if I could, what grief ſhould I forget!
King John, A. 3, S. 4.

—— My grief's ſo great,
That no ſupporter but the huge firm earth
Can hold it up: here I and ſorrows ſit;
Here is my throne, bid kings come bow to it.
King John, A. 3, S. 1.

I will inſtruct my ſorrows to be proud:
For grief is proud, and makes his owner ſtout;
To me, and to the ſtate of my great grief,
Let kings aſſemble. *King John*, A. 3, S. 1.

—— 'Tis better to be lowly born,
And range with humble livers in content,
Than to be perk'd up in a gliſtering grief,
And wear a golden ſorrow. *Henry VIII.* A. 2, S. 3.

Theſe eyes—like lamps whoſe waſting oil is ſpent,
Wax dim, as drawing to their exigent:
Weak ſhoulders, over-borne with burthening grief,

And

And pithless arms, like to a wither'd vine,
That droops his sapless branches to the ground.
Henry VI. P. 1, A. 2, S. 5.

A heavier task could not have been impos'd,
Than I to speak my griefs unspeakable.
Comedy of Errors, A. 1, S. 1.

Grief hath chang'd me, since you saw me last;
And careful hours, with time's deformed hand
Have written strange defeatures in my face.
Comedy of Errors, A. 5, S. 1.

Moderate lamentation is the right of the dead, excessive grief the enemy to the living.
All's well that ends well, A. 1, S. 1.

Long may'st thou live, to wail thy children's loss;
And see another, as I see thee now,
Deck'd in thy rights, as thou art stall'd in mine!
Long die thy happy days before thy death;
And, after many length and hours of grief,
Die neither mother, wife, nor England's queen!
Richard III. A. 1, S. 3.

I then, all smarting, with my wounds being cold,
To be so pester'd with a popinjay,
Out of my grief and my impatience,
Answer'd, neglectingly, I know not what.
Henry IV. P. 1, A. 1, S. 3.

When I was about thy years, Hal, I was not an eagle's talon in the waist; I could have crept into any alderman's thumb-ring: a plague of sighing and grief! it blows a man up like a bladder.
Henry IV. P. 1, A. 2, S. 4.

You see me here, you gods, a poor old man,
As full of grief as age; wretched in both!
If it be you that stir these daughters hearts
Against their father, fool me not so much
To bear it tamely. *Lear*, A 2, S. 4.

—— She

——— She ſhook
The holy water from her heavenly eyes,
And clamour moiſten'd her: then away ſhe ſtarted
To deal with grief alone. *Lear*, A. 4, S. 3.

—— How ſtiff is my vile ſenſe,
That I ſtand up, and have ingenious feeling
Of my huge ſorrows! Better I were diſtract:
So ſhould my thoughts be ſever'd from my griefs;
And woes, by wrong imaginations, loſe
The knowledge of themſelves.
Lear, A. 4, S. 6.

——— Your father loſt a father;
That father loſt, loſt his; and the ſurvivor bound
In filial obligation, for ſome term
To do obſequious ſorrow: but to perſever
In obſtinate condolement, is a courſe
Of impious ſtubbornneſs; 'tis unmanly grief:
It ſhews a will moſt incorrect to heaven.
Hamlet, A. 1, S. 2.

'Tis not alone my inky cloak, good mother,
Nor cuſtomary ſuits of ſolemn black,
Nor windy ſuſpiration of forc'd breath,
No, nor the fruitful river in the eye,
Nor the dejected haviour of the viſage,
Together with all forms, modes, ſhews of grief[1],
That can denote me truly. *Hamlet*, A. 1, S. 2.

—— Come, fellow, be thou honeſt:
Do thou thy maſter's bidding: Look!
I draw the ſword myſelf: take it; and hit

[1] ——— *ſhews of grief.*] Thus the folio—the firſt quarto reads *chapes*, I ſuppoſe, for *ſhapes*. STEEVENS.

"Chape of grief," is *grief put on*. *Chape* is a French word, and ſignifies a veſtment, a garment. The poet ſpeaks of grief dreſt out to catch the eye. This the concluding line of the ſpeech will ſhew. *Chape* ſhould therefore ſtand. A. B.

The

The innocent manſion of my love, my heart:
Fear not, 'tis empty of all things, but grief.
Cymbeline, A. 3, S. 4.

I am not prone to weeping; as our ſex
Commonly are; the want of which vain dew,
Perchance, ſhall dry your pities: but I have
That honourable grief lodg'd here, which burns
Worſe than tears drown. *Winter's Tale*, A. 2, S. 1.

—— He's ſomething ſtain'd
With grief, that's beauty's canker.
Tempeſt, A. 1, S. 2.

GROANS.

—— Thy groans
Did make wolves howl, and penetrate the breaſts
Of ever-angry bears. *Tempeſt*, A. 1, S. 2.

With mirth and laughter let old wrinkles come;
And let my liver rather heat with wine,
Than my heart cool with mortifying groans.
Merchant of Venice, A. 1, S. 1.

—— A poor ſequeſter'd ſtag,
That from the hunter's aim had ta'en a hurt,
Did come to languiſh; and, indeed, my lord,
The wretched animal heav'd forth ſuch groans,
That their diſcharge did ſtretch his leathern coat,
Almoſt to burſting. *As you like it*, A. 2, S. 1.

GUILT.

Thieves are not judg'd, but they are by to hear,
Although apparent guilt be ſeen in them:
And ſhall the figure of God's majeſty,
His captain, ſteward, deputy elect,
Anointed, crowned, planted many years,
Be judg'd by ſubject and inferior breath,
And he himſelf not preſent?
Richard II. A. 4, S. 1.

—— Dread

——— Dread lord,
I ſhould be guiltier than my guiltineſs,
To think I can be undiſcernible,
When I perceive your grace, like power divine,
Hath look'd upon my paſſes.
Meaſure for Meaſure, A. 5, S. 1.

——— Cloſe pent-up guilts,
Rive your concealing continents, and cry
Theſe dreadful ſummoners grace.—I am a man,
More ſinn'd againſt, than ſinning.
Lear, A. 3, S. 2.

——— Pray can I not,
Though inclination be as ſharp as will;
My ſtronger guilt defeats my ſtrong intent;
And, like a man to double buſineſs bound,
I ſtand in pauſe where I ſhall firſt begin,
And both neglect. *Hamlet*, A. 3, S. 3.

He who ſhall ſpeak for her, is afar off guilty,
But that he ſpeaks[1]. *Winter's Tale*, A. 2, S. 1.

H.

HAND.

AS we under heaven are ſupreme head,
So, under him, that great ſupremacy,
Where we do reign, we will alone uphold,
Without the aſſiſtance of a mortal hand:
So tell the pope. *King John*, A. 3, S. 1.

[1] *He who ſhall ſpeak for her, is afar off guilty,*
But that he ſpeaks.] *Afar off guilty*, ſignifies, *guilty in a remote degree.* JOHNSON.
I think we ſhould read,
"He who ſhall ſpeak for her afar off, is guilty
"But that he ſpeaks."
Meaning, *he who barely inſinuates that ſhe is innocent, &c.* A. B.

——— More validity,
More honourable ſtate, more courtſhip lives
In carrion flies, than Romeo: they may ſeize
On the white wonder of dear Juliet's hand,
And ſteal immortal bleſſings from her lips.

Romeo and Juliet, A. 3, S. 3.

I had rather chop this hand off at a blow,
And with the other fling it at thy face,
Than bear ſo low a ſail, to ſtrike to thee.

Henry VI. P. 3, A. 5, S. 1.

—— Hide thee, thou bloody hand;
Thou perjur'd, and thou ſimular man of virtue
That art inceſtuous: caitiff, to pieces ſhake,
That under covert and convenient ſeeming
Haſt practis'd on man's life!—

Lear, A. 3, S. 2.

—— I take thy hand: this hand,
As ſoft as dove's down, and as white as it;
Or Ethiopian's tooth, or the fann'd ſnow,
That's bolted by the northern blaſts twice o'er.

Winter's Tale, A. 4, S. 3.

How uſe doth breed a habit in a man!
This ſhadowy deſart, unfrequented woods,
I better brook than flouriſhing peopled towns.

Two Gentlemen of Verona, A. 5, S. 3.

O, heaven, that ſuch companions thou'dſt unfold,
And put in every honeſt hand a whip,
To laſh the raſcals naked through the world,
Even from the Eaſt to the Weſt!

Othello, A. 4, S. 2.

Three crabbed months had ſoured themſelves to death,
Ere I could make thee open thy white hand,
And clap thyſelf my love[1]. *Winter's Tale*, A. 1, S. 2.

HAR-

[1] *And clap thyſelf my love.*] This reading may be explained. She opened her hand, to *clap* the palm of it into his, as people do when

HARMONY.

—— Soft ſtillneſs, and the night,
Become the touches of ſweet harmony.
Merchant of Venice, A. 5, S. 1.

HATE.

——— I give no reaſon, nor I will not,
More than a lodg'd hate, and a certain loathing,
I bear Anthonio, that I follow thus
A loſing ſuit againſt him.
Merchant of Venice, A. 4, S. 1.

HEART.

For when my outward action doth demonſtrate
The native act and figure of my heart
In compliment extern, 'tis not long after
But I will wear my heart upon my ſleeve
For daws to peck at. *Othello*, A. 1, S. 1.

Theſe ſentences, to ſugar or to gall,
Being ſtrong on both ſides, are equivocal:
But words are words; I never yet did hear
That the bruiſed heart was pierced through the ear[1].
Othello, A. 1, S. 3.

when they confirm a bargain. Hence the phraſe, to *clap up a bargain*, i. e. make one with no other ceremony than a junction of hands. The old copy reads,

" Clepe thyſelf my love." STEEVENS.

" Clepe thyſelf," *i. e. name thyſelf*, is ſurely the reading that ſhould be preferred. A king ſhould not be made to talk of *clapping up a bargain*. A. B.

[1] *But words are words; I never yet did hear That the bruiſed heart was pierced through the ear.*] It is obvious that the text ſhould be reſtored thus:

" That the bruis'd heart was pieced through the ear."

i. e. that the wounds of ſorrow were never cured, or a man made *heart-whole*, merely by the words of conſolation.

WARBURTON.

The other commentators are for retaining *pierced*. " Pierced," however,

——— 'Twas pretty, though a plague,
To ſee him every hour; to ſit and draw
His arched brows, his hawking eye, his curls,
In our heart's table.

All's well that ends well, A. 1, S. 1.

——— You were us'd
To ſay, extremity was the trier of ſpirits;
That common chances common men could bear;
That, when the ſea was calm, all boats alike
Shew'd maſterſhip in floating: you us'd to load me
With precepts, that would make invincible
The heart that conn'd them. *Coriolanus*, A. 4, S. 1.

Fee me an officer, beſpeak him a fortnight before; I will have the heart of him, if he forfeit; for were he out of Venice, I can make what merchandize I will. *Merchant of Venice*, A. 3, S. 1.

He hath a heart as ſound as a bell, and his tongue is the clapper; for what his heart thinks, his tongue ſpeaks. *Much ado about nothing*, A. 3, S. 2.

You are my true and honourable wife;
As dear to me as are the ruddy drops
That viſit my ſad heart. *Julius Cæſar*, A. 2, S. 1.

Her vine, the merry chearer of the heart,
Unpruned dies: her hedges even-pleach'd,
Like priſoners wildly over-grown with hair,
Put forth diſorder'd twigs: her fallow leas
The darnel, hemlock, and rank fumitory,
Doth root upon. *Henry V.* A. 5, S. 2.

There's not a piece of feather in our hoſt,
(Good argument, I hope, we ſhall not fly)

however, ſhould without the ſmalleſt queſtion be *berced*. *Bercé* is a figurative expreſſion, and uſed very frequently by the French. "*Il m'a bercé des vaines eſperances*"—*he ſoothed me with vain hopes*. The ſenſe of our author's lines is this—I did never hear that the afflicted heart could be ſoothed ("*berced*"), or lulled into forgetfulneſs by the help of words. A. B.

And time hath worn us into ſlovenry:
But, by the maſs, our hearts are in the trim:
And my poor ſoldiers tell me—yet ere night
They'll be in freſher robes. *Henry V.* A. 4, S. 3.

O god of battles! ſteel my ſoldiers hearts!
Poſſeſs them not with fear; take from them now
The ſenſe of reckoning, if the oppoſed numbers
Pluck their hearts from them! *Henry V.* A. 4, S. 1.

The commonwealth is ſick of their own choice,
Their over-greedy love hath ſurfeited:—
An habitation giddy and unſure
Hath he, that buildeth on the vulgar heart.
Henry IV. P. 2, A. 1, S. 3.

——— There is my dagger,
And here my naked breaſt; within, a heart
Dearer than Plutus' mine, richer than gold:
If that thou be'ſt a Roman, take it forth;
I, that deny'd thee gold, will give my heart:
Strike as thou didſt at Cæſar; for, I know,
When thou didſt hate him worſt, thou lov'dſt him better
Than ever thou lov'dſt Caſſius.
Julius Cæſar, A. 4, S. 3.

—— Then burſt his mighty heart;
And, in his mantle muffling up his face,
Even at the baſe of Pompey's ſtatue,
Which all the while run blood, great Cæſar fell.
O, what a fall was there, my countrymen!
Then I, and you, and all of us fell down,
Whilſt bloody treaſon flouriſh'd over us.
Julius Cæſar, A. 3, S. 2.

—— Fret, till your proud heart break;
Go, ſhew your ſlaves how cholerick you are,
And make your bondmen tremble. Muſt I budge?
Muſt I obſerve you? Muſt I ſtand and crouch
Under your teſty humour? *Julius Cæſar,* A. 4, S. 3.

I come not, friends, to ſteal away your hearts;
I am no orator, as Brutus is:
But, as you know me all, a plain blunt man,
That love my friend. *Julius Cæſar*, A. 3, S. 2.

You may as well go ſtand upon the beach,
And bid the main flood bate his uſual height;
You may as well forbid the mountain pines
To wag their high tops, and to make no noiſe,
When they are fretted with the guſts of heaven;
You may as well do any thing moſt hard,
As ſeek to ſoften that (than which what's harder?)
His Jewiſh heart! *Merchant of Venice*, A. 4, S. 1.

—— My heart will burſt, an if I ſpeak—
And I will ſpeak, that ſo my heart may burſt.—
Butchers and villains, bloody cannibals!
How ſweet a plant have you untimely cropp'd!
Henry VI. P. 3, A. 5, S. 5.

A heavy heart bears not an humble tongue:
Excuſe me ſo, coming ſo ſhort of thanks.
Love's Labour Loſt, A. 5, S. 2.

My heart beats thicker than a feverous pulſe;
And all my powers do their beſtowing loſe,
Like vaſſalage at unawares encount'ring
The eye of majeſty. *Troilus and Creſſida*, A, 3, S. 2.

—— If my heart were great,
I would burſt at this: Captain I'll be no more;
But I will eat and drink, and ſleep as ſoft
As captain ſhall. *All's well that ends well*, A. 4, S. 3.

— Even now my burden'd heart would break,
Should I not curſe them. Poiſon be their drink!
Their muſic, frightful as the ſerpent's hiſs;
And boading ſcritch-owls make the concert full!
Henry VI. P. 2, A. 3, S. 2.

He's truly valiant, that can wiſely ſuffer
The worſt that man can breathe; and make his wrongs

His outſides! to wear them like his raiment careleſsly;
And ne'er prefer his injuries to his heart,
To bring it into danger. *Timon of Athens*, A. 3, S. 5.

——— Thou viſible God,
That ſolder'ſt cloſe impoſſibilities,
And mak'ſt them kiſs! that ſpeak'ſt with every tongue
To every purpoſe! O thou touch of hearts!
Think, thy ſlave man rebels; and by thy virtue
Set them into confounding odds, that beaſts
May have the world in empire!
Timon of Athens, A. 4, S. 3.

Send to her by the man that ſlew her brothers,
A pair of bleeding hearts; thereon engrave
Edward and York;
If this inducement move her not to love,
Send her a letter of thy noble deeds;
Tell her, thou mad'ſt away her uncle Clarence,
Her uncle Rivers; ay, and, for her ſake,
Mad'ſt quick conveyance with her good aunt Anne.
Richard III. A. 4, S. 4.

Think upon what hath chanc'd; and, at more time,
The interim having weigh'd it [1], let us ſpeak
Our free hearts each to other. *Macbeth*, A. 1, S. 3.

——— Uncurable diſcomfit
Reigns in the hearts of all our preſent parts [2].
Henry VI. P. 2, A. 5, S. 2.

[1] *The interim having weigh'd it.*] This *intervening portion* of time is almoſt perſonified; it is repreſented as a cool, impartial judge; as the *pauſer reaſon*. STEEVENS.

Mr. Steevens is miſtaken. Macbeth does not ſay, that the interim is to weigh the matter, but that they are to weigh the buſineſs during the interim. The conſtruction is—"We, in the "interim having pondered on what hath chanced." A. B.

[2] ——— *all our preſent parts.*] Should we not read, *party?* TYRWHIT.

"Parts," *i. e.* Diviſions or companies. A. B.

You draw me, you hard-hearted adamant,
But yet you draw not iron, for my heart
Is true as ſteel.

Midſummer Night's Dream, A. 2, S. 2.

——— Hold, hold, my heart;
And you, my ſinews, grow not inſtant old,
But bear me ſtiffly up!—Remember thee?
Ay, thou poor ghoſt, while memory holds a ſeat
In this diſtracted globe. *Hamlet*, A. 1, S. 5.

With cunning haſt thou filch'd my daughter's heart,
Turn'd her obedience, which is due to me,
To ſtubborn harſhneſs.

Midſummer Night's Dream, A. 1, S. 1.

—— Now to my mother,—
O, heart, loſe not thy nature; let not ever
The ſoul of Nero enter this firm boſom:
Let me be cruel, not unnatural:
I will ſpeak daggers to her, but uſe none.

Hamlet, A. 3, S. 2.

I would to God, my heart were flint, like Edward's,
Or Edward's ſoft and pitiful, like mine;
I am too childiſh—fooliſh for this world.

Richard III. A. 1, S. 3.

I dy'd for hope [1], ere I could lend thee aid:
But cheer thy heart, and be thou not diſmay'd.

Richard III. A. 5, S. 3.

Leave wringing of your hands; peace, ſit you down,
And let me wring your heart: for ſo I ſhall

[1] *I dy'd for hope.*] *i. e.* I died for wiſhing well to you. But Mr. Theobald, with great ſagacity, conjectured *holpe* or *aid*; which gives the line this fine ſenſe---*I died in giving thee aid, before I could give thee aid.* WARBURTON.

Holpe appears to be right- -"For *holpe*" means, for, or through *want of aid*, and not, as Dr. W. ſuppoſes, *in giving aid*. The ſenſe is, *I died through want of ſupport, in endeavouring to ſupport you.* It is the faſhion to cry down Theobald, but his emendations are often happy. A. B.

If

If it be made of penetrable ſtuff;
If damned cuſtom have not braz'd it ſo,
That it be proof and bulwark againſt ſenſe.
Hamlet, A. 3, S. 4.

—— I will call him to ſo ſtrict account,
That he ſhall render every glory up,
Yea even the ſlighteſt worſhip of his time,
Or I will tear the reckoning from his heart.
Henry IV. P. 1, A. 3, S. 2.

—— What art thou? Have not I
An arm as big as thine? a heart as big?
Thy words, I grant, are bigger; for I wear not
My dagger in my mouth. *Cymbeline*, A. 4, S. 2.

—— O thou day o' the world,
Chain mine arm'd neck; leap thou, attire and all,
Through proof of harneſs to my heart, and there
Ride on the pants triumphing.
Antony and Cleopatra, A. 4, S. 8.

—— Then he ſpeaks
What's in his heart; and that is there, which looks
With us to break his neck [1]. *Coriolanus*, A. 3, S. 3.

HEAVEN.

Bid farewell, and go: when you ſu'd ſtaying,
Then was the time for words: No going then;—
Eternity was in our lips, and eyes;

[1] —— *which looks*
With us to break his neck.] A familiar phraſe of that time, ſignifying, *works with us.* WARBURTON.

To look, is to *wait*, or *expect*. The ſenſe, I believe, is, *What he has in his heart, is waiting there to help us to break his neck.* JOHNSON.

"Which looks with us," means, I believe, *it ſeems to us.* He is a free ſpeaker (ſays Brutus), and there is that in his heart, which, as it ſeems to us, will occaſion his downfal; or, as Shakeſpeare expreſſes it, help to break his neck. A. B.

Bliſs

Bliſs in our brows bent; none our parts ſo poor,
But was a race of heaven.
Antony and Cleopatra, A. 1, S. 3.

—— Confeſs yourſelf to heaven;
Repent what's paſt; avoid what is to come;
And do not ſpread the compoſt on the weeds,
To make them ranker. *Hamlet*, A. 3, S. 4.

What ſhould ſuch fellows as I do, crawling between earth and heaven? *Hamlet*, A. 3, S. 1.

—— Good my brother,
Do not, as ſome ungracious paſtors do,
Shew me the ſteep and thorny way to heaven;
Whilſt, like a puft and reckleſs libertine,
Himſelf the primroſe path of dalliance treads,
And recks not his own read. *Hamlet*, A. 1, S. 3.

Still am I call'd—unhand me, gentlemen;
By heaven I'll make a ghoſt of him that lets me.
Hamlet, A. 1, S. 4.

—— What committed!
Heaven ſtops the noſe at it, and the moon winks;
The bawdy wind, that kiſſes all it meets,
Is huſh'd within the hollow mine of earth,
And will not hear it. *Othello*, A. 4, S. 2.

The means that heaven yields muſt be embrac'd,
And not neglected; elſe, if heaven would,
And we would not heaven's offer, we refuſe
The proffer'd means of ſuccour and redreſs.
Richard II. A. 3, S. 2.

— When the ſearching eye of heaven is hid
Behind the globe, and lights the lower world,
Then thieves and robbers range abroad unſeen,
But when, from under this terreſtrial ball,
He fires the proud tops of the eaſtern pines,
Then murders, treaſons, and deteſted ſins,
Stand bare and naked, trembling at themſelves.
Richard II. A. 3, S. 2.

Methinks,

Methinks, king Richard and myſelf ſhould meet
With no leſs terror than the elements
Of fire and water, when their thund'ring ſhock
At meeting tears the cloudy cheeks of heaven.

Richard II. A. 3, S. 3.

Now bind my brows with iron; and approach
The rugged'ſt hour that time and ſpight dare bring,
To frown upon the enrag'd Northumberland!
Let heaven kiſs earth! Now let not nature's hand
Keep the wide flood confin'd! let order die!

Henry IV. P. 2, A. 1, S. 1.

Heaven witneſs with me, when I here came in,
And found no courſe of breath within your majeſty,
How cold it ſtruck my heart! If I do feign,
O, let me in my preſent wildneſs die;
And never live to ſhew the incredulous world
The noble change that I have purpoſed!

Henry IV. P. 2, A. 4, S. 4.

When beggars die there are no comets ſeen;
The heavens themſelves blaze forth the death of
princes. *Julius Cæſar*, A. 2, S. 2.

—— Look, how the floor of heaven
Is thick inlay'd with pattens of bright gold;
There's not the ſmalleſt orb, which thou behold'ſt,
But in his motion like an angel ſings,
Still quiring to the young-ey'd cherubims.

Merchant of Venice, A. 5, S. 1.

To gild refined gold, to paint the lily,
To throw a perfume on the violet,
To ſmooth the ice, or add another hue
Unto the rainbow, or with taper-light
To ſeek the beauteous eye of heaven to garniſh,
Is waſteful, and ridiculous exceſs.

King John, A. 4, S. 2.

—— Shall

——— Shall we ſerve heaven
With leſs reſpect than we do miniſter
To our groſs ſelves? *Meaſure for Meaſure*, A. 2, S. 2.

Merciful heaven!
Thou rather with thy ſharp and ſulphurous bolt
Split'ſt the unwedgeable and knarled oak,
Than the ſoft myrtle.
Meaſure for Meaſure, A. 2, S. 2.

——— Heaven is in my mouth,
And in my heart, the ſtrong and ſwelling evil
Of my conception. *Meaſure for Meaſure*, A. 2, S. 4.

He, who the ſword of heaven will bear,
Should be as holy as ſevere;
Pattern in himſelf to know,
Grace to ſtand, and virtue go [1].
Meaſure for Meaſure, A. 3, S. 2.

When heaven doth weep, doth not the earth o'erflow?
If the winds rage, doth not the ſea wax mad,
Threat'ning the welkin with his big-ſwoln face?
And wilt thou have a reaſon for this evil?
I am the ſea; hark, how her ſighs do blow!
She is the weeping welkin, I the earth:

[1] *Pattern in himſelf to know,*
Grace to ſtand, and virtue go.] Theſe lines I cannot underſtand, but believe that they ſhould be read thus:
"Patterning himſelf to know,
"In grace to ſtand, in virtue go."

To pattern is to work after a pattern, and perhaps in Shakeſpeare's licentious diction, ſimply to *work*. JOHNSON.

By a ſlight alteration this paſſage will be rendered ſufficiently clear, and even acquire ſome degree of elegance. I read,
"He, who the ſword of heaven will bear,
"Should be as holy as ſevere:
"Pattern in himſelf, to ſhow
"Grace and virtue. Stand or go."

"Stand or go" will mean, that he may make a pauſe, when aſſailed by vice, or paſs onward, when ſolicited by virtue.
A. B.

Then

Then muſt my ſea be moved with her ſighs;
Then muſt my earth with her continual tears
Become a deluge, overflow'd and drown'd.
Titus Andronicus, A. 3, S. 1.

——— Hence, be gone;—
But if thou, jealous, doſt return to pry
On what I further ſhall intend to do,
By heaven, I will tear thee joint by joint,
And ſtrew this hungry church-yard with thy limbs.
Romeo and Juliet, A. 5, S. 3.

There's nothing ſituate under heaven's eye,
But hath his bound, in earth, in ſea, in ſky:
The beaſts, the fiſhes, and the winged fowls,
Are their males ſubject, and at their controls.
Comedy of Errors, A. 2, S. 1.

—— Victorious prince of York,
Before I ſee thee ſeated in that throne
Which now the houſe of Lancaſter uſurps,
I vow by heaven, theſe eyes ſhall never cloſe.
Henry VI. P. 3, A. 1, S. 1.

—— It is preſumption in us, when
The help of heaven we count the act of men.
Dear ſir, to my endeavours give conſent;
Of heaven, not me, make an experiment.
All's well that ends well, A. 2, S. 1.

Our remedies oft in ourſelves do lie,
Which we aſcribe to heaven: the fated ſky
Gives us free ſcope; only, doth backward pull
Our ſlow deſigns, when we ourſelves are dull.
All's well that ends well, A. 1, S. 1.

A flouriſh, trumpets!—Strike alarum, drums!
Let not the heavens hear theſe tell-tale women
Rail on the Lord's anointed. *Richard III.* A. 4, S. 4.

——— Heavens, deal ſo ſtill!
Let the ſuperfluous, and luſt-dieted man,
That ſlaves your ordinance, that will not ſee

Becauſe

Becauſe he doth not feel, feel your power quickly;
So diſtribution ſhould undo exceſs,
And each man have enough. *Lear*, A. 4, S. 1.

Upon ſuch ſacrifices, my Cordelia,
The gods themſelves throw incenſe. Have I caught thee?
He that parts us, ſhall bring a brand from heaven,
And fire us hence, like foxes. *Lear*, A. 5, S. 3.

HONESTY.

I could not ſtir him:
He ſaid, he was gentle, but unfortunate[1];
Diſhoneſtly afflicted, but yet honeſt.
Cymbeline, A. 4, S. 2.

Here's ado,
To lock up honeſty and honour from
The acceſs of gentle viſitors!
Winter's Tale, A. 2, S. 2.

What a fool honeſty is! and truſt, his ſworn-brother, a very ſimple gentleman!
Winter's Tale, A. 4, S. 3.

If I thought it were not a piece of honeſty to acquaint the king withal, I would do't; I hold it the more knavery to conceal it; and therein am I conſtant to my profeſſion. *Winter's Tale*, A. 4, S. 3.

Rich honeſty dwells like a miſer, ſir, in a poor houſe; as your pearl, in your foul oyſter.
As you like it, A. 5, S. 4.

Methinks, thou art more honeſt now, than wiſe;
For, by oppreſſing and betraying me,
Thou might'ſt have ſooner got another ſervice:

[1] —— *gentle, but unfortunate.*] *Gentle*, is *well-born*, of birth above the vulgar. JOHNSON.

"Gentle" ſhould here be written *gentile*. It is ſo found in moſt of our old writers. *Gentil*, Fr. A. B.

For

For many ſo arrive at ſecond maſters,
Upon their firſt lord's neck.

Timon of Athens, A. 4, S. 4.

Honeſty coupled to beauty, is to have honey a ſauce to ſugar. *As you like it*, A. 3, S. 3.

Thoſe, that ſhe makes fair, ſhe ſcarce makes honeſt; and thoſe, that ſhe makes honeſt, ſhe makes very ill favouredly. *As you like it*, A. 1, S. 2.

——— She is too mean
To have her name repeated; all her deſerving
Is a reſerved honeſty, and that
I have not heard examined.

All's well that ends well, A. 3, S. 5.

The honour of a maid is her name; and no legacy is ſo rich as honeſty.

All's well that ends well, A. 3, S. 5.

Ay, ſir; to be honeſt, as this world goes,
Is to be one man picked out of ten thouſand.
For if the ſun breeds maggots in a dead dog,
Being a god, kiſſing carrion. *Hamlet*, A. 2, S. 2.

There is no terror, Caſſius, in your threats;
For I am arm'd ſo ſtrong in honeſty,
That they paſs by me, as the idle wind,
Which I reſpect not. *Julius Cæſar*, A. 4, S. 3.

I know thou art full of love and honeſty,
And weigh'ſt thy words before thou giv'ſt them breath—
Therefore theſe ſtops of thine fright me the more:
For ſuch things, in a falſe diſloyal knave,
Are tricks of cuſtom; but, in a man that's juſt,
They are cloſe delations, working from the heart,
That paſſion cannot rule. *Othello*, A. 3, S. 3.

——— O wretched fool,
That liv'ſt to make thine honeſty a vice!
O monſtrous world! Take note, take note, O world,

To

To be direct and honeſt, is not ſafe.—
I thank you for this profit. *Othello*, A. 3, S. 3.

HONOUR.

Have you not ſet mine honour at the ſtake,
And baited it with all the unmuzzled thoughts
That tyrannous heart can think?
Twelfth Night, A. 3, S. 1.

He after honour hunts, I after love.
Two Gentlemen of Verona, A. 1, S. 1.

I conjure thee, by all the parts of man,
Which honour does acknowledge—
That thou declare
What incidency thou doſt gueſs of harm
Is creeping toward me. *Winter's Tale*, A. 1, S. 2.

——— He
The ſacred honour of himſelf, his queen's,
His hopeful ſon's, his babe's betrays to ſlander,
Whoſe ſting is ſharper than the ſword's.
Winter's Tale, A. 2, S. 3.

—— For Polixenes,
(With whom I am accus'd) I do confeſs,
I lov'd him, as in honour he required;
With ſuch a kind of love, as might become
A lady like me. *Winter's Tale*, A. 3, S. 2.

—— For life, I prize it
As I weigh grief, which I would ſpare: for honour,
'Tis a derivative from me to mine,
And only that I ſtand for. *Winter's Tale*, A. 3, S. 2.

— This thou ſhouldſt have done,
And not have ſpoken of it! In me, 'tis villainy;
In thee, it had been good ſervice. Thou muſt know,
'Tis not my profit that does lead mine honour;
Mine honour, it. Repent that e'er thy tongue
Hath ſo betray'd thine act: being done unknown,
I ſhould

I ſhould have found it afterwards well done;
But muſt condemn it now.
Antony and Cleopatra, A. 2, S. 7.

Let witchcraft join with beauty, luſt with both!
Tie up the libertine in a field of feaſts,
Keep his brain fuming; Epicurean cooks,
Sharpen with cloyleſs ſauce his appetite;
That ſleep and feeding may prorogue his honour,
Even till a lethe'd dullneſs.
Antony and Cleopatra, A. 2, S. 1.

Then bid adieu to me, and ſay, the tears
Belong to Egypt: good now, play one ſcene
Of excellent diſſembling: and let it look
Like perfect honour. *Ant. and Cleop.* A. 1, S. 3.

—— Your honour calls you hence;
Therefore be deaf to my unpitied folly,
And all the gods go with you! Upon your ſword
Sit laurell'd victory! and ſmooth ſucceſs
Be ſtrew'd before your feet!
Antony and Cleopatra, A. 1, S. 3.

I, beyond all limit of what elſe i' the world,
Do love, prize, honour you. *Tempeſt*, A. 3, S. 1.

— Like the ſtag, when ſnow the paſture ſheets,
The barks of trees thou browſedſt: on the Alps,
It is reported, thou didſt eat ſtrange fleſh,
Which ſome did die to look on: and all this
(It wounds thine honour, that I ſpeak it now)
Was borne ſo like a ſoldier, that thy cheek
So much as lank'd not.
Antony and Cleopatra, A. 1, S. 4.

Weigh what loſs your honour may ſuſtain,
If with too credent ear you liſt his ſongs;
Or loſe your heart; or your chaſte treaſure open
To his unmaſter'd importunity.
Fear it, Ophelia, fear it, my dear ſiſter;

And keep you in the rear of your affection,
Out of the ſhot and danger of deſire.

Hamlet, A. 1, S. 3.

—— Rightly, to be great
Is not to ſtir without great argument;
But greatly to find quarrel in a ſtraw,
When honour's at the ſtake. *Hamlet*, A. 4, S. 4.

A ſcar nobly got, or a noble ſcar, is a good livery of honour. *All's well that ends well*, A. 4, S. 5.

——— Perſeverance, dear my lord,
Keeps honour bright: to have done, is to hang
Quite out of faſhion, like a ruſty mail
In monumental mockery.

Troilus and Creſſida, A. 3, S. 3.

What is honour? A word. What is that word, honour? Air. A trim reckoning!—Who hath it? He that dy'd o' Wedneſday. Doth he feel it? No. Doth he hear it? No. Is it inſenſible then? Yea, to the dead. But will it not live with the living? No. Why? Detraction will not ſuffer it: therefore I'll none of it: Honour is a mere ſcutcheon, and ſo ends my catechiſm. *Henry IV.* P. 1, A. 5, S. 1.

——— Take the inſtant way,
For honour travels in a ſtreight ſo narrow,
Where one but goes a-breaſt: keep then the path,
For emulation hath a thouſand ſons,
That one by one purſue; if you give way,
Or hedge aſide from the direct forthright,
Like to an entered tide, they all ruſh by,
And leave you hindmoſt.

Troilus and Creſſida, A. 3, S. 3.

—— Speak to me, ſon:
Thou haſt affected the fine ſtrains of honour,
To imitate the graces of the gods;
To tear with thunder the wide cheeks o' the air,

And

And yet to charge thy ſulphur with a bolt
That ſhould but rive an oak. *Coriolanus*, A. 5, S. 3.

—— Men, like butterflies,
Shew not their mealy wings, but to the ſummer;
And not a man, for being ſimply man,
Hath any honour; but's honour'd for thoſe honours
That are without him, as place, riches, favour,
Prizes of accident as oft as merit.
Troilus and Creſſida, A. 3, S. 3.

—— I have heard you ſay,
Honour and policy, like unſever'd friends,
I' the war do grow together: grant that, and tell me,
In peace, what each of them by the other loſe,
That they combine not there?
Coriolanus, A. 3, S. 2.

— Whiles the honourable captain there
Drops bloody ſweat from his war-wearied limbs,
And, in advantage ling'ring, looks for reſcue,
You, his falſe hopes, the truſt of England's honour,
Keep off aloof with worthleſs emulation.
Henry VI. P. 1, A. 4, S. 4.

Mine honour keeps the weather of my fate:
Life every man holds dear; but the dear man
Holds honour far more precious-dear than life.
Troilus and Creſſida, A. 5, S. 3.

Have patience, ſir; O, let it not be ſo;
Herein you war againſt your reputation,
And draw within the compaſs of ſuſpect
The unviolated honour of your wife.
Comedy of Errors, A. 3, S. 1.

By heaven, methinks, it were an eaſy leap,
To pluck bright Honour from the pale-fac'd moon;
Or dive into the bottom of the deep,
Where fathom-line could never touch the ground,
And pluck up drowned Honour by the locks.
Henry IV. P. 1, A. 1, S. 3.

Your fire-new ſtamp of honour is ſcarce current:
O, that your young nobility could judge,
What 'twere to loſe it, and be miſerable!
They that ſtand high, have many blaſts to ſhake them.
Richard III. A. 1, S. 3.

—— Honour but of danger wins a ſcar;
As oft it loſes all.
All's well that ends well, A. 3, S. 2.

—— He took upon him,
Without the privity o' the king, to appoint
Who ſhould attend on him. He makes up the file [1]
Of all the gentry; for the moſt part ſuch
Too, whom as great a charge as little honour
He meant to lay upon. *Henry VIII.* A. 1, S. 1.

Preſumptuous dame, ill-natur'd Eleanor!
Haſt thou not worldly pleaſures at command,
Above the reach or compaſs of thy thought?
And wilt thou ſtill be hammering treachery,
To tumble down thy huſband, and thyſelf,
From top of honour to diſgrace's feet?
Henry VI. P. 2, A. 1, S. 2.

He had the wit, which I can well obſerve
To-day in our young lords; but they may jeſt,
Till their own ſcorn return to them unnoted,
Ere they can hide their levity in honour.
All's well that ends well, A. 1, S. 2.

—— That is honour's ſcorn,
Which challenges itſelf as honour's born,
And is not like the ſire.
All's well that ends well, A. 2, S. 3.

[1] —— *the file.*] That is, the liſt. JOHNSON.
Rather the *company*. We now ſay, *a file of ſoldiers*. By "makes up the file," the poet means, not only that Wolſey gave in the names of the gentry who were to attend on the King, but that he actually appointed them to ſuch attendance. A. B.

I'll

I'll to the king,
And from a mouth of honour[1] quite cry down
This Ipſwich fellow's inſolence; or proclaim,
There's difference in no perſons.

Henry VIII. A. 1, S. 1.

It is in us to plant thine honour, where
We pleaſe to have it grow: check thy contempt:
Obey our will, which travails in thy good.

All's well that ends well, A. 2, S. 3.

Set honour in one eye, and death i' the other,
And I will look on both indifferently:
For, let the gods ſo ſpeed me, as I love
The name of honour more than I fear death.

Julius Cæſar, A. 1, S. 2.

——— Let higher Italy
(Thoſe 'bated, that inherit but the fall
Of the laſt monarchy) ſee, that you come
Not to woo honour, but to wed it.

All's well that ends well, A. 2, S. 1.

——— Honours beſt thrive,
When rather from our acts we them derive
Than our fore-goers.

All's well that ends well, A. 2, S. 3.

——— She is young, wiſe, fair;
In theſe to nature ſhe's immediate heir;
And theſe breed honour.

All's well that ends well, A. 2, S. 3.

Hearing your high majeſty is touch'd
With that malignant cauſe wherein the honour

[1] —*from a mouth of honour.*] I will cruſh this baſe-born fellow by the due influence of my rank, or ſay that all diſtinction of perſons is at an end. JOHNSON.

By "a mouth of honour," I would rather underſtand, *a plain and honourable recital of facts*—and not that Buckingham was boaſting of his rank. A. B.

Of my dear father's gift ſtands chief in power,
I come to tender it.

All's well that ends well, A. 2, S. 1.

More of his ſoldierſhip I know not; except, in that country, he had the honour to be the officer at a place there call'd Mile-end, to inſtruct for the doubling of files. *All's well that ends well,* A. 4, S. 3.

—— Manhood and honour
Should have hearts, would they but fat their thoughts
With this cramm'd reaſon: reaſon and reſpect
Make livers pale, and luſtyhood, deject.

Troilus and Creſſida, A. 2, S. 2.

——— His honour,
Clock to itſelf, knew the true minute when
Exception bid him ſpeak, and, at that time,
His tongue obey'd his hand.

All's well that ends well, A. 1, S. 2.

Well, 'tis no matter; honour pricks me on. Yea, but how if honour prick me off when I come on? how then? Can honour ſet to a leg? No. Or an arm? No. Or take away the grief of a wound? No. Honour hath no ſkill in ſurgery then? No.

Henry IV. P. 1. A. 5, S. 1.

By heaven, fond wretch, thou know'ſt not what thou ſpeak'ſt;
Or elſe thou art ſuborn'd againſt his honour
In hateful practice. *Meaſure for Meaſure,* A. 5, S. 1.

Though I could 'ſcape ſhot-free at London, I fear the ſhot here; here's no ſcoring, but upon the pate. —Soft! who art thou? Sir Walter Blunt;—there's honour for you: here's no vanity!—I am as hot as molten lead, and as heavy too: Heaven keep lead out of me! *Henry IV.* P. 1, A. 5, S. 3.

If Percy be alive, I'll pierce him. If he do come in my way, ſo: if he do not,—if I come in his, willingly, let him make a carbonado of me. I like not

not ſuch grinning honour as Sir Walter hath: give me life: which if I can ſave, ſo; if not, honour comes unlook'd for, and there's an end.

Henry IV. P. 1, A. 5, S. 3.

I will intreat you, when you ſee my ſon,
To tell him, that his ſword can never win
The honour that he loſes.

All's well that ends well, A. 3, S. 2.

A jewel in a ten-times barr'd-up cheſt
Is—a bold ſpirit in a loyal breaſt.
Mine honour is my life; both grow in one;
Take honour from me, and my life is done.

Richard II. A. 1, S. 1.

—— I am not covetous for gold;
Nor care I, who doth feed upon my coſt;
It yerns me not, if men my garments wear;
Such outward things dwell not in my deſires:
But, if it be a ſin to covet honour,
I am the moſt offending ſoul alive.

Henry V. A. 4, S. 3.

—— If they wrong her honour,
The proudeſt of them ſhall well hear of it.

Much ado about nothing, A. 4, S. 1.

Thoſe that leave their valiant bones in France,
Dying like men, though buried in your dunghills,
They ſhall be fam'd; for there the ſun ſhall greet them,
And draw their honours reeking up to heaven;
Leaving their earthly parts to choak your clime.

Henry V. A. 4, S. 3.

Though we lay thoſe honours on this man,
To eaſe ourſelves of divers ſlanderous loads,
He ſhall but bear them as the aſs bears gold,
To groan and ſweat under the buſineſs,
Either led or driven, as we point the way.

Julius Cæſar, A. 4, S. 1.

— New-made honour doth forget men's names;
[1] 'Tis too reſpective, and too ſociable,
For your converſing. *King John*, A. 1, S. 1.

——— I quake,
Leſt thou a feverous life ſhouldſt entertain,
And ſix or ſeven winters, more reſpect
Than a perpetual honour.
Meaſure for Meaſure, A. 3, S. 1.

O, that eſtates, degrees, and offices,
Were not deriv'd corruptly! and that clear honour
Were purchas'd by the merit of the wearer!
How many then ſhould cover, that ſtand bare?
How many be commanded, that command?
Merchant of Venice, A. 2, S. 9.

——— What, ſhall one of us,
That ſtruck the foremoſt man of all this world,
But for ſupporting robbers; ſhall we now
Contaminate our fingers with baſe bribes?
And ſell the mighty ſpace of our large honours,
For ſo much traſh, as may be graſped thus?—
I had rather be a dog, and bay the moon,
Than ſuch a Roman *Julius Cæſar*, A. 4, S. 3.

——— If, you can report,
And prove it too, againſt mine honour aught,
My bond to wedlock, or my love and duty
Againſt your ſacred perſon, in God's name,
Turn me away; and let the foul'ſt contempt
Shut door upon me, and ſo give me up
To the ſharpeſt kind of juſtice.
Henry VIII. A. 2, S. 4.

[1] *'Tis too reſpective.*] i. e. *reſpectful.* STEEVENS.
"Reſpective" is not, in this place, *reſpectful*, but *particular*, too much attached to ſelf. A. B.

HOPE,

HOPE.

Even here I will put off my hope, and keep it
No longer for my flatterer. *Tempest*, A. 3, S. 3.

Hope is a lover's ſtaff; walk hence with that,
And manage it againſt deſpairing thoughts.
Two Gentlemen of Verona, A. 3, S. 1.

——— Were it good,
To ſet the exact wealth of all our ſtates
All at one caſt? to ſet ſo rich a main
On the nice hazard of one doubtful hour?
It were not good: for therein ſhould we read
The very bottom and the ſoul of hope[1].
Henry IV. P. 1, A. 4, S. 1.

— When this looſe behaviour I throw off,
And pay the debt I never promiſed,
By how much better than my word I am,
By ſo much ſhall I falſify men's hopes.
Henry IV. P. 1, A. 1, S. 2.

——— In God's name, march:
True hope is ſwift, and flies with ſwallow's wings;
Kings it makes gods, and meaner creatures kings.
Richard III. A. 5, S. 2.

O momentary grace of mortal men,
Which we more hunt for than the grace of God!
Who builds his hope in air of your fair looks,
Lives like a drunken ſailor on a maſt;

[1] ——— *therein ſhould we read*
The very bottom and the ſoul of hope.] To *read the bottom and ſoul of hope, and the bound of fortune*, though all the copies, and all the editors have received it, ſurely cannot be right. I can think on no other word than *riſque*.
——— "therein ſhould we riſque
"The very bottom, &c." JOHNSON.

Change is unneceſſary. "To read" is to *diſcover*. We now talk of *reading a man*, *i. e.* that we are able to diſcover,—that we can eaſily ſee through his deſigns. A. B.

Ready,

Ready, with every nod, to tumble down
Into the fatal bowels of the deep.

Richard III. A. 3, S. 4.

Lord cardinal, if thou think'ſt on heaven's bliſs,
Hold up thy hand, make ſignal of thy hope.—
He dies, and makes no ſign.—

Henry VI. P. 2, A. 3, S. 3.

The ample propoſition, that hope makes
In all deſigns begun on earth below,
Fails in the promis'd largeneſs: checks and diſaſters
Grow in the reins of actions higheſt rear'd:
As knots, by the conflux of meeting ſap,
Infect the ſound pine, and divert his grain,
Tortive and errant from his courſe of growth.

Troilus and Creſſida, A. 1, S. 3.

——— O, how wretched
Is that poor man, that hangs on princes favours!
There is, betwixt that ſmile we would aſpire to,
That ſweet aſpect of princes, and our ruin,
More pangs and fears than wars or women have;
And when he falls, he falls like Lucifer;
Never to hope again. *Henry VIII.* A. 3, S. 2.

I will deſpair, and be at enmity
With cozening hope: he is a flatterer,
A paraſite, a keeper back of death,
Who gently would diſſolve the bands of life.

Richard II. A. 2, S. 2.

——— A cauſe on foot
Lives ſo in hope, as in an early ſpring
We ſee the appearing buds; which, to prove fruit,
Hope gives not ſo much warrant as deſpair;
That froſts will bite them.

Henry IV. P. 2, A. 1, S. 3.

The miſerable have no other medicine,
But only hope. *Meaſure for Meaſure,* A. 3, S. 1.

I ſome-

I ſometimes do believe, and ſometimes do not;
As thoſe that fear they hope, and know they fear [1].
As you like it, A. 5, S. 4.

HORROR.

Be ſtirring as the time; be fire with fire;
Threaten the threatner, and out-face the brow
Of bragging horror. *King John*, A. 5, S. 1.

HORSE.

I would my horſe had the ſpeed of your tongue;
And ſo good a continuer.
Much ado about nothing, A. 1, S. 1.

Where think'ſt thou he is now? Stands he, or ſits he?
Or does he walk? or is he on his horſe?
O happy horſe to bear the weight of Antony!
Do bravely, horſe! for wot'ſt thou whom thou mov'ſt?
The demy Atlas of this earth, the arm
And burgonet of man.
Antony and Cleopatra, A. 1, S. 5.

[1] *As thoſe that fear they hope, and know they fear.*] This ſtrange nonſenſe ſhould be read thus:

"As thoſe that fear their hap, and know their fear."

i. e. As thoſe that fear the iſſue of a thing, when they know their fear to be well grounded. WARBURTON.

The depravation of the line is evident, but I do not think the learned commentator's emendation very happy. I read thus:

"As thoſe that fear with hope, and hope with fear."

JOHNSON.

The author of the Reviſal would read:

"As thoſe that fear their hope, and know their fear."

Blackſtone,

"As thoſe that feign they hope, and know they fear."

Muſgrave,

"As thoſe that fear, then hope, and know their fear."

I read,—

"As thoſe that hope they fear, then know they fear." I am puzzled, or perplexed like to thoſe perſons, who at one time form to themſelves imaginary notions or fears, who then hope thoſe fears are groundleſs, and who afterwards are convinced that they are ſo. A. B.

O, for

O, for a horſe with wings!—Hear'ſt thou, Piſanio?
He is at Milford-Haven: read, and tell me
How far 'tis thither. If one of mean affairs
May plod it in a week, why may not I
Glide thither in a day? *Cymbeline*, A. 3, S. 2.

I jeſt to Oberon, and make him ſmile,
When I a fat and bean-fed horſe beguile,
Neighing in likeneſs of a filly foal:
And ſometimes lurk I in a goſſip's bowl,
In very likeneſs of a roaſted crab.
Midſummer Night's Dream, A 2, S. 1.

—— Come, let me take my horſe,
Who is to bear me like a thunder-bolt,
Againſt the boſom of the Prince of Wales:
Harry to Harry ſhall, hot horſe to horſe—
Meet, and ne'er part, till one drop down a corſe.
Henry IV. P. 1, A. 4, S. 1.

Give me another horſe,—bind up my wounds—
Have mercy, Jeſu!—Soft, I did but dream.
Richard III. A. 5, S. 3.

I think there be ſix Richmonds in the field;
Five have I ſlain to-day, inſtead of him:—
A horſe! a horſe! my kingdom for a horſe!
Richard III. A. 5, S. 4.

—— O, he's as tedious
As is a tired horſe, a railing wife;
Worſe than a ſmoky houſe:—I had rather live
With cheeſe and garlick, in a windmill, far;
Than feed on cates, and have him talk to me.
Henry IV. P. 1, A. 3, S. 1.

O, how it yern'd my heart, when I beheld,
In London ſtreets, that coronation day,
When Bolingbroke rode on roan Barbary!
That horſe, that thou ſo often haſt beſtrid.
Richard II. A. 5, S. 5.

That's

That's a colt, indeed, for he doth nothing but talk of his horſe; and he makes it a great appropriation to his own good parts, that he can ſhoe him himſelf. *Merchant of Venice*, A. 1, S. 2.

—— Reformation muſt be ſudden too,
My noble lords: for thoſe, that tame wild horſes,
Pace 'em not in their hands to make 'em gentle;
But ſtop their mouths with ſtubborn bits, and ſpur 'em,
Till they obey the manage. *Henry VIII.* A. 5, S. 2.

HUMILITY.

In peace, there's nothing ſo becomes a man,
As modeſt ſtillneſs, and humility:
But when the blaſt of war blows in our ears,
Then imitate the action of the tyger;
Stiffen the ſinews, ſummon up the blood,
Diſguiſe fair nature with hard-favour'd rage.
Henry V. A. 3, S. 1.

The lion, dying, thruſteth forth his paw,
And wounds the earth, if nothing elſe, with rage
To be o'erpower'd; and wilt thou, pupil-like,
Take thy correction mildly? kiſs the rod?
And fawn on rage with baſe humility?
Richard II. A. 5, S. 1.

—— You are meek, and humble-mouth'd;
You ſign your place and calling, in full ſeeming,
With meekneſs and humility: but your heart
Is cramm'd with arrogancy, ſpleen, and pride.
Henry VIII. A. 2, S. 4.

——— Who were below him
He uſed as creatures of another place;
And bow'd his eminent top to their low ranks,
Making them proud of his humility.
All's well that ends well, A. 1, S. 2.

—— I ſtole

—— I ſtole all courteſy from heaven;
And dreſs'd myſelf in ſuch humility,
That I did pluck allegiance from men's hearts,
Loud ſhouts and ſalutations from their mouths,
Even in the preſence of the crowned king.

Henry IV. P. 1, A. 3, S. 2.

I.

IDLENESS.

THE even mead, that erſt brought ſweetly forth
The freckled cowſlip, burnet, and green clover,
Wanting the ſcythe, all uncorrected, rank,
Conceives by idleneſs; and nothing teems,
But hateful docks, rough thiſtles, keckſies, burs,
Loſing both beauty and utility.

Henry V. A. 5, S. 2.

JEALOUSY.

Think'ſt thou I'd make a life of jealouſy,
To follow ſtill the changes of the moon
With freſh ſuſpicions? No, to be once in doubt,
Is—once to be reſolv'd. *Othello*, A. 3, S. 3.

——— No, Iago;
I'll ſee, before I doubt: when I doubt, prove;
And, on the proof, there is no more but this,—
Away at once with love, or jealouſy.

Othello, A. 3, S. 3.

I do beſeech you,
Though I—perchance, am vicious in my gueſs,
(As, I confeſs, it is my nature's plague
To ſpy into abuſes; and, oft, my jealouſy
Shapes faults that are not) that your wiſdom yet,

From

From one that ſo imperfectly conceits,
Would take no notice. *Othello*, A. 3, S. 3.

Beware, my lord, of jealouſy;
It is the green-ey'd monſter, which doth mock
The meat it feeds on. *Othello*, A. 3, S. 3.

—— Trifles, light as air,
Are, to the jealous, confirmations ſtrong
As proofs of holy writ. *Othello*, A. 3, S. 3.

Look to your wife; obſerve her well with Caſſio;
Wear your eye—thus, not jealous nor ſecure;
I would not have your free and noble nature,
Out of ſelf-bounty, be abus'd; look to't.
Othello, A. 3, S. 3.

—— Jealous ſouls will not be anſwer'd ſo;
They are not ever jealous for the cauſe,
But jealous for they are jealous: 'tis a monſter
Begot upon itſelf, born on itſelf.
Othello, A. 3, S. 4.

Oh, how haſt thou with jealouſy infected
The ſweetneſs of affiance! ſhew men dutiful?
Why, ſo didſt thou: ſeem they grave and learned?
Why, ſo didſt thou: come they of noble family?
Why, ſo didſt thou: ſeem they religious?
Why, ſo didſt thou. *Henry V*. A. 2, S. 2.

The venom clamours of a jealous woman
Poiſon more deadly than a mad dog's tooth.
Comedy of Errors, A. 5, S. 1.

—— Beſhrew my jealouſy!
It ſeems, it is as proper to our age
To caſt beyond ourſelves in our opinions,
As it is common for the younger ſort
To lack diſcretion. *Hamlet*, A. 2, S. 1.

—— Jealous Oberon would have the child
Knight of his train, to trace the foreſts wild:

 But

But ſhe per-force, withholds the loved boy,
Crowns him with flowers, and makes him all her joy.
Midſummer Night's Dream, A. 2, S. 1.

——— If I ſhall be condemn'd
Upon ſurmiſes; all proofs ſleeping elſe,
But what your jealouſies awake, I tell you,
'Tis rigour, and not law. *Winter's Tale*, A. 3, S. 2.

——— This jealouſy
Is for a precious creature: as ſhe's rare,
Muſt it be great, and, as his perſon's mighty,
Muſt it be violent. *Winter's Tale*, A. 1, S. 2.

JEST, JESTER.

I cannot hide what I am: I muſt be ſad when I have cauſe, and ſmile at no man's jeſts; eat when I have ſtomach, and wait for no man's leiſure; ſleep when I am drowſy, and tend on no man's buſineſs; laugh when I am merry, and claw no man in his humour. *Much ado about nothing*, A. 1, S. 3.

She told me, not thinking I had been myſelf, that I was the prince's jeſter; and that I was duller than a great thaw; huddling jeſt upon jeſt, with ſuch impoſſible conveyance, upon me, that I ſtood like a man at a mark, with a whole army ſhooting at me.
Much ado about nothing, A. 2, S. 1.

A jeſt's proſperity lies in the ear
Of him that hears it, never in the tongue
Of him that makes it.
Love's Labour Loſt, A. 5, S. 2.

Nature hath fram'd ſtrange fellows in her time:
Some that will evermore peep through their eyes,
And laugh, like parrots, at a bag-piper;
And other of ſuch vinegar aſpect,
That they'll not ſhow their teeth in way of ſmile,
Though Neſtor ſwear the jeſt be laughable.
Merchant of Venice, A. 1, S. 1.

Now

Now could thou and I rob the thieves, and go merrily to London, it would be argument for a week[1], laughter for a month, and a good jeſt for ever.

Henry IV. P. 1, A. 2, S. 2.

JEW.

You call me—miſbeliever, cut-throat dog,
And ſpit upon my Jewiſh gaberdine,
And all for uſe of that which is mine own.

Merchant of Venice, A. 1, S. 3.

Hath not a Jew eyes? hath not a Jew hands; organs, dimenſions, ſenſes, affections, paſſions? fed with the ſame food, hurt with the ſame weapons, ſubject to the ſame diſeaſes, heal'd by the ſame means, warm'd and cool'd by the ſame winter and ſummer, as a Chriſtian is?

Merchant of Venice, A. 3, S. 1.

JEWEL.

The jewel that we find, we ſtoop and take it,
Becauſe we ſee it; but what we do not ſee,
We tread upon, and never think of it.

Meaſure for Meaſure, A. 2, S. 1.

A diamond gone, coſt me two thouſand ducats in Frankfort! two thouſand ducats in that; and other precious, precious jewels. I would, my daughter were dead at my foot, and the jewels in her ear!

Merchant of Venice, A. 3, S. 1.

Good name, in man, and woman, dear my lord,
Is the immediate jewel of their ſouls;
Who ſteals my purſe, ſteals traſh; 'tis ſomething, nothing;

[1] *Argument for a week.*] *Argument* is ſubject matter for a drama. STEEVENS.

"This will be argument for a week" muſt mean, *this will furniſh converſation for a week.* A. B.

'Twas mine, 'tis his, and has been ſlave to thouſands:
But he, that filches from me my good name,
Robs me of that which not enriches him,
And makes me poor indeed. *Othello*, A. 3, S. 3.

IGNORANCE.

Ignorance itſelf is a plummet o'er me[1]: uſe me as you will. *Merry Wives of Windſor*, A. 5, S. 5.

—— If he have power,
Then vail your ignorance[2]: if none, awake
Your dangerous lenity. *Coriolanus*, A. 3, S. 1.

ILL.

There's nothing ill can dwell in ſuch a temple.
Tempeſt, A. 1, S. 2.

[1] *Ignorance itſelf is a plummet o'er me.*] Though this be perhaps not unintelligible, yet it is an odd way of confeſſing his defection. I ſhould wiſh to read,

"Ignorance itſelf has a plume o'er me."

that is, I am ſo depreſſed, that ignorance itſelf plucks me, and decks itſelf with the ſpoils of my weakneſs. JOHNSON.

If any alteration be neceſſary, I think, ignorance itſelf is a *planet* o'er me, would have a chance to be right. Thus Bobadil excuſes his cowardice; ſure I was ſtruck with a *planet*, for I had no power to touch my weapon. FARMER.

Perhaps Falſtaff's meaning may be this, ignorance itſelf is a plummet *o'er me*, i. e. *above me*,---ignorance itſelf is not ſo low as I am by the length of a *plummet line*. TYRWHIT.

Falſtaff certainly means, that ignorance triumphs over him. We muſt therefore read, *plumet*, Fr. a garland. "Ignorance "itſelf is a plumet o'er me," i. e. *ignorance wears the garland.* A. B.

[2] *Then vail your ignorance.*] The ſenſe of the paſſage is, If this man has power, let the *ignorance* that gave it him, *vail* or bow down before him. JOHNSON.

Dr. Johnſon's interpretation ſeems wrong. *To vail*, is here to *hide*, and *ignorance* is uſed for *weakneſs*. If this man has really the power he pretends to (ſays Coriolanus), then hide or conceal your weakneſs; but if he has, in fact, no authority, then exerciſe yours. A. B.

IMAGE.

If I had thought, the ſight of my poor image
Would thus have wrought you, (for the ſtone is mine)
I'd not have ſhew'd it [1]. *Winter's Tale*, A. 5, S. 3.

IMAGINATION.

When he ſhall hear ſhe dy'd upon his words,
The idea of her life ſhall ſweetly creep
Into his ſtudy of imagination.
Much ado about nothing, A. 4, S. 1.

Princes have but their titles for their glories,
An outward honour for an inward toil;
And, for unfelt imaginations,
They often feel a world of reſtleſs cares.
Richard III. A. 1, S. 4.

Alas, poor Yorick!—I knew him, Horatio; a fellow of infinite jeſt, of moſt excellent fancy: he hath borne me on his back a thouſand times; and now, how abhorr'd in my imagination it is! my gorge riſes at it. Here hung thoſe lips, that I have kiſs'd I know not how oft. *Hamlet*, A. 5, S. 1.

[1] *If I had thought the ſight of my poor image*
Would thus have wrought you, (for the ſtone is mine)
I'd not have ſhew'd it.] I do not know whether we ſhould not read without a parentheſis,
"——for the ſtone i' th' mine
"I'd not have ſhew'd it."
A mine of *ſtone*, or marble, would not, perhaps, at preſent, be eſteemed an accurate expreſſion, but it may ſtill have been uſed by Shakeſpeare, as it has been uſed by Hollingſhed.
TYRWHIT.

To change an accurate expreſſion for an expreſſion confeſſedly not accurate, has ſomewhat of retrogradation. JOHNSON.

"Stone i' th' mine," is ſurely the more forcible and elegant reading; but Mr. Tyrwhit explains his reading wrong. "Stone "i' th' mine," is *diamond*, not *marble*. A. B.

The lunatic, the lover, and the poet,
Are of imagination all compact.
Midsummer Night's Dream, A. 5, S. 1.

The poet's eye in a fine frenzy rolling,
Doth glance from heaven to earth, from earth to heaven;
And, as imagination bodies forth
The forms of things unknown, the poets pen
Turns them to shapes, and gives to airy nothing
A local habitation, and a name.
Midsummer Night's Dream, A. 5, S. 1.

[1] —— How this grace *(viewing a picture)*
Speaks its own standing! what a mental power
This eye shoots forth! how big imagination
Moves in this lip! to the dumbness of the gesture
One might interpret[2]. *Timon of Athens*, A. 1, S. 1.

INFANT.

[1] —— *How this grace Speaks its own standing!*] This relates to the attitude of the figure; and means that it stands judiciously on its own centre. And not only so, but that it has a graceful standing likewise. WARBURTON.

This sentence seems to me obscure, and however explained, not very forcible. *This grace speaks its own standing*, is only, *The gracefulness of this figure shews how it stands.* I am inclined to think something is corrupted. JOHNSON.

This passage, to my apprehension at least, *speaks its own meaning*, which is, how the graceful attitude of this figure proclaims that it stands firm on its centre, or gives evidence in favour of its own fixure! STEEVENS.

No one, I presume, is ignorant of the meaning of *grace* among painters; nor is he to be informed, that without this very essential requisite, a picture, however finely coloured, would be held, by connoisseurs, in little esteem. I am therefore inclined to explain the passage thus—*Here is grace indeed. Here she shews her standing*—*i. e.* her rank and importance. A. B.

[2] —— *to the dumbness of the gesture One might interpret.*] The allusion is to the puppet-shows, or motions, as they were termed in our author's time.

The

INFANT.

——— Firſt the infant,
Mewling and puking in the nurſe's arms:
And then the whining ſchool-boy, with his ſatchel,
And ſhining morning face, creeping like ſnail
Unwillingly to ſchool. *As you like it,* A. 2, S. 7.

This royal infant, (heaven ſtill move about her!)
Though in her cradle, yet now promiſes
Upon this land a thouſand thouſand bleſſings,
Which time ſhall bring to ripeneſs; ſhe ſhall be
(But few now living can behold that goodneſs)
A pattern to all princes living with her,
And all that ſhall ſucceed. *Henry VIII.* A. 5, S. 4.

INGRATITUDE.

In common worldly things, 'tis call'd—ungrateful
With dull unwillingneſs to repay a debt,
Which with a bounteous hand was kindly lent;
Much more, to be thus oppoſite with heaven,
For it requires the royal debt it lent you.
Richard III. A. 2, S. 2.

And do you now put on your beſt attire?
And do you now cull out a holiday?
And do you now ſtrew flowers in his way,
That comes in triumph over Pompey's blood?
Run to your houſes, fall upon your knees,

The perſon who ſpoke for the puppets was called an interpreter. MALONE.

The ſenſe of the paſſage is—*this is nothing more than a picture; yet ſuch is the livelineſs of the repreſentation, that the figure ſeems almoſt to ſpeak, and we readily comprehend the painter's meaning.* I do not ſee that this has any reference to *puppet-ſhows, motions,* or *interpreters,* A. B.

Pray to the gods to intermit the plague
That needs muſt light on this ingratitude.

Julius Cæſar, A. 1, S. 1.

——— Theſe old fellows
Have their ingratitude in them hereditary:
Their blood is cak'd, 'tis cold, it ſeldom flows;
'Tis lack of kindly warmth, they are not kind;
And nature, as it grows again toward earth,
Is faſhion'd for the journey, dull and heavy.

Timon of Athens, A. 2, S. 2.

Ingratitude! thou marble-hearted fiend,
More hideous, when thou ſhew'ſt thee in a child,
Than the ſea-monſter! *Lear*, A. 1, S. 4.

Blow, blow, thou winter wind,
Thou art not ſo unkind
As man's ingratitude;
[1] Thy tooth is not ſo keen,
Becauſe thou art not ſeen,
Although thy breath be rude.

As you like it, A. 2, S. 7.

—— Filial

[1] *Thy tooth is not ſo keen,*
Becauſe thou art not ſeen.] Dr. Warburton obſerves—the *winter wind*, the ſong ſays, is to be preferred to *man's ingratitude*. But why? *Becauſe it is not ſeen.* But this was not only an aggravation of the injury, as it was done in ſecret, *not ſeen*, but was the very circumſtance that made the keenneſs of the ingratitude of his faithleſs courtiers. I would therefore read,

"Becauſe thou art not ſheen,"

i. e. ſhining, ſmiling, like an ungrateful court-ſervant.

WARBURTON.

Sir T. Hanmer alters the line to

"Thou cauſeſt not that teen."

Dr. Farmer reads,

"Becauſe the heart's not ſeen."

And Muſgrave,

"Becauſe thou art foreſeen."

But all, I think, are wrong. The lines are certainly very unmeaning as they at preſent ſtand. A trifling alteration, however,

——— Filial ingratitude!
Is it not as this mouth ſhould tear this hand,
For lifting food to't?—But I will puniſh home:—
No, I will weep no more.— *Lear*, A. 3, S. 4.

I hate ingratitude more in a man,
Than lying, vainneſs, babbling drunkenneſs,
Or any taint of vice, whoſe ſtrong corruption
Inhabits our frail blood. *Twelfth Night*, A. 3, S. 4.

I N K.

He hath never fed on the dainties that are bred in a book; he hath not eat paper, as it were; he hath not drunk ink: his intellect is not repleniſhed.
Love's Labour Loſt, A. 4, S. 2.

Taunt him with the licence of ink: if thou thou'ſt him ſome thrice, it ſhall not be amiſs; let there be gall enough in thy ink; though thou write with a gooſe-pen, no matter. *Twelfth Night*, A. 3, S. 2.

I N N O C E N C E.

We were as twinn'd lambs, that did friſk i' the ſun,
And bleat the one at the other; what we chang'd,
Was innocence for innocence; we knew not
The doctrine of ill-doing.
Winter's Tale, A. 1, S. 2.

ever, will do away the objection raiſed againſt them by Dr. Warburton, and give them the ſenſe and elegance they want. I read,

Thy tooth is not ſo keen:—
Beſide, thou art not ſeen,
Altho' thy breath be rude.

The meaning of the whole will be—winter wind, thy tooth is not ſo keen as man's ingratitude; and though thy breath be rude, yet as thou art not ſeen, thou canſt not inſult us by thy frowns, by haughty and ſupercilious looks. A. B.

—— He may soften at the sight o' the child;
The silence often of pure innocence
Persuades, when speaking fails.

Winter's Tale, A. 2, S. 2.

——— Hence bashful cunning!
And prompt me, plain and holy innocence!

Tempest, A. 3, S. 1.

INSOLENCE.

—— Now breathless wrong
Shall sit and pant in your great chairs of ease;
And pursy insolence shall break his wind,
With fear, and horrid flight.

Timon of Athens, A. 5, S. 5.

[1] I'll canvass thee in thy broad cardinal's hat,
If thou proceed in this thy insolence.

Henry VI. P. 1, A. 1, S. 3.

INSTINCT.

Thou know'st, I am as valiant as Hercules: but beware instinct; the lion will not touch the true prince. Instinct is a great matter; I was a coward on instinct. *Henry IV.* P. 1, A. 2, S. 4.

[1] *I'll canvass thee in thy broad cardinal's hat.*] This means, I believe, *I'll tumble thee into thy great hat, and shake thee, as bran and meal are shaken in a sieve.* STEEVENS.

Mr. Steevens is mistaken, I think, in supposing *that the cardinal is to be tumbled into his great hat, and shaken as meal is shaken in a sieve.*

To *canvas a matter*, is to sift, examine, or inquire particularly into it. The meaning of, "I'll canvas thee in thy broad cardinal's hat," is—I will make inquiry into thy conduct, and lay thee open to the world, notwithstanding the hat thou wearest, and which thou mayst perhaps imagine will serve to protect thee.

A. B.

—— 'Tis

——— 'Tis wonderful,
That an invisible instinct should frame them
To royalty unlearn'd; honour untaught;
Civility not seen from other; valour,
That wildly grows in them, but yields a crop
As if it had been sow'd! *Cymbeline*, A. 4, S. 2.

JOVE.

I have lim'd her: but it is Jove's doing, and Jove make me thankful! What can be said? Nothing that can be, can come between me and the full prospect of my hopes. Well, Jove, not I, is the doer of this, and he is to be thanked.
Twelfth Night, A. 3, S. 4.

——— Jove!
When on my three-foot stool I sit, and tell
The warlike feats I have done, his spirits fly out
Into my story: say,—Thus mine enemy fell;
And thus I set my foot on his neck; even then
The princely blood flows in his cheek, he sweats,
Strains his young nerves, and puts himself in posture
That acts my words. *Cymbeline*, A. 3, S. 3.

For thou dost know, O Damon dear,
This realm dismantled was
Of Jove himself; and now reigns here
A very, very—peacock[1]. *Hamlet*, A. 3, S. 2.

[1] *A very, very—peacock.*] This alludes to a fable of the birds choosing a king- instead of the eagle, a peacock. POPE.
I think Hamlet is setting his father's and uncle's characters in contrast to each other; and means to say, that by his father's death the state was stripped of a god-like monarch, and that now in his stead reigned the most despicable, poisonous animal that could be; a mere paddock or toad. THEOBALD.
I am persuaded that the poet wrote, "a very, very,—meacock," *i. e.* a cowardly, effeminate fellow. A. B.

JOY,

JOY, JOYS.

——— O my ſoul's joy!
If after every tempeſt come ſuch calmneſs,
May the winds blow till they have waken'd death!
And let the labouring bark climb hills of ſeas,
Olympus high, and duck again as low
As hell's from heaven! *Othello.* A. 2, S. 1.

How much better is it to weep at joy, than to joy at weeping! *Much ado about nothing*, A. 1, S. 1.

There appears much joy in him; even ſo much, that joy could not ſhew itſelf modeſt enough, without a badge of bitterneſs.

Much ado about nothing, A. 1, S. 1.

— There is ſuch confuſion in my powers,
As after ſome oration fairly ſpoke
By a beloved prince, there doth appear
Among the buzzing pleaſed multitude;
Where every ſomething, being blent together,
Turns to a wild of nothing, ſave of joy,
Expreſt, and not expreſt.

Merchant of Venice, A. 3, S. 2.

I have no joy of this contract to-night:
It is too raſh, too unadvis'd, too ſudden;
Too like the lightning, which doth ceaſe to be,
Ere one can ſay—it lightens.

Romeo and Juliet, A. 2, S. 2.

——— Note him:
He was not ſad; for he would ſhine on thoſe
That make their looks by his: he was not merry,
Which ſeem'd to tell them, his remembrance lay
In Egypt with his joy.

Antony and Cleopatra, A. 1, S. 5.

ISLE.

This royal throne of kings, this ſcepter'd iſle,
This earth of majeſty, this ſeat of Mars,

This

This other Eden, demy paradiſe;
This fortreſs, built by nature for herſelf,
This happy breed of men, this little world;
This precious ſtone ſet in the ſilver ſea,
Which ſerves it in the office of a wall,
Is now leas'd out (I die pronouncing it)
Like to a tenement, or pelting farm.
Richard II. A. 2, S. 1.

ISSUE.

Thou elviſh-mark'd abortive, roaſting hog!
Thou that waſt ſeal'd in thy nativity
The ſlave of nature, and the ſon of hell!
Thou ſlander of thy mother's heavy womb!
Thou loathed iſſue of thy father's loins!
Thou rag of honour! *Richard III.* A. 1, S. 3.

—— Care not for iſſue;
The crown will find an heir: great Alexander
Left his to the worthieſt: ſo his ſucceſſor
Was like to be the beſt. *Winter's Tale*, A. 5, S. 1.

Kings are no leſs unhappy, their iſſue not being gracious, than they are in loſing them, when they have approved their virtues.
Winter's Tale, A. 4, S. 1.

JUDGMENT.

For my voice,—I have loſt it with hallowing and ſinging of anthems. To approve my youth further, I will not: the truth is, I am only old in judgment and underſtanding; and he that will caper with me for a thouſand marks, let him lend me the money, and have at him. *Henry IV.* P. 2, A. 1, S. 2.

You all did love him once, not without cauſe;
What cauſe withholds you then to mourn for him?—
O judgment, thou art fled to brutiſh beaſts,
And men have loſt their reaſon!—Bear with me;

My heart is in the coffin there with Cæſar,
And I muſt pauſe till it come back to me.
Julius Cæſar, A. 3, S. 2.

——— His ſilver hairs
Will purchaſe us a good opinion,
And buy men's voices to commend our deeds:
It ſhall be ſaid, his judgment rul'd our hands,
Our youths, and wildneſs, ſhall no whit appear,
But all be bury'd in his gravity.
Julius Cæſar, A. 2, S. 1.

——— I charge you by the law,
Whereof you are a well-deſerving pillar,
Proceed to judgment. *Merchant of Venice*, A. 4, S. 1.

Under your good correction, I have ſeen,
When, after execution, judgment hath
Repented o'er his doom.
Meaſure for Meaſure, A. 2, S. 2.

——— How would you be,
If he, which is the top of judgment, ſhould
But judge you, as you are?
Meaſure for Meaſure, A. 2, S. 2.

When I that cenſure him do ſo offend,
Let mine own judgment pattern out my death,
And nothing come in partial.
Meaſure for Meaſure, A. 2, S. 1.

To promiſe is moſt courtly and faſhionable: performance is a kind of will, or teſtament, which argues a great ſickneſs in his judgment that makes it.
Timon of Athens, A. 5, S. 1.

But when we in our viciouſneſs grow hard,
(O miſery on't) the wiſe gods ſeal our eyes;
In our own filth drop our clear judgments; make us
Above our errors; laugh at us, while we ſtrut
To our confuſion. *Antony and Cleopatra*, A. 3, S. 11.

——— Beware
Of entrance to a quarrel; but, being in,

Bear

Bear it that the opposer may beware of thee.
Give every man thine ear, but few thy voice;
Take each man's censure, but reserve thy judgment.
Hamlet, A. 1, S. 3.

His years but young, but his experience old;
His head unmellow'd, but his judgment ripe.
Two Gentlemen of Verona, A. 2, S. 4.

My sallad days[1]!
When I was green in judgment: cold in blood,
To say, as I said then!—
Antony and Cleopatra, A. 1, S. 5.

——— Whether defect of judgment
To fail in the disposing of those chances
Which he was lord of; or whether nature,

[1] *My sallad days!*
When I was green in judgment: cold in blood,
To say, as I said then!] This puzzles Mr. Theobald. He says, Cleopatra may speak very naturally here with contempt of her judgment at that period: but how truly with regard to the coldness of her blood, may admit some question. And then employs his learning to prove, that at this *cold* season of her *blood*, she had seen twenty good years. Shakespeare's best justification, is restoring his own sense, which is done merely by a different pointing:

My sallad days;
When I was green in judgment. Cold in blood!
To say as I said then.

Cold in blood is an upbraiding expostulation to her maid. *Those*, says she, *were my sallad days*, *when I was green in judgment*; *but your blood is as cold as my judgment*, *if you have the same opinion of things now as I had then.* WARBURTON.

I would prefer *ballad days*. What are sallad days? Does *sallad* give any particular or appropriate idea of youth? or do the editors read sallad, because Cleopatra is here speaking of her *green* judgment? *Green*, in this place, however, has not the smallest reference to *colour*, it certainly means *unripe*; and do we say of sallad that it is unripe? The true reading, I should suppose, is *ballad days*, i. e. Days when she was little given to thought or reflection. We now say, "our dancing days," when we speak of the earliest and liveliest part of our life.
A. B.

Not

Not to be other than one thing, not moving
From the casque to the cushion, but commanding
peace
Even with the same austerity and garb
As he controll'd the war: but, one of these,
(As he hath spices of them all, not all,
For I dare so far free him) made him fear'd,
So hated, and so banish'd: but he has a merit,
To choak it in the utterance [1].

Coriolanus, A. 4, S. 7.

JUSTICE.

—— Let us be clear'd
Of being tyrannous, since we so openly
Proceed in justice; which shall have due course,
Even to the guilt, or the purgation.—

Winter's Tale, A. 3, S. 2.

See how yon' justice rails upon yon' simple thief: Hark, in thine ear: change places; and handy-dandy, which is the justice, which is the thief?—Thou hast seen a farmer's dog bark at a beggar? and the creature run from the cur? There thou might'st behold the great image of authority: a dog's obey'd in office. *Lear*, A. 4, S. 6.

—— The usurer hangs the cozener.
Through tatter'd clothes small vices do appear;
Robes and furr'd gowns hide all. Plate sin with
gold,

[1] —— *he has a merit,*
To choak it in the utterance.] He has a merit for no other purpose, than to destroy it by boasting it. JOHNSON.

Dr. Johnson has mistaken the sense. *It* is not the relative to *merit*, but to *defect*:—one of those *defects* in Coriolanus, which Aufidius had enumerated a little before. *Whatever defect he may have* (says Aufidius), *he has a merit to countervail it.*

A. B.

And the ſtrong lance of juſtice hurtleſs breaks:
Arm it in rags, a pigmy's ſtraw doth pierce it.
Lear, A. 4, S. 6.

Let the great gods,
That keep this dreadful pother o'er our heads,
Find out their enemies now. Tremble, thou wretch,
That haſt within thee undivulged crimes,
Unwhipt of juſtice. *Lear*, A. 3, S. 2.

Cries out upon abuſes, ſeems to weep
Over his country's wrongs; and, by this face,
This ſeeming brow of juſtice, did he win
The hearts of all that he did angle for.
Henry IV. P. 1, A. 4, S. 3.

Thus hath the courſe of juſtice wheel'd about,
And left thee but a very prey to time;
Having no more but thought of what thou wert,
To torture thee the more, being what thou art.
Richard III. A. 4, S. 4.

—— Then the juſtice;
In fair round belly, with good capon lin'd,
With eyes ſevere, and beard of formal cut,
Full of wiſe ſaws and modern inſtances.
As you like it, A. 2, S. 7.

——— We hear,
Such goodneſs of your juſtice, that our ſoul
Cannot but yield you forth to public thanks,
Fore-running more requital.
Meaſure for Meaſure, A. 5, S. 1.

—— Worthy prince, diſhonour not your eye
By throwing it on any other object,
Till you have heard me in my true complaint,
And give me juſtice.
Meaſure for Meaſure, A. 5, S. 1.

—— The

——— The nature of our people,
Our city's inſtitutions, and the terms
For common juſtice you are pregnant in.
Meaſure for Meaſure, A. 1, S. 1.

—— He did plot the duke of Gloſter's death;
Sluic'd out his innocent ſoul through ſtreams of blood;
Which blood, like ſacrificing Abel's, cries,
Even from the tongueleſs caverns of the earth,
To me, for juſtice, and rough chaſtiſement.
Richard II. A. 1, S. 1.

—— As thou urgeſt juſtice, be aſſur'd,
Thou ſhalt have juſtice, more than thou deſir'ſt.
Merchant of Venice, A. 4, S. 1.

——— Our decrees,
Dead to infliction, to themſelves are dead;
And liberty plucks juſtice by the noſe.
Meaſure for Meaſure, A. 1, S. 4.

——— His life is parallel'd
Even with the ſtroke and line of his great juſtice.
Meaſure for Meaſure, A. 4, S. 2.

——— What's open made to juſtice,
That juſtice ſeizes.
Meaſure for Meaſure, A. 2, S. 1.

K.

KING, KINGDOM.

YOU would have ſold your king to ſlaughter,
His princes and his peers to ſervitude,
His ſubjects to oppreſſion and contempt,
And his whole kingdom unto deſolation.

Touching

Touching our perſon, ſeek we no revenge;
But we our kingdom's ſafety muſt ſo tender,
Whoſe ruin you three ſought, that to her laws
We do deliver you. *Henry V.* A. 2, S. 2.

We give expreſs charge, that, in our marches through the country, there be nothing compelled from the villages, nothing taken but paid for; none of the French upbraided, or abuſed in diſdainful language; for when lenity and cruelty play for a kingdom, the gentleſt gameſter is the ſooneſt winner.
Henry V. A. 3, S. 6.

[1] O, for a muſe of fire, that would aſcend
The brighteſt heaven of invention!
A kingdom for a ſtage, princes to act,
And monarchs to behold the ſwelling ſcene!
Then ſhould the warlike Harry, like himſelf,
Aſſume the port of Mars; and, at his heels,
Leaſh'd in like hounds, ſhould famine, ſword, and fire,
Crouch for employment. *Henry V. Chorus.*

——— So work the honey bees;
Creatures, that, by a rule in nature, teach
The art of order to a peopled kingdom.
They have a king, and officers of ſorts:

[1] *O for a muſe of fire that would aſcend*
The brighteſt heaven of invention!] This goes upon the notion of the peripatetic ſyſtem, which imagines ſeveral heavens one above another; the laſt, and higheſt of which, was one of fire. WARBURTON.

It alludes likewiſe to the aſpiring nature of fire, which by its levity at the ſeparation of the chaos, took the higheſt ſeat of all the elements. JOHNSON.

The commentators have here, I believe,
" *Diſcover'd meanings which were never meant.*"
" A muſe of fire that would aſcend the brighteſt heaven of in-" vention"—means, I apprehend, *vigour of fancy,—ſuch as is capable of bold and daring flights*; without any alluſion to the peripatetic ſyſtem, or to the aſpiring nature of fire. A. B.

Where ſome, like magiſtrates, correct at home;
Others like merchants, venture trade abroad;
Others like ſoldiers, armed in their ſtings,
Make boot upon the ſummer's velvet buds;
Which pillage they with merry march bring home.

Henry V. A. 1, S. 2.

I'll give my jewels for a ſet of beads;
My gorgeous palace for a hermitage;
My gay apparel for an alms-man's gown;
My figur'd goblets, for a diſh of wood;
My ſcepter, for a palmer's walking ſtaff;
My ſubjects, for a pair of carved ſaints;
And my large kingdom, for a little grave.

Richard II. A. 3, S. 3.

O my poor kingdom, ſick with civil blows!
When that my care could not with-hold thy riots,
What wilt thou do, when riot is thy care?
O, thou wilt be a wilderneſs again,
Peopled with wolves, thy old inhabitants!

Henry IV. P. 2, A. 4, S. 4.

The watry kingdom, whoſe ambitious head
Spits in the face of heaven, is no bar
To ſtop the foreign ſpirits; but they come,
As o'er a brook, to ſee fair Portia.

Merchant of Venice, A. 2, S. 7.

Your breath firſt kindled the dead coal of wars
Between this chaſtis'd kingdom and myſelf,
And brought in matter that ſhould feed this fire,
And now 'tis far too huge to be blown out
With that ſame weak wind which enkindled it.

King John, A. 5, S. 2.

Alas! how ſhould you govern any kingdom,
That know not how to uſe ambaſſadors;
Nor how to be contented with one wife;
Nor how to uſe your brothers brotherly;

Nor

Nor how to ſtudy for the people's welfare;
Nor how to ſhrowd yourſelf from enemies?
Henry VI. P. 3, A. 4, S. 3.

This unhair'd ſaucineſs, and boyiſh troops[1],
The king doth ſmile at. *King John*, A, 5, S. 2.

Let Rome in Tyber melt! and the wide arch
Of the rang'd empire fall! Here is my ſpace;
Kingdoms are clay: our dungy earth alike
Feeds beaſt as man. *Antony and Cleopatra*, A. 1, S. 1.

A true devoted pilgrim is not weary
To meaſure kingdoms with his feeble ſteps;
Much leſs ſhall ſhe, that hath love's wings to fly.
Two Gentlemen of Verona, A. 2, S. 7.

I am all the ſubjects that you have,
Who firſt was mine own king. *Tempeſt*, A. 1, S. 2.

Oh, two ſuch ſilver currents, when they join,
Do glorify the banks that bound them in:
And two ſuch ſhores to two ſuch ſtreams made one,
Two ſuch controlling bounds ſhall you be, kings,
To theſe two princes, if you marry them.
King John, A. 2, S. 2.

Shall that victorious hand be feebled here,
That in your chambers gave you chaſtiſement?
No: Know, the gallant monarch is in arms;

[1] *This unheard of ſaucineſs, and boyiſh troops.*] Thus the printed copies in general; but *unheard* is an epithet of very little force or meaning here. Faulconbridge talks of the Dauphin's *boyiſh troops*, of *dwarfiſh war*, *pigmy arms*, &c. which, according to my emendation, ſort very well with *unhair'd*, i. e. *unbearded* ſaucineſs. THEOBALD.

Yet another reading might be recommended:
"This *unair'd* ſaucineſs,"
i. e. *untravelled* rudeneſs. STEEVENS.

"Unair'd is," I think, the reading to be preferred. *Unair'd*, however, is not, in this place, to be taken in the ſenſe of *untravelled*. It rather means *unſeaſoned*, *inordinate*. A. B.

And like an eagle o'er his airy towers,
To ſouſe annoyance that comes near his neſt.
King John, A. 5, S. 2.

Hear him but reaſon in divinity,
And, all-admiring, with an inward wiſh
You would deſire the king were made a prelate:
Hear him debate of common-wealth affairs,
You would ſay,—it hath been all-in-all his ſtudy.
Henry V. A. 1, S. 1.

You are too much miſtaken in this king:
Queſtion your grace the late ambaſſadors,——
With what great ſtate he heard their embaſſy,
How well ſupply'd with noble counſellors,
How modeſt in exception, and, withal,
How terrible in conſtant reſolution,——
And you ſhall find, his vanities fore-ſpent
Were but the outſide of the Roman Brutus,
Covering diſcretion with a coat of folly.
Henry V. A. 2, S. 4.

Truly, for mine own part, if I were as tedious as a king, I could find in my heart to beſtow it all of your worſhip. *Much ado about nothing*, A. 3, S. 5.

Not all the water in the rough rude ſea
Can waſh the balm from an anointed king;
The breath of worldly men cannot depoſe
The deputy elected by the Lord.
Richard II. A. 3, S. 2.

Rich men look ſad, and ruffians dance and leap,—
The one, in fear to loſe what they enjoy,
The other, to enjoy by rage and war:
Theſe ſigns forerun the death or fall of kings.
Richard II. A. 2, S. 4.

—— Sometimes am I king,
Then treaſon makes me wiſh myſelf a beggar,
And ſo I am: then cruſhing penury
Perſuades me, I was better when a king;

Then am I king'd again: and, by-and-by,
Think, that I am unking'd by Bolingbroke,
And ſtraight am nothing. *Richard II.* A. 5, S. 5.

So doth the greater glory dim the leſs:
A ſubſtitute ſhines brightly as a king,
Until a king be by; and then his ſtate
Empties itſelf, as doth an inland brook,
Into the main of waters.
Merchant of Venice, A. 5, S. 1.

—— I will no more return,
Till Angiers, and the right thou haſt in France,
Together with that pale, that white-fac'd ſhore,
Whoſe foot ſpurns back the ocean's roaring tides,
Salute thee for her king. *King John*, A. 2, S. 1.

—— Nor is there living
A man, that more deteſts, more ſtirs againſt,
Defacers of a publick peace than I do.
Pray heaven the king may never find a heart
With leſs allegiance in it! *Henry VIII.* A. 5, S. 2.

Firſt let me tell you whom you have condemn'd:
Not me begotten of a ſhepherd ſwain,
But iſſu'd from the progeny of kings,
Virtuous, and holy; choſen from above,
By inſpiration of celeſtial grace,
To work exceeding miracles on earth.
Henry VI. P. 1, A. 5, S. 5.

The king is a noble gentleman; and my familiar, I do aſſure you, very good friend:—for I muſt tell thee, it will pleaſe his grace (by the world) ſometime to lean upon my poor ſhoulder; and with his royal finger, thus dally with my excrement, with my muſtachio. *Love's Labour Loſt*, A. 5, S. 1.

—— That it ſhould come to this!
But two months dead! nay, not ſo much, not two:
So excellent a king; that was, to this,
Hyperion to a ſatyr: ſo loving to my mother,

That he might not let e'en the winds of heaven [1]
Visit her face too roughly. *Hamlet*, A. 1, S. 2.

The king doth wake to-night, and take his rouse,
Keeps wassel, and the swaggering up-spring reels;
And, as he drains his draughts of rhenish down,
The kettle-drum, and trumpet, thus bray out
The triumph of his pledge. *Hamlet*, A. 1, S. 4.

—— Do not fear our person;
There's such divinity doth hedge a king,
That treason can but peep to what it would,
Acts little of his will. *Hamlet*, A. 4, S. 5.

My lord of Burgundy,
We first address towards you, who with this king
Have rivall'd for our daughter; what, in the least,
Will you require in present dower with her,
Or cease your quest of love [2]? *Lear*, A. 1, S. 1.

The

[1] *That he permitted not the winds of heaven.*] This is a sophistical reading, copied from the players, for want of understanding the poet, whose text is corrupt in the old impressions; all of which concur in reading,

" —— so loving to my mother,
" That he might not beteene the winds of heaven
" Visit her face too roughly."

"Beteene" is a corruption without doubt, but not so inveterate a one, but that, by the change of a single letter, and the separation of two words, mistakenly jumbled together, I am verily persuaded, I have retained the poet's reading.---That he might not *let e'en* the winds of heaven, &c. THEOBALD.

Mr. Theobald observes, that "beteene" is undoubtedly a corruption, and Mr. Steevens appears to be of the same opinion, by admitting "*let e'en*" to a place in the text,---but they are both mistaken. To "beteen" is to *enrage*, to *anger*. We must read the passage thus:

" —— so loving to my mother,
" That the beteened winds of heaven might not
" Visit her face too roughly."

i. e. Such was his love of my mother, that he would not permit the angry winds of heaven, at any time, to blow upon her.

A. B.

[2] —— *quest of love.*] *Quest of love*, is *amorous expedition.*

The

The king will always think him in our debt;
And think we think ourſelves unſatisfy'd,
Till he hath found a time to pay us home.
And ſee already how he doth begin
To make us ſtrangers to his looks of love.
Henry IV. P. 1, A. 1, S. 3.

——— The harlot king
Is quite beyond mine arm, out of the blank
And level of my brain, plot proof, but ſhe
I can hook to me. *Winter's Tale*, A. 2, S. 3.

Kent baniſh'd thus! and France in choler parted!
And the king gone to-night! ſubſcrib'd his power[1]!
Confin'd to exhibition! All this done
Upon the gad! *Lear*, A. 1, S. 2.

— Thus king Henry throws away his crutch,
Before his legs be firm to bear his body:
Thus is the ſhepherd beaten from thy ſide,
And wolves are gnarling who ſhall gnaw thee firſt.
Henry VI. P. 2, A. 3, S. 1.

— Time ſerves, wherein you may redeem
Your baniſh'd honours, and reſtore yourſelves
Into the good thoughts of the world again:
Revenge the jeering, and diſdain'd contempt,
Of this proud king. *Henry IV.* P. 1, A. 1, S. 3.

The term originated from romance. A queſt was the expedition in which a knight was engaged. This phraſe is often met with in the Fairy Queen. STEEVENS.

"Queſt," in this place, is *requeſt*, *ſolicitation.* "Ceaſe your "queſt of love." *Ceaſe your love ſolicitations.* A. B.

1 ——— *ſubſcrib'd his power.*] *Subſcrib'd* for *transferred*, *alienated.* WARBURTON.

To ſubſcribe, is to transfer by ſigning, or *ſubſcribing* a writing of teſtimony. We now uſe the term, He *ſubſcribed* forty pounds to the new building. JOHNSON.

"Subſcrib'd his power," is, *his power contracted or limited.* Or, we may read,—"*proſcrib'd his power*"—*his power is taken from him—there is an interdiction, a ſtop to all his power.* The folio reads *preſcrib'd.* A. B.

Gives not the hawthorn bufh a fweeter fhade
To fhepherds, looking on their filly fheep,
Than doth a rich embroider'd canopy
To kings, that fear their fubjects' treachery?
O, yes, it doth, a thoufand fold it doth.

Henry VI. P. 3, A. 2, S. 5.

——— She, which late
Was in my nobler thoughts moft bafe, is now
The praifed of the king; who, fo ennobled,
Is, as 'twere, born fo.

All's well that ends well, A. 2, S. 3.

I'll win this lady Margaret. For whom?
Why, for my king: tufh! that's a wooden thing[1].

Henry VI. P. 1, A. 5, S. 4.

K I S S.

Good my lord, forbear;
The ruddinefs upon her lip is wet;
You'll mar it, if you kifs it; ftain your own
With oily painting. *Winter's Tale*, A. 5, S. 3.

——— Ere I could
Give him that parting kifs, which I had fet
Betwixt two charming words, comes in my father
And, like the tyrannous breathing of the north,
Shakes all our buds from growing.

Cymbeline, A. 1, S. 4.

——— O, a kifs
Long as my exile, fweet as my revenge!
Now by the jealous queen of heaven, that kifs
I carried from thee, dear; and my true lip
Hath virgin'd it e'er fince.—You gods! I prate,

[1] ——— *a wooden thing*.] Is an aukward bufinefs,---an undertaking not likely to fucceed. STEEVENS.

"A wooden thing" is a *mad thing*. "Tufh! that's a wooden "thing"---*Hold, the thought is madnefs.* A. B.

And

And the moſt noble mother of the world
Leave unſaluted. *Coriolanus*, A. 5, S. 3.

I found not Caſſio's kiſſes on her lips:
He that is robb'd, not wanting what is ſtolen,
Let him not know it, and he's not robb'd at all.
Othello, A. 3, S. 3.

And let him, for a pair of reechy kiſſes [1],
Make you to ravel all this matter out,
That I eſſentially am not in madneſs,
But mad in craft. *Hamlet*, A. 3, S. 4.

KNAVE.

——— You ſhall mark
Many a duteous and knee-crooking knave,
That, doting on his own obſequious bondage,
Wears out his time, much like his maſter's aſs,
For nought but provender, and, when he's old, caſhier'd;
Whip me ſuch honeſt knaves. *Othello*, A. 1, S. 1.

Fetch forth the ſtocks, ho!
You ſtubborn ancient knave [2], you reverend braggart,
We'll teach you. *Lear*, A. 2, S. 2.

1 ——— *reechy kiſſes.*] *Reechy* is ſmoky. The author meant to convey a coarſe idea, and was not very ſcrupulous in his choice of an epithet. The ſenſe, however, is applied with greater propriety to the neck of a cook-maid in Coriolanus. STEEVENS.
" Reechy," in this place, is rather *ſmoking* than *ſmoky*.— " Reechy kiſſes" are *hot*, *burning* kiſſes. A. B.

2 ——— *ancient knave.*] Two of the quartos read *miſcreant* knave, and one of them *unreverent*, inſtead of *reverend*. STEEVENS.

" Unreverent" is right. *Unreverent* is *rude*, *diſreſpectful*. Cornwal would ſay, " you old rogue, you irreverent braggart!" A. B.

KNIGHT.

KNIGHT.

It is a merry knight.—[1] Will you go an heirs?
Merry Wives of Windſor, A. 2, S. 1.

Theſe knights will hack[2]; and ſo thou ſhouldſt not alter the article of thy gentry.
Merry Wives of Windſor, A. 2, S. 1.

[1] *Will you go an-heirs?*] This nonſenſe is ſpoken to Shallow.—We ſhould read—*will you go on*, HERIS? *i. e.* will you go on, Maſter?---Heris, an old Scotch word for maſter. WARBURTON.

Mr. Steevens would read, *will you go on heroes?* or, *will you go on hearts?* and Mr. Malone thinks it ſhould be, *will you go and hear us?*

Herie, in Spenſer, is *worſhip*, *worſhipful*, probably from *herus*, the head of a family; and one who is conſequently intitled to reſpect. Shallow, it muſt be remarked is a country juſtice, the hoſt may therefore ſay to him, will you go on *herie*, or *herus?* meaning, will you go firſt, as you are worſhipful, or diſtinguiſhed by being a juſtice? A. B.

[2] *Theſe knights will hack, and ſo thou ſhouldſt not alter the article of thy gentry.*] Dr. Warburton is of opinion, that we ſhould read *lack*, but I do not clearly ſee his meaning. Dr. Johnſon thinks, that hack is ſaid in alluſion to the hacking off the ſpurs of recreant knights. Hanmer ſays, that *hack* means to turn hackney, or proſtitute; and Blackſtone, that the word *hack* muſt ſignify, to become cheap and vulgar.

"*Theſe knights will hack*" is certainly very harſh. I am therefore much inclined to read, "theſe knights will jack," *i. e.* play the jack, in alluſion to the proverb---*Jack will never make a gentleman.* The ſenſe is, This honour conferred on your huſband will ſignify nothing; he will ſtill be *Jack* in his manners---it will not alter the article of thy gentility. A. B.

L.

L A D Y.

MY dear lady Disdain! are you yet living?
Much ado about nothing, A. 1, S. 1.

Thou didst swear to me upon a parcel-gilt goblet, sitting in my dolphin-chamber, at the round table by a sea-coal fire, on Wednesday, in Whitsun-week, when the prince broke thy head for likening his father to a singing-man of Windsor; thou didst swear to me then, as I was washing thy wound, to marry me, and make me my lady thy wife.
Henry IV. P. 2, A. 2, S. 1.

— That's the lady; all the world desires her:
From the four corners of the earth they come,
To kiss this shrine, this mortal breathing saint.
Merchant of Venice, A. 2, S. 7.

Fair ladies, mask'd, are roses in their bud;
Dismask'd, their damask sweet commixture shewn,
Are angels vailing clouds, or roses blown.
Love's Labour Lost, A. 5, S. 2.

——— Constant you are;
But yet a woman; and for secresy,
No lady closer; for I well believe,
Thou wilt not utter what thou dost not know;
And so far will I trust thee.
Henry IV. P. 1, A. 2, S. 3.

——— 'Tis thought,
That Marcius shall be consul: I have seen
The dumb men throng to see him, and the blind
To hear him speak: matrons flung gloves,
Ladies and maids their scarfs and handkerchiefs,
Upon him as he pass'd: the nobles bended,

As

As to Jove's ſtatue; and the commons made
A ſhower, and thunder, with their caps, and ſhouts.
Coriolanus A. 2, S. 2.

—— She, ſweet lady, dotes,
Devoutly dotes, dotes in idolatry,
Upon this ſpotted and inconſtant man.
Midſummer Night's Dream, A. 1, S. 1.

[1] O well-a-day, lady, if he be not drawn now!
Henry V. A. 2, S. 1.

LANGUAGE.

Thoſe girls of Italy, take heed of them;
They ſay, our French lack language to deny,
If they demand.
All's well that ends well, A. 2, S. 1.

You taught me language; and my profit on't
Is, I know how to curſe: [2] the red plague rid you.
Tempeſt, A. 1, S. 2.

LAUGH-

[1] *O well-a-day, if he be not hewn now!*] I cannot underſtand the drift of this expreſſion. If he be not *hewn*, muſt ſignify, if he be not *cut down*, and in that caſe, the very thing is ſuppoſed which Quickly was apprehenſive of. But I rather think her fright ariſes from ſeeing the ſwords drawn, and I have ventured to make a ſlight alteration accordingly. *If he be not drawn*, for, *if he has not his ſword drawn*, is an expreſſion familiar to our poet. THEOBALD.

I have not diſturbed Mr. Theobald's emendation; but yet I think we might read—if he be not *hewing*. To hack and *hew* is a common vulgar expreſſion. STEEVENS.

"Hewn" ſhould be "hewin." *Hewin*, or *hewid*, in Chaucer, is *coloured*. Mrs. Quickly would ſay—*if he be not coloured*, if he be not in a *paſſion*.

That *drawn* is not the proper word, may be ſeen by turning to a ſubſequent ſcene of the play, in which Piſtol is made to ſay, "O braggard vile, &c." and at which ſpeech, in the old copies, is the following ſtage direction—(*they drawe.*) A. B.

[2] —— *the red plague.*] I ſuppoſe from the redneſs of the body, univerſally inflamed. JOHNSON.

The *eryſipelas* was anciently called the *red plague*. STEEVENS.

By

LAUGHTER.

I will devise matter enough out of this Shallow, to keep prince Harry in continual laughter, the wearing out of six fashions (which is four terms, or two actions), and he shall laugh without intervallums.

Henry IV. P. 2, A. 5, S. 1.

The brain of this foolish-compounded clay, man, is not able to invent any thing that tends to laughter, more than I invent, or is invented on me: I am not only witty in myself, but the cause that wit is in other men. *Henry IV.* P. 2, A. 1, S. 2.

LAWS.

——— O perilous mouths,
That bear in them one and the self-same tongue,
Either of condemnation or approof!
Bidding the law make court'sy to their will.

Measure for Measure, A. 2, S. 4.

—— Your scope is as mine own;
So to inforce or qualify the laws,
As to your soul seems good.

Measure for Measure, A. 1, S. 1.

The pound of flesh, which I demand of him,
Is dearly bought, 'tis mine, and I will have it:
If you deny me, fie upon your law!

Merchant of Venice, A. 4, S. 1.

——— I beseech you,
Wrest once the law to your authority:
To do a great right, do a little wrong.

Merchant of Venice, A. 4, S. 1.

By *red plague*, I understand *lightning*. The "red plague rid "you," is, as though he should say, *lightning blast you*. Lightning is called by the poets, the red-wing'd messenger of Jove. Caliban may be supposed to have observed the dreadful effects of lightning; but how should he know any thing about the erysipelas? A. B.

It

It is the curſe of kings, to be attended
By ſlaves, that take their humours for a warrant
To break within the bloody houſe of life:
And, on the winking of authority,
To underſtand a law. *King John*, A. 4, S. 2.

We muſt not make a ſcare-crow of the law,
Setting it up to fear the birds of prey,
And let it keep one ſhape, till cuſtom make it
Their perch, and not their terror.
Meaſure for Meaſure, A. 2, S. 1.

It is the law, not I, condemns your brother:
Were he my kinſman, brother, or my ſon,
It would be thus with him.
Meaſure for Meaſure, A. 2, S. 2.

We have ſtrict ſtatutes and moſt biting laws,
Which for theſe fourteen years we have let ſleep;
Even like an o'er-grown lion in a cave,
That goes not out to prey.
Meaſure for Meaſure, A. 1, S. 4.

L I F E.

——— Haply, this life is beſt,
If quiet life be beſt, ſweeter to you,
That have a ſharper known; well correſponding
With your ſtiff age; but, unto us, it is
A cell of ignorance: travelling a-bed;
A priſon for a debtor that not dares
To ſtride a limit. *Cymbeline*, A. 3, S. 3.

—— You, my lord, beſt know,
(Who leaſt will ſeem to do ſo) my paſt life
Hath been as continent, as chaſte, as true,
As I am now unhappy. *Winter's Tale*, A. 3, S. 2.

—— What ſhould be the fear?
I do not ſet my life at a pin's fee;

And,

And, for my ſoul, what can it do to that,
Being a thing immortal as itſelf? *Hamlet*, A. 1, S. 4.

O thou good Kent, how ſhall I live, and work,
To match thy goodneſs? my life will be too ſhort,
And every meaſure fail me [1]. *Lear*, A. 4, S. 7.

— This our life, exempt from publick haunt,
Finds tongues in trees, books in the running brooks,
Sermons in ſtones, and good in every thing.
As you like it, A. 2, S. 1.

The web of our life is of a mingled yarn, good and ill together: our virtues would be proud, if our faults whipp'd them not; and our crimes would deſpair, if they were not cheriſh'd by our virtues.
All's well that ends well, A. 4, S. 3.

——— At my birth,
The front of heaven was full of fiery ſhapes;
Theſe ſigns have marked me extraordinary;
And all the courſes of my life do ſhew,
I am not in the roll of common men.
Henry IV. P. 1, A. 3, S. 1.

[2] —— My life is ſpann'd already;
I am the ſhadow of poor Buckingham;
Whoſe figure even this inſtant cloud puts on,
By dark'ning my clear ſun. *Henry VIII*. A. 1, S. 1.

Beaufort's red ſparkling eyes blab his heart's malice,
And Suffolk's cloudy brow his ſtormy hate;

1 —— *every meaſure fail me*.] All good which I ſhall allot thee, or *meaſure out* to thee, will be ſcanty. JOHNSON.
"Meaſure" here is *effort*, *endeavour*. A. B.

2 ——— *My life is ſpann'd already*.] To ſpan is to *gripe*, or *incloſe in the hand*; to *ſpan* is alſo to meaſure by the palm and fingers. The meaning, therefore, may either be, that hold is taken of my life; my life is in the gripe of my enemies, or that my time is meaſured, the length of my life is now determined. JOHNSON.
"My life is ſpann'd," *i. e. my life is ſhort*. We now ſay, *contracted to a ſpan*, for any ſhort ſpace of time. A. B.

Sharp

Sharp Buckingham unburdens with his tongue
The envious load that lies upon his heart;
And dogged York, that reaches at the moon,
Whofe over-weening arm I have pluck'd back,
By falfe accufe doth level at my life.

Henry VI. P. 2, A. 3, S. 1.

I cannot tell, what you and other men
Think of this life; but, for my fingle felf,
I had as lief not be, as live to be
In awe of fuch a thing as I myfelf.
I was born free as Cæfar; fo were you:
We both have fed as well; and we can both
Endure the winter's cold as well as he.

Julius Cæfar, A. 1, S. 2.

—— I am married to a wife,
Which is as dear to me as life itfelf;
But life itfelf, my wife, and all the world,
Are not with me efteem'd above thy life.

Merchant of Venice, A. 4, S. 1.

Thou art too noble to conferve a life
In bafe appliances. *Meafure for Meafure*, A. 3, S. 1.

——— Reafon thus with life,—
If I do lofe thee, I do lofe a thing,
That none but fools would keep.

Meafure for Meafure, A. 3, S. 1.

Nay, take my life and all, pardon not that:
You take my houfe, when you do take the prop
That doth fuftain my houfe; you take my life
When you do take the means whereby I live.

Merchant of Venice, A. 4, S. 1.

Make me to fee it; or (at leaft) fo prove it,
That the probation bear no hinge, nor loop,
To hang a doubt on: or, woe upon thy life!

Othello, A. 3. S. 3.

—— For all, that life can rate
Worth name of life, in thee hath eftimate;

Youth,

Youth, beauty, wiſdom, courage, virtue, all
That happineſs and prime [1], can happy call.

All's well that ends well, A. 2, S. 1.

L I O N.

——— I met a lion,
Who glar'd upon me, and went ſurly by,
Without annoying me:
And, yeſterday, the bird of night did ſit,
Even at noon-day, upon the market-place,
Hooting, and ſhrieking.
I do believe they are portentous things
Unto the climate, that they point upon.

Julius Cæſar, A. 1, S. 3.

To whom do lions caſt their gentle looks?
Not to the beaſt that would uſurp their den.
Whoſe hand is that the foreſt bear doth lick?
Not his, that ſpoils her young before her face.

Henry VI. P. 3, A. 2, S. 2.

Thus yields the cedar to the axe's edge,
Whoſe arms gave ſhelter to the princely eagle,
Under whoſe ſhade the ramping lion ſlept;
Whoſe top branch over-peer'd Jove's ſpreading tree,
And kept low ſhrubs from winter's powerful wind.

Henry VI. P. 3, A. 5, S. 2.

Methought, he bore him in the thickeſt troop,
As doth a lion in a herd of neat;

[1] ——— *prime.*] *Youth*; the ſpring or morning of life. JOHNSON.

Should we not read *pride?* Dr. Johnſon explains prime to mean *youth*; and indeed I do not ſee any other plauſible interpretation that can be given of it. But how does that ſuit with the context? *Happineſs and pride*, may ſignify, I think, the *pride of happineſs*, the proudeſt ſtate of happineſs. TYRWHIT.

I think we ſhould read,

" That happineſs *in* prime can happy call."

i. e. happineſs in the greateſt degree. A. B.

Or as a bear, encompaſs'd round with dogs;
Who having pinch'd a few, and made them cry,
The reſt ſtand all aloof, and bark at him.

Henry VI. P. 3, A. 2, S. 1.

LIVER.

[1] I had rather heat my liver with drinking.

Antony and Cleopatra, A. 1, S. 2.

LOVE, LOVER.

——— Gentle lady,
When I did firſt impart my love to you,
I freely told you, all the wealth I had
Ran in my veins, I was a gentleman;
And then I told you true.

Merchant of Venice, A. 3, S. 2.

Heaven, and fortune, bar me happy hours!
Day, yield me not thy light; nor, night, thy reſt;
Be oppoſite all planets of good luck
To my proceeding, if, with pure heart's love,
Immaculate devotion, holy thoughts,
I tender not thy beauteous princely daughter!

Richard III. A. 4, S. 4.

——— The leiſure, and the fearful time
Cuts off the ceremonious vows of love,
And ample interchange of ſweet diſcourſe,

[1] *I had rather heat my liver with drinking.*] To know why the lady is ſo averſe from *heating her liver*, it muſt be remembered, that a heated liver is ſuppoſed to make a pimpled face.

JOHNSON.

Dr. Johnſon is miſtaken, I believe, in ſuppoſing that the lady is thinking of a pimpled face. The ſeat of love was by ancient writers ſuppoſed to be in the liver. The ſoothſayer ſays to Charmion, "You ſhall be more beloving than belov'd." If that is the caſe, replies ſhe, I had rather heat my liver with drinking than with love. A. B.

Which

Which ſo long ſundred friends ſhould dwell upon,
God give us leiſure for theſe rites of love!

Richard III. A. 5, S. 3.

—— Perhaps, he loves you now;
And now no ſoil, nor cautel, doth beſmirch
The virtue of his will: but, you muſt fear,
His greatneſs weigh'd, his will is not his own;
For he himſelf is ſubject to his birth.

Hamlet, A. 1, S. 3.

O, Hamlet, what a falling off was there!
From me, whoſe love was of that dignity,
That it went hand in hand even with the vow
I made to her in marriage; and to decline
Upon a wretch, whoſe natural gifts were poor
To thoſe of mine! *Hamlet*, A. 1, S. 5.

Haſte me to know it; that I, with wings as ſwift
As meditation, or the thoughts of love,
May ſweep to my revenge. *Hamlet*, A. 1, S. 5.

This is the very ecſtaſy of love:
Whoſe violent property foredoes itſelf,
And leads the will to deſperate undertakings,
As oft as any paſſion under heaven,
That does afflict our natures. *Hamlet*, A. 2, S. 1.

[1] The inſtances, that ſecond marriage move,
Are baſe reſpects of thrift, but none of love.

Hamlet, A. 3, S. 2.

There lives within the very flame of love
A kind of wick, or ſnuff, that will abate it;
And nothing is at a like goodneſs ſtill;
For goodneſs, growing to a pleuriſy,
Dies in his own too much. *Hamlet*, A. 4, S. 7.

[1] *The inſtances.*] The *motives.* JOHNSON.
We ſhould rather explain "inſtances" by *circumſtances.* We cannot well ſay, *the motives that move.* A. B.

All fancy-sick she is, and pale of cheer
With sighs of love.
Midsummer Night's Dream, A. 3, S. 2.

You thief of love! what, have you come by night,
And stol'n my love's heart from him?
Midsummer Night's Dream, A. 3, S. 2.

Lovers and madmen have such seething brains,
Such shaping fantasies that apprehend
More than cool reason ever comprehends.
Midsummer Night's Dream, A. 5, S. 1.

Before the time I did Lysander see,
Seem'd Athens as a paradise to me:
O then, what graces in my love do dwell,
That he hath turn'd a heaven unto a hell!
Midsummer Night's Dream, A. 1, S. 1.

As waggish boys themselves in game forswear,
So the boy Love is perjur'd every where.
Midsummer Night's Dream, A. 1, S. 1.

Ah me! for aught that I could ever read,
Could ever hear by tale or history,
The course of true love never did run smooth.
Midsummer Night's Dream, A. 1, S. 1.

Things base and vile, holding no quantity,
Love can transpose to form and dignity.
Love looks not with the eyes, but with the mind;
And therefore is wing'd Cupid painted blind.
Midsummer Night's Dream, A. 1, S. 1.

Your wrongs do set a scandal on my sex:
We cannot fight for love, as men may do;
We should be woo'd, and were not made to woo.
Midsummer Night's Dream, A. 2, S. 2.

O spirit of love, how quick and fresh art thou!
That, notwithstanding thy capacity
Receiveth as the sea, nought enters there,
But falls into abatement and low price,
Even in a minute! *Twelfth Night*, A. 1, S. 1.

——She

——— She never told her love,
But let concealment, like a worm i' the bud,
Feed on her damaſk cheek.

Twelfth Night, A. 2, S. 4.

O, what a deal of ſcorn looks beautiful
In the contempt and anger of his lip!
A murd'rous guilt ſhews not itſelf more ſoon
Than love that would ſeem hid.

Twelfth Night, A. 3, S. 1.

—— Such as I am, all true lovers are;
Unſtaid and ſkittiſh in all motions elſe,
Save, in the conſtant image of the creature
That is belov'd. *Twelfth Night*, A. 2, S. 4.

——— I cannot love him:
Yet I ſuppoſe him virtuous, know him noble,
Of great eſtate, of freſh and ſtainleſs youth;
And in dimenſion, and the ſhape of nature,
A gracious perſon. *Twelfth Night*, A. 1, S. 5.

Write loyal cantons of contemned love,
Halloo your name to the reverberate hills,
And make the babbling goſſip of the air
Cry out Olivia! *Twelfth Night*, A. 1, S. 5.

If luſty Love ſhould go in queſt of beauty,
Where ſhould he find it fairer than in Blanch?
If zealous Love ſhould go in ſearch of virtue,
Where ſhould he find it purer than in Blanch?
If Love ambitious ſought a match of birth,
Whoſe veins bound richer blood than lady Blanch?

King John, A. 2, S. 2.

He counſels a divorce: a loſs of her,
That, like a jewel, has hung twenty years
About his neck, yet never loſt her luſtre;
Of her, that loves him with that excellence
That angels love good men with; even of her,
That, when the greateſt ſtroke of fortune falls,
Will bleſs the king. *Henry VIII.* A. 2, S. 2.

——— Farewell,
Thou pure impiety, and impious purity!
For thee I'll lock up all the gates of love.
Much ado about nothing, A. 4, S. 1.

I never tempted her with word too large;
But, as a brother to a ſiſter, ſhew'd
Baſhful ſincerity and comely love.
Much ado about nothing, A. 4, S. 1.

I will not be ſworn, but love may transform me to an oyſter; but I'll take my oath on it, till he have made an oyſter of me, he ſhall never make me ſuch a fool. *Much ado about nothing*, A. 2, S. 3.

I do much wonder, that one man, ſeeing how much another man is a fool when he dedicates his behaviours to love, will, after he hath laugh'd at ſuch ſhallow follies in others, become the argument of his own ſcorn, by falling in love.
Much ado about nothing, A. 2, S. 3.

Love me! why, it muſt be requited. I hear how I am cenſured: they ſay, I will bear myſelf proudly, if I perceive the love come from her; they ſay too, that ſhe will rather die than give any ſign of affection.—I did never think to marry:—I muſt not ſeem proud. *Much ado about nothing*, A. 2, S. 3.

——— Loving goes by haps:
Some Cupid kills with arrows, ſome with traps.
Much ado about nothing, A. 3, S. 1.

——— She cannot love,
Nor take no ſhape nor project of affection,
She is ſo ſelf-endeared.
Much ado about nothing, A. 3, S. 1.

They ſay, the lady is fair; 'tis a truth I can bear them witneſs; and virtuous; 'tis ſo, I cannot reprove it: and wiſe—but for loving me:—By my troth, it is no addition to her wit;—nor no great argument

argument of her folly, for I will be horribly in love with her. *Much ado about nothing*, A. 2, S. 3.

If I do not take pity of her, I am a villain; if I do not love her, I am a Jew: I will go get her picture. *Much ado about nothing*, A. 2, S. 3.

If e'er my will did trefpafs 'gainft his love,
Either in difcourfe, or thought, or actual deed;
Or that mine eyes, mine ears, or any fenfe,
Delighted them in any other form;
Or that I do not yet, and ever did,
And ever will,—though he do fhake me off
To beggarly divorcement,—love him dearly,
Comfort forfwear me! *Othello*, A. 4, S. 2.

—— I would do much
To [1] atone them, for the love I bear to Caffio.
Othello, A. 4, S. 1.

I had rather hear my dog bark at a crow, than a man fwear he loves me.
Much ado about nothing, A. 1, S. 1.

How fweetly do you minifter to love,
That know love's grief by his complexion!
Much ado about nothing, A. 1, S. 1.

Prove, that ever I lofe more blood with love, than I will get again with drinking, pick out mine eyes with a ballad-maker's pen, and hang me up at the door of a brothel-houfe for the fign of blind Cupid.
Much ado about nothing, A. 1, S. 1.

Friendfhip is conftant in all other things,
Save in the office and affairs of love:
Therefore, all hearts in love ufe their own tongues;

1 —— *atone them*.] Make them *one*; reconcile them. JOHNSON.
"*Atone* them" feems harfh. Perhaps we may read,
"*Attune* them,"
i. e. Create an harmony between them—reconcile them. A. B.

Let every eye negotiate for itſelf,
And truſt no agent.
Much ado about nothing, A. 2, S. 1.

—— Were 't to renounce his baptiſm,
All ſeals and ſymbols of redeemed ſin,—
His ſoul is ſo enfetter'd to her love,
That ſhe may make, unmake, do what ſhe liſt,
Even as her appetite ſhall play the god
With his weak function. *Othello*, A. 2, S. 3.

[1] What! keep a week away? ſeven days and nights!
Eight ſcore eight hours? and lovers abſent hours,
More tedious than the dial eight ſcore times,
O weary reckoning! *Othello*, A. 3, S. 4.

You know me well: and herein ſpend but time,
To wind about my love with circumſtance:
And, out of doubt, you do me now more wrong,
In making queſtion of my uttermoſt,
Than if you had made waſte of all I have.
Merchant of Venice, A. 1, S. 1.

Bring me the faireſt creature northward born,
Where Phœbus' fire ſcarce thaws the iſicles,
And let us make inciſion for your love,
To prove whoſe blood is reddeſt, his, or mine.
Merchant of Venice, A. 2, S. 1.

I tell thee, lady, this aſpect of mine
Hath fear'd the valiant; by my love, I ſwear,
The beſt regarded virgins of our clime
Have lov'd it too: I would not change this hue,
Except to ſteal your thoughts, my gentle queen.
Merchant of Venice, A. 2, S. 1.

[1] *What! keep a week away?---Seven days and nights!*]

Hui! univorſum triduum! TERENCE.

A. B.

There

There may as well be amity and life
'Tween ſnow and fire, as treaſon and my love.
Merchant of Venice, A. 3, S. 2.

—— Ten times faſter Venus' pigeons fly
To ſeal love's bonds new made, than they are wont,
To keep obliged faith unforfeited!
Merchant of Venice, A. 2, S. 6.

O love, be moderate, allay thy ecſtaſy,
In meaſure rain thy joy, ſcant this exceſs.
I feel too much thy bleſſing, make it leſs.
Merchant of Venice, A. 3, S. 2.

——— Now he goes,
With no leſs preſence [1], but with much more love,
Than young Alcides, when he did redeem
The virgin tribute paid by howling Troy
To the ſea-monſter. *Merchant of Venice*, A. 3, S. 2.

I am undone; there is no living, none,
If Bertram be away. It were all one,
That I ſhould love a bright particular ſtar,
And think to wed it, he is ſo above me.
All's well that ends well, A. 1, S. 1.

——— Fair ſoul,
In your fine frame hath love no quality?
If the quick fire of youth light not your mind,
You are no maiden, but a monument.
All's well that ends well, A. 4, S. 2.

I am aſhamed, that women are ſo ſimple
To offer war where they ſhould kneel for peace;
Or ſeek for rule, ſupremacy, or ſway,
When they are bound to ſerve, love, and obey.
Taming of the Shrew, A. 5, S. 2.

[1] *With no leſs preſence.*] With the ſame *dignity of mien.* JOHNSON.

I think it would be better to read *preſcience*, *i. e.* no leſs confident of ſucceſs. A. B.

Never

Never durſt poet touch a pen to write,
Until his ink were temper'd with love's ſighs;
O, then his lines would raviſh ſavage ears,
And plant in tyrants mild humility.

Love's Labour Loſt, A. 4, S. 3.

—— Love, firſt learned in a lady's eyes,
Lives not alone immured in the brain;
But with the motion of all elements,
Courſes as ſwift as thought in every power.

Love's Labour Loſt, A. 4, S. 3.

What? what? I love! I ſue! I ſeek a wife!
A woman, that is like a German clock,
Still a repairing; ever out of frame;
And never going aright, being a watch,
But being watch'd that it may ſtill go right?

Love's Labour Loſt, A. 3, S. 1.

Adieu, valour! ruſt, rapier! be ſtill, drum! for your manager is in love; yea, he loveth. Aſſiſt me, ſome extemporal god of rhime, for, I am ſure, I ſhall turn ſonnetteer. *Love's Labour Loſt*, A. 1, S. 2.

Love's tongue proves dainty Bacchus groſs in taſte.
As ſweet and muſical,
As bright Apollo's lute, ſtrung with his hair;
[1] And, when Love ſpeaks, the voice of all the gods
Makes heaven drowſy with the harmony.

Love's Labour Loſt, A. 4, S. 3.

[1] *And, when Love ſpeaks, the voice of all the gods*
Makes heaven drowſy with the harmony.] All the editions agree in reading as above, and the commentators have endeavoured to explain it. But why the *voice of love* ſhould make heaven *drowſy*, I do not rightly underſtand. It may very naturally be ſuppoſed to have a totally different effect. We ſhould ſurely read,

"And, when Love ſpeaks, the voice of all the gods
"Wakes drowſy heaven with the harmony."

i. e. Heaven inſtantly becomes enlivened by it—all at once is harmony. It is a ſound to "raviſh all the gods!" &c. A. B.

For

For wiſdom's ſake, a word that all men love;
Or for love's ſake, a word that loves all men;
Or for men's ſake, the authors of theſe women;
Or women's ſake, by whom we men are men;
Let us once loſe our oaths, to find ourſelves.

Love's Labour Loſt, A. 4, S. 3.

—— Love is full of unbefitted ſtrains;
All wanton as a child, ſkipping, and vain;
Form'd by the eye, and, therefore, like the eye,
Full of ſtrange ſhapes, of habits, and of forms.

Love's Labour Loſt, A. 5, S. 2.

If froſts, and faſts, hard lodging, and thin weeds,
Nip not the gaudy bloſſoms of your love,
Then at the expiration of the year,
Come challenge me. *Love's Labour Loſt*, A. 5, S. 2.

—— Tell this youth what 'tis to love.
It is to be made all of ſighs and tears;—
It is to be all made of faith and ſervice;—
It is to be all made of fantaſy,
All made of paſſion, and all made of wiſhes.

As you like it, A. 5, S. 2.

That ſame wicked baſtard of Venus, that was begot of thought, conceived of ſpleen, and born of madneſs; that blind raſcally boy, that abuſes every one's eyes, becauſe his own are out, let him judge, how deep I am in love. *As you like it*, A. 4, S. 1.

There is a man haunts the foreſt, that abuſes our young plants with carving Roſalind on their barks; if I could meet that fancy-monger, I would give him ſome good counſel, for he ſeems to have the quotidian of love upon him.

As you like it, A. 3, S. 2.

He that will divide a minute into a thouſand parts, and break but a part of the thouſandth part of a minute in the affairs of love, it may be ſaid of him, that

that Cupid hath clapt him o' the ſhoulder; but I warrant him heart-whole. *As you like it*, A. 4, S. 1.

Your hoſe ſhould be ungarter'd, your bonnet unbanded, your ſleeve unbuttoned, your ſhoe untied, and every thing about you demonſtrating a careleſs deſolation. But you are no ſuch man; you are rather point-device in your accoutrements; as loving yourſelf, than ſeeming the lover of any other.

As you like it, A. 3, S. 2.

It is as eaſy to count atomies, as to reſolve the propoſitions of a lover. *As you like it*, A. 3, S. 2.

Say, that you love me not; but ſay not ſo
In bitterneſs: the common executioner,
Whoſe heart the accuſtom'd ſight of death makes
hard,
Falls not the axe upon the humbled neck,
But firſt begs pardon. *As you like it*, A. 3, S. 5.

O coz, coz, coz, my pretty little coz, that thou didſt know how many fathom deep I am in love! But it cannot be ſounded; my affection hath an unknown bottom, like the bay of Portugal.

As you like it, A. 4, S. 1.

Me believe it? you may as ſoon make her that you love believe it; which, I warrant, ſhe is apter to do, than to confeſs ſhe does; that is one of the points in the which women ſtill give the lie to their conſciences.

As you like it, A. 3, S. 2.

If ever (as that ever may be near)
You meet in ſome freſh cheek the power of fancy [1];
Then ſhall you know the wounds inviſible
That love's keen arrows make.

As you like it, A. 3, S. 5.

1 ——— *power of fancy*.] *Fancy* is here uſed for *love*.
JOHNSON.

I rather think that *fancy*, in this place, is *thought*, *deep reflection*.
A. B.

I have neither the ſcholar's melancholy, which is emulation; nor the muſician's, which is fantaſtical; nor the courtier's, which is proud; nor the ſoldier's, which is ambitious; nor the lawyer's, which is politick; nor the lady's, which is nice; nor the lover's, which is all theſe. *As you like it*, A. 4, S. 1.

Think not I love him, though I aſk for him;
'Tis but a peeviſh boy:—yet he talks well;—
But what care I for words? yet words do well,
When he that ſpeaks them pleaſes thoſe that hear.
As you like it, A. 3, S. 5.

Miſtreſs, know yourſelf, down on your knees,
And thank heaven, faſting, for a good man's love:
For I muſt tell you friendly in your ear,—
Sell when you can; you are not for all markets.
As you like it, A. 3, S. 5.

The oath of a lover is no ſtronger than the word of a tapſter; they are both the confirmers of falſe reckonings. *As you like it*, A. 3, S. 4.

——— Then, the lover;
Sighing like furnace, with a woful ballad
Made to his miſtreſs' eye-brow.
As you like it, A. 2, S. 7.

If thou remember'ſt not the ſlighteſt folly
That ever love did make thee run into,
Thou haſt not lov'd. *As you like it*, A. 2, S. 4.

If thou haſt not ſat, as I do now,
Wearying thy hearer in thy miſtreſs' praiſe,
Thou haſt not lov'd. *As you like it*, A. 2, S. 4.

If thou haſt not broke from company,
Abruptly, as my paſſion now makes me,
Thou haſt not lov'd. *As you like it*, A. 2, S. 4.

——Know, my love, as eaſy mayſt thou fall
A drop of water in the breaking gulph,
And take unmingled thence that drop again,

Without

Without addition, or diminiſhing,
As take from me thyſelf, and not me too.

Comedy of Errors, A. 2, S. 2.

— Since the heavens have ſhap'd my body ſo,
Let hell make crook'd my mind, to anſwer it.
I had no father, I am like no father:
I have no brother, I am like no brother:
And this word—love, which grey-beards call divine,
Be reſident in men like one another,
And not in me. *Henry VI.* P. 3, A. 5, S. 6.

Love forſwore me in my mother's womb:
And, for I ſhould not deal in her ſoft laws,
She did corrupt frail nature with ſome bribe
To ſhrink mine arm up like a wither'd ſhrub;
To make an envious mountain on my back,
Where ſits deformity to mock my body;
And am I then a man to be belov'd?

Henry VI. P. 3, A. 3, S. 2.

— She, whom all men praiſed, and whom myſelf,
Since I have loſt, have lov'd, was in mine eye
The duſt that did offend it.

All's well that ends well, A. 5, S. 3.

I know I love in vain, ſtrive againſt hope;
Yet, in this captious and intenable ſieve,
I ſtill pour in the waters of my love,
And lack not to loſe ſtill.

All's well that ends well, A. 1, S. 3.

To each of you one fair and virtuous miſtreſs
Fall, when love pleaſe!—[1] marry, to each but one!

All's well that ends well, A. 2, S. 3.

—— This

[1] —— *marry, to each but one!*] I cannot underſtand this paſſage in any other ſenſe than as a ludicrous exclamation, in conſequence of Helena's wiſh of *one* fair and virtuous miſtreſs *to each* of the lords. If that be ſo, it cannot belong to Helena; and might properly enough be given to Parolles. Tyrwhit.

The

[1] —— This has no holding,
To ſwear by him whom I proteſt to love,
That I will work againſt him.

All's well that ends well, A. 4, S. 2.

—— Holy father; throw away that thought;—
Believe not that the dribbling dart of love
Can pierce a complete boſom.

Meaſure for Meaſure, A. 1, S. 4.

O, bid me leap, rather than marry Paris,
From off the battlements of yonder tower;
Or walk in thieviſh ways; or bid me lurk
Where ſerpents are; chain me with roaring bears;
Or hide me nightly in a charnel houſe,
Things that, to hear them told, have made me tremble;
And I will do it without fear or doubt,
To live an unſtain'd wife to my ſweet love.

Romeo and Juliet, A. 4, S. 1.

It was the lark, the herald of the morn,
No nightingale: look, love, what envious ſtreaks
Do lace the ſevering clouds in yonder eaſt:
Night's candles are burnt out, and jocund day
Stands tip-toe on the miſty mountains tops.

Romeo and Juliet, A. 3, S. 5.

The entire ſpeech belongs to Helena. "But one" means, *with an exception to Bertram.* She would inſinuate, that *love* is not to give him a miſtreſs, as ſhe herſelf aſſumes love's power, and means to lay claim to Bertram. A. B.

[1] —— *this has no holding,*
To ſwear by him whom I proteſt to love,
That I will work againſt him.] This paſſage appears to me corrupt. She ſwears not *by* him whom ſhe *loves*, but by *Jupiter*. I believe we may read to *ſwear* to *him*. There is, ſays ſhe, no *holding*, no conſiſtency to ſwear to one that I *love him*, when I ſwear it only to *injure* him. JOHNSON.

Helena certainly ſwears *by Jupiter*, and not *to her lover*, as Dr. Johnſon ſuppoſes. I read,

"—— this has no holding,
"To ſwear by him, and to proteſt I love
"Whom I will work againſt." A. B.

Wilt

Wilt thou be gone! it is not yet near day:
It was the nightingale, and not the lark,
That pierc'd the fearful hollow of thine ear;
Nightly ſhe ſings on yon pomegranate tree:
Believe me, love, it was the nightingale.

Romeo and Juliet, A. 3, S. 5.

——— O, my love! my wife!
Death, that hath ſuck'd the honey of thy breath,
Hath had no power yet upon thy beauty:
Thou art not conquer'd; beauty's enſign yet
Is crimſon in thy lips, and in thy cheeks,
And death's pale flag is not advanced there.

Romeo and Juliet, A. 5, S. 3.

——— I beſeech thee, youth,
Pull not another ſin upon my head,
By urging me to fury:—O be gone!
By heaven, I love thee better than myſelf;
For I come hither arm'd againſt myſelf.

Romeo and Juliet, A. 5, S. 3.

—— Love's heralds ſhould be thoughts,
Which ten times faſter glide than the ſun's beams
Driving back ſhadows over low'ring hills:
Therefore do nimble-pinion'd doves draw love,
And therefore hath the wind-ſwift Cupid wings.

Romeo and Juliet, A. 2, S. 5.

Doſt thou love me? I know, thou wilt ſay—Ay;
And I will take thy word; yet, if thou ſwear'ſt,
Thou mayſt prove falſe; at lovers' perjuries,
They ſay, Jove laughs.

Romeo and Juliet, A. 2, S. 2.

—— O brawling love! O loving hate!
O any thing, of nothing firſt created!
O heavy lightneſs! ſerious vanity!
Miſſhapen chaos of well-ſeeming forms!
Feather of lead, bright ſmoke, cold fire, ſick health!
Still-waking ſleep. *Romeo and Juliet*, A. 1, S. 1.

Love is a ſmoke rais'd with the fume of ſighs;
Being purg'd, a fire ſparkling in lover's eyes [1];
Being vex'd, a ſea nouriſh'd with lover's tears:
What is it elſe? a madneſs moſt diſcreet,
A choaking gall, and a preſerving ſweet.

Romeo and Juliet, A. 1, S. 1.

If that the Dauphin there, thy princely ſon,
Can in this book of beauty read, I love,
Her dowry ſhall weigh equal with a queen:
As ſhe in beauty, education, blood,
Holds hand with any princeſs of the world.

King John, A. 2, S. 2.

I have done penance for contemning love;
Whoſe high imperious thoughts have puniſh'd me
With bitter faſts, with penitential groans,
With nightly tears, and daily heart-ſore ſighs.

Two Gentlemen of Verona, A. 2, S. 4.

What ſhould it be, that he reſpects in her,
But I can make reſpective in myſelf,
If this fond love were not a blinded god?

Two Gentlemen of Verona, A. 4, S. 3.

This weak impreſs of love is as a figure
Trenched in ice; which with an hour's heat
Diſſolves to water, and doth loſe his form.

Two Gentlemen of Verona, A. 3, S. 2.

Here is my hand for my true conſtancy;
And when that hour o'er-ſlips me in the day,
Wherein I ſigh not, Julia, for thy ſake,

[1] *Being purg'd, a fire ſparkling in lover's eyes.*] The author may mean, being *purged of ſmoke*, but it is, perhaps, a meaning never given to the word in any other place. I would rather read, *being urged, a fire ſparkling*. Being incited and inforced. To *urge* the fire is the technical term. JOHNSON.

I do not believe that "purg'd" has any reference to *ſmoke*. "Being purg'd," is *being pure*. Love, ſays the poet, is for the moſt part as a ſmoke; but when pure, it is as a fire, &c.
A. B.

The next ensuing hour some foul mischance
Torment me for my love's forgetfulness!

Two Gentlemen of Verona, A. 2, S. 2.

——— Hinder not my course:
I'll be as patient as a gentle stream,
And make a pastime of each weary step,
Till the last step have brought me to my love.

Two Gentlemen of Verona, A. 2, S. 7.

——— Now my love is thaw'd;
Which, like a waxen image 'gainst a fire,
Bears no impression of the thing it was.

Two Gentlemen of Verona, A. 2, S. 4.

I to myself am dearer than a friend;
For love is still more precious in itself:
And Silvia, witness heaven, that made her fair,
Shews Julia but a swarthy Ethiope.

Two Gentlemen of Verona, A. 2, S. 6.

[1] O, sweet-suggesting love, if thou hast sinn'd,
Teach me, thy tempted subject, to excuse it!

Two Gentlemen of Verona, A. 2, S. 6.

Even as one heat another heat expels,
Or as one nail by strength drives out another,
So the remembrance of my former love
Is by a newer object quite forgotten.

Two Gentlemen of Verona, A. 2, S. 4.

——— Love's a mighty lord,
And hath so humbled me, as, I confess,

[1] *O, sweet-suggesting love.*] To *suggest* is to *tempt*, in our author's language. The sense is, *O, tempting love, if thou hast influenced me to sin, teach me to excuse it.* Dr. Warburton reads, *If I have sinn'd*; but, I think, not only without necessity, but with less elegance. JOHNSON.

"Sweet-suggesting" has something more than *tempting* in it. It means *inspiring*, or *soul-inspiring*. Beside, *tempted* occurs in the following line. We should surely read—*If I have sinn'd.* A. B.

There is no woe to his correction,
Nor, to his service, no such joy on earth!
Two Gentlemen of Verona, A. 2, S. 4.

Were't not affection chains thy tender days
To the sweet glances of thy honour'd love,
I rather would entreat thy company,
To see the wonders of the world abroad,
Than living dully sluggardiz'd at home,
Wear out thy youth with shapeless idleness.
Two Gentlemen of Verona, A. 1, S. 1.

—— As in the sweetest bud
The eating canker dwells, so eating love
Inhabits in the finest wits of all.
Two Gentlemen of Verona, A. 1, S. 1.

—— Love, where scorn is bought with groans;
Coy looks, with heart-sore sighs.
Two Gentlemen of Verona, A. 1, S. 1.

—— As the most forward bud
Is eaten by the canker ere it blow,
Even so by love the young and tender wit
Is turn'd to folly.
Two Gentlemen of Verona, A. 1, S. 1.

Love is your master, for he masters you;
And he that is so yoked by a fool,
Methinks should not be chronicled for wise.
Two Gentlemen of Verona, A. 1, S. 1.

Fie, fie! how wayward is this foolish love,
That, like a testy babe, will scratch the nurse,
And presently, all humbled, kiss the rod.
Two Gentlemen of Verona, A. 1, S. 2.

L U S T.

That incestuous, that adulterate beast,
With witchcraft of his wit, with traiterous gifts,
(O wicked wit, and gifts, that have the power

So to ſeduce!) won to his ſhameful luſt
The will of my moſt ſeeming-virtuous queen:

Hamlet, A. 1, S. 5.

[1] —— His captain's heart,
Which in the ſcuffles of great fights hath burſt
The buckles on his breaſt, reneges all temper;
And is become the bellows, and the fan,
To cool a gypſy's luſt.

Antony and Cleopatra, A. 1, S. 1.

LIE, LYING.

Manhood is melted into courteſies, valour into compliment, and men are only turned into tongue, and trim ones too: he is now as valiant as Hercules, that only tells a lie, and ſwears it.

Much ado about nothing, A. 4, S. 1.

O ſir, we quarrel in print, by the book; I will name you the degrees. The firſt, the retort courteous; the ſecond, the quip modeſt; the third, the reply churliſh; the fourth, the reproof valiant; the fifth, the counter-check quarrelſome; the ſixth, the lie with circumſtance; the ſeventh, the lie direct; and you may avoid that too, with an if. I knew when ſeven juſtices could not take up a quarrel; but when the parties were met themſelves, one of them thought but of an If, as, If you ſaid ſo, then I ſaid ſo; and they ſhook hands, and ſwore brothers. Your If is the only peace-maker; much virtue in If.

As you like it, A. 5, S. 4.

I did diſlike the cut of a certain courtier's beard; he ſent me word, if I ſaid his beard was not cut well, he was in the mind it was: this is called the retort courteous. If I ſent him word again, it was not well

[1] —— *his captain's heart, &c.*] I ſhould prefer—his *captain-heart, i. e.* his bold, and daring ſpirit.
The mark of the genitive caſe obſcures the meaning. A. B.

cut,

cut, he would ſend me word, he cut it to pleaſe himſelf: this is called the quip modeſt. If again, it was not well cut, he diſabled my judgment: this is called the reply churliſh. If again, it was not well cut, he would anſwer, I ſpake not true: this is called the reproof valiant. If again, it was not well cut, he would ſay I lie: this is called the counter-check quarrelſome; and ſo to the lie circumſtantial, and the lie direct. *As you like it*, A. 5, S. 4.

Let me have no lying; it becomes none but tradeſmen. *Winter's Tale*, A. 4, S. 3.

—— Will poor folk lie,
That have afflictions on them; knowing 'tis
A puniſhment, or trial? Yes, no wonder,
When rich ones ſcarce tell true: to lapſe in fullneſs
Is ſorer, than to lie for need; and falſehood
Is worſe in kings, than beggars.
Cymbeline, A. 3, S. 6.

Lord, lord, how this world is given to lying!—I grant you, I was down, and out of breath; and ſo was he: but we roſe both at an inſtant, and fought a long hour by Shrewſbury clock. If I may be believ'd, ſo; if not, let them, that ſhould reward valour, bear the ſin upon their own heads.
Henry IV. P. 1, A. 5, S. 4.

M.

MADNESS.

—— SINCE I ſaw thee,
The affliction of my mind amends, with which,
I fear a madneſs held me. *Tempeſt*, A. 5, S. 1.

——— Sometimes am I
All wound with adders, who with cloven tongues,
Do hiſs me into madneſs. *Tempeſt*, A. 2, S. 2.

Not a ſoul
But felt a fever of the mad, and play'd
Some tricks of deſperation. *Tempeſt*, A. 1, S. 2.

——— Mother, for love of grace,
Lay not that flattering unction to your ſoul,
That not your treſpaſs, but my madneſs, ſpeaks;
It will but ſkin and film the ulcerous place;
Whiles rank corruption, mining all within,
Infects unſeen. *Hamlet*, A. 3, S. 4.

This is mere madneſs:
And thus awhile the fit will work on him;
Anon, as patient as the female dove,
When that her golden couplets are diſclos'd,
His ſilence will ſit drooping. *Hamlet*, A. 5, S. 1.

My pulſe, as yours, doth temperately keep time,
And makes as healthful muſic: it is not madneſs,
That I have utter'd: bring me to the teſt,
And I the matter will reword; which madneſs
Would gambol from. *Hamlet*, A. 3, S. 4.

——— He was met even now
As mad as the vex'd ſea: ſinging aloud;
Crown'd with rank fumiter, and furrow weeds,
With harlocks, hemlocks, nettles, cuckow-flowers,
Darnel, all the idle weeds that grow
In our ſuſtaining corn. *Lear*, A. 4, S. 4.

[1] How pregnant ſometimes his replies are! a happineſs that often madneſs hits on, which reaſon and ſanity could not ſo proſperouſly be delivered of.
Hamlet, A. 2, S. 2.

[1] *How pregnant, &c.*] *Pregnant* is ready, dexterous, apt.
STEEVENS.

"Pregnant" is ſomething more than dexterous, or apt. It here means, *full of conſequence.* A. B.

Mad

Mad let us grant him then: and now remains,
That we find out the cauſe of this effect;
Or, rather ſay, the cauſe of this defect;
For this effect, defective, comes by cauſe.
Hamlet, A. 2, S. 2.

That he is mad, 'tis true: 'tis true 'tis pity;
And pity 'tis, 'tis true: a fooliſh figure;
But farewell it, for I will uſe no art.
Hamlet, A. 2, S. 2.

What, if it tempt you toward the flood, my lord?
Or to the dreadful ſummit of the cliff,
That bettles o'er his baſe into the ſea?
And there aſſume ſome other horrible form,
Which might deprive your ſovereignty of reaſon
And draw you into madneſs? *Hamlet*, A. 1, S. 4.

——— He made me mad,
To ſee him ſhine ſo briſk, and ſmell ſo ſweet,
And talk ſo like a waiting-gentlewoman,
Of guns, and drums, and wounds, (God ſave the mark!)
And telling me, the ſovereign'ſt thing on earth,
Was parmacity for an inward bruiſe.
Henry IV. P. 1, A. 1, S. 3.

Be Kent unmannerly, when Lear is mad.
Think'ſt thou that duty ſhall have dread to ſpeak,
When power to flattery bows? To plainneſs honour's bound,
When majeſty ſtoops to folly. *Lear*, A. 1, S. 1.

Her madneſs hath the oddeſt frame of ſenſe,
Such a dependency of thing on thing,
As e'er I heard in madneſs.
Meaſure for Meaſure, A. 5, S. 1.

MAJESTY.

Now will it beſt avail your majeſty,
To croſs the ſeas, and to be crown'd in France:

The presence of a king engenders love
Amongst his subjects, and his loyal friends.
Henry VI. P. 1, A. 3, S. 1.

—— The cease of majesty
Dies not alone; but, like a gulf, doth draw
What's near it, with it: it is a massy wheel,
Fix'd on the summit of the highest mount,
To whose huge spokes ten thousand lesser things
Are mortis'd and adjoin'd, which, when it falls,
Each small annexment, petty consequence,
Attends the boisterous ruin. *Hamlet*, A. 3, S. 3.

—— To beg
Enfranchisement immediate on his knees:
Which on the royal party granted once,
His glittering arms he will commend to rust,
His barbed steeds to stables, and his heart
To faithful service of your majesty.
Richard II. A. 3, S. 3.

—— O majesty!
When thou dost pinch thy bearer, thou dost sit
Like a rich armour worn in heat of day,
That scalds with safety.
Henry IV. P. 2, A. 4, S. 4.

With many holiday and lady terms
He question'd me; among the rest, demanded
My prisoners, in your majesty's behalf.
Henry IV. P. 1, A. 1, S. 3.

MALICE.

Kneel not to me:
The power that I have on you, is to spare you:
The malice towards you, to forgive you; live,
And deal with others better. *Cymbeline*, A. 5, S. 5.

Fie, uncle Beaufort! I have heard you preach,
That malice was a great and grievous sin:

And will not you maintain the thing you teach,
But prove a chief offender in the ſame?
Henry VI. P. 1. A. 3, S. 1.

MAN.

—— Eſpous'd to death, with blood he ſeal'd
A teſtament of noble-ending love.
The pretty and ſweet manner of it forc'd
Thoſe waters from me, which I would have ſtopp'd;
But I had not ſo much of man in me,
But all my mother came into mine eyes,
And gave me up to tears. *Henry V.* A. 4, S. 6.

—— In ſuch caſes,
Men's natures wrangle with inferior things,
Though great ones are their object. 'Tis ev'n ſo.
For let our finger ach, and it endues
Our other healthful members, ev'n to a ſenſe
Of pain [1]. *Othello*, A. 3, S. 4.

Yet ſhe muſt die, elſe ſhe'll betray more men.
Put out the light, and then—Put out the light!
If I quench thee, thou flaming miniſter,
I can again thy former light reſtore
Should I repent me:—but once put out thy light,
Thou cunning'ſt pattern of excelling nature,
I know not where is that Promethean heat,
That can thy light relumine. *Othello*, A. 5, S. 2.

Bring me unto my trial when you will.
Dy'd he not in his bed? where ſhould he die?

[1] *For let our finger ach, and it endues*
Our other healthful members, with a ſenſe
Of pain.] I believe it ſhould be rather *ſubdues* our other healthful members to a ſenſe of pain. JOHNSON.

"Endues," I believe, ſhould be *induces*; i. e. *brings on*, *ſuper-induces*. The paſſage ſhould be printed thus:
"For let our finger ach, and it induces
"A ſenſe of pain e'en to our healthful members."
A. B.

Can

Can I make men live, whe'r they will or no?—
Oh! torture me no more, I will confefs.

Henry VI. P. 2, A. 3, S. 3.

Gratiano fpeaks an infinite deal of nothing, more than any man in all Venice: his reafons are as two grains of wheat hid in two bufhels of chaff; you fhall feek all day ere you find them; and, when you have them, they are not worth the fearch.

Merchant of Venice, A. 1, S. 1.

If to do, were as eafy as to know what were good to do, chapels had been churches, and poor men's cottages, prince's palaces.

Merchant of Venice, A. 1, S. 2.

The painting is almoft the natural man;
For fince difhonour trafficks with man's nature,
He is but outfide: thefe pencil'd figures are
Even fuch as they give out.

Timon of Athens, A. 1, S. 1.

A barren-fpirited fellow, one that feeds
On objects, arts, and imitations;
Which, out of ufe, and ftal'd by other men,
Begin his fafhion: do not talk of him,
But as a property. *Julius Cæfar*, A. 4, S. 1.

Oh, what may man within him hide,
Though angel on the outward fide!

Meafure for Meafure, A. 3, S. 2.

——— Difhoneft wretch!
Wilt thou be made a man out of my vice?

Meafure for Meafure, A. 3, S. 1.

——— When maidens fue,
Men give like gods.

Meafure for Meafure, A. 1, S. 5.

Could great men thunder
As Jove himfelf does, Jove would ne'er be quiet,

For

For every pelting [1], petty officer,
Would uſe his heaven for thunder.

Meaſure for Meaſure, A. 2, S. 2.

——— Man! proud man,
(Dreſt in a little brief authority;
Moſt ignorant of what he's moſt aſſur'd,
His glaſſy eſſence) like an angry ape,
Plays ſuch fantaſtic tricks before high heaven,
As make the angels weep.

Meaſure for Meaſure, A. 2, S. 2.

Great men may jeſt with ſaints: 'tis wit in them;
But, in the leſs, foul profanation.

Meaſure for Meaſure, A. 2, S. 2.

——— Men ſo noble,
However faulty, yet ſhould find reſpect
For what they have been: 'tis a cruelty,
To load a falling man. *Henry VIII.* A. 5, S. 2.

——— Men, that make
Envy, and crooked malice, nouriſhment,
Dare bite the beſt. *Henry VIII.* A. 5, S. 2.

—— This imperious man will work us all
From princes into pages; all men's honours
Lie like one lump before him, to be faſhion'd
Into what pitch he pleaſe. *Henry VIII.* A. 2, S. 2.

——— He was a man
Of an unbounded ſtomach, ever ranking
Himſelf with princes; one, that by ſuggeſtion
Ty'd all the kingdom: ſimony was fair play;
His own opinion was his law: I' the preſence
He would ſay untruths; and be ever double,
Both in his words and meaning: he was never,
But where he meant to ruin, pitiful:

[1] ——— *pelting.*] *i. e.* Paltry. STEEVENS.
"Pelting" is *noiſy, turbulent.* See note on King Lear, page 45.
A. B.

His

His promiſes were, as he then was, mighty;
But his performance, as he is now, nothing.
Henry VIII. A. 4, S. 2.

[1] I ſee, that men make hopes in ſuch affairs,
That we'll forſake ourſelves. Give me that ring.
All's well that ends well, A. 4, S. 2.

—— The jewel, beſt enamelled,
Will loſe his beauty; and the gold 'bides ſtill,
That others touch; yet often touching will
Wear gold: and ſo no man, that hath a name,
But falſehood and corruption doth it ſhame.
Comedy of Errors, A. 2, S. 1.

— Wiſe men ne'er ſit and wail their loſs,
But cheerly ſeek how to redreſs their harms.
What though the maſt be now blown over-board,
The cable broke, our holding anchor loſt,
And half our ſailors ſwallow'd in the flood?
Yet lives our pilot ſtill. *Henry VI.* P. 3, A. 5, S. 4.

A lioneſs, with udders all drawn dry,
Lay couching, head on ground, with cat-like watch,
When that the ſleeping man ſhould ſtir; for 'tis

[1] *I ſee that men make hopes in ſuch affairs.*] The folio editions read:

"—— make ropes in ſuch a ſcarre."

The emendation was introduced by Mr. Rowe. Ray ſays, that *ſcarre* is a cliff of a rock, or a naked rock on dry land, from the Saxon *carre*, cautes. STEEVENS.

"Make ropes in ſuch a ſcarre." The paſſage is undoubtedly corrupt; but the reading propoſed by Mr. Rowe is poor and bald indeed! If for "ropes" we read *japes*, and for "ſcarre" *ſcathe*, both which words were eaſily miſtaken in tranſcribing, we ſhall, I believe, diſcover the meaning of the ſpeech. *Jape* is *jeſt*, and *ſcathe* is *injury*. I read,

"I ſee that men make japes of ſuch a ſcathe:
"That we'll forſake ourſelves."

i. e. "I know that men are apt to make a jeſt of ſuch injuries, and to think that they may rely on our weakneſs for ſucceſs."

This is the language which a woman of virtue may well be ſuppoſed to hold to the man who is endeavouring to ſeduce her.
A. B.

The

The royal diſpoſition of that beaſt,
To prey on nothing that doth ſeem as dead.
As you like it, A. 4, S. 3.

Under an oak, whoſe boughs were moſs'd with age,
And high top bald with dry antiquity,
A wretched ragged man, o'ergrown with hair,
Lay ſleeping on his back. *As you like it*, A. 4, S. 3.

Men are April when they woo, December when they wed: maids are May when they are maids, but the ſky changes when they are wives.
As you like it, A. 4, S. 1.

When a man's verſes cannot be underſtood, nor a man's good wit ſeconded with the forward child, underſtanding, it ſtrikes a man more dead than a great reckoning in a little room.
As you like it, A. 3, S. 3.

If ever I thank any man, I'll thank you: but that they call compliment, is like the encounter of two dog-apes. *As you like it*, A. 2, S. 5.

—— Now 'tis odds beyond arithmetick;
And manhood is call'd foolery, when it ſtands
Againſt a falling fabrick. *Coriolanus*, A. 3, S. 1.

A man of ſovereign parts he is eſteem'd:
Well fitted in the arts, glorious in arms:
Nothing becomes him ill that he would well.
Love's Labour Loſt, A. 2, S. 1.

——— Man—how dearly ever parted,
Cannot make boaſt to have that which he hath,
Nor feels not what he owes, but by reflection;
As when his virtues ſhining upon others
Heat them, and they retort that heat again
To the firſt giver. *Troilus and Creſſida*, A. 3, S. 3.

——— O ſtrange men!
That can ſuch ſweet uſe make of what they hate,
When

When ſaucy truſting of the cozen'd thoughts
Defiles the pitchy night!
All's well that ends well, A. 4, S. 4.

A moſt incomparable man; breath'd, as it were,
To an untirable and continuate goodneſs:
He paſſes [1]. *Timon of Athens*, A. 1, S. 1.

Smooth runs the water, where the brook is deepeſt;
And in his ſimple ſhew he harbours treaſon.
The fox barks not, when he would ſteal the lamb.
No, no, my ſovereign; Gloſter is a man
Unſounded yet, and full of deep deceit.
Henry VI. P. 2, A. 3, S. 1.

—— Plagues incident to men,
Your potent and infectious fevers heap
On Athens, ripe for ſtroke! thou cold ſciatica,
Cripple our ſenators, that their limbs may halt
As lamely as their manners!
Timon of Athens, A. 4, S. 1.

—— He ne'er drinks
But Timon's ſilver treads upon his lip;
And yet, (O, ſee the monſtrouſneſs of man,
When he looks out in an ungrateful ſhape!)
He does deny him. *Timon of Athens*, A. 3, S. 2.

Timon will to the woods, where he ſhall find
The unkindeſt beaſt more kinder than mankind.
The gods confound (hear me, ye good gods all)
The Athenians both within and out that wall!
And grant, as Timon grows, his hate may grow
To the whole race of mankind, high, and low!
Timon of Athens, A. 4, S. 1.

[1] *He paſſes.*] *i. e.* He exceeds:—Goes beyond common bounds.
STEEVENS.

Shakeſpeare had compared Timon to an horſe breathed or exerciſed for the courſe. He ſtill preſerves the ſimile, and ſays, that Timon *paſſes*, i. e. gets before or outſtrips others in goodneſs.
A. B.

—— Be

——— Be abhorr'd
All feasts, societies, and throngs of men!
His semblable, yea, himself, Timon disdains:
Destruction fang mankind!

Timon of Athens, A. 4, S. 3.

I am misanthropos, and hate mankind.
For thy part, I do wish thou wert a dog,
That I might love thee something.

Timon of Athens, A. 4, S. 3.

Promise me friendship, but perform none: if
Thou wilt not promise, the gods plague thee, for
Thou art a man! if thou dost perform, confound thee,
For thou art a man! *Timon of Athens*, A. 4, S. 3.

Upon my life, she finds, although I cannot,
Myself to be a marvellous proper man.
I'll be at charges for a looking-glass;
And entertain a score or two of taylors,
To study fashions to adorn my body.

Richard III. A. 1, S. 2.

——— Common mother, thou
Whose womb unmeasurable, and infinite breast,
Teems, and feeds all; whose self-same mettle,
Whereof thy proud child, arrogant man, is puft,
Engenders the black toad, and adder blue,
The gilded newt, and eyeless venom'd worm,
Yield him, who all thy human souls doth hate,
From forth thy plenteous bosom one poor root!

Timon of Athens, A. 4, S. 3.

Sweet prince, the untainted virtue of your years
Hath not yet div'd into the world's deceit:
No more can you distinguish of a man,
Than of his outward shew; which, God he knows,
Seldom, or never, jumpeth with the heart.

Richard III. A. 3, S. 1.

Let's

[1] Let's levy men, and beat him back again.
Henry VI. P. 3, A. 4, S. 8.

By heaven, I cannot flatter; I defy
The tongues of foothers; but a braver place
In my heart's love, hath no man than yourfelf.
Henry IV. P. 1, A. 4, S. 1.

What! old acquaintance! could not all this flefh
Keep in a little life? Poor Jack, farewell!
I could have better fpar'd a better man.
Henry IV. P. 1, A. 5, S. 4.

I tax not you, you elements, with unkindnefs,
I never gave you kingdoms, call'd you children,
You owe me no fubfcription; why then let fall
Your horrible pleafure; here I ftand, your flave,
A poor, infirm, weak, and defpis'd old man.
Lear, A. 3, S. 2.

Is man no more than this? Confider him well: thou oweft the worm no filk, the beaft no hide, the fheep no wool, the cat no perfume:——thou art the thing itfelf: unaccommodated man is no more but fuch a poor, bare, forked animal as thou art.
Lear, A. 3, S. 4.

What's the matter? If it be fummer news,
Smile to't before: if winterly, thou need'ft

[1] *Let's levy men, and beat him back again.*] This line expreffes a fpirit of war fo unfuitable to the character of Henry, that I would give the firft cold fpeech to the king, and the brifk anfwer to Warwick. JOHNSON.

Every judicious reader muft concur in this opinion. STEEVENS.

It matters little to whom the line is given. Dr. Johnfon's reafon for taking it from Henry, however, is not very forcible. A king who had been imprifoned, and who had recently regained his liberty, might very well throw out a wifh for "levying forces," and for beating back the man who was endeavouring to deprive him of his crown. This is furely highly natural, though a "fpirit of war" were no way confonant to his general character. A. B.

But

But keep that countenance ſtill.—Speak man, thy tongue
May take off ſome extremity, which to read
Would be even mortal to me.

Cymbeline, A. 3, S. 4.

It hath been taught us from the primal ſtate,
That he, which is, was wiſh'd until he were;
And the ebb'd man, ne'er lov'd, till ne'er worth love,
Comes dear'd, by being lack'd.

Antony and Cleopatra, A. 1, S. 4.

A great man, I'll warrant; I know, by the picking on's teeth. *Winter's Tale*, A. 4, S. 3.

—— He cannot be a perfect man,
Not being try'd, and tutor'd in the world.

Two Gentlemen of Verona, A. 1, S. 3.

—— Give me that man
That is not paſſion's ſlave, and I will wear him
In my heart's core, ay, in my heart of heart,
As I do thee. *Hamlet*, A. 3, S. 2.

What a piece of work is man! How noble in reaſon! how infinite in faculties! in form, and moving, how expreſs and admirable! in action, how like an angel! in apprehenſion, how like a god! the beauty of the world! the paragon of animals! And yet, to me, what is this quinteſſence of duſt?

Hamlet, A. 2, S. 2.

—— From his cradle,
He was a ſcholar, and a ripe, and good one:
Exceeding wiſe, fair ſpoken, and perſuading:
Lofty and ſour, to them that lov'd him not;
But, to thoſe men that ſought him, ſweet as ſummer;
And, to add greater honours to his age
Than man could give him, he dy'd, fearing God.

Henry VIII. A. 4, S. 2.

——— She wiſh'd
That heaven had made her ſuch a man: ſhe thank'd me:
And bad me, if I had a friend that lov'd her,
I ſhould but teach him how to tell my ſtory,
And that would woo her. *Othello*, A. 1, S. 3.

Good my complexion[1]! doſt thou think, though I am capariſon'd like a man, I have a doublet and hoſe in my diſpoſition? *As you like it*, A. 3, S. 2.

Men ſhould be what they ſeem;
Or, thoſe that be not, would they might ſeem none!
Othello, A. 3, S. 3.

He was a man, take him for all in all,
I ſhall not look upon his like again.
Hamlet, A. 1, S. 2.

O maſters! if I were diſpos'd to ſtir
Your hearts and minds to mutiny and rage,
I ſhould do Brutus wrong, and Caſſius wrong,
Who, you all know, are honourable men:
I will not do them wrong; I rather chooſe

[1] *Good my complexion!*] This is a mode of expreſſion, Mr. Theobald ſays, *which he cannot reconcile to common ſenſe.* Like enough; and ſo too the Oxford editor. But the meaning is, *hold good my complexion*, i. e. let me not bluſh. WARBURTON.

Dr. Warburton's explanation may be juſt, but as he gives no example of ſuch a meaning affixed to the words in queſtion, we are ſtill at liberty to ſuſpend our faith, till ſome luckier critic ſhall decide. All I can add is, that *paint* for the face was in Shakeſpeare's time called complexion. Shakeſpeare likewiſe uſes *complexion* for *diſpoſition*. STEEVENS.

I believe we ſhould read,

"Good! cry complexion!"

Celia ſays, "wonderful, wonderful, out of all cry;" to this Roſalind makes anſwer, "then cry complexion," *i. e.* ſay it is my temperament, my conſtitution; for though I am capariſoned like a man, I have not the manners, the diſpoſition of one.
A. B.

To wrong the dead, to wrong myſelf, and you,
Than I will wrong ſuch honourable men.
Julius Cæſar, A. 3, S. 2.

O what men dare do! what men may do! what
Men daily do! not knowing what they do!
Much ado about nothing, A. 4, S. 1.

Goodman Verges, ſir, ſpeaks a little of the matter: an old man, ſir, and his wits are not ſo blunt, as, God help, I would deſire they were.
Much ado about nothing, A. 3, S. 5.

—— Thy fall hath left a kind of blot,
To mark the full-fraught man the beſt endu'd,
With ſome ſuſpicion. I will weep for thee;
For this revolt of thine, methinks, is like
Another fall of man. *Henry V.* A. 2, S. 2.

Thou haſt ſo wrong'd my innocent child and me,
That I am forc'd to lay my reverence by;
And, with grey hairs, and bruiſe of many days,
Do challenge thee to tryal of a man.
Much ado about nothing, A. 5, S. 1.

Yes, I thank God, I am as honeſt as any man living, that is an old man, and no honeſter than I.
Much ado about nothing, A. 3, S. 5.

Thou trembleſt; and the whiteneſs in thy cheek
Is apter than thy tongue to tell thy errand.
Even ſuch a man, ſo faint, ſo ſpiritleſs,
So dull, ſo dead in look, ſo woe-begone,
Drew Priam's curtain in the dead of night,
And would have told him, half his Troy was burn'd.
Henry IV. P. 2, A. 1, S. 1.

My lord of York, it better ſhew'd with you,
When that your flock, aſſembled by the bell,
Encircled you, to hear with reverence
Your expoſition on the holy text;

Than now to ſee you here an iron man,
Cheering a rout of rebels with your drum.
Henry IV. P. 2, A. 4, S. 2.

There is a hiſtory in all men's lives,
Figuring the nature of the times deceas'd;
The which obſerv'd, a man may propheſy,
With a near aim, of the main chance of things
As yet not come to life. *Henry IV.* P. 2, A. 3, S. 1.

Let me have men about me that are fat;
Sleek-headed men, and ſuch as ſleep o' nights:
Yon Caſſius has a lean and hungry look;
He thinks too much: ſuch men are dangerous.
Julius Cæſar, A. 1, S. 2.

Theſe growing feathers pluck'd from Cæſar's wing,
Will make him fly an ordinary pitch;
Who elſe would ſoar above the view of men,
And keep us all in ſervile fearfulneſs.
Julius Cæſar, A. 1, S. 1.

Now could I, Caſca, name to thee a man
Moſt like this dreadful night;
That thunders, lightens, opens graves, and roars
As doth the lion in the capitol:
A man no mightier than thyſelf, or me,
In perſonal action; yet prodigious grown,
And fearful, as theſe ſtrange eruptions are.
Julius Cæſar, A. 1, S. 3.

This was the nobleſt Roman of them all:
His life was gentle; and the elements
So mix'd in him, that nature might ſtand up,
And ſay to all the world, This was a man!
Julius Cæſar, A. 5, S. 5.

You are not wood, you are not ſtones, but men;
And, being men, hearing the will of Cæſar,
It will inflame you, it will make you mad:

'Tis

'Tis good you know not that you are his heirs;
For if you ſhould, O, what would come of it!

Julius Cæſar, A. 3, S. 2.

Thrift is bleſſing, if men ſteal it not.

Merchant of Venice, A. 1, S. 3.

God made him, and therefore let him paſs for a man. *Merchant of Venice*, A. 1, S. 2.

There are a ſort of men, whoſe viſages
Do cream and mantle, like a ſtanding pond;
And do a wilful ſtillneſs entertain,
With purpoſe to be dreſt in an opinion
Of wiſdom, gravity, profound conceit;
As who ſhould ſay, I am Sir Oracle,
And when I ope my lips, let no dog bark!

Merchant of Venice, A. 1, S. 1.

Ships are but boards, ſailors but men: there be land rats, and water rats, water thieves, and land thieves; I mean, pirates; and then, there is the peril of waters, winds, and rocks.

Merchant of Venice, A. 1, S. 3.

——— I'll hold thee any wager
When we are both apparell'd like young men,
I'll prove the prettier fellow of the two,
And wear my dagger with the braver grace.

Merchant of Venice, A. 3, S. 4.

France friend with England! what becomes of me?
Fellow, begone; I cannot brook thy ſight;
This news hath made thee a moſt ugly man.

King John, A. 3, S. 1.

——— Seldom, when
The ſteeled gaoler is the friend of men.

Meaſure for Meaſure, A. 4, S. 2.

[1] Is there any man has rebus'd your worship?
Taming of the Shrew, A. 1, S. 2.

MANNERS.

I do presume, sir, that you are not fallen
From the report that goes upon your goodness;
And therefore, goaded with most sharp occasions,
Which lay nice manners by, I put you to
The use of your own virtues.
All's well that ends well, A. 5, S. 1.

——— Harsh rage,
Defect of manners, want of government,
Pride, haughtiness, opinion, and disdain:
The least of which, haunting a nobleman,
Loseth men's hearts. *Henry IV.* P. 1, A. 3, S. 1.

——— Ungracious wretch,
Fit for the mountains, and the barbarous caves,
Where manners ne'er were preach'd! out of my sight.
Twelfth Night, A. 4, S. 1.

——— In companions
That do converse and waste the time together,
Whose souls do bear an equal yoke of love,
There must needs be a like proportion
Of lineaments, of manners, and of spirit.
Merchant of Venice, A. 3, S. 4.

Alack, what heinous sin is it in me,
To be ashamed to be my father's child!
But though I am a daughter to his blood,
I am not to his manners.
Merchant of Venice, A. 2, S. 3.

[1] *Is there any man has rebus'd your worship?*] What is the meaning of *rebus'd*? or is it a false print for *abus'd*?
TYRWHIT.

" Rebus'd your worship." Has a *rebus* been made on your worship?—has any wit been exercised on you? A. B.

MARRIAGE.

—— O curſe of marriage,
That we can call theſe delicate creatures ours,
And not their appetites! I had rather be a toad,
And live upon the vapour of a dungeon,
Than keep a corner in the thing I love,
For others' uſes. *Othello*, A. 3, S. 3.

—— Marriage is a matter of more worth,
Than to be dealt in by attorneyſhip;
For what is wedlock forced, but a hell,
An age of diſcord and continual ſtrife?
Whereas the contrary bringeth forth bliſs,
And is a pattern of celeſtial peace.
Henry VI. P. 1, A. 5, S. 6.

They'll ſit by the fire, and preſume to know
What's done i' the capitol: who's like to riſe,
Who thrives, and who declines: ſide factions, and give out
Conjectural marriages; making parties ſtrong,
And feebling ſuch, as ſtand not in their liking.
Coriolanus, A. 1, S. 1.

I may chance have ſome odd quirks and remnants of wit broken on me, becauſe I have rail'd ſo long againſt marriage: but doth not the appetite alter? A man loves the meat in his youth, that he cannot endure in his age.
Much ado about nothing, A. 2, S. 3.

MELANCHOLY.

Sweet recreation barr'd what doth enſue,
But moody and dull melancholy,
Kinſman to grim and comfortleſs deſpair[1];

 And,

[1] *Kinſman to grim and comfortleſs deſpair.*] Shakeſpeare could never make melancholy a *male* in this line, and a *female* in the next,

And, at her heels, a huge infectious troop
Of pale diſtemperatures, and foes to life?

Comedy of Errors, A. 5, S. 1.

It is a melancholy of mine own, compounded of many ſimples, extracted from many objects, and, indeed, the ſundry contemplation of my travels, in which my often rumination wraps me in a moſt humorous ſadneſs. *As you like it*, A. 4, S. 1.

He will look upon his boot, and ſing; mend the ruff, and ſing; aſk queſtions, and ſing; pick his teeth, and ſing: I know a man that had this trick of melancholy, ſold a goodly manor for a ſong.

All's well that ends well, A. 3, S. 2.

Why haſt thou loſt the freſh blood in thy cheeks;
And given my treaſures, and my rights of thee
To thick-ey'd muſing, and curs'd melancholy?

Henry IV. P. 1, A. 2, S. 3.

—— She pin'd in thought;
And, with a green and yellow melancholy,
She ſat like patience on a monument,
Smiling at grief. *Twelfth Night*, A. 2, S. 4.

O ſovereign miſtreſs of true melancholy,
The poiſonous damp of night diſpunge upon me;
That life, a very rebel to my will,
May hang no longer on me.

Antony and Cleopatra, A. 4, S. 9.

O, melancholy!
Who ever yet could ſound thy bottom? find
The ooze, to ſhew what coaſt thy ſluggiſh crare
Might eaſilieſt harbour in? *Cymbeline*, A. 4, S. 2.

next. This was the fooliſh inſertion of the firſt editors. I have, therefore, put it into hooks as ſpurious WARBURTON.

All the commentators have objected to "kinſman," and juſtly —why then ſhould we not read *kindred?* A. B.

MEMORY.

MEMORY.

——— Remember thee?
Yea, from the table of my memory,
I'll wipe away all trivial fond records,
All ſaws of books, all forms, all preſſures paſt,
That youth and obſervation copied there;
And thy commandment all alone ſhall live
Within the book and volume of my brain,
Unmix'd with baſer matter. *Hamlet*, A. 1, S. 5.

O thou, that doſt inhabit in my breaſt,
Leave not the manſion ſo long tenantleſs;
Leſt, growing ruinous, the building fall,
And leave no memory of what it was!
Two Gentlemen of Verona, A. 5, S. 3.

Nay, then let the devil wear black, for I'll have a ſuit of ſables. O heavens! die two months ago, and not forgotten yet? Then there's hope, a great man's memory may out-live his life half a year. But, by'r lady, he muſt build churches then.
Hamlet, A. 3, S. 2.

MERCY.

—— Mercy is above this ſcepter'd ſway,
It is enthroned in the hearts of kings;
It is an attribute to God himſelf.
Merchant of Venice, A. 4, S. 1.

How ſhalt thou hope for mercy, rend'ring none?
Merchant of Venice, A. 4, S. 1.

——— Whereto ſerves mercy,
But to confront the viſage of offence?
And what's in prayer, but this two-fold force,—
To be fore-ſtalled, ere we come to fall,
Or pardon'd, being down? Then I'll look up;
My fault is paſt. *Hamlet*, A. 3, S. 3.

The quality of mercy is not ſtrain'd;
It droppeth, as the gentle rain from heaven

Upon

Upon the place beneath: it is twice bleſſed;
It bleſſeth him that gives, and him that takes:
'Tis mightieſt in the mightieſt.

Merchant of Venice, A. 4, S. 1.

Earthly power doth ſhew likeſt God's,
When mercy ſeaſons juſtice.

Merchant of Venice, A. 4, S. 1.

Mercy is not itſelf, that oft looks ſo;
Pardon is ſtill the nurſe of ſecond woe.

Meaſure for Meaſure, A. 2, S. 1.

——— Think on that,
And mercy then will breathe within your lips,
Like man new made. *Meaſure for Meaſure*, A. 2, S. 2.

——— Lawful mercy
Is nothing kin to foul redemption.

Meaſure for Meaſure, A. 2, S. 4.

Againſt all ſenſe you do importune her:
Should ſhe kneel down in mercy of this fact,
Her brother's ghoſt his paved bed would break,
And take her hence in horror.

Meaſure for Meaſure, A. 5, S. 1.

—— Stain not thy tomb with blood:
Wilt thou draw near the nature of the gods?
Draw near them then in being merciful:
Sweet mercy is nobility's true badge.

Titus Andronicus, A. 1, S. 2.

The mercy, that was quick in us but late,
By your own counſel is ſuppreſs'd and kill'd:
You muſt not dare, for ſhame, to talk of mercy;
For your own reaſons turn into your boſoms,
As dogs upon their maſters, worrying them.

Henry V. A. 2, S. 2.

If I begin the battery once again,
I will not leave the half-atchiev'd Harfleur,
Till in her aſhes ſhe lie buried.
The gates of mercy ſhall be all ſhut up;

And

And the fleſh'd ſoldier,—rough and hard of heart,—
In liberty of bloody hand, ſhall range
With conſcience wide as hell. *Henry V.* A. 3, S. 3.

Though juſtice be thy plea, conſider this,—
That, in the courſe of juſtice, none of us
Should ſee ſalvation: we do pray for mercy;
And that ſame prayer doth teach us all to render
The deeds of mercy. *Merchant of Venice*, A. 4, S. 1.

When vice makes mercy, mercy's ſo extended,
That, for the fault's love is the offender friended.
Meaſure for Meaſure, A. 4, S. 2.

MERIT, MERITS.

——— Who ſhall go about
To cozen fortune, and be honourable
Without the ſtamp of merit?
Merchant of Venice, A. 2, S. 9.

——— 'Tis mad idolatry,
To make the ſervice greater than the God;
And the will dotes, that is inclinable
To what infectiouſly itſelf affects,
Without ſome image of the affected merit.
Troilus and Creſſida, A. 2, S. 2.

So turns ſhe every man the wrong ſide out;
And never gives to truth and virtue, that
Which ſimpleneſs and merit purchaſeth.
Much ado about nothing, A. 3, S. 1.

Be it known, that we, the greateſt, are miſthought
For things that others do; and, when we fall,
We anſwer others' merits in our names,
Are therefore to be pitied.
Antony and Cleopatra, A. 5, S. 2.

MERRIMENT.

Where be your gibes now? your gambols? your ſongs? your flaſhes of merriment, that were wont

to

to ſet the table on a roar? Not one now, to mock your own grinning? quite chap-fallen? Now get you to my lady's chamber, and tell her, let her paint an inch thick, to this favour ſhe muſt come; make her laugh at that. *Hamlet*, A. 5, S. 1.

MIND.

—— My heart's ſubdu'd
Even to the very quality of my lord:
I ſaw Othello's viſage in his mind;
And to his honours, and his valiant parts,
Did I my ſoul and fortunes conſecrate.
Othello, A. 1, S. 3.

— When the mind is quicken'd, out of doubt,
The organs, tho' defunct and dead before,
Break up their drowſy grave, and newly move
With caſted ſlough and freſh legerity.
Henry V. A. 4, S. 1.

You have ſome ſick offence within your mind,
Which, by the right and virtue of my place,
I ought to know of: and, upon my knees,
I charm you, by my once commended beauty,
By all your vows of love, and that great vow
Which did incorporate and make us one,
That you unfold to me, yourſelf, your half,
Why you are heavy. *Julius Cæſar*, A. 2, S. 1.

—— I have within my mind
A thouſand raw tricks of theſe bragging jacks,
Which I will practiſe. *Merchant of Venice*, A. 3, S. 4.

That churchman bears a bounteous mind indeed,
A hand as fruitful as the land that feeds us;
His dews fall every where. *Henry VIII.* A. 1, S. 3.

—— If we ſhall ſtand ſtill,
In fear our motion will be mock'd or carp'd at,
We ſhould take root here where we ſit, or ſit
State ſtatues only. *Henry VIII.* A. 1, S. 2.

When

When theſe ſo noble benefits ſhall prove
Not well diſpos'd, the mind growing once corrupt
They turn to vicious forms, ten times more ugly
Than ever they were fair. *Henry VIII.* A. 1, S. 2.

With every minute you do change a mind;
And call him noble, that was now your hate,
Him vile, that was your garland.
Coriolanus, A. 1, S. 1.

Our purſes ſhall be proud, our garments poor:
For 'tis the mind that makes the body rich;
And as the ſun breaks through the darkeſt clouds,
So honour peereth in the meaneſt habit.
Taming of the Shrew, A. 4, S. 3.

I thought king Henry had reſembled thee,
In courage, courtſhip, and proportion:
But all his mind is bent to holineſs,
To number Ave-Maries on his beads:
His champions are—the prophets and apoſtles;
His weapons, holy laws of ſacred writ.
Henry VI. P. 2, A. 1, S. 3.

Follow I muſt, I cannot go before,
While Gloſter bears this baſe and humble mind.
Were I a man, a duke, and next of blood,
I would remove theſe tedious ſtumbling blocks,
And ſmooth my way upon their headleſs necks.
Henry VI. P. 2, A. 1, S. 2.

——— He cannot flatter, he!—
An honeſt mind and plain,—He muſt ſpeak truth:
An they will take it, ſo; if not, he's plain.
Theſe kind of knaves I know, which in this plainneſs
Harbour more craft, and more corrupter ends,
Than twenty ſilly ducking obſervants[1],
That ſtretch their duties nicely. *Lear*, A. 2, S. 2.

——— When

[1] *Than twenty ſilly ducking obſervants.*] The epithet *ſilly* cannot be right. Firſt, becauſe Cornwal, in this beautiful ſpeech, is

——— When the mind's free,
The body's delicate: the tempeſt in my mind
Doth from my ſenſes take all feeling elſe,
Save what beats there. *Lear*, A. 3, S. 4.

Pray, do not mock me:
I am a very fooliſh fond old man,
Fourſcore and upward; and, to deal plainly,
I fear, I am not in my perfect mind.
Lear, A. 4, S. 7.

O, what a noble mind is here o'erthrown!
The courtier's, ſoldier's, ſcholar's, eye, tongue, ſword;
The expectancy and roſe of the fair ſtate,
The glaſs of faſhion, and the mould of form,
The obſerv'd of all obſervers! quite, quite down!
Hamlet, A. 3, S. 1.

— Though nature with a beauteous wall
Doth oft cloſe in pollution, yet of thee
I will believe, thou haſt a mind that ſuits
With this thy fair and outward character.
Twelfth Night, A. 1, S. 2.

——— Fair youth,
Think us no churls; nor meaſure our good minds
By this rude place we live in. *Cymbeline*, A. 3, S. 6.

is not talking of the *different ſucceſs* of theſe two kinds of paraſites, but of their *different corruptions of heart*. Second, becauſe he ſays, theſe ducking obſervants *know how* to ſtretch their duties nicely. I am perſuaded we ſhould read,

"Twenty *ſilky* ducking obſervants."

Which not only alludes to the *garb* of a court ſycophant, but admirably well denotes the ſmoothneſs of his character.

WARBURTON.

Silly means only *ſimple*, or ruſtic. *Nicely*, is *fooliſhly*.

STEEVENS.

"Silky" is ſurely the proper epithet. "Nicely" muſt mean, to *the extremeſt point—as far as duty can go*. A. B.

—— What

——— What is in thy mind,
That makes thee ſtare thus? Wherefore breaks that
ſigh
From the inward of thee? One but painted thus,
Would be interpreted a thing perplex'd
Beyond ſelf-explication. *Cymbeline*, A. 3, S. 4.

MIRACLE.

They ſay, miracles are paſt; and we have our philoſophical perſons, to make modern and familiar, things ſupernatural and cauſeleſs.

All's well that ends well, A. 2, S. 3.

I am a rogue, if I were not at half ſword with a dozen of them two hours together: I have 'ſcap'd by miracle. I am eight times thruſt through the doublet; four through the hoſe; my buckler cut through and through; my ſword hack'd like a hand-ſaw, ecce ſignum. *Henry IV.* P. 1, A. 2, S. 4.

MIRTH.

From the crown of his head to the ſole of his foot, he is all mirth; he hath twice or thrice cut Cupid's bow ſtring, and the little hangman [1] dare not ſhoot at him. *Much ado about nothing*, A. 3, S. 2.

MISCHANCE.

——— I was, I muſt confeſs,
Great Albion's queen in former golden days:
But now miſchance hath trod my title down,
And with diſhonour laid me on the ground.
Henry VI. P. 3, A. 3, S. 3.

[1] *The little hangman dare not ſhoot at him.*] This character of Cupid came from the Arcadia of Sir Philip Sidney. FARMER.
I would read "twangman," *i. e.* bowman. Why Cupid ſhould be called *hangman*, I do not well ſee. A. B.

MISERY.

MISERY.

Misery acquaints a man with ſtrange bed-fellows.
Tempeſt, A. 2, S. 2.

—— Do not tempt my miſery,
Leſt that it make me ſo unſound a man,
As to upbraid you with thoſe kindneſſes
That I have done for you. *Twelfth Night*, A. 3, S. 4.

——— Willing miſery
Out-lives incertain pomp, is crown'd before:
The one is filling ſtill, never complete;
The other at high wiſh. *Timon of Athens*, A. 4, S. 3.

Make my miſery ſerve thy turn; ſo uſe it,
That my revengeful ſervices may prove
As benefits to thee; for I will fight
Againſt my canker'd country with the ſpleen
Of all the under fiends. *Coriolanus*, A. 4, S. 5.

——— Being alone,
Left and abandon'd of his velvet friends;
'Tis right, quoth he; thus miſery doth part
The flux of company. *As you like it*, A. 2, S. 1.

I do remember an apothecary,——
And hereabouts he dwells,——whom late I noted
In tatter'd weeds, with overwhelming brows,
Culling of ſimples; meagre were his looks,
Sharp miſery had worn him to the bones:
And in his needy ſhop a tortoiſe hung,
An alligator ſtuff'd, and other ſkins
Of ill-ſhap'd fiſhes. *Romeo and Juliet*, A. 5, S. 1.

——— He covets leſs
Than miſery itſelf would give; rewards
His deeds with doing them; and is content
To ſpend his time to end it [1]. *Coriolanus*, A. 1, S. 2.

MOCK,

[1] COM. ——— *and is content*
To ſpend his time, to end it.
MEN. *He's right noble.*] The laſt words of Cominius's ſpeech

MOCK, MOCKERY.

—— On old Hyem's chin, and icy crown,
An odorus chaplet of ſweet ſummer buds
Is, as in mockery, ſet.
Midſummer Night's Dream, A. 2, S. 2.

Can you not hate me, as I know you do,
But you muſt join, in ſouls [1], to mock me too?
Midſummer Night's Dream, A. 3, S. 2.

MODESTY.

—— By my modeſty,
(The jewel in my dower) I would not wiſh
Any companion in the world but you.
Tempeſt, A. 3, S. 1.

ſpeech are altogether unintelligible. Shakeſpeare, I ſuppoſe, wrote the paſſage thus:

—— and is content
To ſpend his time.

To which Menenius, the warm friend of Coriolanus, replies,

To end it, he's right noble. WARBURTON.

I know not whether my conceit will be approved, but I cannot forbear to think our author wrote,

—— He rewards
His deeds with doing them, and is content
To ſpend his time, to ſpend it.

To do great acts, for the ſake of doing them; to ſpend his life for the ſake of ſpending it. JOHNSON.

The whole, I believe, may ſtand, and without any change, though there is certainly a fault in the expreſſion.—He is content to ſpend his time (life) to end it. That is, he is content to paſs his life in ſuch a way (*i. e.* in war) as may poſſibly put an end to his life. A. B.

[1] —— *join in ſouls.*] Sir T. Hanmer would read, *in flouts*; Dr. Warburton, *inſolents*; Mr. Tyrwhit, *ill ſouls*; and Sir W. Blackſtone, *in ſcouls*; but I do not think that either reading is right. Perhaps we may read,

"But you muſt inſult join, and mock'ry too!"

Can you not be content to hate me, as I know you do? Why muſt you add inſolence and mockery to that hate? A. B.

O, for ſuch means!
Though peril to my modeſty [1], not death on't,
I would adventure. *Cymbeline*, A. 3, S. 4.

You do impeach your modeſty too much,
To leave the city, and commit yourſelf
Into the hands of one that loves you not.
Midſummer Night's Dream, A. 2, S. 2.

Have you no modeſty, no maiden ſhame,
No touch of baſhfulneſs?
Midſummer Night's Dream, A. 3, S. 2.

We wound our modeſty, and make foul the clearneſs of our deſervings, when of ourſelves we publiſh them. *All's well that ends well*, A. 1, S. 3.

——— Can it be,
That modeſty may more betray our ſenſe
Than woman's lightneſs?
Meaſure for Meaſure, A. 2, S. 2.

——— Take pain
To allay with ſome cold drops of modeſty
Thy ſkipping ſpirit; leſt, through thy wild behaviour,
I be miſconſtru'd in the place I go to,
And loſe my hopes, *Merchant of Venice*, A. 2, S. 2.

If I know more of any man alive,
Than that which maiden modeſty doth warrant,
Let all my ſins lack mercy!
Much ado about nothing, A. 4, S. 1.

——— O thou public commoner!
I ſhould make very forges of my cheeks,
That would to cinders burn up modeſty,
Did I but ſpeak thy deed. *Othello*, A. 4, S. 2.

[1] *Though peril to my modeſty.*] I read,
"*Through peril.*"
I would for ſuch means adventure through peril of modeſty; I would riſque every thing but real diſhonour. JOHNSON.

By "though peril" Imogen means—though my prudence may be queſtioned---though modeſty may take the alarm. A. B.

MONARCHS.

— Were I crown'd the moſt imperial monarch,
Thereof moſt worthy; were I the faireſt youth
That ever made eye ſwerve: had force and knowledge
More than was ever man's, I would not prize them
Without her love. *Winter's Tale*, A. 4, S. 3.

——— The gates of monarchs
Are arch'd ſo high, that giants may jet through
And keep their impious turbands on, without
Good-morrow to the ſun.—Hail, thou fair heaven!
We houſe i' the rock, yet uſe thee not ſo hardly
As prouder livers do. *Cymbeline*, A. 3, S. 3.

MONEY.

How like a fawning publican he looks!
I hate him for he is a chriſtian:
But more, for that, in low ſimplicity,
He lends out money gratis, and brings down
The rate of uſance here with us in Venice.
Merchant of Venice, A. 1, S. 3.

Send for money, knight; if thou haſt her not i' the end, call me cut [1]. *Twelfth Night*, A. 2, S. 3.

[1] *Call me cut.*] This contemptuous diſtinction is preſerved in the *Merry Wives of Windſor*.
"He will maintain you like a gentlewoman."
"Ay, that I will, come cut and long tail, under the degree of a ſquire." STEEVENS.
"Call me cut," *i. e. call me wine-bibber—call me drunkard.* This is highly natural. Men are very apt to rail againſt the vices that themſelves are addicted to. We now ſay of a man who has been drinking to exceſs, that he is *cut*. The meaning of *cut*, in "come cut and long tail," is, however, totally different. See note on Merry Wives of Windſor. A. B.

MONSTER.

Think, my lord!—By heaven, he echoes me,
As if there were ſome monſter in his thought
Too hideous to be ſhewn. *Othello*, A. 3, S. 3.

[1] —— Moſt monſter-like, be ſhewn
For poor'ſt diminutives to dolts; and let
Patient Octavia plough thy viſage up
With her prepared nails.
Antony and Cleopatra, A. 4, S. 10.

MOON.

I do wander every where,
Swifter than the moones ſphere;

[1] —— *moſt monſter-like, be ſhewn*
For poor'ſt diminutives, for dolts.] As the alluſion here is to monſters carried about in ſhews, it is plain that the words, for *pooreſt diminutives*, muſt mean, for the leaſt piece of money; we muſt therefore read the next word——
"For *doits*,"
i. e. farthings, which ſhews what he meant by *pooreſt diminutives.*
WARBURTON.

There was ſurely no occaſion for the poet to *ſhew what he meant* by *pooreſt diminutives*. The expreſſion is clear enough, and certainly acquires no additional force from the explanation. I rather believe we ſhould read,
"For pooreſt diminutives, *to dolts*."
This aggravates the contempt of her ſuppoſed ſituation; to be ſhewn as monſters are, not only for the ſmalleſt pieces of money, but to the moſt ſtupid and vulgar ſpectators. TYRWHIT.

I have adopted this truly ſenſible emendation. STEEVENS.

I cannot help thinking but that our author, by *diminutives*, rather means *perſons* than *things*, and that we ſhould read,
"—— monſter-like, be *ſhew*,
"For pooreſt diminutives, for *dolts*.
i. e. become a ſhew for the *rabble* and for *fools*. The French ſay, *le menu peuple*, for *le bas peuple*. *Menu*, in French, is *little*, *diminutive*. *Menu peuple*, if tranſlated literally, is therefore the *little people*, or, as Shakeſpeare chooſes to call them (in imitation of his neighbours) *diminutives*. In Troilus and Creſſida, Therſites ſays of Patroclus,—"How the poor world is peſtered with ſuch water-flies; diminutives of nature!" A. B.

And

And I ſerve the fairy queen,
To dew her orbs upon the green.
Midſummer Night's Dream, A. 2, S. 1.

—— The moon, the governeſs of floods,
Pale in her anger, waſhes all the air,
That rheumatic diſeaſes do abound:
And, thorough this diſtemperature, we ſee
The ſeaſons alter.
Midſummer Night's Dream, A. 2, S. 2.

—— How ſlow
This old moon wanes! ſhe lingers my deſires,
Like to a ſtep-dame or a dowager,
[1] Long withering out a young man's revenue.
Midſummer Night's Dream, A. 1, S. 1.

Now the hungry lion roars,
And the wolf beholds the moon;
Whilſt the heavy ploughman ſnores,
All the weary taſk fordone.
Midſummer Night's Dream, A. 5, S. 2.

—— In ſilence ſad,
Trip we after the night's ſhade:
We the globe can compaſs ſoon,
Swifter than the wand'ring moon.
Midſummer Night's Dream, A. 4, S. 1.

MORNING.

But, look, the morn, in ruſſet mantle clad,
Walks o'er the dew of yon high eaſtern hill.
Hamlet, A. 1, S. 1.

A goodly day not to keep houſe, with ſuch
Whoſe roof's as low as ours! ſtoop, boys: this gate

[1] *Long withering out a young man's revenue.*] So in Chapman's tranſlation of the 4th book of Homer:
"There the goodly plant lies withering out his grace."
STEEVENS.

We ſhould read "lithering," *i. e.* lingering. *Lither* is idle. lazy, ſluggiſh. A. B.

Inftructs you how to adore the heavens, and bows
you
To morning's holy office. *Cymbeline*, A. 3, S. 3.

This morning, like the fpirit of a youth
That means to be of note, begins by times.
Antony and Cleopatra, A. 4, S. 4.

The grey-ey'd morn fmiles on the frowning night
Checkering the eaftern clouds with ftreaks of light;
And flecked darknefs [1] like a drunkard reels
From forth day's path-way, made by Titan's
wheels. *Romeo and Juliet*, A. 2, S. 3.

See, how the morning opes her golden gates,
And takes her farewell of the glorious fun!
How well refembles it the prime of youth,
Trimm'd like a yonker, prancing to his love!
Henry VI. P. 3, A. 2, S. 1.

MOTHER.

——— Who might be your mother,
[2] That you infult, exult, and all at once,
Over the wretched? *As you like it*, A. 3, S. 5.

MURDER,

[1] *And flecked darknefs.*] *Flecked* is fpotted, dappled, ftreaked. Lord Surrey ufes the word in his tranflation of the 4th Æneid.

"Her quivering cheeks *flecked* with deadly ftain."

STEEVENS.

"Flecked" is undoubtedly *fpotted.* But flecked, in this place, fhould be *flick'ring*, i. e. *fluttering*. Darknefs, or night, is always reprefented with wings. To fay, therefore, that night went off flowly ("flickering"), or hefitatingly, like a drunkard, is beautiful, and perfectly juft. The text is certainly faulty, for if flecked, or *fpotted darknefs*, be likened to a *reeling man*, where is the truth of the comparifon? A. B.

[2] *That you infult, exult, and all at once.*] By examining the crime of the perfon accufed, we fhall difcover that the line is to be read thus:

"That you infult, exult, and rail at once."

But the Oxford editor improves it, and for *rail at once*, reads *domineer*. WARBURTON.

There

MURDER, MURDERER.

Within this boſom never enter'd yet
The dreadful motion of a murd'rous thought,
And you have ſlander'd nature in my form;
Which, howſoever rude exteriorly,
Is yet the cover of a fairer mind
Than to be butcher of an innocent child.

King John, A. 4, S. 2.

O God, which this blood mad'ſt, revenge his death!
O earth, which this blood drink'ſt, revenge his death!
Either, heaven, with lightning ſtrike the murderer dead,
Or, earth, gape open wide, and eat him quick.

Richard III. A. 1, S. 2.

——— The great King of kings
Hath in the table of his law commanded,
That thou ſhalt do no murder; wilt thou then
Spurn at his edict, and fulfil a man's?

Richard III. A. 1, S. 4.

Perjury, perjury, in the higheſt degree,
Murder, ſtern murder, in the dir'ſt degree;
All ſeveral ſins, all us'd in each degree,
Throng to the bar,
Methought the ſouls of all that I had murder'd
Came to my tent, and every one did threat
To-morrow's vengeance on the head of Richard.

Richard III. A. 5, S. 3.

——— I'll have theſe players
Play ſomething like the murder of my father,
Before mine uncle: I'll obſerve his looks;

There is no neceſſity for introducing "rail," and which is beſide included in the word inſult. We have only to make a tranſpoſition of the words:

"That you at once inſult, exult,—and all,
"Over the wretched."

i. e. and *that too* over the wretched. A. B.

I'll tent him to the quick; if he do blench,
I know my courſe. *Hamlet*, A. 2, S. 2.

——— I have heard,
That guilty creatures, ſitting at a play,
Have by the very cunning of the ſcene
Been ſtruck ſo to the ſoul, that preſently
They have proclaim'd their malefactions:
For murder, though it have no tongue, will ſpeak
With moſt miraculous organ, *Hamlet*, A. 2, S. 2.

It cannot be, but thou haſt murder'd him;
So ſhould a murderer look, ſo dead, ſo grim.
Midſummer Night's Dream, A. 3, S. 2.

——— O, what form of prayer
Can ſerve my turn? Forgive me my foul murder!
That cannot be: ſince I am ſtill poſſeſs'd
Of thoſe effects for which I did the murder,
My crown, mine own ambition, and my queen.
Hamlet, A. 3, S. 3.

A murderer, and a villain: a vice of kings:
A cut-purſe of the empire and the rule;
That from a ſhelf the precious diadem ſtole,
And put it in his pocket! *Hamlet*, A. 3, S. 4.

This play is the image of a murder done in Vienna: 'tis a knaviſh piece of work: but what of that? your majeſty, and we that have free ſouls, it toucheth us not: let the gall'd jade wince, our withers are unwrung. *Hamlet*, A. 3, S. 2.

MUSICK.

Where ſhould this muſick be? i' the air, or the earth?
Tempeſt, A. 1, S. 2.

This muſick crept by me upon the waters;
Allaying both their fury, and my paſſion,
With its ſweet air. *Tempeſt*, A. 1, S. 2.

Give

Give me ſome muſick; muſick, moody food
Of us that trade in love.

Antony and Cleopatra, A. 2, S. 5.

If muſick be the food of love, play on,
Give me exceſs of it; that ſurfeiting,
The appetite may ſicken, and ſo die.

Twelfth Night, A. 1, S. 1.

Except I be by Silvia in the night,
There is no muſick in the nightingale.

Two Gentlemen of Verona, A. 3, S. 1.

Prepoſterous aſs! that never read ſo far
To know the cauſe why muſick was ordain'd!
Was it not, to refreſh the mind of man,
After his ſtudies, or his uſual pain?

Taming of the Shrew, A. 3, S. 1.

——— The poet
Did feign that Orpheus drew trees, ſtones, and floods,
Since nought ſo ſtockiſh, hard, and full of rage,
But muſick for the time doth change his nature.

Merchant of Venice, A. 5, S. 1.

How ſweet the moon-light ſleeps upon this bank!
Here will we ſit, and let the ſounds of muſick
Creep in our ears. *Merchant of Venice*, A. 5, S. 1.

Come, ho, and wake Diana with a hymn;
With ſweeteſt touches pierce your miſtreſs' ear,
And draw her home with muſick.

Merchant of Venice, A. 5, S. 1.

I am never merry, when I hear ſweet muſick.

Merchant of Venice, A. 5, S. 1.

——— He may win:
And what is muſick then? then muſick is
Even as the flouriſh when true ſubjects bow
To a new-crowned monarch.

Merchant of Venice, A. 3, S. 2.

The man that hath no muſick in himſelf,
Nor is not mov'd with concord of ſweet ſounds,

Is

Is fit for treaſons, ſtratagems, and ſpoils;
Let no ſuch man be truſted.
Merchant of Venice, A. 5, S. 1.

Let muſick ſound, while he doth make his choice,
Then if he loſe, he makes a ſwan-like end,
Fading in muſick. *Merchant of Venice*, A. 3, S. 2.

There is much muſic, excellent voice, in this little organ; yet cannot you make it ſpeak. Why, do you think, that I am eaſier to be play'd on than a pipe? Call me what inſtrument you will, though you can fret me, you cannot play upon me.
Hamlet, A. 3, S. 2.

Let there be no noiſe made, my gentle friends,
[1] Unleſs ſome dull and favourable hand
Will whiſper muſick to my weary ſpirit.
Henry IV. P. 2, A. 4, S. 4.

MYSTERY.

Why, look you now, how unworthy a thing you make of me! you would play upon me; you would ſeem to know my ſtops; you would pluck out the heart of my myſtery; you would ſound me from my loweſt note to the top of my compaſs.
Hamlet, A. 3, S. 2.

[1] *Unleſs ſome dull and favourable hand.*] Thus the old editions read it, evidently corrupt. Shakeſpeare ſeems to have wrote,
"Unleſs ſome doleing favourable hand."
doleing, *i. e.* a hand uſing ſoft melancholy airs. WARBURTON.
I rather think that *dull* ſignifies melancholy, gentle, ſoothing. JOHNSON.
"Dull and favourable hand." The terms *dull* and *favourable* are too much oppoſed to be right. Shakeſpeare may have Anglicifed the word *dolce*, and written,
"Unleſs ſome dolce and favourable hand."
dolce, i. e. *ſoft*, *ſoothing*.
The Italian expreſſion, *con dolce maniera*, ſignifies, to play in a ſoft and agreeable manner. A. B.

NAIAD.

N.

NAIAD.

YOU nymphs, call'd Naiads, of the wand'ring brooks[1],
With your ſedg'd crowns, and ever harmleſs looks,
Leave your criſp channels. *Tempeſt*, A. 4, S. 1.

NAME.

With thy bleſſings ſteel my lance's point,
That it may enter Mowbray's waxen coat[2],
And furbiſh new the name of John of Gaunt.
Richard II. A. 1, S. 3.

——— To abide a field,
Where nothing but the ſound of Hotſpur's name
Did ſeem defenſible[3]. *Henry IV.* P. 2, A. 2, S. 3.

NATION.

[1] ——— *wand'ring brooks.*] The modern editors read *winding brooks.* The old copy *windring.* I ſuppoſe we ſhould read *wand'ring*, as it is here printed. STEEVENS.

Perhaps we ſhould read, *windered brooks*, *i. e.* brooks whoſe ſides were decked, or ornamented, with flowers. *Windered*, in Chaucer, is *gay, trim, ornamented.* A. B.

[2] ——— *waxen coat.*] *Waxen* may mean *ſoft*, and conſequently *penetrable.* STEEVENS.

A "waxen coat" is not a coat made of wax, nor even a *ſoft* coat. The ſpeech is figurative. Waxen is employed as a participle preſent, and means *growing.*—*Coat* is uſed for *conſequence, importance*, in alluſion to enſigns armorial. Bolingbroke's meaning is,—that he hopes to overturn, or put down, the growing greatneſs of Mowbray, and to raiſe up the name of Gaunt. A. B.

[3] *Did ſeem defenſible.*] *Defenſible* does not, in this place, mean *capable of defence*, but *bearing ſtrength, furniſhing the means of defence.* MALONE.

The

NATION.

——— Remember where we are;
In France, amongſt a fickle wavering nation:
If they perceive diſſenſion in our looks,
And that within ourſelves we diſagree,
How will their grudging ſtomachs be provok'd
To wilful diſobedience, and rebel!

Henry VI. P. 1, A. 4, S. 1.

He hath diſgraced me, and hindered me of half a million; laugh'd at my loſſes, mock'd at my gains, ſcorn'd my nation, thwarted my bargains, cool'd my friends, heated mine enemies, and what's his reaſon! I am a Jew. *Merchant of Venice*, A. 3, S. 1.

This heavy-headed revel, eaſt and weſt,
Makes us traduc'd, and tax'd of other nations:
They clepe us drunkards, and with ſwiniſh phraſe
Soil our addition; and, indeed, it takes
From our atchievements, though perform'd at height,
The pitch and marrow of our attribute.

Hamlet, A. 1, S. 4.

NATURE.

—— Nature is made better by no mean,
But nature makes that mean; ſo, o'er that art
Which, you ſay, adds to nature, is an art
That nature makes. *Winter's Tale*, A. 4, S. 3.

——— Once a day, I'll viſit
The chapel where they lie; and tears, ſhed there,
Shall be my recreation: ſo long as nature
Will bear up with this exerciſe, ſo long
I daily vow to uſe it. *Winter's Tale*, A. 3, S. 2.

The meaning is, that nothing but the name of Hotſpur gave ſtrength or ſupport to the cauſe. So in Richard III.
"Beſide, the king's name is a tower of ſtrength, &c."

A. B,

This

This is as ſtrange a maze as e'er men trod:
And there is in this buſineſs more than nature
Was ever conduct of. *Tempeſt*, A. 5, S. 1.

How bleſs'd are we, that are not ſingle men!
Yet nature might have made me as theſe are,
Therefore I will not diſdain. *Wint. Tale*, A. 4, S. 3.

——— Nature wants ſtuff
To vie ſtrange forms with fancy; yet, to imagine
An Antony, were nature's piece 'gainſt fancy,
Condemning ſhadows quite.
Antony and Cleopatra, A. 5, S. 2.

How ſometimes nature will betray its folly,
Its tenderneſs: and make itſelf a paſtime
To harder boſoms! *Winter's Tale*, A. 1, S. 2.

O thou goddeſs,
Thou divine nature, thou thyſelf thou blazon'ſt
In theſe two princely boys! They are as gentle
As zephyrs, blowing below the violet,
Not wagging his ſweet head, and yet as rough,
Their royal blood enchaf'd, as the rud'ſt wind,
That by the top doth take the mountain pine,
And make him ſtoop to the vale.
Cymbeline, A. 4, S. 2.

—— Though train'd up thus meanly
I' the cave, wherein they bow, their thoughts do hit
The roofs of palaces; and nature prompts them,
In ſimple and low things, to prince it, much
Beyond the trick of others. *Cymbeline*, A. 3, S. 3.

Too much of water haſt thou, poor Ophelia,
And therefore I forbid my tears: but yet
It is our trick; nature her cuſtom holds,
Let ſhame ſay what it will: when theſe are gone
The woman will be out. *Hamlet*, A. 4, S. 7.

——— Hath nature given them eyes
To ſee this vaulted arch, and the rich crop
Of ſea and land, which can diſtinguiſh 'twixt

The

The fiery orbs above, and the twinn'd ſtones [1]
Upon the number'd beach? and can we not
Partition make with ſpectacles ſo precious
'Twixt fair and foul? *Cymbeline*, A. 1, S. 7.

Uſe can almoſt change the ſtamp of nature,
And either maſter the devil, or throw him out
With wond'rous potency. Once more, good night!
And when you are deſirous to be bleſt,
I'll bleſſing beg of you. *Hamlet*, A. 3, S. 4.

—— Here lay Duncan,
His ſilver ſkin lac'd with his golden blood;
And his gaſh'd ſtabs look'd like a breach in nature,
For ruin's waſteful entrance: there the murderers

[1] —— *and the twinn'd ſtones*
Upon the number'd beach?] I have no idea in what ſenſe the beach, or ſhore, ſhould be called *number'd*. I have ventured, againſt all the copies, to ſubſtitute,

"Upon th' unnumber'd beach?"

i. e. the infinite extenſive beach. THEOBALD.

"Upon th' unnumber'd beach?" Senſe, and the antitheſis, oblige us to read this nonſenſe thus:

"Upon the *humbled* beach?"

i. e. becauſe daily inſulted by the flow of the tide. WARBURTON.

I know not well how to regulate this paſſage. *Number'd* is, perhaps, *numerous*. *Twinn'd ſtones* I do not underſtand. *Twinn'd ſhells*, or *pairs of ſhells*, are very common. For twinn'd we might read twin'd, that is, *twiſted*, *convolved*; but this ſenſe is more applicable to ſhells than to ſtones. JOHNSON.

I would read thus:

"—— which can diſtinguiſh 'twixt
"The fiery orbs above, and the twinn'd ſtones
"Unnumber'd on the beach?"

Unnumber'd ſeems to include both *ſtars* and *ſtones*. *Twinn'd ſtones*, may mean, *ſtones in ſhape and number like the ſtars*.

The ſenſe, I believe, is this; *Man*, ſays the poet, can diſtinguiſh between the fiery orbs above, and the ſtones upon the beach, which are ſpherical like thoſe orbs, and which alſo reſemble them in number; and cannot we, aſſiſted as we are by *reaſon*, by the faculties of the ſoul; or as he expreſſes it, having "*ſpectacles ſo precious*," diſtinguiſh between virtue and vice,—betwixt fair and foul? A. B.

Steep'd

Steep'd in the colours of their trade, their daggers
Unmannerly breech'd with gore [1].

Macbeth, A. 2, S. 3.

Let your own discretion be your tutor: suit the action to the word, the word to the action; with this special observance, that you o'erstep not the modesty of nature; for any thing so overdone is from the purpose of playing, whose end, both at the first, and now, was, and is, to hold the mirror as 'twere up to nature; to shew virtue her own feature, scorn her own image, and the very age and body of the time his form and pressure. *Hamlet*, A. 3, S. 2.

That nature, which contemns its origin,
Cannot be border'd certain in itself;
She that herself will sliver and disbranch

[1] *Unmannerly breech'd with gore.*] An *unmannerly dagger*, and a *dagger breech'd*, or, as in some editions, *breach'd with gore*, are expressions not easily to be understood. There are undoubtedly two faults in this passage, which I have endeavoured to take away by reading,

"—— daggers
"Unmannerly drench'd with gore."

I saw, drenched with the king's blood, the fatal daggers, not only instruments of murder, but evidences of cowardice. JOHNSON.

"Unmannerly breech'd with gore."

This nonsensical account of the state in which the daggers were found, must surely be read thus:

"Unmannerly reech'd with gore."

Reech'd, soiled with a dark yellow, which is the colour of any reechy substance, and must be so of steel stained with blood. WARBURTON.

"This passage (says Mr. Heath) seems to have been the *crux* " *criticorum*. Every one has tried his skill at it, and I may venture to say, no one has succeeded."

The whole matter is, I think, that some of the lines have been transposed at the press. I regulate the passage thus:

"—— Here lay Duncan,
"His silver skin lac'd with his golden blood;
"And his gash'd stabs look'd like a breach in nature,
"(Unmannerly breach!) for ruin's wasteful entrance.—
"There the murderers, steep'd in the colours of their trade,
"Their daggers drenched with gore." A. B.

From

From her maternal ſap, perforce muſt wither,
And come to deadly uſe. *Lear*, A. 4, S. 2.

Fie on't? O fie! 'tis an unweeded garden,
That grows to ſeed; things rank and groſs in nature,
Poſſeſs it merely. *Hamlet*, A. 1, S. 2.

—— Nature, creſcent, does not grow alone
In thews, and bulk; but, as this temple waxes,
The inward ſervice of the mind and ſoul
Grows wide withal. *Hamlet*, A. 1, S. 3.

—— What may this mean,——
That thou, dead corſe, again, in complete ſteel,
Reviſit'ſt thus the glimpſes of the moon,
Making night hideous; and we fools of nature
So horridly to ſhake our diſpoſition,
With thoughts beyond the reaches of our ſouls?
Hamlet, A. 1, S. 4

—— 'Tis often ſeen,
Adoption ſtrives with nature; and choice breeds
A native ſlip to us from foreign ſeeds.
All's well that ends well, A. 1, S. 3.

Why ſhould you want? Behold, the earth hath roots;
Within this mile break forth an hundred ſprings:
The oaks bear maſt, the briars ſcarlet hips;
The bounteous huſwife, nature, on each buſh
Lays her full meſs before you.
Timon of Athens, A. 4, S. 3.

Fiery? the fiery duke?—Tell the hot duke, that—
No, but not yet:—may be, he is not well:
Infirmity doth ſtill neglect all office,
Whereto our health is bound; we are not ourſelves,
When nature, being oppreſs'd, commands the mind
To ſuffer with the body. *Lear*, A. 2, S. 4.

O, reaſon not the need: our baſeſt beggars
Are in the pooreſt thing ſuperfluous:
Allow not nature more than nature needs,
Man's life is cheap as beaſt's. *Lear*, A. 2, S. 4.

—— Nothing

——— Nothing could have ſubdu'd nature
To ſuch a lowneſs, but his unkind daughters.—
Is it the faſhion, that diſcarded fathers
Should have thus little mercy on their fleſh?
Judicious puniſhment! 'twas this fleſh begot
Thoſe pelican daughters. *Lear*, A. 3, S. 4.

Beſides this nothing that he ſo plentifully gives me, the ſomething that nature gave me, his countenance ſeems to take from me: he lets me feed with his hinds, bars me the place of a brother, and, as much as in him lies, mines my gentility with my education. *As you like it*, A. 1, S. 1.

Julio Romano; who, had he himſelf eternity, and could put breath into his work, would beguile nature of her cuſtom [1], ſo perfectly he is her ape.
Winter's Tale, A. 5, S. 2.

——— Nature never lends
The ſmalleſt ſcruple of her excellence,
But, like a thrifty goddeſs, ſhe determines
Herſelf the glory of her creditor,
Both thanks and uſe.
Meaſure for Meaſure, A. 1, S. 1.

NECESSITY.

——— Art cold?
I am cold myſelf.—Where is this ſtraw, my fellow?
The art of our neceſſities is ſtrange,
That can make vile things precious. Come, your
hovel. *Lear*, A. 3, S. 2.

——— His demand
Springs not from Edward's well-meant honeſt love,

[1] *Of her cuſtom*,] That is, *of her trade*,—would draw her cuſtomers from her. JOHNSON.
"Her cuſtom" is rather *her excellence*; *her powers*, *as uſually ſeen*. The meaning is, that he would rival nature. A. B.

But from deceit, bred by neceſſity,
For how can tyrants ſafely govern home,
Unleſs abroad they purchaſe great alliance?
Henry VI. P. 3, A. 3, S. 3.

All places that the eye of heaven viſits,
Are to a wiſe man ports and happy havens;
Teach thy neceſſity to reaſon thus;
There is no virtue like neceſſity.
Think not, the king did baniſh thee;
But thou the king. *Richard II.* A. 1, S. 3.

It follows then, the cat muſt ſtay at home:
Yet that is but a curs'd neceſſity[1];
Since we have locks to ſafeguard neceſſaries,
And pretty traps to catch the petty thieves.
Henry V. A. 1, S. 2.

——— Greet him from me;
Bid him ſuppoſe ſome good neceſſity
Touches his friend[2]. *Timon of Athens*, A. 2, S. 2.

[1] *Yet that is but a curs'd neceſſity.*] So the old quarto. The folios read *cruſh'd*; neither of the words convey any tolerable idea; but give us a counter reaſoning, and not at all pertinent. We ſhould read, "*'ſcus'd* neceſſity," that is, though there be a ſeeming neceſſity, yet it is one that may be well *excuſed* and *got over.* WARBURTON.

Neither the old readings, nor the emendation, ſeem very ſatisfactory. A *curs'd* neceſſity has no ſenſe; a 'ſcus'd neceſſity is ſo harſh, that one would not admit it if any thing elſe can be found. A *cruſh'd* neceſſity may mean, a neceſſity which is *ſubdued* and *overpowered* by contrary reaſons. We might read a *crude* neceſſity, but it is too harſh. JOHNSON.

Mr. Steevens is for adhering to the reading of the quarto, "curs'd neceſſity," but it is impoſſible that it ſhould be right. I would read a *carv'd* neceſſity, *i. e.* a neceſſity *cut out* for the occaſion—a pretended neceſſity. A. B.

[2] *Bid him ſuppoſe ſome good neceſſity Touches his friend.*] *Good*, as it may afford Ventidius an opportunity of exerciſing his bounty, and relieving his friend, in return for his former kindneſs; or ſome *honeſt* neceſſity, not the conſequence of a *villainous* and ignoble *bounty*. I rather think this latter is the meaning. MALONE.

Good is here uſed for *real, abſolute,* no way *feigned.* A. B.

NEPTUNE.

NEPTUNE.

I, like a forefter, the groves may tread,
Even till the eaftern gate all fiery-red,
Opening on Neptune with fair bleffed beams,
Turns into yellow gold his falt-green ftreams.
Midfummer Night's Dream, A. 3, S. 2.

His mother was a votrefs of my order;
And, in the fpiced Indian air, by night,
Full often hath fhe goffipp'd by my fide;
And fat with me on Neptune's yellow fands,
Marking the embarked traders on the flood.
Midfummer Night's Dream, A. 2, S. 2.

NEWS.

You have heard of the news abroad; I mean, the whifper'd ones, for they are yet but ear-kiffing arguments[1]? *Lear*, A. 2, S. 1.

—— The firft bringer of unwelcome news
Hath but a lofing office; and his tongue
Sounds ever after as a fullen bell,
Remember'd knolling a departed friend.
Henry IV. P. 2, A. 1, S. 1.

I faw a fmith ftand with his hammer, thus,
The whilft his iron did on the anvil cool,
With open mouth fwallowing a taylor's news;
Who, with his fhears and meafure in his hand,
Standing on flippers (which his nimble hafte
Had falfely thruft upon contrary feet)

1 —— *ear-kiffing arguments.*] Subjects of difcourfe, topicks. JOHNSON.

Ear-kiffing arguments means, that they are yet in reality only *whifpered ones*, STEEVENS.

"*Ear-kiffing arguments*" may mean, *news that is only talked of* —*news that is not confirmed.* To fay that the news is whifpered, is faying nothing as to its *truth*. Befide, he had obferved, that the news was *whifpered* immediately before. A. B.

Told of a thousand warlike French,
That were embattled and rank'd in Kent.

King John, A. 4, S. 2.

[1] ——— Some news is come,
That turns their countenances.

Coriolanus, A. 4, S. 6.

NIGHT.

'Tis now the very witching time of night;
When church-yards yawn, and hell itself breathes out
Contagion to this world: now could I drink hot blood,
And do such business as the bitter day
Would quake to look on. *Hamlet*, A. 3, S. 2.

Now it is the time of night,
That the graves, all gaping wide,
Every one lets forth his spright,
In the church-way paths to glide.

Midsummer Night's Dream, A. 5, S. 2.

The iron tongue of midnight hath told twelve:
This palpable gross play hath well beguil'd
The heavy gait of night.

Midsummer Night's Dream, A. 5, S. 1.

——— Night's swift dragons cut the clouds full fast,
And yonder shines Aurora's harbinger;
At whose approach, ghosts, wandering here and there,
Troop home to church-yards.

Midsummer Night's Dream, A. 3, S. 2.

[1] *— Some news is come,*
That turns their countenances.] *i. e.* That renders their aspect *sour*. This allusion to the acescence of milk occurs again in Timon of Athens. MALONE.

I cannot think that *turns* has, in this place, any thing to do with *sour*. It only means *that the news had affected them—that they changed countenance on it.* A. B.

Hie

Hie therefore, Robin, overcast the night,
The starry welkin cover thou anon
With drooping fog, as black as Acheron.

Midsummer Night's Dream, A. 3, S. 2.

Dark night, that from the eye his function takes,
The ear more quick of apprehension makes;
Wherein it doth impair the seeing sense,
It pays the hearing double recompense.

Midsummer Night's Dream, A. 3, S. 2.

——— I have intreated him along
With us to watch the minutes of this night:
That, if again this apparition come,
He may approve our eyes [1], and speak to it.

Hamlet, A. 1, S. 1.

——— Are you not he,
That fright the maidens of the villag'ry;
And sometimes make the drink to bear no barm;
Mislead night-wanderers, laughing at their harm?

Midsummer Night's Dream, A. 2, S. 1.

I know a bank whereon the wild thyme blows,
Where ox-lips and the nodding violet grows;
Quite over-canopy'd with luscious woodbine,
With sweet musk-roses, and with eglantine:
There sleeps Titania, some time of the night,
Lull'd in these flowers with dances and delight.

Midsummer Night's Dream, A. 2, S. 2.

True;
When the day serves, before black-corner'd night [2],
Find what thou want'st by free and offer'd light.

Timon of Athens, A. 5, S. 1.

[1] ——— *approve our eyes.*] Add a new testimony to that of our eyes. JOHNSON.

"Approve our eyes." Have proof that we were no way mistaken, that we have not been fanciful. He had said in the first line of the speech,—Horatio says, 'tis but our phantasy. A. B.

[2] *When the day serves, before black-corner'd night.*] We should read,

" ——— black

The moon ſhines bright:—In ſuch a night as this,
When the ſweet wind did gently kiſs the trees,
And they did make no noiſe; in ſuch a night,
Troilus, methinks, mounted the Trojan wall,
And ſigh'd his ſoul toward the Grecian tents,
Where Creſſid lay that night.

Merchant of Venice, A. 5, S. 1.

——— Urchins
Shall, [1] for that vaſt of night that they may work,
All exerciſe on thee. *Tempeſt*, A. 1, S. 2.

——— This fearful night,
There is no ſtir or walking in the ſtreets;
And the complexion of the element,
It favours like the work we have in hand,
Moſt bloody, fiery, and moſt terrible.

Julius Cæſar, A. 1, S. 3.

"——— black cornette night."
A *cornette* is a woman's head-dreſs for the night. So in another place he calls her—*black brow'd night*. WARBURTON.

Black-corner'd night is probably corrupt, but black-cornette can hardly be right, for it ſhould be *black-cornetted night*. I cannot propoſe any thing, but muſt leave the place in its preſent ſtate. JOHNSON.

I believe that Shakeſpeare, by this expreſſion, meant only night, which is as obſcure as a *dark corner*. STEEVENS.

"Black-corner'd night" is a very unmeaning expreſſion. I would read,

"——— black, coaled night."
I know not if the reading may be admitted, but I think it has much of Shakeſpeare's manner. Or he may have written *collied*. A. B.

[1] —— *for that vaſt of night that they may work.*] The *vaſt of night* means the night which is naturally empty and deſerted, without action; or when all things lying in ſleep and ſilence, makes the world appear one great uninhabited *waſte*. STEEVENS.

I underſtand *vaſt*, in this place, to mean *length of time*—*for*, is *during*. *Fairies* (ſays he) *ſhall, during the whole extent, or ſpace of night, and in which they are allowed to work, all exerciſe on thee.* Our author, it may be remembered, uſes *vaſty* for extent of place. A. B.

From camp to camp, through the foul womb of night,
The hum of either army ſtilly ſounds,
That the fix'd centinels almoſt receive
The ſecret whiſpers of each other's watch:
Fire anſwers fire; and through their paly flames
Each battle ſees the other's umber'd face.
Henry V. A. 4, *Chorus.*

The confident, and over-luſty French
Do the low-rated Engliſh play at dice;
And chide the cripple tardy-gaited night,
Who like a foul and ugly witch, doth limp
So tediouſly away. *Henry V.* A. 4, *Chorus.*

Steed threatens ſteed, in high and boaſtful neighs,
Piercing the night's dull ear; and from the tents,
The armourers, accompliſhing the knights,
With buſy hammers cloſing rivets up,
Give dreadful note of preparation.
Henry V. A. 4, *Chorus.*

——— Here nothing breeds,
Unleſs the nightly owl, or fatal raven.
They told me, here, at dead time of the night,
A thouſand fiends, a thouſand hiſſing ſnakes,
Ten thouſand ſwelling toads, as many urchins,
Would make ſuch fearful and confuſed cries,
As any mortal body, hearing it,
Should ſtraight fall mad, or elſe die ſuddenly.
Titus Andronicus, A. 2, S. 3.

Gallop apace you fiery-footed ſteeds,
Towards Phœbus' manſion; ſuch a waggoner
As Phaeton would whip you to the weſt,
And bring in cloudy night immediately.
Romeo and Juliet, A. 3, S. 2.

——— If the midnight bell
Did, with his iron tongue and brazen mouth,
Sound on unto the drowsy race of night [1].
King John, A. 3, S. 3.

The time of night when Troy was set on fire;
The time when scritch-owls cry, and ban-dogs howl [2].
Henry VI. P. 2, A. 1, S. 4.

[3] Brief as the lightning in the colly'd night,
That, in a spleen, unfolds both heaven and earth,
And

[1] *Sound on unto the drowsy race of night.*] Some of the commentators have taken infinite pains to prove that the present reading, *sound on*, is faulty, and that we ought to read, "sound one," &c. while the others have as stoutly maintained that the text should undoubtedly remain unchanged. I am of opinion, however, that both these readings are wrong, and have therefore ventured to alter the passage thus:

" ——— If the midnight bell
" Had, with his iron tongue and brazen mouth,
" Sounden unto the drowsy race of night."

To suppose that the king was unable to communicate his thoughts to Hubert, at any other time than when the bell was *sounding on*, is truly ridiculous and absurd. But that he should consider midnight as the proper season for conversing with him on the dreadful business in hand, is highly beautiful and just. He therefore says, if the bell *had sounded*, or *sounden*, then, &c.

In old language, the participle is frequently formed by the termination *en*, as it is now by *ed*. A. B.

[2] ——— *ban-dogs howl.*] The etymology of the word *ban-dogs* is unsettled. They seem, however, to have been designed by poets to signify some terrific beings, whose office it was *to make night hideous*, like those mentioned in the first book of Horace:

" Serpentes, atque videres
" Infernos errare canes." STEEVENS.

" Ban-dog," or band-dog, is a dog kept in bands, or tied up. A mastiff. A. B.

[3] *Brief as the lightning in the collied night,*
That, in a spleen, unfolds both heaven and earth,
And ere a man hath power to say,—behold!
The jaws of darkness do devour it up.] Though the word *spleen* be here employed oddly enough, yet I believe it right.

And ere a man hath power to ſay,—behold!
The jaws of darkneſs do devour it up.
Midſummer Night's Dream, A. 1, S. 1.

NOBLENESS, NOBILITY.

[1] ——— When did he regard
The ſtamp of nobleneſs in any perſon,
Out of himſelf? *Henry VIII.* A. 3, S. 2.

I am join'd with no foot but with nobility, and tranquillity; burgomaſters and great moneyers; ſuch as can hold in; [2] ſuch as will ſtrike ſooner than ſpeak, and

right. Shakeſpeare, hurried on by the grandeur and multitude of his ideas, aſſumes every now and then an uncommon licence in the uſe of his words. Here he uſes the word *ſpleen* for a *ſudden, haſty fit*. WARBURTON.

It is ſcarcely poſſible that *ſpleen* ſhould be right. I read *ſhene*, *i. e.* ſhining, *Chauc. Spenſ.* Shakeſpeare uſes it as a ſubſtantive, —*flaſh*, *ſudden blaze*. A. B.

[1] ——— *When did he regard*
The ſtamp of nobleneſs in any perſon,
Out of himſelf?] The expreſſion is bad, and the thought falſe. It ſuppoſes Wolſey to be *noble*, which was not ſo. We ſhould read,

" ——— When did he regard
" The ſtamp of nobleneſs in any perſon;
" Out of't himſelf?"

i. e. When did he regard *nobleneſs* of blood in another; having none of his own to value himſelf upon? WARBURTON.

I do not think this correction proper. The meaning of the preſent reading is eaſy. *When did he, however careful to carry his own dignity to the utmoſt height, regard any dignity of another?* JOHNSON.

I conceive the meaning to be—that from his pride he never paid a proper reſpect to nobleneſs, but when he was abſolutely obliged to it. "Out of himſelf" is, *of himſelf, of his own accord*. That this is the ſenſe is evident. It is impoſſible, as Warburton rightly obſerves (though he has printed and pointed the paſſage wrong), that the Chamberlain ſhould be talking of Wolſey's being *noble*. A. B.

[2] *Such as will ſtrike ſooner than ſpeak; and ſpeak ſooner than drink;*

and ſpeak ſooner than drink, and drink ſooner than pray. *Henry IV.* P. 1, A. 2, S. 1.

NOSE.

——— His chin, new reap'd,
Shew'd like a ſtubble land at harveſt home:
He was perfumed like a milliner;
And 'twixt his finger and his thumb he held
A pouncet-box, which ever and anon
He gave his noſe. *Henry IV.* P. 1, A. 1, S. 3.

drink; and drink ſooner than pray.] According to the ſpecimen given us in this play, of this diſſolute gang, we have no reaſon to think they were *leſs ready to drink than ſpeak.* We ſhould certainly read,—They will ſtrike ſooner than ſpeak; and ſpeak ſooner than think; and think ſooner than pray.

WARBURTON.

I am in doubt about this paſſage. There is yet a part unexplained. What is the meaning of *ſuch as can hold in?* It cannot mean ſuch as can keep their own ſecret, for they will, he ſays, *ſpeak* ſooner than *think*; and though we ſhould read, by tranſpoſition, *ſuch as will ſpeak ſooner than ſtrike,* the climax will not proceed regularly. I muſt leave it as it is.

JOHNSON.

"Drink" is certainly wrong, and for the reaſon given by Dr. Warburton; but *think* is ſcarcely right. *Drink,* I am of opinion, has been printed in miſtake for *drien,* the old word for *ſuffer.* I read the paſſage thus:

"Such as will ſtrike ſooner than ſpeak, and ſpeak ſooner than "drien (ſuffer); and drien (ſuffer) ſooner than pray." Here the climax is perfectly regular.

"Hold in" ſhould, I think, be *hold on,* i. e. ſuch as will purſue their courſe,—ſuch as are not eaſily terrified. This agrees with the reading above propoſed, and gives conſiſtency to the entire ſpeech. A. B.

OATH.

O.

OATH.

HE professes no keeping of oaths; in breaking them, he is stronger than Hercules. He will lie, sir, with such volubility, that you would think truth were a fool: drunkenness is his best virtue: for he will be swine-drunk.

All's well that ends well, A. 4, S. 3.

Not for Bohemia, nor the pomp that may
Be thereat glean'd; for all the sun sees, or
The close earth wombs, or the profound sea hides
In unknown fathoms, will I break my oath.

Winter's Tale, A. 4, S. 3.

If thou wert any way given to virtue, I would swear by thy face; my oath should be, by this fire: but thou art altogether given over; and wert indeed, but for the light in thy face, the son of utter darkness. *Henry IV*. P. 1, A. 3, S. 3.

A thousand oaths, an ocean of his tears,
And instances as infinite of love,
Warrant me welcome.

Two Gentlemen of Verona, A. 2, S. 7.

His words are bonds, his oaths are oracles;
His love sincere, his thoughts immaculate;
His tears, pure messengers sent from his heart;
His heart as far from fraud, as heaven from earth.

Two Gentlemen of Verona, A. 2, S. 7.

He has betray'd your business, and given up,
For certain drops of salt, your city Rome
(I say, your city) to his wife and mother:

Breaking

Breaking his oath and resolution, like
A twist of rotten silk. *Coriolanus*, A. 5, S. 5.

——— You swore to us,—
And you did swear that oath at Doncaster,—
That you did nothing purpose 'gainst the state;
Nor claim no further than your new-fall'n right,
The seat of Gaunt, dukedom of Lancaster:
To this we sware our aid. *Henry IV.* P. 1, A. 5, S. 1.

That's a brave man! he writes brave verses, speaks brave words, swears brave oaths, and breaks them bravely. *As you like it*, A. 3, S. 4.

—— Were it not against our laws,
Against my crown, my oath, my dignity,
Which princes, would they, may not disannul,
My soul should sue as advocate for thee.
Comedy of Errors, A. 1, S. 1.

——— Pernicious woman,
Think'st thou thy oaths
Were testimonies against his worth and credit,
That's seal'd in approbation?
Measure for Measure, A. 5, S. 1.

With mine own hands I give away my crown,
With mine own tongue deny my sacred state,
With mine own breath release all duteous oaths:
All pomp and majesty I do forswear.
Richard II. A. 4. S. 1.

Were I a common laugher, or did use
To stale with ordinary oaths my love
To every new protester; if you know
That I do fawn on men, and hug them hard,
And after scandal them; hold me dangerous.
Julius Cæsar, A. 1, S. 2.

No, not an oath:
Swear priests and cowards, and men cautelous,
Old feeble carrions, and such suffering souls
That welcome wrongs; unto bad causes swear

Such

Such creatures as men doubt: but do not ſtain
The even virtue of our enterprize,
Nor the inſuppreſſive mettle of our ſpirits,
To think, that, or our cauſe, or our performance,
Did need an oath. *Julius Cæſar*, A. 2, S. 1.

So ſoon as ever thou ſeeſt him, draw; and, as thou draw'ſt, ſwear horribly: for it comes to paſs oft, that a terrible oath, with a ſwaggering accent ſharply twang'd off, gives manhood more approbation than even proof itſelf would have earn'd him.

Twelfth Night, A. 3, S. 4.

OBLIVION.

Your deſert ſpeaks loud; and I ſhould wrong it,
To lock it in the wards of covert boſom,
When it deſerves with characters of braſs
A forted reſidence, 'gainſt the tooth of time
And razure of oblivion.

Meaſure for Meaſure, A. 5, S. 1.

——— Laſt ſcene of all,
Is ſecond childiſhneſs, and mere oblivion;
Sans teeth, ſans eyes, ſans taſte, ſans every thing.

As you like it, A. 2, S. 7.

Time hath, my lord, a wallet at his back,
Wherein he puts alms for oblivion,
A great-ſiz'd monſter of ingratitudes;
Thoſe ſcraps are good deeds paſt; which are devour'd
As faſt as they are made.

Troilus and Creſſida, A. 3, S. 3.

The noble iſle doth want her proper limbs;
Her face deface'd with ſcars of infamy,
Her royal ſtock graft with ignoble plants,
And almoſt ſhoulder'd in the ſwallowing gulph
Of dark forgetfulneſs and deep oblivion.

Richard III. A. 3, S. 7.

Sir, you and I muſt part,—but that's not it:
Sir, you and I have lov'd,—but there's not it;
That you know well: ſomething it is I would,—
O, my oblivion is a very Antony,
And I am all forgotten.
Antony and Cleopatra, A. 1, S. 3.

OBSTRUCTION.

Ay, but to die, and go we know not where;
To lie in cold obſtruction, and to rot;
This ſenſible warm motion to become
A kneaded clod. *Meaſure for Meaſure*, A. 3, S. 1.

OCCUPATION.

O you mortal engines, whoſe rude throats
The immortal Jove's dread clamours counterfeit,
Farewel! Othello's occupation's gone!
Othello, A. 3, S. 3.

——— Contract, ſucceſſion,
[1] Bourn, bound of land, tilth, vineyard, none,
No uſe of metal, corn, or wine, or oil:
No occupation. *Tempeſt*, A. 2, S. 1.

ODOUR.

That ſtrain again;—it had a dying fall:
O, it came o'er my ear like the ſweet ſouth,
That breathes upon a bank of violets,
Stealing and giving odour.—
Twelfth Night, A. 1, S. 1.

[1] *Bourn, bound of land*] A *bourn*, in this place, ſignifies *limit*, a *meer*, a *land-mark*. STEEVENS.

"Bourn" is properly a *little river*, though ſometimes uſed for a *boundary*. It muſt have its original meaning here, the more eſpecially as "bound of land" immediately follows it.

Borne is a limit, a *boundary*. See note on King Lear, page 37. A. B.

OFFENCES.

OFFENCES.

That I have ta'en away this old man's daughter,
It is moſt true; true, I have married her;
The very head and front of my offending
Hath this extent, no more. *Othello*, A. 1, S. 3.

If my offence be of ſuch mortal kind,
That, neither ſervice paſt, nor preſent ſorrows,
Nor purpos'd merit in futurity,
Can ranſom me into his love again,
But to know ſo muſt be my benefit;
So ſhall I clothe me in a forc'd content,
And ſhut myſelf up in ſome other courſe [1],
To fortune's alms. *Othello*, A. 3, S. 4.

Who is here ſo baſe, that would be a bond-man? If any, ſpeak; for him have I offended. Who is here ſo rude, that would not be a Roman? If any, ſpeak; for him have I offended. Who is here ſo vile, that will not love his country? If any, ſpeak; for him have I offended. *Julius Cæſar*, A. 3, S. 2.

King of England ſhalt thou be proclaim'd
In every borough as we paſs along;
And he, that caſts not up his cap for joy,
Shall for the offence make forfeit of his head.
Henry VI. P. 3, A. 2, S. 1.

[1] *And ſhoot myſelf up in ſome other courſe.*] The quarto 1630, and the folio read,

"And ſhut myſelf up."

I cannot help thinking this reading the true one. The idea ſeems taken from the confinement of a monaſtic life.
STEEVENS.

I think the quarto right which reads *ſhoot*, inſtead of *ſhut*. To ſay that a man will ſhut himſelf up in a courſe of life, is language ſuch as Shakeſpeare would never make uſe of, even in his moſt whimſical or licentious moments. MONCK MASON.

I think the poet may have written,

"And ſhape myſelf upon ſome other courſe."

To ſhape one's courſe, is a very common expreſſion, and is uſed by Shakeſpeare elſewhere. A. B.

The nature of his great offence is dead,
And deeper than oblivion we do bury
The incensing relicks of it.
All's well that ends well, A. 5, S. 3.

My life, sir, in any case: not that I am afraid to die; but that, my offences being many, I would repent out the remainder of nature: let me live, sir, in a dungeon, i' the stocks, or any where, so I may live. *All's well that ends well*, A. 4, S. 3.

This is most strange! that she should in this time
Commit a thing so monstrous, to dismantle
So many folds of favour! sure, her offence
Must be of such unnatural degree,
That monsters it, [1] or your fore-vouch'd affection
Fall into taint [2]. *Lear*, A. 1, S. 1.

I am

[1] *That monsters it.*] This uncommon verb occurs again in Coriolanus.

"To hear my nothings monster'd," STEEVENS.

"Monsters it" should, I think, be *masters it*; and I am the more inclined to this opinion, as *monstrous* occurs a line or two before. I read the passage thus:

"—— that she should
"Commit a thing so monstrous, to dismantle
"So many folds of favour! sure, her offence
"Must be of most unnatural degree,
"That masters it."

"That masters it," *i. e. that masters your favour or kindness.* If we do not admit this reading, where is the antecedent to *it?*
A. B.

[2] —— *or your fore-vouch'd affection*
Fall into taint.] Such is the reading of the folio. The common books read,—"fall'n into taint." Or, signifies *before*, and *or ever*, is, *before ever*; the meaning of the folio may therefore be, *sure her crime must be monstrous before your affection can be affected with hatred.* JOHNSON.

I believe the reading of the first quarto,
"—— or you for vouch'd affection
"Fall'n into taint,"
to be the true one. In support of the reading of the quarto, in preference to that of the folio, it should be observed, that Lear had not *vouch'd*, had *not* made any particular declaration of his affection

I am myſelf indifferent honeſt; but yet I could accuſe me of ſuch things, that it were better, my mother had not borne me: I am very proud, revengeful, ambitious; with more offences at my beck, than I have thoughts to put them in, imagination to give them ſhape, or time to act them in.

Hamlet, A. 3, S. 1.

ORNAMENT.

——— In religion,
What damned error, but ſome ſober brow
Will bleſs it, and approve it with a text,
Hiding the groſſneſs with fair ornament?

Merchant of Venice, A. 3, S. 2.

The world is ſtill deceiv'd with ornament:
In law, what plea ſo tainted and corrupt,
But, being ſeaſon'd with a gracious voice,
Obſcures the ſhow of evil?

Merchant of Venice, A. 3, S. 2.

affection for Cordelia; while, on the other hand, Goneril and Regan have made, in this ſcene, an oſtentatious profeſſion of their love for their father. MALONE.

The reading of the folio is right. *Taint*, I think, is *ſuſpicion.*

"——— or your fore-vouch'd affection
"Fall into taint."

That is, *the affection which you had before expreſſed will be queſtioned or diſbelieved—its ſincerity will be doubted.*

Mr. Malone is wrong, in ſaying that Lear had not made any declaration of his affection for Cordelia. He ſays of her, in one place, "Now our joy, although the laſt, not leaſt," and in another, "We lov'd her moſt," &c. A. B.

P.

PASSION, PASSIONS.

IS this the noble Moor, whom our full ſenate
Call—all-in-all ſufficient? This the noble nature
Whom paſſion could not ſhake? whoſe ſolid virtue
The ſhot of accident, nor dart of chance,
Could neither graze, nor pierce? *Othello*. A. 4, S. 1.

——— By heaven
My blood begins my ſafer guides to rule;
And paſſion having my beſt judgment collied [1],
Aſſays to lead the way. *Othello*, A. 2, S. 3.

——— I will go to Benedick,
And counſel him to fight againſt his paſſion:
And, truly, I'll deviſe ſome honeſt ſlanders
To ſtain my couſin with.
Much ado about nothing, A. 3, S. 1.

The colour of the king doth come and go,
Between his purpoſe and his conſcience,
Like heralds 'twixt two dreadful battles ſet:
His paſſion is ſo ripe, it needs muſt break.
King John, A. 4, S. 2.

[1] *And paſſion having my beſt judgment collied.*] Thus the folio reads, and I believe rightly. Othello means, that paſſion has diſcoloured his judgment. To *colly*, anciently, ſignified to *beſmut*, to *blacken as with coal*. Hanmer reads, *cholered*.
STEEVENS.

I think we ſhould read "colliding." To *collide* is to *claſh*, to *ſtrike againſt*. The line may ſtand thus:
"And paſſion now colliding 'gainſt my judgment."
i. e. Paſſion claſhing or ſtriking againſt my judgment, aſſays, &c.
A. B.

O, that

O, that my tongue were in the thunders mouth!
Then with a paſſion would I ſhake the world;
And rouze from ſleep that fell anatomy,
Which cannot hear a lady's feeble voice.
King John, A. 3, S. 4.

—— Such ſmiling rogues as theſe,
Like rats, oft bite the holy cords in twain
Too intrinſecate t' unlooſe: ſmooth every paſſion
That in the nature of their lords rebels;
Bring oil to fire, ſnow to their colder moods;
Renege, affirm, and turn their halcyon beaks
With every gale and vary of their maſters.
Lear, A. 2. S. 2.

Now and then an ample tear trill'd down
Her delicate cheek: it ſeem'd, ſhe was a queen
Over her paſſion; who, moſt rebel-like,
Sought to be king o'er her. *Lear*, A. 4, S. 3.

O, it offends me to the ſoul, to hear a robuſtious perriwig-pated fellow tear a paſſion to tatters, to very rags, to ſplit the ears of the groundlings; who, for the moſt part, are capable of nothing but inexplicable dumb ſhews and noiſe: I would have ſuch a fellow whipp'd for o'er-doing Termagant; it out-herods Herod: pray you avoid it. *Hamlet*, A. 3, S. 2.

For Hecuba!
What's Hecuba to him, or he to Hecuba,
That he ſhould weep for her? What would he do,
Had he the motive and the cue for paſſion,
That I have? he would drown the ſtage with tears,
And cleave the general ear with horrid ſpeech;
Make mad the guilty and appal the free,
Confound the ignorant: and amaze, indeed,
The very faculty of eyes and ears.
Hamlet, A. 2, S. 2.

That old and antique ſong we heard laſt night;
Methought, it did relieve my paſſion much;

More than light airs, and recollected terms,
Of these most brisk and giddy-paced times.

Twelfth Night, A. 2, S. 4.

Cesario, by the roses of the spring,
By maidhood, honour, truth, and every thing,
I love thee so, that, maugre all my pride,
Nor wit, nor reason, can my passion hide.

Twelfth Night, A. 3, S. 1.

Her passions are made of nothing but the finest part of pure love: we cannot call her winds and waters, sighs and tears [1]; they are greater storms and tempests than almanacks can report.

Antony and Cleopatra, A. 1, S. 2.

O, what a rogue and peasant slave am I!
Is it not monstrous, that this player here,
But in a fiction, in a dream of passion,
Could force his soul so to his own conceit,
That from her working, all his visage warm'd;
Tears in his eyes, distraction in's aspect,
A broken voice, and his whole function suiting
With forms to his conceit? And all for nothing!

Hamlet, A. 2, S. 2.

PATIENCE.

I know not how to pray your patience,
Yet I must speak: choose your revenge yourself;
Impose me to what penance your invention
Can lay upon my sin.

Much ado about nothing, A. 5, S. 1.

[1] *We cannot call her winds and waters, sighs and tears.*] I believe Shakespeare wrote,

"We cannot call her sighs and tears, winds and waters."

MALONE.

Mr. Malone is wrong in proposing any change. "Her winds "and waters (that is, her sighs and tears), says Enobarbus, "appear to be more than sighs and tears: they seem storms and "tempests." This sense is destroyed by transposition. A. B.

—— I know not how,
But I do find it cowardly and vile,
For fear of what might fall, ſo to prevent
The time of life :—arming myſelf with patience,
To ſtay the providence of ſome high powers,
That govern us below. *Julius Cæſar*, A. 5, S. 1.

In ſuffering thus thy brother to be ſlaughter'd,
Thow ſhew'ſt the naked path-way to thy life,
Teaching ſtern murder how to butcher thee:
That which in mean men we entitle—patience,
Is pale cold cowardice in noble breaſts.
Richard II. A. 1, S. 2.

—— Since he ſtands obdurate,
And that no lawful means can carry me
Out of his envy's reach, I do oppoſe
My patience to his fury; and am arm'd
To ſuffer, with a quietneſs of ſpirit,
The very tyranny and rage of his.
Merchant of Venice, A. 4, S. 1.

And am I thus rewarded?
Bring me a conſtant woman to her huſband,
One that ne'er dream'd a joy beyond his pleaſure;
And to that woman, when ſhe has done moſt,
Yet will I add an honour,—a great patience.
Henry VIII. A. 3, S. 1.

Ah, you bleſſed miniſters above,
Keep me in patience; and with ripen'd time,
Unfold the evil which is here wrapt up
In countenance! *Meaſure for Meaſure*, A. 5, S. 1.

[1] —— (Alas!) to make me
A fix'd figure, for the time of ſcorn

[1] —— *but, alas! to make me*
A fixed figure, for the time of ſcorn
To point his ſlow unmoving finger at.] Much has been written on this paſſage. Mr. Steevens is for the preſent reading, and would very willingly explain it. Mr. Rowe had changed "time

To point his ſlow unmoving finger at,—
O! O!
Yet could I bear that too; well, very well:
But there, where I have garner'd up my heart;
Where either I muſt live, or bear no life;
The fountain from the which my current runs
Or elſe dries up; to be diſcarded thence!
Or keep it as a ciſtern for foul toads
To knot and gender in!—turn thy complexion there!
Patience, thou young and roſe-lipp'd cherubim;
Ay, there, look grim as hell! *Othello*, A. 4, S. 2.

Good maſter muſtard-ſeed, I know your patience well[1]. *Midſummer Night's Dream*, A. 3, S. 1.

PEACE.

—— Let it not diſgrace me,
If I demand, before this royal view,

"time of ſcorn" to "hand of ſcorn," and he has been followed by ſucceeding editors. Mr. Malone thinks that Shakeſpeare might have written, "ſcorn of time," and Mr. Monck Maſon is of opinion, that "time of ſcorn" is a ſtrange expreſſion.

"Time of ſcorn" is undoubtedly nonſenſe; and if we admit the "hand of ſcorn" of Rowe, we ſhall loſe a very conſiderable beauty, becauſe we muſt then read—"the ſlow unmoving finger "of ſcorn," inſtead of the "ſlow unmoving finger of time."

I read,

"A fixed figure and in ſcorn, for time
"To point his ſlow unmoving finger at."

Nothing can be more poetical or beautiful, than thus to depicture *Time*. "Slow unmoving," for the imperceptible gradation of time. A. B.

[1] *Patience*.] The Oxford edition reads, "I know your *parentage* well." I believe the correction is right. JOHNSON.

Parentage was not eaſily corrupted to *patience*. I fancy the true word is *paſſions*, *ſufferings*. FARMER.

By *patience* is meant, ſtanding ſtill in a muſtard pot, to be eaten with the beef, on which it was a conſtant attendant. COLLINS.

"Patience" is right. It is ſpoken ironically, and in reference to the hot and biting quality of muſtard ſeed. A. B.

What

What rule, or what impediment, there is,
Why that the naked, poor, and mangled peace,
Dear nurſe of arts, plenties, and joyful births,
Should not, in this beſt garden of the world,
Our fertile France, put up her lovely viſage?
Henry V. A. 5, S. 2.

Cry, havock, kings! back to the ſtained field,
You equal potents, fiery-kindled ſpirits!
Then let confuſion of one part confirm
The other's peace. *King John*, A. 2, S. 2.

Still in thy right hand carry gentle peace,
To ſilence envious tongues. Be juſt, and fear not:
Let all the ends, thou aim'ſt at, be thy country's,
Thy God's, and truth's; then if thou fall'ſt, O Cromwell,
Thou fall'ſt a bleſſed martyr.
Henry VIII. A. 3, S. 2.

Peace ſhall go ſleep with Turks and infidels,
And, in this ſeat of peace, tumultuous wars
Shall kin with kin, and kind with kind confound;
Diſorder, horror, fear, and mutiny,
Shall here inhabit, and this land be call'd
The field of Golgotha. *Richard II.* A. 4, S. 1.

—— Her own ſhall bleſs her;
Her foes ſhake like a field of beaten corn,
And hang their heads with ſorrow: good grows with her
In her days, every man ſhall eat in ſafety,
Under his own vine, what he plants; and ſing
The merry ſongs of peace to all his neighbours.
Henry VIII. A. 5, S. 4.

Peace ſhould ſtill her wheaten garland wear,
And ſtand a comma [1] 'tween their amities.
Hamlet, A. 5, S. 2.

[1] *And ſtand a comma*, &c.]
"Stand a comma" is ſurely very unmeaning. Johnſon, however,

Peace, chewet, peace[1]. *Henry IV.* P. 1, A. 5, S. 1.

And for we think, the eagle-winged pride
Of ſky-aſpiring and ambitious thoughts,
With rival-hating envy, ſet you on
To wake our peace, which in our country's cradle
Draws the ſweet infant breath of gentle ſleep;
Which ſo rouz'd up with boiſterous untun'd drums,
And hard-reſounding trumpets dreadful bray,
And grating ſhock of wrathful iron arms,
Might from our quiet confines fright fair peace[2].
Richard II. A. 1, S. 3.

PEARL.

——— She is mine own;
And I as rich in having ſuch a jewel,
As twenty ſeas, if all their ſand were pearl,
The water nectar, and the rocks pure gold.
Two Gentlemen of Verona, A. 2, S. 4.

ever, would retain it, and Warburton would read, "ſtand a "commerce," and Hanmer, "ſtand a cement." I think we ſhould read, "ſtand a compact." A. B.

[1] *Peace, chewet, peace.*] Mr. Theobald ſays, that a *chewet* is a noiſy chattering bird. Mr. Steevens ſays, that it is a pudding; —and the latter is certainly right. I believe, however, that the poet's word was *chevin* (the *chub fiſh*). "Peace, chevin, peace," peace, jolthead, peace. A. B.

[2] *To wake our peace, which in our country's cradle*
Draws the ſweet infant breath of gentle ſleep;
Which ſo rouz'd up with boiſterous untun'd drums,
Might from our quiet confines fright fair peace.] This, pretty as it is in the image, is abſurd in the ſenſe: for peace awake is ſtill peace, as well as when aſleep. The difference is, that peace aſleep, gives one the notion of a happy people ſunk in ſloth and luxury, which is not the idea the ſpeaker would raiſe, and from which ſtate the ſooner it was awaked the better. WARBURTON.

Perhaps, "wake our eaſe," *i. e. diſturb our tranquillity*, may be the true reading. *Eaſe* and *peace* being nearly alike in ſound, the tranſcriber might be deceived by it. A. B.

That

That ſame dew, which ſometime on the buds
Was wont to ſwell, like round and orient pearls,
Stood now within the pretty flouret's eyes,
Like tears that did their own diſgrace bewail.
Midſummer Night's Dream, A. 4, S. 1.

——— When Phœbe doth behold
Her ſilver viſage in the watry glaſs,
Decking with liquid pearl the bladed graſs.
Midſummer Night's Dream, A. 1, S. 1.

I muſt go ſeek ſome dew-drops here,
And hang a pearl in every cowſlip's ear.
Midſummer Night's Dream, A. 2, S. 1.

——— Then muſt you ſpeak
Of one, that lov'd not wiſely, but too well;
Of one, not eaſily jealous, but, being wrought,
Perplex'd in the extreme; of one, whoſe hand,
Like the baſe Judean, threw a pearl away
Richer than all his tribe; of one, whoſe ſubdu'd eyes,
Albeit unuſed to the melting mood,
Drop tears as faſt as the Arabian trees
Their med'cinable gum. *Othello*, A. 5, S. 2.

PENITENCE.

By penitence the Eternal's wrath's appeas'd.
Two Gentlemen of Verona, A. 5, S. 3.

PENURY.

Take the baſeſt and moſt pooreſt ſhape,
That ever penury in contempt of man,
Brought near to beaſt: my face I'll grime with filth;
Blanket my loins; elf all my hair in knots;
And with preſented nakedneſs out-face
The winds, and perſecutions of the ſky.
Lear, A. 2, S. 3.

PHŒBUS.

PHŒBUS.

——— Pale primroſes,
That die unmarried, ere they can behold
Bright Phœbus in his ſtrength.
Winter's Tale, A. 4, S. 3.

—— Stalls, bulks, windows,
Are ſmother'd up, leads fill'd, and ridges hors'd
With variable complexions; all agreeing
In earneſtneſs to ſee him: ſeld-ſhown flamens
Do preſs among the popular throngs, and puff
To win a vulgar ſtation: our veil'd dames
Commit the war of white and damaſk, in
Their nicely gawded cheeks, to the wanton ſpoil
Of Phœbus' burning kiſſes. *Coriolanus*, A. 2, S. 1.

Under the allowance of your grand aſpect,
Whoſe influence, like the wreath of radiant fire
On flickering Phœbus' front [1]. *Lear*, A. 2, S. 2.

PICTURE.

Doſt thou love pictures? we will fetch thee ſtraight
Adonis, painted by a running brook;
And Cytherea all in ſedges hid;
Which ſeem to move and wanton with her breath,
Even as the waving ſedges play with wind.
Taming of the Shrew, *Induct.*

PITY.

'Tis well known, that whiles I was protector,
Pity was all the fault that was in me;

[1] *On flickering Phœbus' front.*] Dr. Johnſon, in his Dictionary, ſays this word means to *flutter*. Stoneyhurſt, in his tranſlation of the fourth book of Virgil's Æneid, deſcribes Iris,

"From the ſky down flickering, &c." STEEVENS.

To "flicker" is likewiſe to *fleer*, to *look proudly*. Phœbus cannot well be ſaid to *flutter*, but he certainly may be ſaid to *fleer*. Kent is laughing at Cornwal, and compares his "grand "aſpect" to the proud looks of Apollo. A. B.

For

For I ſhould melt at an offender's tears,
And lowly words were ranſom for their fault.

Henry VI. P. 2, A. 3, S. 1.

I am an humble ſuitor to your virtues;
For pity is the virtue of the law,
And none but tyrants uſe it cruelly.

Timon of Athens, A. 3, S. 5.

Where an unclean mind carries virtuous qualities, there commendations go with pity, they are virtues and traitors too.

All's well that ends well, A. 1, S. 1.

—— That we have been familiar,
Ingrate forgetfulneſs ſhall poiſon, rather
Than pity note how much.—Therefore, be gone.
Mine ears againſt your ſuits are ſtronger, than
Your gates againſt my force. *Coriolanus*, A. 5, S. 2.

My pity hath been balm to heal their wounds,
My mildneſs hath allay'd their ſwelling griefs,
My mercy dry'd their water-flowing tears:
I have not been deſirous of their wealth,
Nor much oppreſs'd them with great ſubſidies.

Henry VI. P. 3, A. 4, S. 8.

Say—pardon, king; let pity teach thee how:
The word is ſhort, but not ſo ſhort as ſweet;
No word like, pardon, for kings' mouth ſo meet.

Richard II. A. 5, S. 3.

If ever you have look'd on better days;
If ever ſat at any good man's feaſt;
If ever from your eye-lids wip'd a tear,
And know what 'tis to pity, and be pitied;
Let gentleneſs my ſtrong enforcement be.

As you like it, A. 2, S. 7.

——— Thou art come to anſwer
A ſtony adverſary, an inhuman wretch

Uncapable

Uncapable of pity, void and empty
From any dram of mercy.
Merchant of Venice, A. 4, S. 1.

—— If we ſuffer
(Out of our eaſineſs, and childiſh pity
To one man's honour) this contagious ſickneſs,
Farewell all phyſick: and what follows then?
Commotions, uproars, with a general taint
Of the whole ſtate. *Henry VIII.* A. 5, S. 2.

O, now you weep; and, I perceive you feel
The dint of pity [1]: theſe are gracious drops.
Kind ſouls, what, weep you, when you but behold
Our Cæſar's veſture wounded? Look you here!
Here is himſelf, marr'd, as you ſee, with traitors.
Julius Cæſar, A. 3, S. 2.

But ſoft, but ſee, or rather do not ſee,
My fair roſe wither: yet look up; behold;
That you in pity may diſſolve to dew,
And waſh him freſh again with true-love tears.
Richard II. A. 5, S. 1.

I am the moſt unhappy woman living.—
Shipwreck'd upon a kingdom, where no pity,
No friends, no hope, no kindred weep for me,
Almoſt, no grave allow'd me:—like the lily,
That once was miſtreſs of the field, and flouriſh'd,
I'll hang my head, and periſh.
Henry VIII. A. 3, S. 1.

[1] —— *and I perceive you feel*
The dint of pity.] Is the impreſſion of pity.

The word is in common uſe among our ancient writers. So in Preſton's Cambyſes:

"Your grace therein may hap receive, with others, for your haſte,
"The *dent* of death, &c." STEEVENS.

Dint, with Shakeſpeare, and in this place, is rather *force* or *power*. *Dent* is undoubtedly *ſtroke* or *impreſſion*. A. B.

Thou

Thou know'ſt no law of God nor man;
No beaſt ſo fierce, but knows ſome touch of pity.
Richard III. A. 1, S. 2.

—— Our very eyes
Are ſometimes like our judgments, blind. Good faith,
I tremble ſtill with fear: but if there be
Yet left in heaven as ſmall a drop of pity
As a wren's eye, fear'd gods, a part of it!
Cymbeline, A. 4, S. 2.

—— Come on, poor babe;
Some powerful ſpirit inſtruct the kites and ravens,
To be thy nurſes! Wolves, and bears, they ſay,
Caſting their ſavageneſs aſide, have done
Like offices of pity. *Winter's Tale*, A. 2, S. 3.

PLAYER.

O, there be players, that I have ſeen play,—and heard others praiſe, and that highly,—not to ſpeak it profanely, that, neither having the accent of chriſtians, nor the gait of chriſtian, pagan, nor man, have ſo ſtrutted, and bellow'd, that I have thought ſome of nature's journeymen had made men, and not made them well, they imitated humanity ſo abominably. *Hamlet*, A. 3, S. 2.

PLEASURE, PLEASURES.

—— Pleaſure, and revenge,
Have ears more deaf than adders to the voice
Of any true deciſion. *Troilus and Creſſida*, A. 2, S. 2.

What our contempts do often hurl from us,
We wiſh it ours again; the preſent pleaſure,
By revolution lowering, does become
The oppoſite of itſelf.
Antony and Cleopatra, A. 1, S. 2.

—— Grave ſir, hail! I come
To anſwer thy beſt pleaſure; be't to fly,

To

To ſwim, to dive into the fire, to ride
On the curl'd clouds. *Tempeſt*, A. 1, S. 2.

The miſtreſs, which I ſerve, quickens what's dead,
And makes my labours pleaſures.
Tempeſt, A. 3, S. 1.

PLOTS.

——— Let us know,
Our indiſcretion ſometime ſerves us well,
When our deep plots do fail: and that ſhould teach us,
There's a divinity that ſhapes our ends,
Rough-hew them how we will. *Hamlet*, A. 5, S. 2.

POESY.

—— Much is the force of heaven-bred poeſy.
Two Gentlemen of Verona, A. 3, S. 2.

I had rather be a kitten, and cry—mew,
Than one of theſe ſame metre ballad-mongers;
I had rather hear a brazen canſtick turn'd,
Or a dry wheel grate on the axle-tree;
And that would nothing ſet my teeth on edge,
Nothing ſo much as mincing poetry.
Henry IV. P. 1, A. 3, S. 1.

POISON.

——— I ſee that thou art poor;
Hold, there is forty ducats: let me have
A dram of poiſon; ſuch ſoon-ſpeeding geer
As will diſperſe itſelf through all the veins,
That the life-weary taker may fall dead.
Romeo and Juliet, A. 5, S. 1.

——— He, that ſtrikes
The veniſon firſt, ſhall be the lord o' the feaſt;
To him the other two ſhall miniſter;

And

And we will fear no poiſon, which attends
In place of greater ſtate. *Cymbeline*, A. 3, S. 3.

——— If there be cords, or knives,
Poiſon, or fire, or ſuffocating ſtreams,
I'll not endure it.—Would, I were ſatisfied!
Othello, A. 3, S. 3.

I feel my maſter's paſſion! [1] this ſlave,
Unto his honour, has my lord's meat in him:
Why ſhould it thrive, and turn to nutriment,
When he is turn'd to poiſon?
Timon of Athens, A. 3, S. 1.

P O M P.

——— This holy fox,
Or wolf, or both, (for he is equal ravenous,
As he is ſubtle)
Only to ſhew his pomp as well in France
As here at home, ſuggeſts the king our maſter
To this laſt coſtly treaty. *Henry VIII.* A. 1, S. 1.

Lo, now my glory ſmear'd in duſt and blood!
My parks, my walks, my manors that I had,
Even now forſake me; and of all my lands,
Is nothing left me but my body's length!
Why what is pomp, rule, reign, but earth and duſt?
Henry VI. P. 3, A. 5, S. 2.

[1] ——— *this ſlave,*
Unto his honour.] What Flaminius ſeems to mean is,—This ſlave (to the honour of his character) has, &c.
STEEVENS.

How can the conduct and behaviour of Lucullus be ſaid, in any way, to redound to his honour? We ſhould ſurely point thus:

"——— this ſlave
"Unto his honour."

i. e. This ſlave, who is continually talking of honourable actions;—who has always piqued himſelf on his honour. A. B.

Ah, Humphrey, can I bear this ſhameful yoke?
Trow'ſt thou, that e'er I'll look upon the world;
Or count them happy, that enjoy the ſun?
No; dark ſhall be my light, and night my day;
To think upon my pomp, ſhall be my hell.
Henry VI. P. 2, A. 2, S. 4.

—— Take phyſic, pomp:
Expoſe thyſelf to feel what wretches feel;
That thou may'ſt ſhake the ſuperflux to them,
And ſhew the heavens more juſt. *Lear*, A. 3, S. 4.

—— Why ſhould the poor be flatter'd?
No, let the candy'd tongue lick abſurd pomp;
And crook the pregnant hinges of the knee,
Where thrift may follow fawning.
Hamlet, A. 3, S. 2.

PRAISE.

Thou ſhalt find ſhe will out-ſtrip all praiſe,
And make it halt behind her. *Tempeſt*, A. 4, S. 1.

He gave you all the duties of a man;
Trimm'd up your praiſes with a princely tongue;
Spoke your deſervings like a chronicle;
Making you ever better than his praiſe,
By ſtill diſpraiſing praiſe, valu'd with you.
Henry IV. P. 1, A. 5, S. 2.

Ah! when the means are gone, that buy this praiſe,
The breath is gone whereof this praiſe is made:
Feaſt-won, faſt-loſt [1]: one cloud of winter ſhowers,
Theſe flies are couch'd.
Timon of Athens, A. 2, S. 2.

[1] *Feaſt-won, faſt-loſt.*] I do not underſtand this. I think we ſhould read,

"Faſt won, faſt loſt."

i. e. Your friends are ſuch as may be eaſily acquired, and who are eaſily loſt. A. B.

A giving

A giving hand, though foul, ſhall have fair praiſe,
And, out of queſtion, ſo it is ſometimes;
Glory grows guilty of deteſted crimes.
Love's Labour Loſt, A. 4, S. 1.

Your praiſe is come too ſwiftly home before you,
Know you not, maſter, to ſome kind of men
Their graces ſerve them but as enemies?
As you like it, A. 2, S. 3.

Methinks ſhe is too low for a high praiſe, too brown for a fair praiſe, and too little for a great praiſe.
Much ado about nothing, A. 1, S. 1.

How many things by ſeaſon ſeaſon'd are
To their right praiſe, and true perfection?
Merchant of Venice, A. 5, S. 1.

Like one of two contending in a prize,
That thinks he hath done well in people's eyes,
Hearing applauſe, and univerſal ſhout
Giddy in ſpirit, ſtill gazing, in a doubt
Whether thoſe peals of praiſe be his or no.
Merchant of Venice, A. 3, S. 2.

PRAYERS.

——— I'll bribe you with true prayers,
That ſhall be up at heaven, and enter there,
Ere the ſun riſe. *Meaſure for Meaſure*, A. 2, S. 2.

——— He cannot thrive,
Unleſs her prayers, whom heaven delights to hear,
And loves to grant, reprieve him from the wrath
Of greateſt juſtice.
All's well that ends well, A. 3, S. 4.

PRECEPT.

[1] ——— Then I precepts gave her,
That she should lock herself from his resort,
Admit no messengers. *Hamlet*, A. 2, S. 2.

PRESENCE.

It ill beseems this presence, to cry aim
To these ill-tuned repetitions [2].
King John, A. 2, S. 1.

PREY.

So looks the pent-up lion o'er the wretch
That trembles under his devouring paws:

[1] *And then I precepts gave her.*] Thus the folio. The two elder quartos read, *prescripts.* STEEVENS.

"Prescripts" is right—signifying *inhibition*, *restraint*. That it is the true reading the context will fully shew. Polonius says, that he had already observed to his daughter,

"Lord Hamlet is a prince: out of thy sphere—
"This must not be!"

Now this we may consider as a precept, or hint, to Ophelia how she should behave. He then goes on,

"And then I prescripts (or orders) gave her,
"That she should lock herself from his resort," &c.

A. B.

[2] *It ill beseems this presence, to cry aim*
To these ill-tuned repetitions.] Dr. Warburton has well observed on one of the former plays, that to *cry aim* is to *encourage*. I once thought that it was borrowed from archery; and that *aim!* having been the word of command, as we now say *present!* to cry aim had been to *incite notice*, or raise *attention*. But I rather think that the old word of applause was *j'aime*, *I love it*, and that to applaud was to cry j'aime, which the English, not easily pronouncing *je*, sunk into *aime* or *aim*. JOHNSON.

I think it highly probable that we should read, "cry aien," *i. e.* cry *again! aien* is *again.*—See Chaucer and other old writers. *Cry aim* may, indeed, in other places, have the sense which Dr. Warburton has given to it. A. B.

And

And ſo he walks, inſulting o'er his prey;
And ſo he comes, to rend his limbs aſunder.
Henry VI. P. 3, A. 1, S. 3.

——— Ravens, crows, and kites,
Fly o'er our heads, and downward look on us,
As we were ſickly prey; their ſhadows ſeem
A canopy moſt fatal, under which
Our army lies ready to give up the ghoſt.
Julius Cæſar, A. 5, S. 1.

P R I D E.

—— Infants prattle of thy pride,
Thou art a moſt pernicious uſurer;
Froward by nature, enemy to peace;
Laſcivious, wanton, more than well beſeems
A man of thy profeſſion and degrees.
Henry VI. P. 1, A. 3, S. 1.

——— Who cries out on pride,
That can therein tax any private party?
Doth it not flow as hugely as the ſea,
Till that the very very means do ebb?
As you like it, A. 2, S. 7.

What fire is in mine ears? can this be true?
Stand I condemn'd for pride and ſcorn ſo much?
Contempt, farewell! and maiden pride, adieu!
No glory lives behind the back of ſuch.
Much ado about nothing, A. 3, S. 1.

——— Come all to ruin; let
Thy mother rather feel thy pride, than fear
Thy dangerous ſtoutneſs: for I mock at death
With as big heart as thou. Do as thou liſt.
Thy valiantneſs was mine, thou ſuck'dſt it from me;
But owe thy pride thyſelf. *Coriolanus*, A. 3, S. 2.

—— He that's proud, eats up himſelf:
Pride is his own glaſs, his own trumpet, his

Own chronicle; and whate'er praiſes itſelf
But in the deed, devours the deed i' the praiſe.
Troilus and Creſſida, A. 2, S. 3.

——— Pride hath no other glaſs
To ſhew itſelf, but pride; for ſupple knees
Feed arrogance, and are the proud man's fees.
Troilus and Creſſida, A. 3, S. 3.

If thou didſt put this ſour cold habit on
To caſtigate thy pride, 'twere well: but thou
Doſt it enforcedly; thou'dſt courtlier be again,
Wert thou not beggar. *Timon of Athens*, A. 4, S. 3.

PRINCE.

The hearts of princes kiſs obedience,
So much they love it; but, to ſtubborn ſpirits,
They ſwell, and grow as terrible as ſtorms.
Henry VIII. A. 3, S. 1.

The Hyrcanian deſerts, and the vaſty wilds
Of wide Arabia, are as thorough-fares now,
For princes to come view fair Portia.
Merchant of Venice, A. 2, S. 7.

——— Now he was
The ivy, which had hid my princely trunk,
And ſuck'd my verdure out on't.
Tempeſt, A. 1, S. 2.

——— The ſhepherd's homely curds,
His cold thin drink out of his leather bottle,
His wonted ſleep under a freſh tree's ſhade,
All which ſecure and ſweetly he enjoys,
Is far beyond a prince's delicates,
His viands ſparkling in a golden cup,
His body couched in a curious bed,
When care, miſtruſt, and treaſon waits on him.
Henry VI. P. 3, A. 2, S. 5.

The

The ſtrawberry grows underneath the nettle;
And wholeſome berries thrive and ripen beſt,
Neighbour'd by fruit of baſer quality:
And ſo the prince obſcur'd his contemplation
Under the veil of wildneſs. *Henry V.* A. 1, S. 1.

By the Lord, I knew ye as well as he that made ye. Why, hear ye, my maſters: was it for me to kill the heir apparent? ſhould I turn upon the true prince?
Henry IV. P. 1, A. 2, S. 4.

——— Like groſs terms,
The prince will, in the perfectneſs of time,
Caſt off his followers: and their memory
Shall as a pattern or a meaſure live,
By which his grace muſt mete the lives of others;
Turning paſt evils to advantages.
Henry IV. P. 2, A. 4, S. 4.

PROMONTORY.

——I do but dream on ſovereignty;
Like one that ſtands upon a promontory,
And ſpies a far-off ſhore where he would tread,
Wiſhing his foot were equal with his eye;
And chides the ſea that ſunders him from thence.
Henry VI. P. 3, A. 3, S. 2.

——— Thou remember'ſt
Since once I ſat upon a promontory,
And heard a mermaid, on a dolphin's back,
Uttering ſuch dulcet and harmonious breath,
That the rude ſea grew civil at her ſong.
Midſummer Night's Dream, A. 2. S. 2.

——— The ſtrong-bas'd promontory
Have I made ſhake; and by the ſpurs pluck'd up
The pine and cedar. *Tempeſt,* A. 5, S. 1.

PROMOTION.

Thou art not for the faſhion of theſe times,
Where none will ſweat, but for promotion;
And having that, do choak their ſervice up
Even with the having. *As you like it*, A. 2, S. 3.

Q.

QUEEN.

TO be a queen in bondage is more vile,
Than is a ſlave in baſe ſervility;
For princes ſhould be free.
Henry VI. P. 1, A. 5, S. 4.

O, would to God, that the incluſive verge
Of golden metal, that muſt round my brow,
Were red-hot ſteel, to ſear me to the brain!
Anointed let me be with deadly venom;
And die, ere men can ſay—God ſave the queen!
Richard III. A. 4, S. 1.

What, doſt thou turn away, and hide thy face?
I am no loathſome leper, look on me.
What, art thou, like the adder, waxen deaf?
Be poiſonous too, and kill thy forlorn queen.
Henry VI. P. 2, A. 3, S. 2.

What! ſhall king Henry be a pupil ſtill,
Under the ſurly Gloſter's governance?
Am I a queen in title and in ſtyle,
And muſt be made a ſubject to a duke?
Henry VI. P. 2, A. 1, S. 3.

Go thy ways, Kate: thou art, alone,
If thy rare qualities, ſweet gentleneſs,

Thy

Thy meeknefs, faint-like, wife-like government;
Obeying in commanding,—and thy parts
Sovereign and pious elfe, could fpeak thee out [1],
The queen of earthly queens.

Henry VIII. A. 2, S. 4.

—— I fee, queen Mab hath been with you.
She is the fairies' midwife; and fhe comes
In fhapes no bigger than an agat-ftone
On the fore-finger of an alderman,
Drawn with a team of little atomies
Athwart men's nofes as they lie afleep:
Her waggon-fpokes made of long fpinners' legs;
The cover, of the wings of grafhoppers;
The traces, of the fmalleft fpiders' web;
The collars, of the moonfhine's watry beams;
Her whip, of cricket's bone; the lafh, of film:
Her waggoner, a fmall grey-coated gnat,
Not half fo big as a round little worm
Prick'd from the lazy finger of a maid:
Her chariot is an empty hazel-nut,
Made by the joiner fquirrel, or old grub,
Time out of mind the fairies' coach-makers.
And in this ftate fhe gallops night by night
Through lovers' brains, and then they dream of love;
On courtiers' knees, that dream on court'fies ftraight:
O'er lawyers' fingers, who ftraight dream on fees:
O'er ladies' lips, who ftraight on kiffes dream;
Which oft the angry Mab with blifters plagues,
Becaufe their breaths with fweetmeats tainted are.
Sometimes fhe gallops o'er a courtier's nofe,
And then dreams he of fmelling out a fuit:
And fometimes comes fhe with a tithe-pig's tail,

[1] —— *could fpeak thee out.*] If thy feveral qualities had tongues to fpeak thy praife. JOHNSON.

Thefe qualities do fufficiently fpeak, or plead, for the queen in the king's breaft: but he here means, by *fpeak thee out*, that if thefe qualities were known to the world, Catherine would be confidered as the queen of earthly queens. A. B.

Tickling a parson's nose as a' lies asleep,
Then dreams he of another benefice:
Sometimes she driveth o'er a soldier's neck,
And then dreams he of cutting foreign throats,
Of breaches, ambuscadoes, Spanish blades,
Of healths five fathom deep; and then anon
Drums in his ear; at which he starts, and wakes;
And, being thus frighted, swears a prayer or two,
And sleeps again. *Romeo and Juliet*, A. 1, S. 4.

Good expedition be my friend, and comfort
The gracious queen [1], part of his theme, but nothing
Of his ill-ta'en suspicion! *Winter's Tale*, A. 1, S. 2.

——— We say, the king
Is wise, and virtuous; and his noble queen
Well struck in years [2]. *Richard III.* A. 1, S. 1.

[1] *Good expedition be my friend, and comfort The gracious queen.*] But how could this expedition comfort the queen? On the contrary, it would increase her husband's suspicion. We should read,

"—— and comfort
"The gracious queen's."

i. e, be expedition my friend, and be comfort the queen's friend. WARBURTON.

Dr. Warburton's conjecture is, I think, just; but what shall be done with the following words, of which I can make nothing? JOHNSON.

The obscurity of this passage arises from the wrong pointing. I read,

"Good expedition be my friend and comfort.
"The gracious queen part of his theme, but nothing
"Of his ill-ta'en suspicion!"

The meaning is—may expedition be my friend and comforter; and may the queen again become his (Leontes') theme, but without suspicion. A. B.

[2] *Well struck in years.*] This odd expression in our language was preceded by one as uncouth, though of a similar kind.

"Well *shot* in years he seem'd." *Spenser's F. Q.*

The meaning of neither is very obvious. STEEVENS.

This is said with a sneer, and purposely rendered ambiguous. It may mean, "somewhat old," or as we now say, *stricken in years*: or that the queen is *no girl*, but so far advanced in age, as to be capable of advising the king. A. B.

RAGE,

R.

RAGE.

I Remember when the fight was done,
When I was dry with rage, and extreme toil,
Breathlefs and faint, leaning upon my fword,
Came there a certain lord, neat, and trimly drefs'd,
Frefh as a bridegroom. *Henry IV.* P. 1, A. 1, S. 3.

Be gone.
Put not your worthy rage into your tongue;
One time will owe another[1]. *Coriolanus*, A. 3, S. 1.

RANK.

——— I do know but one
That unaffailable holds on his rank[2],
Unfhak'd of motion. *Julius Cæfar*, A. 3, S. 1.

RARENESS.

[1] *Put not your worthy rage into your tongue;*
One time will owe another.] I know not whether to *owe*, in this place, means to *poffefs by right*, or to *be indebted:* either fenfe may be admitted. *One time*, in which the people are feditious, will *give us power* in fome *other time*: or this time of the people's predominance will *own them in debt:* that is, will lay them open to the law, and expofe them hereafter to more fervile fubjection. JOHNSON.

I am of opinion that Dr. Johnfon has miftaken the fenfe; and that we fhould read, *we'll*, inftead of *will.*

"Put not your worthy rage into your tongue;
"One time we'll owe (*i. e.* own) another."

That is, at *another time*, at a more convenient feafon, we'll own *another kind of tongue:*—we'll hold a very different language. A. B.

[2] ——— *holds on his rank.*] Perhaps, *holds on his race*; continues his courfe. We commonly fay, to *hold a rank*, and to *hold on a courfe.* JOHNSON.

"*Holds*

RARENESS.

Thus did I keep my perſon freſh, and new;
My preſence, like a robe pontifical,
Ne'er ſeen but wonder'd at: and ſo my ſtate,
Seldom, but ſumptuous, ſhewed like a feaſt;
And won, by rareneſs, ſuch ſolemnity.

Henry IV. P. 1, A. 3, S. 2.

If all the year were playing holidays,
To ſport would be as tedious as to work;
But, when they ſeldom come, they wiſh'd-for come,
And nothing pleaſeth but rare accidents.

Henry IV. P. 1, A. 1, S. 2.

RASHNESS.

If Cleopatra heard you, your reproof
Were well deſerv'd of raſhneſs [1].

Antony and Cleopatra, A. 2, S. 2.

REASON.

Though with their high wrongs I am ſtruck to the quick,
Yet, with my nobler reaſon, 'gainſt my fury
Do I take part. *Tempeſt*, A. 5, S. 1.

" *Holds on*" here means, *reſts on, relies on*; and the words *unaſſailable* and *unſhaken*, ſufficiently prove that ſuch is the ſenſe. A. B.

[1] —— *your reproof*
Were well deſerv'd of raſhneſs.] In the old edition,
" —— your proof
" Were well deſerv'd."
Which Mr. Theobald, with his uſual triumph, changes to *approof*, which he explains *allowance.* JOHNSON.

I think "*approof*" is right. *Approof*, with the writers of Shakeſpeare's time, is *commendation.* Your commendation of Octavia (ſays Cæſar) would, if Cleopatra heard you, be conſtrued into folly; *raſhneſs* here is *folly.* A. B.

Who

Who was ſo firm, ſo conſtant, that this coil
Would not infect his reaſon? *Tempeſt*, A. 1, S. 2.

——— Their underſtanding
Begins to ſwell; and the approaching tide
Will ſhortly fill the reaſonable ſhore,
That now lies foul and muddy. *Tempeſt*, A. 5, S. 1.

——— I perceive, theſe lords
At this encounter do ſo much admire,
That they devour their reaſon; and ſcarce think,
Their eyes do offices of truth. *Tempeſt*, A. 5, S. 1.

——— Reaſon, my ſon
Should chooſe himſelf a wife; but as good reaſon,
The father (all whoſe joy is nothing elſe
But fair poſterity) ſhould hold ſome counſel
In ſuch a buſineſs. *Winter's Tale*, A. 4, S. 3.

Is not your father grown incapable
Of reaſonable affairs? Is he not ſtupid
With age, and altering rheums? Can he ſpeak, hear?
Know man from man? diſpute his own eſtate?
Winter's Tale, A. 4, S. 3.

I'll yet follow
The wounded chance of Antony [1], though my reaſon
Sits in the wind againſt me.
Antony and Cleopatra, A. 3, S. 8.

——— Reaſon thus with reaſon fetter:
Love ſought is good, but given unſought, is better.
Twelfth Night, A. 3, S. 1.

I, of ladies moſt deject and wretched,
That ſuck'd the honey of his muſick vows,

[1] *The wounded chance of Antony.*] I know not whether the author, who loves to draw his images from the ſports of the field, might not have written
"The wounded *chaſe* of Antony."
The alluſion is to a deer wounded and chaſed, whom all other deer avoid. I will, ſays Enobarbus, follow Antony, though *chaſed* and *wounded*. JOHNSON.

"Wounded chance," *i. e. fallen fortunes.* A. B.

Now

Now ſee the noble and moſt ſovereign reaſon,
Like ſweet bells jangled, out of tune and harſh.
Hamlet, A. 3, S. 1.

——— How ſtand I then,
That have a father kill'd, a mother ſtain'd,
Excitements of my reaſon, and my blood,
And let all ſleep? while, to my ſhame, I ſee
The imminent death of twenty thouſand men,
That, for a fantaſy, and trick of fame,
Go to their graves like beds. *Hamlet*, A. 4, S. 4.

Sure, he, that made us with ſuch large diſcourſe,
Looking before, and after, gave us not
That capability and god-like reaſon
To fuſt in us unus'd. *Hamlet*, A. 4, S. 4.

——— Do not baniſh reaſon
For inequality: but let your reaſon ſerve
To make the truth appear, where it ſeems hid.
Meaſure for Meaſure, A. 5, S. 1.

If Cæſar hide himſelf, ſhall they not whiſper,
Lo, Cæſar is afraid?
Pardon me, Cæſar; for my dear, dear love
To your proceeding bids me tell you this;
And reaſon to my love is liable [1].
Julius Cæſar, A. 2, S. 2.

——— She hath proſperous art
When ſhe will play with reaſon and diſcourſe,
And well ſhe can perſuade.
Meaſure for Meaſure, A. 1, S. 3.

What, upon compulſion? No, were I at the ſtrappado, or all the racks in the world, I would not tell you on compulſion. Give you a reaſon on com-

[1] *And reaſon to my love is liable.*] And reaſon, or propriety of conduct and language, is ſubordinate to my love. JOHNSON.
Rather—Reaſon *falls in with*, or *agrees*, to what my love has ſuggeſted. A. B.

pulſion! if reaſons were as plenty as black-berries, I would give no man a reaſon upon compulſion, I.

Henry IV. P. 1, A. 2, S. 4.

REBELLION.

——— Their weapons only
Seem'd on our ſide, but, for their ſpirits and ſouls,
This word rebellion, it had froze them up.

Henry IV. P. 2, A. 1, S. 1.

For the mutable, rank-ſcented many, let them
Regard me as I do not flatter, and
Therein behold themſelves: I ſay again,
In ſoothing them, we nouriſh 'gainſt our ſenate
The cockle of rebellion. *Coriolanus*, A. 3, S. 1.

—— Your ſon had only but the corps,
But ſhadows, and the ſhews of men, to fight:
For that ſame word, rebellion, did divide
The action of their bodies from their ſouls;
And they did fight with queaſineſs, conſtrain'd,
As men drink potions. *Henry IV.* P. 2, A. 1, S. 1.

——— If that rebellion
Came like itſelf, in baſe and abject routs,
Led on by bloody youth, guarded with rage,
And countenanc'd by boys, and beggary;
I ſay, if damn'd commotion ſo appear'd,
In his true, native, and moſt proper ſhape,
You, reverend father, and theſe noble lords,
Had not been here, to dreſs the ugly form
Of baſe and bloody inſurrection
With your fair honours. *Henry IV.* P. 2, A. 4, S. 1.

Fly, noble Engliſh, you are bought and ſold;
Unthread the rude eye of rebellion [1],
And welcome home again diſcarded faith.

King John, A. 5, S. 4.

REMEM-

[1] *Unthread the rude eye of rebellion.*] Though all the copies concur

REMEMBRANCE.

Praiſing what is loſt,
Makes the remembrance dear.

All's well that ends well, A. 5, S. 3.

There's roſemary, that's for remembrance; pray you, love, remember: and there is panſies, that's for thoughts [1]. *Hamlet*, A. 4, S. 5.

REPENTANCE.

Well, I'll repent, and that ſuddenly, while I am in ſome liking; I ſhall be out of heart ſhortly, and

concur in this reading, how poor is the metaphor of *unthreading* the *eye* of a *needle!* And beſides, as there is no mention made of a needle, how remote and obſcure is the alluſion without it! We ſhould read,

"Untread the rude way of rebellion." THEOBALD.

The metaphor is certainly harſh, but I do not think the paſſage corrupted. JOHNSON.

"Unthread the rude *eye* of rebellion," is particularly harſh indeed; but Shakeſpeare certainly wrote *tie*. *Unthread*, has no alluſion to a needle, but means *looſen*. The word is uſed in that ſenſe by Milton. We muſt read,

"Unthread the tie of rude rebellion."

i. e. looſen the knot of rebellion.

Mr. Steevens, indeed, obſerves in ſupport of the ordinary reading, that "Shakeſpeare elſewhere uſes the expreſſion, *thread-*"*ing dark-ey'd night*." But this is nothing to the purpoſe: *threading dark-ey'd night*, is *traverſing* or *going about during the night*. To *thread* is to *paſs through*, to *unthread* is to *looſen*.

A ſimilar expreſſion is to be found in Henry IV. "*Unknit* "this churliſh *knot* of war." A. B.

[1] *There's roſemary, that's for remembrance; and there's panſies, that's for thoughts.*] There is probably ſome mythology in the choice of theſe herbs, but I cannot explain it. *Panſies* is for *thoughts*, becauſe of its name, *penſées*; but why *roſemary* indicates *remembrance*, except that it is an evergreen, and carried at funerals, I have not diſcovered. JOHNSON.

Roſemary has always been conſidered as an excellent *cephalic*. The reaſon why roſemary indicates remembrance, is, becauſe it is ſuppoſed to ſtrengthen the brain. It is well known that in inveterate head-achs, the memory is frequently loſt. A. B.

then I ſhall have no ſtrength to repent. An I have not forgotten what the inſide of a church is made of, I am a pepper-corn, a brewer's horſe.

Henry IV. P. 1, A. 3, S. 3.

Who by repentance is not ſatisfy'd,
Is nor of heaven, nor earth.

Two Gentlemen of Verona, A. 5, S. 3.

—— What then? what reſts?
Try what repentance can: what can it not?
Yet what can it, when one cannot repent?

Hamlet, A. 3, S. 3.

REPUTATION.

Reputation is an idle and moſt falſe impoſition; oft got without merit, and loſt without deſerving: You have loſt no reputation at all, unleſs you repute yourſelf ſuch a loſer. *Othello*, A. 2, S. 3.

——— What's the matter,
[1] That you unlace your reputation thus,
And ſpend your rich opinion, for the name
Of a night brawler? *Othello*, A. 2, S. 3.

The pureſt treaſure mortal times afford,
Is—ſpotleſs reputation; that away,
Men are but gilded loam, or painted clay.

Richard II. A. 1, S. 1.

Thy death-bed is no leſſer than the land,
Wherein thou lieſt in reputation ſick;
And thou, too careleſs, patient as thou art,
Committ'ſt thy anointed body to the cure
Of thoſe phyſicians that firſt wounded thee.

Richard II. A. 2, S. 1.

[1] *That you unlace.*] *Slacken* or *looſen.* Put in danger of dropping, or perhaps ſtrip of its ornaments. JOHNSON.
I would read,
"Unbrace your reputation." A. B.

REVENGE.

REVENGE.

——— As he does conceive
He is dishonour'd by a man which ever
Profess'd to him, why, his revenges must
In that be made more bitter.

Winter's Tale, A. 1, S. 2.

Now might I do it, pat, now he is praying;
And now I'll do't:—and so he goes to heaven:
And so am I reveng'd? that would be scann'd,
A villain kills my father; and, for that,
I, his sole son, do this same villain send
To heaven. *Hamlet*, A. 3, S. 3.

How all occasions do inform against me,
And spur my dull revenge! What is a man,
If his chief good, and market of his time,
Be but to sleep, and feed? a beast, no more.

Hamlet, A. 4, S. 4.

—— No, you unnatural hags,
I will have such revenges on you both,
That all the world shall,—I will do such things,—
What they are, yet I know not; but they shall be
The terrors of the earth. *Lear*, A. 2, S. 4.

No satisfaction, no revenge: nor no ill luck stirring, but what lights o' my shoulders; no sighs but o' my breathing, no tears but o' my shedding.

Merchant of Venice, A. 3, S. 1.

If you prick us, do we not bleed? if you tickle us, do we not laugh? if you poison us, do we not die? and if you wrong us, shall we not revenge? if we are like you in the rest, we will resemble you in that. *Merchant of Venice*, A. 3, S. 1.

O that the slave had forty thousand lives;
One is too poor, too weak for my revenge!

Now

Now do I ſee 'tis true.—Look here, Iago;
All my fond love thus do I blow to heaven.
Othello, A. 3, S. 3.

Had all his hairs been lives, my great revenge
Had ſtomach for them all. *Othello*, A. 5, S. 2.

REVERENCE.

Knavery cannot ſure hide himſelf in ſuch reverence.
Much ado about nothing, A. 2, S. 3.

But yeſterday the word of Cæſar might
Have ſtood againſt the world: now lies he there,
And none ſo poor to do him reverence.
Julius Cæſar, A. 3, S. 2.

I aſk, that I might waken reverence,
And bid the cheek be ready with a bluſh,
Modeſt as morning when ſhe coldly eyes
The youthful Phœbus.
Troilus and Creſſida, A. 1, S. 3.

—— Though mean and mighty, rotting
Together, have one duſt; yet reverence
(That angel of the world) doth make diſtinction
Of place 'twixt high and low. Our foe was princely;
And tho' you took his life, as being our foe,
Yet bury him as a prince. *Cymbeline*, A. 4, S. 2.

RICHES.

Poor and content, is rich, and rich enough;
But riches, fineleſs, is as poor as winter,
To him that ever fears he ſhall be poor.
Othello, A. 3, S. 3.

Well, whiles I am a beggar, I will rail,
And ſay,—there is no ſin; but to be rich;
And being rich, my virtue then ſhall be,
To ſay,—there is no vice, but beggary.
King John, A. 2, S. 2.

—— When thou art old, and rich,
Thou haſt neither heat, affection, limb, nor beauty,
To make thy riches pleaſant.

Meaſure for Meaſure, A. 3, S. 1.

Kent, in the commentaries Cæſar writ,
Is term'd the civil'ſt place of all this iſle;
Sweet is the country, becauſe full of riches;
The people liberal, valiant, active, wealthy;
Which makes me hope you are not void of pity.

Henry VI. P. 2, A. 4, S. 7.

I have often wiſh'd myſelf poorer, that I might come nearer to you. We are born to do benefits: and what better or properer can we call our own, than the riches of our friends? O, what a precious comfort 'tis, to have ſo many, like brothers, commanding one another's fortunes!

Timon of Athens, A. 1, S. 2.

O, the fierce wretchedneſs that glory brings us!
Who would not wiſh to be from wealth exempt,
Since riches point to miſery and contempt?
Who'd be ſo mock'd with glory? or to live
But in a dream of friendſhip?

Timon of Athens, A. 4, S. 2.

RIDDLE.

No egma, no riddle, no l'envoy [1]; no ſalve in the male, ſir: O ſir, plantain, a plain plantain; no l'envoy, no l'envoy, no ſalve, ſir, but a plantain!

Love's Labour Loſt, A. 3, S. 1.

ROME.

[1] *No l'envoy.*] The *l'envoy* is a term borrowed from the old French poetry. It appeared always at the head of a few concluding verſes to each piece, which either ſerved to convey the moral, or to addreſs the poem to ſome particular perſon. It was frequently adopted by the ancient Engliſh writers.

No ſalve in the male, ſir.] What this can mean is not eaſily diſcovered.

R O M E.

Would'ſt thou be window'd in great Rome, and ſee
Thy maſter thus with pleach'd arms, bending down
His corrigible neck [1], his face ſubdu'd
To penetrative ſhame; whilſt the wheel'd ſeat
Of fortunate Cæſar, drawn before him, branded
His baſeneſs that enſued?

Antony and Cleopatra, A. 4, S. 12.

The noble ſiſter of Publicola,
The moon of Rome; chaſte as the iſicle
That's curdled by the froſt from pureſt ſnow,
And hangs on Dian's temple. *Coriolanus*, A. 5, S. 3.

diſcovered. If *mail*, for a *pocket* or *bag*, was a word then in uſe, *no ſalve in the male*, may mean, No ſalve in the mountebank's budget. Or, ſhall we read, *no enigma*, *no riddle*, *no l'envoy*—*in the vale*, *ſir*, *O*, *ſir plantain*. The matter is not great, but one could wiſh for ſome meaning or other. JOHNSON.

I believe we ſhould read and point the paſſage thus:

"No egma, no riddle, no *l'envoy*. No ſalve for the mal, ſir. "O, ſir plantain, a plain plantain; no *l'envoy*, no ſalve, ſir, "but a plantain."

There is a quibble on the word *envoy*, which ſignifies both an *ambaſſador*, and the *addreſs* that Dr. Johnſon has noticed.

When Coſtard and Moth come in, Armado ſays,—"Here is "ſome riddle, come, the *l'envoy*, the *addreſs*---begin." Coſtard plays upon *envoy*, which he ſuppoſes to mean *ambaſſador*, whom he conſiders as a *ſalve*, meaning that an *envoy* is frequently ſent to *heal grievances*, but that *envoy* would not heal a broken pate. He therefore goes on,---"No ſalve for the mal, ſir" *(i. e. this is no ſalve for the ſore, ſir)*. "Plantain, plantain, ſir, no ſalve like a plain plantain."

That ſuch is the quibble, will be ſeen by what follows:

Armad. Doth the inconſiderate take ſalve for *l'envoy*, and the word *envoy* for a ſalve?

Moth. Doth the wiſe conſider them other? is not *l'envoy* a ſalve? A. B.

[1] *His corrigible neck.*] *Corrigible* for *corrected*. STEEVENS.

Corrigible does not here mean *corrected*; but ready, or willing to be corrected. The ſenſe is---would'ſt thou ſee thy maſter bending his neck, and tamely ſubmitting or yielding himſelf to any ignominious puniſhment that the victor may chooſe to inflict on him? A. B.

—— What traſh is Rome,
What rubbiſh, and what offal, when it ſerves
For the baſe matter to illuminate
So vile a thing as Cæſar? *Julius Cæſar*, A. 1, S. 3.

If there be any in this aſſembly, any dear friend of Cæſar's, to him I ſay, that Brutus' love to Cæſar was no leſs than his. If then that friend demand, why Brutus roſe againſt Cæſar, this is my anſwer,—Not that I lov'd Cæſar leſs, but that I lov'd Rome more. Had you rather Cæſar were living, and die all ſlaves; than that Cæſar were dead, to live all free men? *Julius Cæſar*, A. 3, S. 2.

Thou laſt of all the Romans, fare thee well!
It is impoſſible, that ever Rome
Should breed thy fellow.—Friends, I owe more tears
To this dead man, than you ſhall ſee me pay.
Julius Cæſar, A. 5, S. 3.

—— Muſt I back,
Becauſe that John hath made his peace with Rome?
Am I Rome's ſlave? What penny hath Rome borne,
What men provided, what munition ſent,
To underprop this action? *King John*, A. 5, S. 2.

Why, fooliſh Lucius, doſt thou not perceive,
That Rome is but a wilderneſs of tygers;
Tygers muſt prey; and Rome affords no prey,
But me and mine. *Titus Andronicus*, A. 3, S. 1.

In the moſt high and palmy ſtate of Rome,
A little ere the mightieſt Julius fell,
The grave ſtood tenantleſs, and the ſheeted dead
Did ſqueak and gibber in the Roman ſtreets;
Stars ſhone with trains of fire; dews of blood fell;
Diſaſters veil'd the ſun; and the moiſt ſtar,
Upon whoſe influence Neptune's empire ſtands
Was ſick almoſt to doomſday with eclipſe.
Hamlet, A. 1, S. 1.

—— Shall

——— Shall they hoiſt me up,
And ſhew me to the ſhouting varlets
Of cenſuring Rome? rather a ditch in Egypt
Be gentle grave unto me! rather on Nilus' mud
Lay me ſtark-naked, and let the water-flies
Blow me into abhorring!

Antony and Cleopatra, A. 5, S. 2.

——— By the diſcovery,
We ſhall be ſhorten'd in our aim; which was,
To take in many towns [1], ere, almoſt, Rome
Should know we were afoot. *Coriolanus*, A. 1, S. 2.

R O S E.

Say, that ſhe rail; why then I'll tell her plain,
She ſings as ſweetly as a nightingale:
Say, that ſhe frown; I'll ſay, ſhe looks as clear
As morning roſes newly waſh'd with dew:
Say, ſhe be mute, and will not ſpeak a word;
Then I'll commend her volubility,
And ſay,—ſhe uttereth piercing eloquence.

Taming of the Shrew, A. 2, S. 1.

Shall it, for ſhame, be ſpoken in theſe days,
That men of your nobility, and power,
Did 'gage them both in an unjuſt behalf—
As both of you, God pardon it! have done,—
To put down Richard, that ſweet lovely roſe,
And plant this thorn, this canker, Bolingbroke?

Henry IV. P. 1, A. 1, S. 3.

[1] *To take in many towns.*] *To take in*, is here, as in many other places, *to ſubdue*. STEEVENS.

To take in, is here conſidered by Mr. Steevens, I think, in too large and poſitive a ſenſe. By *take in* the poet ſurely means, *include in the plan of operations*, that is, their plan was to make an attack on many towns, *in the hope of ſubduing them*. A. B.

— [1] Since ſhe did neglect her looking-glaſs,
And threw her ſun-expelling maſk away,
The air hath ſtarv'd the roſes in her cheeks,
And pinch'd the lily tincture of her face.

Two Gentlemen of Verona, A. 4, S. 3.

—— Hoary headed froſts
Fall in the freſh lap of the crimſon roſe.

Midſummer Night's Dream, A. 2, S. 2.

—— Earthlier happy is the roſe diſtill'd,
Than that, which withering on the virgin-thorn,
Grows, lives, and dies, in ſingle bleſſedneſs.

Midſummer Night's Dream, A. 1, S. 1.

—— When I have pluck'd thy roſe,
I cannot give it vital growth again,
It needs muſt wither :—I'll ſmell it on the tree.

Othello, A. 5, S. 2.

[1] *But ſince ſhe did neglect her looking-glaſs,*
And threw her ſun-expelling maſk away;
The air hath ſtarv'd the roſes in her cheeks,
And pinch'd the lily-tincture of her face,
That now ſhe is become as black as I.] What is *pinching a tincture? Starved*, in the third line, made the blundering editors write *pinch'd* in the fourth, though they might have ſeen that it was a tanning, ſcorching, not a freezing air, that was ſpoken of. For how could this latter quality in the air ſo affect the whiteneſs of the ſkin as to turn it black? We ſhould read,

"And *pitch'd* the lily tincture," &c.

i. e. turned the white tincture *black*. WARBURTON.

This is no emendation. None ever heard of a face being *pitched* by the weather. The colour of a part *pinched* is livid, as it is commonly termed, *black and blue*. The weather may therefore be juſtly ſaid to *pinch*, when it produces the ſame viſible effect. JOHNSON.

"Pinch'd" ſhould be *pencte*, i. e. *painted*. Since ſhe threw her maſk away, the air hath ſtarved the roſes in her cheeks, and ſo painted or changed her lily complexion, that ſhe is now ſwarthy as I am.

The word is found in Chaucer, and other early writers.

A. B.

SADNESS.

S.

SADNESS.

SUCH a want-wit ſadneſs makes of me,
That I have much ado to know myſelf.
Merchant of Venice, A. 1, S. 1.

In ſooth, I know not why I am ſo ſad;
It wearies me; you ſay it wearies you;
But how I caught it, found it, or came by it,
What ſtuff 'tis made of, whereof it is born,
I am to learn. *Merchant of Venice*, A. 1, S. 1.

Methinks, nobody ſhould be ſad, but I:
Yet, I remember, when I was in France,
Young gentlemen would be as ſad as night,
Only for wantonneſs. *King John*, A. 4, S. 1.

Methinks, your looks are ſad, your chear appall'd [1].
Henry VI. P. 1, A. 1, S. 2.

SALVATION.

For a quart d'ecu he will ſell the fee-ſimple of his ſalvation, the inheritance of it; and cut the intail from all remainders, and a perpetual ſucceſſion for it perpetually. *All's well that ends well*, A. 4, S. 3.

SEA.

——— Know, Iago,
But that I love the gentle Deſdemona,

[1] ——— *your chear appall'd.*] *Chear* is countenance, appearance. STEEVENS.

"Chear" is not *countenance*, but *gaiety*, *cheerfulneſs*.---"Your "chear appall'd," means, *your chearfulneſs abated*. He had already ſaid, "your looks are ſad." A. B.

I would not my unhoufed free condition
Put into circumfcription and confine
For the fea's worth. *Othello*, A. 1, S. 2.

—— O, fhe is fallen
Into a pit of ink! that the wide fea
Hath drops too few to wafh her clean again.
Much ado about nothing, A. 4, S. 1.

—— Suppofe, that you have feen
The well-appointed king at Hampton pier
Embark his royalty; and his brave fleet
With filken ftreamers the young Phœbus fanning,
Play with your fancies; and in them behold,
Upon the hempen tackle, fhip-boys climbing:
Hear the fhrill whiftle, which doth order give
To founds confus'd: behold the threaden fails,
Borne with the invifible and creeping wind,
Draw the huge bottoms through the furrow'd fea,
Breafting the lofty furge. *Henry V.* A. 3, *Chorus.*

—— When I thought
What harm a wind too great might do at fea,
I fhould not fee the fandy hour-glafs run,
But I fhould think of fhallows, and of flats;
And fee my wealthy Andrew dock'd in fand,
Vailing her high top lower than her ribs.
Merchant of Venice, A. 1, S. 1.

The time and my intents are favage-wild;
More fierce, and more inexorable far,
Than empty tygers, or the roaring fea.
Romeo and Juliet, A. 5, S. 3.

We will not from the helm, to fit and weep;
But keep our courfe, though the rough wind fay no,
From fhelves and rocks that threaten us with wreck
As good to chide the waves, as fpeak them fair,
And what is Edward but a ruthlefs fea?
Henry VI. P. 3, A. 5, S. 4.

——— Is't meet, that he
Should leave the helm, and, like a fearful lad,
With tearful eyes add water to the ſea,
And give more ſtrength to that which hath too much,
Whiles, in his moan, the ſhip ſplits on the rock,
Which induſtry and courage might have ſav'd?
Henry VI. P. 3, A. 5, S. 4.

——— The ſea being ſmooth,
How many ſhallow bauble boats dare ſail
Upon her patient breaſt, making their way
With thoſe of nobler bulk?
But let the ruffian Boreas once enrage
The gentle Thetis, and, anon, behold
The ſtrong-ribb'd bark through liquid mountains cut,
Bounding between the two moiſt elements,
Like Perſeus' horſe. *Troilus and Creſſida*, A. 1, S. 3.

——— Great floods have flow'd
From ſimple ſources; and great ſeas have dry'd,
When miracles have by the greateſt been deny'd.
All's well that ends well, A. 2, S. 1.

Was I, for this, nigh wreck'd upon the ſea;
And twice by aukward wind from England's bank
Drove back again unto my native clime?
What boded this, but well fore-warning wind
Did ſeem to ſay,—Seek not a ſcorpion's neſt,
Nor ſet no footing on this unkind ſhore?
Henry VI. P. 2, A. 3, S. 2.

I have ſeen two ſuch ſights, by ſea, and by land; but I am not to ſay, it is a ſea, for it is now the ſky; betwixt the firmament and it, you cannot thruſt a bodkin's point. *Winter's Tale*, A. 3, S. 3.

——— Thou didſt ſmile,
Infuſed with a fortitude from heaven,
When I have deck'd the ſea[1] with drops full ſalt.
Tempeſt, A. 1, S. 2.

SEASON.

[1] ——— *deck'd the ſea.*] To deck the ſea, if explained, to honour,

SEASON.

He is noble, wise, judicious, and best knows
The fits o' the season[1]. *Macbeth*, A. 4, S. 2.

SELF-SLAUGHTER.

——I must die;
And if I do not by thy hand, thou art
No servant of thy master's: against self-slaughter
There is a prohibition so divine,
That cravens my weak hand. *Cymbeline*, A. 3, S. 4.

SENSE.

[2] I have rubb'd this young quat almost to the sense,
And he grows angry. *Othello*, A. 5, S. 1.

Impossible

honour, adorn, or dignify, is indeed ridiculous, but the original import of the verb *deck* is, *to cover*; so in some parts they yet say *deck the table*. This sense may be borne, but perhaps the poet wrote *fleck'd*, which I think is still used in rustic language of drops falling upon water. Dr. Warburton reads *mock'd*, the Oxford edition *braek'd*. JOHNSON.

I have little doubt but that the poet wrote "beck'd the sea," *added rivers to the sea*. *Beck*, in early writers, is a river. "I "have beck'd the sea," for, *I have added rivers to the sea*, is not indeed a very easy language, but it is certainly the language of Shakespeare. A. B.

[1] *The fits o' the season.*] *The fits of the season* should appear to be, from the following passage in Coriolanus, the *violent disorders* of the season, its convulsions:

" —— but that
" The *violent fit* o' th' times craves it as physick."

STEEVENS.

" He is noble, wise, judicious, and best knows
" The fits o' the season."

The meaning is,—He is wise and judicious, and knows how to conduct himself according to the temper of the times.

A. B.

[2] *I've rubb'd this young quat almost to the sense,*
And he grows angry.] This is a passage much contro-

verted

[1] Impoſſible be ſtrange attempts, to thoſe
That weigh their pain in ſenſe; and do ſuppoſe,
What hath been cannot be.

All's well that ends well, A. 1, S. 1.

SERPENT.

verted among the editors. Sir T. Hanmer reads *quab*, a *gudgeon*; not that a gudgeon can be *rubbed* to much *ſenſe*, but that a man groſsly deceived, is often called a gudgeon. Mr. Upton reads *quail*, which he proves, by much learning, to be a very choleric bird. Dr. Warburton retains *gnat*, which is found in the early quarto. Theobald would introduce *knot*, a ſmall bird of that name. I have followed the text of the folio, and third and fourth quartos.

A *quat*, in the midland counties, is a *pimple*, which by rubbing is made to ſmart, or is rubbed to ſenſe. Rodorigo is called a *quat* by the ſame mode of ſpeech, as a low fellow is now termed, in low language, a *ſcab*. JOHNSON.

All the commentators, I believe, have miſtaken the ſenſe of this paſſage. A "quat," in my opinion, is an *intimate*, a *crony*. We now ſay, when we ſpeak of the intimacy of one man with another,—"O! they are quater-couſins."—I therefore read as follows:

"I have *fubb'd* this young quat," &c.

i. e. I have *fubb'd*, or *put off*, this quater-couſin, or aſſociate of mine, as long as poſſible, and now he grows angry. "*Quat*" appears to be an abbreviation of "*quater*," and may have been uſed for *quater-couſin*, or *friend*, in the ſame way that *cuz* is employed for *couſin*, a relation by blood or marriage. A. B.

[1] *Impoſſible be ſtrange attempts, to thoſe*
That weigh their pain in ſenſe; and do ſuppoſe,
What hath been cannot be.] Theſe lines I read with Hanmer:

"Impoſſible be ſtrange attempts to thoſe
"That weigh their pain in ſenſe, and do ſuppoſe,
"What ha'nt been, cannot be."

New attempts ſeem impoſſible to thoſe who eſtimate their *labour* or *enterprizes* by ſenſe, and believe that nothing can be but what they ſee before them. JOHNSON.

There is no neceſſity for alteration. The paſſage is ſufficiently clear as it ſtands. New attempts, ſays Helena, appear ſo very difficult to moſt people, that they are apt to imagine it is impoſſible we ſhould ever ſucceed in them, though it is well known that events or occurrences, equally ſtrange with that on which I am meditating, have frequently been obſerved in the world. If any change is made, it ſhould be as follows:

"Impoſſible

SERPENT.

Who 'ſcapes the lurking ſerpent's mortal ſting?
Not he, that ſets his foot upon her back.
The ſmalleſt worm will turn, being trodden on;
And doves will peck, in ſafeguard of their brood.
Who hath not ſeen them (even with thoſe wings
Which ſometime they have us'd in fearful flight)
Make war with him that climb'd unto their neſt,
Offering their own lives in their young's defence?
Henry VI. P. 3, A. 2, S. 2.

'Tis given out, that, ſleeping in my orchard,
A ſerpent ſtung me; ſo the whole ear of Denmark
Is by a forged proceſs of my death
Rankly abus'd: but know, thou noble youth,
The ſerpent that did ſting thy father's life,
Now wears his crown. *Hamlet,* A. 1, S. 5.

She hath abated me of half my train;
Look'd back upon me; ſtruck me with her tongue,
Moſt ſerpent-like, upon the very heart:
All the ſtor'd vengeances of heaven fall
On her ingrateful top! ſtrike her young bones,
You taking airs, with lameneſs! *Lear,* A. 2, S. 4.

SERVICE.

——— 'Tis the curſe of ſervice;
Preferment goes by letter, and affection,
Not by the old gradation, where each ſecond
Stood heir to the firſt. *Othello,* A. 1, S. 1.

Nym, and Bardolph, are ſworn brothers in filch-

" Impoſſible be ſtrange attempts, to thoſe
" Who weigh their pain in ſenſe; nor do ſuppoſe
" What hath been, can be." A. B.

ing;

ing; and in Calais they ſtole a fire-ſhovel: I knew, by that piece of ſervice, the men would carry coals [1].

Henry V. A. 3, S. 2.

SHADOWS.

——— 'Tis ſuch as you,
That creep like ſhadows by him, and do ſigh
At each his needleſs heavings; ſuch as you
Nouriſh the cauſe of his awaking.

Winter's Tale, A. 2, S. 3.

By the apoſtle Paul, ſhadows to-night
Have ſtruck more terror to the ſoul of Richard,
Than can the ſubſtance of ten thouſand ſoldiers
Armed in proof, and led by ſhallow Richmond.

Richard III. A. 5, S. 3.

SHAME.

O ſhame! where is thy bluſh? Rebellious hell,
If thou canſt mutiny in a matron's bones,
To flaming youth let virtue be as wax,
And melt in her own fire. *Hamlet*, A. 3, S. 4.

——— Bring me
To the dead bodies of my queen, and ſon:
One grave ſhall be for both; upon them ſhall
The cauſes of their death appear, unto
Our ſhame perpetual. *Winter's Tale*, A. 3, S. 2.

[1] *I knew by that piece of ſervice the men would carry coals.*] It appears, that in Shakeſpeare's age, to *carry coals* was, I know not why, to *endure affronts*. JOHNSON.

Cant phraſes are the ephemerons of literature. In the quartos the paſſage ſtands thus:

"I knew by that *they meant* to carry coles."

STEEVENS.

"Carry coals"—there is a quibble here on the Engliſh word *coal*, and the French word *colle*, which ſignifies *ſham*, *bamboozle*, or *cheat*.

"I knew by that they meant to carry coles,"

i. e. I ſaw plainly that they were *bamboozlers*, or *trickſters*. A. B.

O Cæſar,

O Cæſar, what a wounding ſhame is this;
That thou, vouchſafing here to viſit me,
Doing the honour of thy lordlineſs
To one ſo meek [1], that mine own ſervant ſhould
Parcel the ſum of my diſgraces [2] by
Addition of his envy!

Antony and Cleopatra, A. 5, S. 2.

——I have mark'd
A thouſand bluſhing apparitions
To ſtart into her face; a thouſand innocent ſhames
In angel whiteneſs bear away thoſe bluſhes.

Much ado about nothing, A. 4, S. 1.

Thought I, thy ſpirits were ſtronger than thy ſhames,
Myſelf would, on the rearward of reproaches,
Strike at thy life. *Much ado about nothing*, A. 4, S. 1.

I dare aſſure thee, that no enemy
Shall ever take alive the noble Brutus:
The gods defend him from ſo great a ſhame!
When you do find him, or alive, or dead,
He will be found like Brutus, like himſelf.

Julius Cæſar, A. 5, S. 4.

For my part, I may ſpeak it to my ſhame,
I have a truant been to chivalry;
And ſo, I hear, he doth account me too:
Yet this before my father's majeſty,—
I am content, that he ſhall take the odds
Of his great name and eſtimation;

[1] *To one ſo meek.*] *Meek*, I ſuppoſe, means here, *tame*, ſubdued by adverſity. Cleopatra, in any other ſenſe, was not eminent for *meekneſs*. MALONE.

Weak, I think, would be a better word in the mouth of Cleopatra. *One ſo weakened or reduced by adverſity, that my ſervant takes advantage of it.* A. B.

[2] *Parcel the ſum of my diſgraces.*] *To parcel her diſgraces*, might be expreſſed in vulgar language, to *bundle up her calamities*. JOHNSON.

I do not ſee any thing inelegant here. *Parcel* is *augment*. A. B.

 And

And will, to ſave the blood on either ſide,
Try fortune with him in a ſingle fight.

Henry IV. P. 1, A. 5, S. 1.

——— I'll not chide thee;
Let ſhame come when it will, I do not call it:
I do not bid the thunder-bearer ſhoot,
Nor tell tales of thee to high-judging Jove:
Mend, when thou canſt; be better, at thy leiſure.

Lear, A. 2, S. 4.

——— How you ſtorm!
I would be friends with you, and have your love,
Forget the ſhames that you have ſtain'd me with,
Supply your preſent wants, and take no doit
Of uſance for my monies.

Merchant of Venice, A. 1, S. 3.

Hadſt thou but ſhook thy head, or made a pauſe,
When I ſpake darkly what I purpoſed:
Or turn'd an eye of doubt upon my face;
Or bid me tell my tale in expreſs words;
Deep ſhame had ſtruck me dumb.

King John, A. 4, S. 2.

——— I do not ſhame
To tell you what I was, ſince my converſion
So ſweetly taſtes, being the thing I am.

As you like it, A. 4, S. 3.

His grandam's wrongs, and not his mother's ſhames,
Draw thoſe heaven-moving pearls from his poor eyes,
Which heaven ſhall take in nature of a fee;
Ay, with theſe cryſtal beads heaven ſhall be brib'd
To do him juſtice and revenge on you.

King John, A. 2, S. 1.

The God of ſoldiers,
With the conſent of ſupreme Jove, inform
Thy thoughts with nobleneſs; that thou may'ſt prove
To ſhame invulnerable, and ſtick i' the wars

Like

Like a great ſea-mark, ſtanding every flaw,
And ſaving thoſe that eye thee!

Coriolanus, A. 5, S. 3.

If we be conquer'd, let men conquer us,
And not theſe baſtard Brittains; whom our fathers
Have in their own land beaten, bobb'd, and thump'd,
And, on record, left them the heirs of ſhame.

Richard III. A. 5, S. 3.

What a ſlave art thou, to hack thy ſword as thou haſt done; and then ſay, it was in fight! What trick, what device, what ſtarting hole, canſt thou now find out, to hide thee from this open and apparent ſhame? *Henry IV.* P. 1, A. 2, S. 4.

[1] —— A divulged ſhame,
Traduc'd by odious ballads; my maiden's name
Sear'd

[1] —— *A divulged ſhame,*
Traduc'd by odious ballads; my maiden's name
Sear'd otherwiſe; no worſe of worſt extended,
With vileſt torture let my life be ended.] This paſſage is apparently corrupt, and how ſhall it be rectified? I have no great hope of ſucceſs, but ſomething muſt be tried. I read the whole thus:

"—— A divulged theme,
"Traduc'd by odious ballads my maiden name;
"Sear'd otherwiſe, to worſt of worſt extended,
"With vileſt torture let my life be ended."

Firſt, I venture what is deareſt to me, my maiden reputation; but if your diſtruſt *extends* my character to the *worſt* of the *worſt*, and ſuppoſes me *ſeared* againſt the ſenſe of infamy, I will add to the ſtake of infamy the ſtake of life. Yet we may try another experiment.

"Fear otherwiſe to worſt of worſt extended."

That is, let me act under the greateſt terrour poſſible.

Yet once again we will try to find the right way, by the glimmer of Hanmer's emendation:

"—— my maiden name
"Sear'd; otherwiſe the worſt of worſt extended," &c.

JOHNSON.

The great difficulty ſeems to lie in, "*No worſe of worſt extended*," and the paſſage is evidently corrupt. I therefore read,

"—— A di-

Sear'd otherwiſe; no worſe of worſt extended,
With vileſt torture let my life be ended.

All's well that ends well, A. 2, S. 1.

——— At ſuch a point,
When half to half the world oppos'd, he being
The meered queſtion[1]: 'twas a ſhame no leſs
Than was his loſs, to courſe your flying flags,
And leave his navy gazing.

Antony and Cleopatra, A. 3, S. 11.

SICKNESS.

——— I was writing of my epitaph,
It will be ſeen to-morrow; my long ſickneſs
Of health, and living, now begins to mend,
And nothing brings me all things.

Timon of Athens, A 5, S. 2.

"——— A divulged ſhame,
"Traduced by odious ballads; my maiden name
"Sear'd otherwiſe;—and worſe, if worſe, attended
"With vileſt torture let my life be ended."

i. e. I would ſubmit to ſhame, and become the ſubject of odious ballads; my maiden reputation ſhould be otherwiſe feared and branded; and if any thing can be *worſe*, or more dreadful than this, my life ſhould willingly be ended in torture. A. B.

[1] ——— *he being*
The meered queſtion.] The *meered* queſtion is a term I do not underſtand. I know not what to offer, except
"The *mooted* queſtion,"
That is, the *diſputed* point, the ſubject of debate; *mere* is indeed a *boundary*, and the *meered queſtion*, if it can mean any thing, may, with ſome violence of language, mean, the *diſputed boundary*. JOHNSON.

Meered may be a word of our author's own formation, from *mere*. He being the *ſole*, the entire ſubject of diſpute. MALONE.

Shakeſpeare, I ſhould think, wrote *meeteſt*. "He being the "meeteſt queſtion," *i. e.* he being the propereſt perſon to anſwer the attack of Cæſar, not you. A. B.

Like a ficknefs, did I loath this food:
But, as in health, come to my natural tafte,
Now do I wifh it, love it, long for it.
Midfummer Night's Dream, A. 4, S. 1.

SILENCE.

Silence is the perfecteft herald of joy: I were but little happy, if I could fay how much.
Much ado about nothing, A. 2, S. 1.

—— Silence is only commendable
In a neat's tongue dry'd, and a maid not vendible.
Merchant of Venice, A. 1, S. 1.

I think, the beft grace of wit will fhortly turn into filence, and difcourfe grow commendable in none only but parrots.
Merchant of Venice, A. 3, S. 5.

Rome's readieft champions, repofe you here,
Secure from worldly chances and mifhaps!
Here lurks no treafon, here no envy fwells,
Here grow no damned grudges; here no ftorm,
No noife, but filence and eternal fleep.
Titus Andronicus, A. 1, S. 2.

—— Her fmoothnefs,
Her very filence, and her patience,
Speak to the people. *As you like it*, A. 1, S. 3.

—— I pray you all,
If you have hitherto conceal'd this fight,
Let it be tenable in your filence ftill;
And whatfoever elfe fhall hap to-night,
Give it an underftanding, but no tongue.
Hamlet, A. 1, S. 2.

SIN, SINS.

——— Our compell'd ſins
Stand more for number than for accompt.
Meaſure for Meaſure, A. 2, S. 4.

—— Confeſs thee freely of thy ſin;
For to deny each article with oath,
Cannot remove, nor choak, the ſtrong conception
That I do groan withal. *Othello*, A. 5, S. 2.

SLANDER.

I am diſgrac'd, impeach'd, and baffled here;
Pierc'd to the ſoul with ſlander's venom'd ſpear;
The which no balm can cure, but his heart-blood
Which breath'd this poiſon. *Richard II.* A. 1, S. 1.

—— Slander lives upon ſucceſſion;
For ever hous'd, where it once gets poſſeſſion.
Comedy of Errors, A. 3, S. 1.

——— What king ſo ſtrong,
Can tie the gall up in the ſlanderous tongue?
Meaſure for Meaſure, A. 3, S. 2.

Fear no more the lightning-flaſh,
Nor the all-dreaded thunder-ſtone;
Fear not ſlander, cenſure raſh [1];
Thou haſt finiſh'd joy and moan.
Cymbeline, A. 4, S. 2.

Laertes, I muſt common with your grief,
Or you deny me right. Go but apart,
Make choice of whom your wiſeſt friends you will,
And they ſhall hear and judge 'twixt you and me.
Hamlet, A. 4, S. 5.

[1] *Fear not ſlander, cenſure raſh.*] Perhaps,
"Fear not *ſlander*'s cenſure raſh." JOHNSON.
The text, I think, is right. "Cenſure raſh" is *haſty opinion*. *Slander* is ſomething worſe. A. B.

——— 'Tis ſlander;
Whoſe edge is ſharper than the ſword; whoſe tongue
Out-venoms all the worms of Nile; whoſe breath
Rides on the poſting winds and doth belie
All corners of the world; kings, queens, and ſtates,
Maids, matrons, nay, the ſecrets of the grave
This viperous ſlander enters. *Cymbeline*, A. 3, S. 4.

——— For haply, ſlander,
Whoſe whiſper o'er the world's diameter,
As level as the cannon to his blank,
Tranſports his poiſon'd ſhot, may miſs our name,
And hit the woundleſs air. *Hamlet*, A. 4, S. 1.

S L E E P.

——— O'er their brows death-counterfeiting ſleep
With leaden legs and batty wings doth creep.
Midſummer Night's Dream, A. 3, S. 2.

I'll give thee fairies to attend on thee;
And they ſhall fetch thee jewels from the deep,
And ſing, while thou on preſſed flowers doſt ſleep.
Midſummer Night's Dream, A. 3, S. 1.

Sleep, that ſometimes ſhuts up ſorrow's eye,
Steal me a while from mine own company.
Midſummer Night's Dream, A. 3, S. 2.

In revenge of my contempt of love,
Love hath chac'd ſleep from my enthralled eyes,
And made them watchers of mine own heart's ſorrow.
Two Gentlemen of Verona, A. 2, S. 4.

——— I
Do come with words as med'cinal as true;
Honeſt, as either; to purge him of that humour,
That preſſes him from ſleep.
Winter's Tale, A. 2, S. 3.

To ſee his nobleneſs!
Conceiving the diſhonour of his mother,
He ſtraight declined, droop'd, took it deeply,
Threw

Threw off his ſpirit, his appetite, his ſleep,
And downright languiſh'd.

Winter's Tale, A. 2, S. 3.

——— Nor ſleep, nor ſanctuary,
Being naked, ſick; nor fane, nor capitol,
The prayers of prieſts, nor times of ſacrifice,
Embarquements all of fury, ſhall lift up
Their rotten privilege and cuſtom 'gainſt
My hate to Marcius. *Coriolanus*, A. 1, S. 10.

——— Thou Mars! I tell thee,
We have a power of foot; and I had purpoſe
Once more to hew thy target from thy brawn,
Or loſe mine arm for't: thou haſt beat me out
Twelve ſeveral times, and I have nightly ſince
Dreamt of encounters 'twixt thyſelf and me;
We have been down together in my ſleep,
Unbuckling helms, fiſting each other's throat,
And wak'd half dead with nothing.

Coriolanus, A. 4, S. 5.

Canſt thou, O partial ſleep! give thy repoſe
To the wet ſea-boy in an hour ſo rude!
And, in the calmeſt and moſt ſtilleſt night,
With all appliances and means to boot,
Deny it to a king? Then, happy low, lie down!
Uneaſy lies the head that wears a crown.

Henry IV. P. 2, A. 3, S. 1.

——— O gentle ſleep,
Nature's ſoft nurſe, how have I frighted thee,
That thou no more wilt weigh my eye-lids down,
And ſteep my ſenſes in forgetfulneſs?

Henry IV. P. 2, A. 3, S. 1.

Why rather, ſleep, ly'ſt thou in ſmoky cribs,
Upon uneaſy pallets ſtretching thee,
And huſh'd with buzzing night-flies to thy ſlumber;
Than in the perfum'd chambers of the great,

Under the canopies of coſtly ſtate,
And lull'd with ſounds of ſweeteſt melody?
Henry IV. P. 2, A. 3, S. 1.

—— Faſt aſleep? It is no matter;
Enjoy the honey-heavy dew of ſlumber:
Thou haſt no figures, nor no fantaſies,
Which buſy care draws in the brains of men;
Therefore thou ſleep'ſt ſo ſound.
Julius Cæſar, A. 2, S. 1.

Faſt lock'd up in ſleep, as guiltleſs labour
When it lies ſtarkly in the traveller's bones.
Meaſure for Meaſure, A. 4, S. 2.

—— Not poppy, nor mandragora,
Nor all the drowſy ſyrups of the world,
Shall ever med'cine thee to that ſweet ſleep
Which thou ow'dſt yeſterday. *Othello*, A. 3, S. 3.

S M I L E.

——— Ghaſtly looks
Are at my ſervice, like enforced ſmiles;
And both are ready in their offices,
At any time, to grace my ſtratagems.
Richard III. A. 3, S. 5.

What thou wilt,
Thou rather ſhalt enforce it with thy ſmile,
Than hew to't with thy ſword.
Timon of Athens, A. 5, S. 5.

In Richard's time,—What do you call the place?—
A plague upon't!—it is in Gloſterſhire;—
'Twas where the mad-cap duke his uncle kept,
His uncle York;—where I firſt bow'd my knee
Unto this king of ſmiles, this Bolingbroke.
Henry IV. P. 1, A. 1, S. 3.

SNOW.

O thou ſweet king-killer, and dear divorce
'Twixt natural ſon and ſire! thou bright defiler
Of Hymen's pureſt bed! thou valiant Mars!
Thou ever young, freſh, lov'd, and delicate wooer,
Whoſe bluſh doth thaw the conſecrated ſnow
That lies on Dian's lap!

Timon of Athens, A. 4, S. 3.

SOCIETY.

—— This is worſhipful ſociety,
And fits the mounting ſpirit; like myſelf:
For he is but a baſtard to the time,
That doth not ſmack of obſervation.

King John, A. 1, S. 1.

—— So pleaſe you, leave me;
Stick to your journal courſe: the breach of cuſtom
Is breach of all. I am ill; but your being by me
Cannot amend me: ſociety is no comfort
To one not ſociable. *Cymbeline*, A. 4, S. 2.

——— Elſe,
Could ſuch inordinate, and low deſires,
Such barren pleaſures, rude ſociety,
As thou art match'd withal, and grafted to,
Accompany the greatneſs of thy blood,
And hold their level with thy princely heart?

Henry IV. P. 1, A. 3, S. 2.

SOLDIER.

When a ſoldier was the theme, my name
Was not far off: then was I as a tree,
Whoſe boughs did bend with fruit; but, in one
night,
A ſtorm, or robbery, call it what you will,

Shook down my mellow hangings, nay, my leaves,
And left me bare to weather. *Cymbeline*, A. 3, S. 3.

——— Our ſlippery people
(Whoſe love is never link'd to the deſerver,
Till his deſerts are paſt) begin to throw
Pompey the great, and all his dignities
Upon his ſon; who, high in name and power,
Higher than both in blood and life, ſtands up
For the main ſoldier.

Antony and Cleopatra, A. 1, S. 2.

If I be not aſhamed of my ſoldiers, I am a ſouc'd gurnet: I have miſus'd the king's preſs damnably. I have got, in exchange of a hundred and fifty ſoldiers, three hundred and odd pounds.

Henry IV. P. 1, A. 4, S. 2.

—— As the ſoldiers bore dead bodies by,
He call'd them untaught knaves, unmannerly,
To bring a ſlovenly unhandſome corſe,
Betwixt the wind and his nobility.

Henry IV. P. 1, A. 1, S. 3.

——— Debonair, unarm'd,
As bending angels; that's their fame in peace:
But when they would ſeem ſoldiers, they have galls,
Good arms, ſtrong joints, true ſwords; and, Jove's accord,
Nothing ſo full of heart [1].

Troilus and Creſſida, A. 1, S. 3.

[1] ——— *they have galls,*
Good arms, ſtrong joints, true ſwords; and Jove's accord,
Nothing ſo full of heart.] As this paſſage is printed I cannot diſcover any meaning in it. If there be no corruption, the ſemicolon which is placed after *ſwords*, ought rather to be placed after the word *accord*; of which, however, the ſenſe is not very clear. I ſuſpect that the tranſcriber's ear deceived him, and that we ſhould read,

"And Jove's a *god*," &c. MALONE.

"Accord" is certainly right. "Jove's accord" is, *Jove gives ſanction to their proceedings. Jove is their protector.*" A. B.

Their

Their weapons like to lightning came and went;
Our ſoldiers—like the night-owl's lazy flight,
Or like an idle threſher with a flail,—
Fell gently down, as if they ſtruck their friends.
Henry VI. P. 3, A. 2, S. 1.

——— Then, a ſoldier;
Full of ſtrange oaths, and bearded like the pard,
Jealous in honour, ſudden and quick in quarrel,
Seeking the bubble reputation
Even in the cannon's mouth.
As you like it, A. 2, S. 7.

Conſider further,
That when he ſpeaks not like a citizen,
You find him like a ſoldier: do not take
His rougher accents for malicious ſounds;
But, as I ſay, ſuch as become a ſoldier,
Rather than envy you. *Coriolanus*, A. 3, S. 3.

——— In a moment, look to ſee
The blind and bloody ſoldier with foul hand
Defile the locks of your ſhrill-ſhrieking daughters;
Your fathers taken by the ſilver beards,
And their moſt reverend heads daſh'd to the walls;
Your naked infants ſpitted upon pikes;
Whiles the mad mothers, with their howls confus'd,
Do break the clouds, as did the wives of Jewry
At Herod's bloody-hunting ſlaughtermen.
Henry V. A. 3, S. 3.

——— You men of Harfleur,
Take pity of your town, and of your people,
Whiles yet my ſoldiers are in my command;
Whiles yet the cool and temperate wind of grace
O'er-blows the filthy and contagious clouds
Of heady murder, ſpoil, and villainy.
Henry V. A. 3, S. 3.

He was wont to ſpeak plain, and to the purpoſe, like an honeſt man, and a ſoldier; and now is he turned

turned orthographer; his words are a very fantaſtical banquet, juſt ſo many ſtrange diſhes.

Much ado about nothing, A. 2, S. 3.

——— Say to them,
Thou art their ſoldier, and being bred in broils,
Haſt not the ſoft way, which, thou doſt confeſs,
Were fit for thee to uſe, as they to claim,
In aſking their good loves. *Coriolanus*, A. 3, S. 2.

Behold! I have a weapon:
A better never did itſelf ſuſtain
Upon a ſoldier's thigh; I have ſeen the day,
That, with this little arm, and this good ſword,
I have made my way through more impediments
Than twenty times your ſtop. *Othello*, A. 5, S. 2.

Oft have I ſeen the haughty cardinal—
More like a ſoldier, than a man o' the church,
As ſtout, and proud, as he were lord of all,—
Swear like a ruffian, and demean himſelf
Unlike the ruler of a common-weal.

Henry VI. P. 2, A. 1, S. 1.

S O N.

Take but degree away, untune that ſtring,
And, hark, what diſcord follows! the bounded waters
Should lift their boſoms higher than the ſhores,
And make a ſop of all this ſolid globe:
Strength ſhould be lord of imbecility,
And the rude ſon ſhould ſtrike his father dead:
Force ſhould be right.

Troilus and Creſſida, A. 1, S. 3.

—— If the deed were ill,
Be you contented, wearing now the garland,
To have a ſon ſet your decrees at nought;
To pluck down juſtice from your awful bench;

To

To trip the courſe of law, and blunt the ſword
That guards the peace and ſafety of your perſon.
Henry IV. P. 2, A. 5, S. 2.

Queſtion your royal thoughts, make the caſe yours,
Be now the father, and propoſe a ſon:
Hear your own dignity ſo much profan'd,
See your moſt dreadful laws ſo looſely ſlighted,
Behold yourſelf ſo by a ſon diſdained;
And then imagine me taking your part,
And, in your power, ſo ſilencing your ſon.
Henry IV. P. 2, A. 5, S. 2.

If I were mad, I ſhould forget my ſon;
Or madly think, a babe of clouts were he:
I am not mad; too well, too well I feel
The different plague of each calamity.
King John, A. 3, S. 4.

I am not mad;—this hair I tear is mine;
My name is Conſtance; I was Geffrey's wife;
Young Arthur is my ſon, and he is loſt.
King John, A. 3, S. 4.

What doſt thou mean by ſhaking of thy head?
Why doſt thou look ſo ſadly on my ſon?
King John, A. 3, S. 1.

——— Oh, time's extremity!
Haſt thou ſo track'd and ſplitted my poor tongue,
In ſeven ſhort years, that here my only ſon
Knows not my feeble key of untun'd cares?
Comedy of Errors, A. 5, S. 1.

All my followers to the eager foe
Turn back, and fly, like ſhips before the wind,
Or lambs purſu'd by hunger-ſtarved wolves.
My ſons—God knows what hath bechanced them:
But this I know,—they have demean'd themſelves
Like men born to renown, by life, or death.
Henry VI. P. 3, A. 1, S. 4.

Where

Where is thy husband now? where be thy brothers?
Where be thy two sons? wherein dost thou joy?
Who sues, and kneels, and says—God save the queen?
Where be the bending peers that flatter'd thee?
Where be the thronging troops that follow'd thee?
Richard III. A. 4, S. 4.

There thou mak'st me sad, and mak'st me sin,
In envy that my lord Northumberland
Should be the father of so blest a son:
A son, who is the theme of Honour's tongue;
Who is sweet Fortune's minion, and her pride:
Whilst I, by looking on the praise of him,
See riot and dishonour stain the brow
Of my young Harry. *Henry IV.* P. 1, A. 1, S. 1.

——— What might I have been,
Might I a son and daughter now have look'd on,
Such goodly things as you?
Winter's Tale, A. 5, S. 1.

I will buy me a son-in-law in a fair, and toll for this. I'll none of him [1].
All's well that ends well, A. 5, S. 3.

[1] *I will buy me a son-in-law in a fair, and toule for this. I'll none of him.*] Thus the first folio. The second reads,

"I will buy me a son-in law in a fair, and toule him for "this."

The reading of the first copy seems to mean this: I'll buy me a new son-in-law, and *toll* the bell for this, *i. e.* look upon him as a dead man. The second reading, as Dr. Percy suggests, may imply; I'll buy me a son-in-law as they buy a horse in a fair; and *toul* him, *i. e.* enter him on the *toul*, or *toll* book, to prove I came honestly by him. STEEVENS.

The commentators have totally mistaken the meaning of *toule*. We must read and point thus:

"I'll buy me a son-in-law in a fair: a toule. For this, I'll none of him."

A *toule*, or *tole*, is a *toy*. The word is found in Chaucer. Lafeu says, he will go to a fair, and buy a toy, a *puppet* for a son-in-law; he will have nothing to do with Bertram. A. B.

——— Priam's six-gated city
(Dardan, and Thymbria, Ilias, Chetas, Troyan,
And Antenoridas) with massy staples,
And corresponsive and fulfilling bolts [1],
Sperrs up the sons of Troy. *Prol. Troilus and Cressida.*

SORROW.

——— Wisely, good sir, weigh
Our sorrow with our comfort. *Tempest*, A. 2, S. 1.

——— If hearty sorrow
Be a sufficient ransom for offence,
I tender it. *Two Gentlemen of Verona*, A. 5, S. 3.

When it pleaseth their deities to take the wife of a man from him, it shews to man the tailors of the earth; comforting therein, that when old robes are worn out, there are members to make new, and, indeed, the tears live in an onion [2], that should water this sorrow. *Antony and Cleopatra*, A. 1, S. 2.

Sir, you have done enough, and have perform'd
A saint-like sorrow:
Do, as the heavens have done; forget your evil
With them, forgive yourself.
Winter's Tale, A. 5, S. 1.

[1] ——— *fulfilling bolts.*] To *fulfil*, in this place, means to fill till there be no room for more. In this sense it is now obsolete. STEEVENS.

"Fulfilling" cannot, in this place, have the sense that Mr. Steevens has annexed to it,—"fulfilling bolts" must here signify, *bolts that answer the end for which they were made: bolts that fit their sockets well; bolts that render us secure.* A. B.

[2] *The tears that live in an onion.*] So in the Noble Soldier,— "So much water as you might squeeze out of an onion had been "enough," &c. STEEVENS.

So much water as you might squeeze, &c. is not, I think, the precise and definite meaning of *the tears that live in an onion.* I conceive the sense of the passage to be this,—"the tears should "be *forced* tears which are to water this sorrow." That is to say, such tears as an onion is apt to occasion. A. B.

——— Patience

——— Patience and Sorrow ſtrove
Who ſhould expreſs her goodlieſt. You have ſeen
Sunſhine and rain at once: her ſmiles and tears
Were like a better day [1]. Thoſe happy ſmiles,
That play'd on her ripe lip, ſeem'd not to know
What gueſts were in her eyes; which parted thence,
As pearls from diamonds dropt. *Lear*, A. 4, S. 3.

Thou didſt uſurp my place, and doſt thou not
Uſurp the juſt proportion of my ſorrow?
Now thy proud neck bears half my burden'd yoke;
From which even here I ſlip my wearied head,
And leave the burden of it all on thee.
Farewell, York's wife,—and queen of ſad miſchance.
Richard III. A. 4, S. 4.

Sorrow breaks ſeaſons, and repoſing hours,
Makes the night morning, and the noon-tide night.
Richard III. A. 1, S. 4.

—— Remember this another day,
When he ſhall ſplit thy very heart with ſorrow,
And ſay, poor Margaret was a propheteſs.—
Live each of you the ſubjects to his hate,
And he to yours, and all of you to God's!
Richard III. A. 1, S. 3.

1 ——— *her ſmiles and tears*
Were like a better day.] It is plain we ſhould read—"a "wetter May," *i. e.* a ſpring ſeaſon wetter than ordinary.
WARBURTON.

A *better* day is the *beſt* day, and the *beſt day* is a day moſt favourable to the productions of the earth—ſuch are the days in which there is a due mixture of rain and ſunſhine.
STEEVENS.

We ſhould read,
"—— *the* better day."
The ſenſe is then ſufficiently clear.

"You have ſeen, ſays the gentleman, ſunſhine and rain at "once? Cordelia's ſmiles and tears were like *the* better day," *i. e.* like to that day in which ſunſhine prevails over rain.
A. B.

Thy

Thy heart is big; get thee apart and weep.
Paſſion, I ſee, is catching; for mine eyes,
Seeing thoſe beads of ſorrow ſtand in thine,
Begin to water. *Julius Cæſar*, A. 3, S. 1.

Give me that glaſs, and therein will I read.—
No deeper wrinkles yet? Hath ſorrow ſtruck
So many blows upon this face of mine,
And made no deeper wounds?—Oh, flattering glaſs,
Like to my followers in proſperity,
Thou doſt beguile me. *Richard II.* A. 4, S. 1.

——— Be ſad, good brothers,
For, to ſpeak truth, it very well becomes you;
Sorrow ſo royally in you appears,
That I will deeply put the faſhion on,
And wear it in my heart.
Henry IV. P. 2, A. 5, S. 2.

—— I found the prince in the next room,
Waſhing with kindly tears his gentle cheeks;
With ſuch a deep demeanour in great ſorrow,
That tyranny, which never quaff'd but blood,
Would, by beholding him, have waſh'd his knife
With gentle eye-drops. *Henry IV.* P. 2, A. 4, S. 4.

—— 'Tis all men's office to ſpeak patience
To thoſe that wring under the load of ſorrow;
But no man's virtue, nor ſufficiency,
To be ſo moral, when he ſhall endure
The like himſelf.
Much ado about nothing, A. 5, S. 1.

Shorten my days thou can'ſt with ſullen ſorrow,
And pluck nights from me, but not lend a morrow.
Thou can'ſt help time to furrow me with age,
But ſtop no wrinkle in his pilgrimage;
Thy word is current with him for my death;
But, dead, thy kingdom cannot buy my breath.
Richard II. A. 1, S. 3.

Duſt

Duſt was thrown upon his ſacred head;
Which with ſuch gentle ſorrow he ſhook off,—
His face ſtill combating with tears and ſmiles,
The badges of his grief and patience,—
That had not God, for ſome ſtrong purpoſe, ſteel'd
The hearts of men, they muſt perforce have melted.

Richard II. A. 5, S. 2.

Gnarling Sorrow hath leſs power to bite
The man that mocks at it, and ſets it light.

Richard II. A. 1, S. 3.

——The apprehenſion of the good
Gives but the greater feeling to the worſe:
Fell Sorrow's tooth doth never rankle more,
Than when it bites, but lanceth not the ſore.

Richard II. A. 1, S. 3.

——— I hardly yet have learn'd
To inſinuate, flatter, bow, and bend my knee:
Give Sorrow leave a while to tutor me
To this ſubmiſſion. *Richard II.* A. 4, S. 1.

Now will canker Sorrow eat my bud,
And chaſe the native beauty from his cheek,
And he will look as hollow as a ghoſt;
As dim and meagre as an ague's fit.

King John, A. 3, S. 4.

Oh, if thou teach me to believe this ſorrow,
Teach thou this ſorrow how to make me die;
And let belief and life encounter ſo,
As doth the fury of two deſperate men,
Which in the very meeting, fall, and die.

King John, A. 3, S. 1.

If ſuch a one will ſmile, and ſtroke his beard;
And Sorrow, wag [1]! cry; hem, when he ſhould groan;

Patch

[1] *If ſuch a one will ſmile, and ſtroke his beard;*
And Sorrow, wag! cry hem when he ſhould groan.] Such is the reading of all the copies; and on this very difficult paſſage the

Patch grief with proverbs; make misfortune drunk
With candle-wafters; bring him yet to me,
And I of him will gather patience.
Much ado about nothing, A. 5, S. 1.

SOUL.

Excellent wretch! Perdition catch my foul,
But I do love thee! and when I love thee not,
Chaos is come again. *Othello*, A. 3, S. 3.

—— I wonder in my foul,
What you could afk me, that I fhould deny,
Or ftand fo mammering on. What! Michael Caffio,
That came a wooing with you; and fo many a time,
When I have fpoke of you difpraifingly,
Hath ta'en your part: to have fo much to do
To bring him in! *Othello*, A. 3, S. 3.

——— Befhrew me much Emilia,
I was (unhandfome warrior as I am) [1]
Arraigning his unkindnefs with my foul;
But now I find I had fuborn'd the witnefs,
And he's indited falfely. *Othello*, A. 3, S. 4.

the commentators have tried their critical fkill, but without fuccefs. I cannot difcover any meaning in the lines as they at prefent ftand, and fhall therefore propofe a trifling alteration. I read,

"Call Sorrow hag! cry hem when he fhould groan."

A. B.

[1] —— *(unhandfome warrior as I am)*] How this came to be fo blundered, I cannot conceive. It is plain Shakefpeare wrote,

"Unhandfome wrangler as I am." WARBURTON.

Unhandfome warrior, is evidently *unfair affailant*.

JOHNSON.

"Unhandfome warrior" fhould furely be "unhandfome "lawyer," or pleader. The context will fufficiently warrant this reading. *Lawyer* and *warrior* being fomewhat alike in found, the miftake was made in tranfcribing. A. B.

—— Oh place! oh form!
How often dost thou with thy ease, thy habit,
Wrench awe from fools, and tie the wiser souls
To thy false seeming!

Measure for Measure, A. 2, S. 4.

—— Now my soul hath elbow-room,
It would not out at windows, nor at doors.
There is so hot a summer in my bosom,
That all my bowels crumble up to dust.

King John, A. 5, S. 7.

What shall I say to thee, lord Scroop; thou cruel,
Ingrateful, savage, and inhuman creature!
Thou, that didst bear the key of all my counsels,
That knew'st the very bottom of my soul,
That almost might'st have coin'd me into gold,
Would'st thou have practis'd on me for thy use?

Henry V. A. 2, S. 2.

It is too late; the life of all his blood
Is touch'd corruptibly; and his pure brain
(Which some suppose the soul's frail dwelling-house)
Doth, by the idle comments that it makes,
Foretell the ending of mortality.

King John, A. 5, S. 7.

—— Impartial are our eyes and ears:
Were he my brother; nay, my kingdom's heir;
Now by my sceptre's awe I make a vow,
Such neighbour nearness to our sacred blood
Should nothing privilege him, nor partialize
The unstooping firmness of my upright soul.

Richard II. A. 1, S. 1.

—— God forgive the sin of all those souls,
That to their everlasting residence,
Before the dew of ev'ning fall, shall fleet,
In dreadful trial of our kingdom's king!

King John, A. 2, S. 1.

—— Thy

——— Thy currish spirit
Govern'd a wolf, who, hang'd for human slaughter,
Even from the gallows did his fell soul fleet,
And, whilst thou lay'st in thy unhallow'd dam,
Infus'd itself in thee. *Merchant of Venice*, A. 4, S. 1.

— All the souls that were, were forfeit once;
And he that might the vantage best have took,
Found out the remedy.
Measure for Measure, A. 2, S. 2.

Oh, how this discord doth afflict my soul!—
Can you, my lord of Winchester, behold
My sighs and tears, and will not once relent?
Who should be pitiful, if you be not?
Or who should study to prefer a peace,
If holy churchmen take delight in broils?
Henry VI. P. 1, A. 3, S. 1.

——— My soul akes,
To know, when two authorities are up,
Neither supreme, how soon confusion
May enter 'twixt the gap of both, and take
The one by the other. *Coriolanus*, A. 3, S. 1.

Believe this of me, there can be no kernel in this light nut; the soul of this man is his clothes: trust him not in matter of heavy consequence; I have kept of them tame, and know their natures.
All's well that ends well, A. 2, S. 5.

—— O Lord, that lend'st me life,
Lend me a heart replete with thankfulness!
For thou hast given me, in this beauteous face,
A world of earthly blessings to my soul,
If sympathy of love unite our thoughts.
Henry VI. P. 2, A. 1, S. 1.

Go, tread the path that thou shalt ne'er return,
Simple, plain Clarence!—I do love thee so,

That I will ſhortly ſend thy ſoul to heaven,
If heaven will take the preſent at our hands.
Richard III. A. 1, S. 1.

Avaunt, thou dreadful miniſter of hell!
Thou hadſt but power over his mortal body,
His ſoul thou canſt not have.
Richard III. A. 1, S. 2.

The worm of conſcience ſtill be-gnaw thy ſoul!
Thy friends ſuſpect for traitors while thou liv'ſt,
And take deep traitors for thy deareſt friends!
No ſleep cloſe up that deadly eye of thine,
Unleſs it be while ſome tormenting dream
Affrights thee with a hell of ugly devils!
Richard III. A. 1, S. 3.

I do not know that Engliſhman alive,
With whom my ſoul is any jot at odds,
More than the infant that is born to-night;
I thank my God for my humility.
Richard III. A. 2, S. 1.

—— Remember this,—
God, and our good cauſe, fight upon our ſide;
The prayers of holy ſaints, and wronged ſouls,
Like high-rear'd bulwarks, ſtand before our faces.
Richard III. A. 5, S. 3.

I will from henceforth rather be myſelf,
Mighty, and to be fear'd, than my condition;
Which hath been ſmooth as oil, ſoft as young down,
And therefore loſt that title of reſpect,
Which the proud ſoul ne'er pays, but to the proud.
Henry IV. P. 1, A. 1, S. 3.

—— This viſitation
Is but to whet thy almoſt blunted purpoſe.
But, look! amazement on thy mother ſits:
O, ſtep between her and her fighting ſoul;
Conceit in weakeſt bodies ſtrongeſt works.
Hamlet, A. 3, S. 4.

—— Uncivil

—— Uncivil lady,
To whoſe ingrate and unauſpicious altars
My ſoul the faithfull'ſt offerings hath breath'd out,
That e'er devotion tender'd!

Twelfth Night, A. 5, S. 1.

The ſoul and body rive not more at parting,
Than greatneſs going off.

Antony and Cleopatra, A. 4, S. 11.

Even as I was then, is Percy now.
Now by my ſceptre, and my ſoul to boot,
He hath more worthy intereſt to the ſtate
Than thou, the ſhadow of ſucceſſion.

Henry IV. P. 1, A. 3, S. 2.

—— O my gentle Hubert,
We owe thee much; within this wall of fleſh
There is a ſoul, counts thee her creditor,
And with advantage means to pay thy love.

King John, A. 3, S. 3.

—— We have with ſpecial ſoul
Elected him our abſence to ſupply,
Lent him our terror, dreſt him with our love;
And given his deputation all the organs
Of our own power. *Meaſure for Meaſure*, A. 1, S. 1.

——— Sheba was never
More covetous of wiſdom, and fair virtue,
Than this pure ſoul ſhall be: all princely graces
That mould up ſuch a mighty piece as this is,
With all the virtues that attend the good,
Shall ſtill be doubled on her: truth ſhall nurſe her,
Holy and heavenly thoughts ſtill counſel her:
She ſhall be lov'd, and fear'd.

Henry VIII. A. 5, S. 4.

It is the cauſe, it is the cauſe, my ſoul,—
Let me not name it to you, you chaſte ſtars!—
It is the cauſe.—Yet I'll not ſhed her blood,

Nor ſcar that whiter ſkin of hers than ſnow,
And ſmooth as monumental alabaſter.

Othello, A. 5, S. 2.

——— You few that lov'd me,
And dare be bold to weep for Buckingham,
His noble friends, and fellows, whom to leave
Is only bitter to him, only dying,
Go with me, like good angels, to my end;
And, as the long divorce of ſteel falls on me,
Make of your prayers one ſweet ſacrifice,
And lift my ſoul to heaven.

Henry VIII. A. 2, S. 1.

Ten thouſand French have ta'en the ſacrament,
To rive their dangerous artillery [1]
Upon no Chriſtian ſoul but Engliſh Talbot.

Henry VI. P. 1, A. 4, S. 2.

SPEECH.

——— Rude am I in my ſpeech,
And little bleſs'd with the ſet phraſe of peace;
For ſince theſe arms of mine had ſeven years pith,
Till now, ſome nine moons waſted, they have us'd
Their deareſt action in the tented field.

Othello, A. 1, S. 3.

——— But, I do ſee, you are mov'd;
I am to pray you, not to ſtrain my ſpeech

[1] *To rive their dangerous artillery.*] I do not underſtand the phraſe to *rive artillery*; perhaps it might be to drive; we ſay to *drive a blow*, and to *drive at a man*, when we mean to expreſs furious aſſault. JOHNSON.

Rive their artillery, ſeems to mean, charge their artillery ſo much as to endanger their burſting. TOLLET.

"To rive" is properly *to break*; and *to break* has ſometimes the ſenſe of *to open*.

"Rive their artillery on the enemy" is, *break their artillery on the enemy*. The expreſſion is equivalent to the modern one—*open the artillery*. A. B.

To

To groſſer iſſues, nor to larger reach,
Than to ſuſpicion. *Othello*, A. 3, S. 3.

There was ſpeech in their dumbneſs, language in their very geſture; they look'd as they had heard of a world ranſom'd, or one deſtroy'd; a notable paſſion of wonder appear'd in them: but the wiſeſt beholder, that knew no more but ſeeing, could not ſay, if the importance were joy or ſorrow.

Winter's Tale, A. 5, S. 2.

Speak the ſpeech, I pray you, as I pronounc'd it to you, trippingly on the tongue; but if you mouth it, as many of our players do, I had as lieve the town-crier ſpoke my lines. Nor do not ſaw the air too much with your hand, thus; but uſe all gently: for in the very torrent, tempeſt, and (as I may ſay) whirlwind of your paſſion, you muſt acquire and beget a temperance, that may give it ſmoothneſs.

Hamlet, A. 3, S. 2.

His ſpeech was like a tangled chain; nothing impaired, but all diſordered.

Midſummer Night's Dream, A. 5, S. 1.

SPIRIT, SPIRITS.

I do applaud thy ſpirit, Valentine,
And think thee worthy of an empreſs' love.

Two Gentlemen of Verona, A. 5, S. 3.

——— My ſpirits obey; and Time
Goes upright with his carriage. *Tempeſt*, A. 5, S. 1.

If thou doſt play with him at any game,
Thou art ſure to loſe; and, of that natural luck,
He beats thee 'gainſt the odds; thy luſtre thickens
When he ſhines by: I ſay again, thy ſpirit
Is all afraid to govern thee near him;
But, he away, 'tis noble.

Antony and Cleopatra, A. 2, S. 2.

—— Hence
Some, to kill cankers in the musk-rose buds;
Some, war with rear-mice for their leathern wings,
To make my small elves coats; and some, keep back
The clamorous owl, that nightly hoots, and wonders
At our quaint spirits.
Midsummer Night's Dream, A. 2, S. 3.

—— Damned spirits all,
That in cross-ways and floods have burial,
Already to their wormy beds are gone.
Midsummer Night's Dream, A. 3, S. 2.

Forth at your eyes your spirits wildly peep;
And, as the sleeping soldiers in the alarm,
Your bedded hair, like life in excrements,
Starts up, and stands on end. *Hamlet*, A. 3, S. 4.

I am thy father's spirit;
Doom'd for a certain term to walk the night;
And, for the day, confin'd to fast in fires,
Till the foul crimes, done in my days of nature,
Are burnt and purg'd away. *Hamlet*, A. 1, S. 5.

—— I have heard,
The cock, that is the trumpet to the morn,
Doth with his lofty and shrill-sounding throat
Awake the god of day; and, at his warning,
Whether in sea or fire, in earth or air,
The extravagant and erring spirit hies
To his confine. *Hamlet*, A. 1, S. 1.

Angels and ministers of grace defend us!---
Be thou a spirit of health, or goblin damn'd,
Bring with thee airs from heaven, or blasts from hell,
Be thy intents wicked, or charitable,
Thou com'st in such a questionable shape,
That I will speak to thee. *Hamlet*, A. 1, S. 4.

My father's spirit in arms! all is not well;
I doubt some foul play: would the night were come;

Till

Till then ſit ſtill, my ſoul: foul deeds will riſe
(Though all the earth o'erwhelm them) to men's eyes.
Hamlet, A. 1, S. 2.

——— The ſpirit that I have ſeen,
May be a devil: and the devil hath power
To reſume a pleaſing ſhape; yea, and, perhaps
Out of my weakneſs, and my melancholy,
(As he is very potent with ſuch ſpirits)
Abuſes me to damn me. *Hamlet*, A. 2, S. 2.

——— Let me not live,
After my flame lacks oil, to be the ſnuff
Of younger ſpirits, whoſe apprehenſive ſenſes
All but new things diſdain.
All's well that ends well, A. 1, S. 2.

[1] Whoſe haughty ſpirit, winged with deſire,
Will coaſt my crown, and, like an empty eagle,
Tire on the fleſh of me, and of my ſon!
Henry VI. P. 3, A. 1, S. 1.

——— Spirits are not finely touch'd,
But to fine iſſues. *Meaſure for Meaſure*, A. 1, S. 1.

Oh Julius Cæſar, thou art mighty yet!
Thy ſpirit walks abroad, and turns our ſwords
In our own proper entrails.
Julius Cæſar, A. 5, S. 3.

[1] *Whoſe haughty ſpirit, winged with deſire,*
Will coſt my crown, and, like an empty eagle,
Tire on the fleſh.]

Read *coaſt*, i. e. hover over it. WARBURTON.

The word which Dr. Warburton would introduce, appears to violate the metaphor, nor is to *coaſt* uſed as a term in falconry. We may however maintain the integrity of the figure, by inſerting the word *cote*. To *cote* is to come up with, to overtake. STEEVENS.

"Cote" may perhaps be right. To *cote*, however, is not *to come up with, to overtake*, but *to mark, to notice*. Henry's meaning is, that the Duke of York would keep his eye at all times on the crown; that he would never loſe ſight of it. A. B.

We

We all ſtand up againſt the ſpirit of Cæſar;
And in the ſpirit of men there is no blood;
O, that we then could come by Cæſar's ſpirit,
And not diſmember Cæſar! but, alas,
Cæſar muſt bleed for it! *Julius Cæſar*, A. 2, S. 1.

Now ſet the teeth, and ſtretch the noſtril wide;
Hold hard the breath, and bend up every ſpirit
To his full height!—On, on, you nobleſt Engliſh,
Whoſe blood is ſet from fathers of war-proof!
Henry V. A. 3, S. 1.

—— Gracious lord,
Stand for your own; unwind your bloody flag;
Look back unto your mighty anceſtors:
Go, my dread lord, to your great grandſire's tomb,
From whom you claim; invoke his warlike ſpirit;
And your great uncle's, Edward the black prince.
Henry V. A. 1, S. 2.

Who ſets me elſe? by heaven I'll throw at all:
I have a thouſand ſpirits in one breaſt,
To anſwer twenty thouſand ſuch as you.
Richard II. A. 4, S. 1.

I do beſeech ye, if you bear me hard,
Now, whilſt your purpled hands do reek and ſmoke;
Fulfil your pleaſure. Live a thouſand years,
I ſhall not find myſelf ſo apt to die:
No place will pleaſe me ſo, no mean of death,
As, here by Cæſar, and by you cut off,
The choice and maſter ſpirits of this age.
Julius Cæſar, A. 3, S. 1.

That I did love thee, Cæſar; O, 'tis true:
If then thy ſpirit look upon us now,
Shall it not grieve thee, dearer than thy death,
To ſee thy Antony making his peace,
Shaking the bloody fingers of thy foes,
Moſt noble! in the preſence of thy corſe?
Julius Cæſar, A. 3, S. 1.

—— Soul

—— Soul of Rome!
Brave ſon, deriv'd from honourable loins!
Thou, like an exorciſt, haſt conjur'd up
My mortified ſpirit. Now bid me run,
And I will ſtrive with things impoſſible;
Yea, get the better of them.

Julius Cæſar, A. 2, S. 1.

—— What ſhould be in that Cæſar?
Why ſhould that name be ſounded more than yours?
Write them together, yours is as fair a name;
Sound them it doth become the mouth as well;
Weigh them, it is as heavy; conjure with them,
Brutus will ſtart a ſpirit as ſoon as Cæſar.

Julius Cæſar, A. 1, S. 2.

—— He reads much;
He is a great obſerver, and he looks
Quite through the deeds of men: he loves no plays
As thou doſt, Antony; he hears no muſick:
Seldom he ſmiles; and ſmiles in ſuch a ſort,
As if he mock'd himſelf, and ſcorn'd his ſpirit
That could be mov'd to ſmile at any thing.

Julius Cæſar, A. 1, S. 2.

Nor ſtony tower, nor walls of beaten braſs,
Nor airleſs dungeon, nor ſtrong links of iron,
Can be retentive to the ſtrength of ſpirit;
But life, being weary of theſe worldly bars,
Never lacks power to diſmiſs itſelf.

Julius Cæſar, A. 1, S. 3.

—— She is too diſdainful;
I know, her ſpirits are as coy and wild
As haggards of the rock.

Much ado about nothing, A. 3, S. 1.

Happy in this, ſhe is not yet ſo old
But ſhe may learn: happier than this,
She is not bred ſo dull but ſhe can learn;
Happieſt of all, is, that her gentle ſpirit

Commits

Commits itſelf to yours to be directed,
As from her lord, her governor, her king.
Merchant of Venice, A. 3, S. 2.

—— A braver choice of dauntleſs ſpirits,
Than now the Engliſh bottoms have waft o'er,
Did never float upon the ſwelling tide,
To do offence and ſcath in Chriſtendom.
King John, A. 2, S. 1.

I hold you as a thing enſky'd, and ſainted;
By your renouncement, an immortal ſpirit;
And to be talked with in ſincerity,
As with a ſaint. *Meaſure for Meaſure*, A. 1, S. 5.

[1] Methinks, in thee ſome bleſſed ſpirit doth ſpeak;
His powerful ſound within an organ weak.
All's well that ends well, A. 2, S. 1.

Although this lord of weak remembrance, this,
(Who ſhall be of as little memory,
When he is earth'd) hath here almoſt perſuaded
(For he's a ſpirit of perſuaſion [2], only
Profeſſes

[1] *Methinks, in thee ſome bleſſed ſpirit doth ſpeak;*
His powerful ſound within an organ weak.] To *ſpeak a ſound* is a barbariſm. Beſide the conſtruction is vicious with the two ablatives, *in thee*, and *within an organ weak*. The lines, therefore, ſhould be read and pointed,

"Methinks in thee ſome bleſſed ſpirit doth ſpeak;
"His power *full* ſounds within an organ weak."

WARBURTON.

If we change the order of the lines, there is no longer any difficulty.

"O powerful ſound within an organ weak!
"Methinks in thee ſome bleſſed ſpirit doth ſpeak!"

A. B.

[2] *For he's a ſpirit of perſuaſion.*] Of this entangled ſentence I can draw no ſenſe from the preſent reading, and therefore imagine that the author gave it thus:

"For he, a ſpirit of perſuaſion, only
"Profeſſes to perſuade."

Of which the meaning may be either, *that he alone, who is a ſpirit of perſuaſion, profeſſes to perſuade the king*; or that, *he only profeſſes*

Professes to persuade) the king, his son's alive;
'Tis as impossible that he's undrown'd,
As he, that sleeps here, swims. *Tempest*, A. 2, S. 1.

SPLEEN.

[1] ——— At this match,
With swifter spleen than powder can enforce,
The mouth of passage shall we fling wide ope,
And give you entrance. *King John*, A. 2, S. 2.

SPORT, SPORTS.

——— To confound such time,—
That drums him from his sport, and speaks as loud
As his own state, and ours,—'tis to be chid
As we rate boys; who, being mature in knowledge,
Pawn their experience to their present pleasure,
And so rebel to judgment.
Antony and Cleopatra, A. 1, S. 4.

There be some sports are painful; but their labour
Delight in them sets off. *Tempest*, A. 3, S. 1.

fesses to persuade, that is, *without being so persuaded himself, he makes a shew of persuading the king.* JOHNSON.

"(For he's a spirit of persuasion, only
"Professes to persuade.)"

The meaning is, *that in cases like to that of which they are speaking, he is generally admitted, or considered, as a spirit of persuasion, who endeavours to persuade of the truth of the news he brings. That such agreeable reports are readily listened to.* The want of the pronoun *who*, occasions much of the difficulty. Read,

Who professes to persuade. A. B.

[1] ——— *At this match*
With swifter spleen.] Our author uses *spleen* for any violent hurry, or tumultuous speed. So in the Midsummer Night's Dream, he applies *spleen* to the *lightning*. JOHNSON.

"Spleen" is *anger*, but the word is out of its place. We must read the line thus:

"Swifter than powder can in spleen enforce." A. B.

— Never

—— Never, ſince the middle ſummer's ſpring,
Met we on hill, in dale, foreſt, or mead,
By paved fountain, or by ruſhy brook,
Or on the beached margent of the ſea,
To dance our ringlets to the whiſtling wind,
But with thy brawls thou haſt diſturb'd our ſport.
Midſummer Night's Dream, A. 2, S. 2.

—— Let it work;
For 'tis the ſport, to have the engineer
Hoiſt with his own petar: and it ſhall go hard,
But I will delve one yard below their mines,
And blow them at the moon. *Hamlet*, A. 3, S. 4.

Now, by the ground that I am baniſh'd from,
Well could I curſe away a winter's night,
Though ſtanding naked on a mountain top,
Where biting cold would never let graſs grow,
And think it but a minute ſpent in ſport.
Henry VI. P. 2, A. 3, S. 2.

—— His addiction was to courſes vain:
His companions unletter'd, rude, and ſhallow;
His hours fill'd up with riots, banquets, ſports;
And never noted in him any ſtudy,
Any retirement, any ſequeſtration
From open haunts and popularity.
Henry V. A. 1, S. 1.

STARS.

Men at ſome time are maſters of their fates:
The fault, dear Brutus, is not in our ſtars,
But in ourſelves, that we are underlings.
Julius Cæſar, A. 1, S. 2.

—— Thou cold-blooded ſlave,
Haſt thou not ſpoke like thunder on my ſide?
Been ſworn my ſoldier, bidding me depend

Upon

Upon thy ſtars, thy fortune, and thy ſtrength?
And doſt thou now fall over to my foes?

King John, A. 3, S. 1.

Hung be the heavens with black, yield day to night!
Comets, importing change of times and ſtates,
Brandiſh your cryſtal treſſes in the ſky;
And with them ſcourge the bad revolting ſtars,
That have conſented unto Henry's death!

Henry VI. P. 1, A. 1, S. 1.

Henry the fifth! thy ghoſt I invocate;
Proſper this realm, keep it from civil broils!
Combat with adverſe planets in the heavens!
A far more glorious ſtar thy ſoul will make,
Than Julius Cæſar. *Henry VI.* P. 1, A. 1, S. 1.

I am the prince of Wales; and think not, Percy,
To ſhare with me in glory any more:
Two ſtars keep not their motion in one ſphere;
Nor can one England brook a double reign.

Henry IV. P. 1, A. 5, S. 4.

Thy lord? that is my lord, Leonatus.
O, learn'd indeed were that aſtronomer,
That knew the ſtars, as I his characters;
He'd lay the future open. *Cymbeline*, A. 3, S. 2.

S T A T E.

——— Yet, if you there
Did practiſe on my ſtate, your being in Ægypt
Might be my queſtion [1].

Antony and Cleopatra, A. 2, S. 2.

[1] ——— *my queſtion.*] *i. e.* My theme or ſubject of converſation. MALONE.

Mr. Malone here conſiders *queſtion* in a much too limited ſenſe. *My queſtion* muſt, in this place, mean *my buſineſs*. This is a matter, ſays Cæſar (meaning the practiſing on his ſtate), that I ſhould *particularly inquire into*. A. B.

S T O N E.

STONE.

Go to then; your confiderate ftone[1].
Antony and Cleopatra, A. 2, S. 2.

STORM.

This day I'll wear aloft my burgonet,
(As on a mountain top the cedar fhews,
That keeps his leaves in fpight of any ftorm)
Even to affright thee with the view thereof.
Henry VI. P. 2, A. 5, S. 1.

Poor naked wretches, wherefoe'er you are,
That bide the pelting of this pitilefs ftorm,
How fhall your houfelefs heads, and unfed fides,
Your loop'd and window'd raggednefs, defend you
From feafons fuch as thefe? *Lear*, A. 3, S. 4.

SUN.

Miflike me not for my complexion,
The fhadow'd livery of the burnifh'd fun,
To whom I am a neighbour, and near bred.
Merchant of Venice, A. 2, S. 1.

[1] ——— *your confiderate ftone.*] This line is paffed by all the editors, as if they underftood it, and believed it univerfally intelligible. I cannot find in it any very obvious, and hardly any poffible meaning. I would therefore read,

"Go to then, you confiderate ones."

You who diflike my franknefs and temerity of fpeech, and are fo *confiderate* and difcreet, *Go to.* JOHNSON.

I believe, *Go to then, your confiderate ftone,* means only this: *If I muft be chidden, henceforward I will be mute as a marble ftatue, which feems to think, though it can fay nothing.* STEEVENS.

"Confiderate ftone," as Dr. Johnfon obferves, is certainly without meaning. I am perfuaded that it is a mifprint, and that we fhould read: *Go to then; your confederate's tone;* i. e. *Go to then; as your confederate would fay.* By which words, Enobarbus feems to reprove Antony for his mildnefs, and at the fame time to throw out an infinuation that Cæfar is fomewhat too affuming in his manner. A. B.

To ſolemnize this day, the glorious ſun
Stays in his courſe, and plays the alchymiſt;
Turning, with ſplendour of his precious eye,
The meagre cloddy earth to glittering gold.
King John, A. 3, S. 1.

——— It is I,
That lying, by the violet, in the ſun,
Do, as the carrion does, not as the flower,
Corrupt with virtuous ſeaſon.
Meaſure for Meaſure, A. 2, S. 2.

Soft! What light through yonder window breaks?
It is the eaſt, and Juliet is the ſun!
Ariſe, fair ſun, and kill the envious moon,
Who is already ſick and pale with grief,
That thou her maid art far more fair than ſhe.
Romeo and Juliet, A. 2, S. 2.

When the ſun ſhines, let fooliſh gnats make ſport,
But creep in crannies, when he hides his beams.
Comedy of Errors, A. 2, S. 2.

Ne'er through an arch ſo hurry'd the blown tide,
As the re-comforted through the gates. Why, hark
you,
The trumpets, ſackbuts, pſalteries, and fifes,
Tabors, and cymbals, and the ſhouting Romans,
Make the ſun dance. *Coriolanus*, A. 5, S. 4.

The ſun's a thief, and with his great attraction
Robs the vaſt ſea: the moon's an arrant thief,
And her pale fire ſhe ſnatches from the ſun;
The ſea's a thief, whoſe liquid ſurge reſolves
The moon into ſalt tears; the earth's a thief,
That feeds and breeds by a compoſture ſtolen
From general excrement: each thing's a thief.
Timon of Athens, A. 4, S. 3.

—— I was born ſo high,
Our aiery buildeth in the cedar's top,
And dallies with the wind, and ſcorns the ſun.

Richard III. A. 1, S. 3.

The weary ſun hath made a golden ſet,
And, by the bright track of his fiery car,
Gives token of a goodly day to-morrow.

Richard III. A. 5, S. 3.

The ſun will not be ſeen to-day; what's that to me
More than to Richmond? for the ſelf-ſame heaven
That frowns on me, looks ſadly upon him.

Richard III. A. 5, S. 3.

Yet will I imitate the ſun;
Who doth permit the baſe contagious clouds
To ſmother up his beauty from the world,
That, when he pleaſe again to be himſelf,
Being wanted, he may be more wondered at,
By breaking through the foul and ugly miſts
That ſeem to ſtrangle him.

Henry IV. P. 1, A. 1, S. 2.

—— Come, the ſong we had laſt night:
Mark it, Ceſario; it is old, and plain;
The ſpinſters and the knitters in the ſun,
And the free maids that weave their thread with bones,
Do uſe to chaunt it. *Twelfth Night*, A. 2, S. 4.

—— We fairies, that do run
By the triple Hecat's team,
From the preſence of the ſun,
Following darkneſs like a dream,
Now are frolick.

Midſummer Night's Dream, A. 5, S. 2.

At firſt I did adore a twinkling ſtar;
But now I worſhip a celeſtial ſun.

Two Gentlemen of Verona, A. 2, S. 6.

All

All the infections that the ſun ſucks up
From bogs, fens, flats, on Proſper fall, and make him
By inch-meal a diſeaſe! *Tempeſt*, A. 2, S. 2.

O ſun, thy upriſe ſhall I ſee no more:
Fortune and Antony part here; even here
Do we ſhake hands.—All come to this?—The hearts
That ſpaniel'd me at heels, to whom I gave
Their wiſhes, do diſcandy, melt their ſweets
On bloſſoming Cæſar; and this pine is bark'd
That over-topp'd them all.
Antony and Cleopatra, A. 4, S. 10.

——— Once, or twice,
I was about to ſpeak; and tell him plainly,
The ſelf-ſame ſun, that ſhines upon his court,
Hides not his viſage from our cottage, but
Looks on alike. *Winter's Tale*, A. 4, S. 3.

S U R G E.

— Do but ſtand upon the foaming ſhore:
The chiding billow ſeems to pelt the clouds;
The wind-ſhak'd ſurge, with high and monſtrous main,
Seems to caſt water on the burning bear,
And quench the guards of the ever-fix'd pole;
I never did like moleſtation view
On the enchafed flood. *Othello*, A. 2, S. 1.

I ſaw him beat the ſurges under him,
And ride upon their backs. *Tempeſt*, A. 2, S. 1.

For now I ſtand as one upon a rock,
Environ'd with a wilderneſs of ſea;
Who marks the waxing tide grow wave by wave,
Expecting ever when ſome envious ſurge
Will in his briniſh bowels ſwallow him.
Titus Andronicus, A. 3, S. 1.

——— Leak'd is our bark;
And we, poor mates, ſtand on the dying deck,
Hearing the ſurges threat: we muſt all part
Into this ſea of air. *Timon of Athens*, A. 4, S. 2.

——— Say to Athens,
Timon hath made his everlaſting manſion
Upon the beached verge of the ſalt flood,
Which once a day with his emboſſed froth
The turbulent ſurge ſhall cover; thither come,
And let my grave-ſtone be your oracle.
Timon of Athens, A. 5, S. 2.

How fearful
And dizzy 'tis, to caſt one's eyes ſo low!
The crows, and choughs, that wing the midway air,
Shew ſcarce ſo groſs as beetles:
The fiſhermen, that walk upon the beach,
Appear like mice; and yon tall anchoring bark,
Diminiſh'd to her cock; her cock, a buoy
Almoſt too ſmall for ſight: the murmuring ſurge,
That on the unnumber'd idle pebbles chaſes,
Cannot be heard ſo high. *Lear*, A. 4, S. 6.

S W A Y.

——— Confederates,
So dry he was for ſway [1], with the king of Naples
To give him annual tribute, do him homage.
Tempeſt, A. 1, S. 2.

[1] *So dry he was for ſway.*] *i. e.* So thirſty. The expreſſion, I am told, is not uncommon in the midland counties. STEEVENS.
"Dry" is very inelegant. I ſuppoſe we ſhould read *dree*, i. e. ſorrowing. A. B.

T.

TALE.

——BY your gracious patience,
I will a round unvarniſh'd tale deliver
Of my whole courſe of love; what drugs, what charms,
What conjuration, and what mighty magic,
(For ſuch proceeding I am charg'd withal)
I won his daughter with. *Othello*, A. 1, S. 3.

Oh, but they ſay, the tongues of dying men
Inforce attention, like deep harmony:
Though Richard my life's counſel would not hear,
My death's ſad tale may yet undeaf his ear.
Richard II. A. 2, S. 1.

In winter's tedious nights, ſit by the fire
With good old folks; and let them tell thee tales
Of woful ages, long ago betid.
Richard II. A. 5, S. 1.

He hears merry tales, and ſmiles not: I fear, he will prove the weeping philoſopher when he grows old, being ſo full of unmannerly ſadneſs in his youth.
Merchant of Venice, A. 1, S. 2.

It is not ſo; thou haſt miſ-ſpoke, miſ-heard;
Be well adviſed, tell o'er thy tale again:
It cannot be; thou doſt but ſay, 'tis ſo;
I truſt, I may not truſt thee; for thy word
Is but the vain breath of a common man.
King John, A. 3, S. 1.

There's nothing in this world can make me joy:
Life is as tedious as a twice-told tale,
Vexing the dull ear of a drowsy man.
King John, A. 3, S. 4.

—— Aged ears play truant at his tales,
And younger hearings are quite ravished;
So sweet and voluble is his discourse.
Love's Labour Lost, A. 2, S. 1.

I thank him that he cuts me from my tale,
For I profess not talking; only this—
Let each man do his best: and here draw I
A sword, whose temper I intend to stain
With the best blood that I can meet withal.
Henry IV. P. 1, A. 5, S. 2.

——— But that I am forbid
To tell the secrets of my prison-house,
I could a tale unfold, whose lightest word
Would harrow up thy soul; freeze thy young blood;
Make thy two eyes, like stars, start from their spheres;
Thy knotty and combined locks to part,
And each particular hair to stand on end
Like quills upon the fretful porcupine.
Hamlet, A. 1, S. 5.

[1] The wisest aunt, telling the saddest tale,
Sometime for three-foot stool mistaketh me.
Midsummer Night's Dream, A. 2, S. 1.

[1] *The wisest aunt.*] *Aunt* is *procuress*. STEEVENS.

The author of the REMARKS says, "this conjecture is much "too wanton and injurious to the word *aunt*, which, in this place "at least, certainly means no other than an *innocent old woman*." REED.

"Aunt"—this word should be written *aunct*—abbreviation of auncient. It means an old person, *man* or *woman*. A. B.

TALKER.

TALKER.

Farewell: I'll grow a talker for this gear[1].

Merchant of Venice, A. 1, S. 1.

TEARS.

If that the earth could teem with woman's tears,
Each drop she falls would prove a crocodile:—
Out of my sight! *Othello*, A. 4, S. 1.

What! canst thou not forbear me half an hour?
Then get thee gone, and dig my grave thyself;
And bid the merry bells ring to thine ear,
That thou art crowned, not that I am dead;
Let all the tears that should bedew my hearse,
Be drops of balm to sanctify thy head.

Henry IV. P. 2, A. 4, S. 4.

If you have tears, prepare to shed them now.
You all do know this mantle: I remember
The first time ever Cæsar put it on;
'Twas on a summer's evening, in his tent;
That day he overcame the Nervii.

Julius Cæsar, A. 3, S. 2.

You men of Angiers, open wide your gates,
And let young Arthur, duke of Bretagne, in;
Who, by the hand of France, this day hath made
Much work for tears in many an English mother.

King John, A. 2, S. 2.

—— Look, the good man weeps!
He's honest, on mine honour. God's blest mother!
I swear, he is true-hearted; and a soul
None better in my kingdom.—Get you gone,

[1] *I'll grow a talker for this gear.*] *Gear* appears to me to have no meaning here. I would therefore read,

"I'll grow a talker for this *year*." MALONE.

"Gear" should, in this place, be written *gere*, i. e. a jest. Anthonio says, "a good jest; I shall become a talker." A. B.

And do as I have bid you.—He has ſtrangled
His language in his tears. *Henry VIII.* A. 5, S. 1.

I am about to weep; but, thinking that
We are a queen (or long have dream'd ſo), certain
The daughter of a king, my drops of tears
I'll turn to ſparks of fire. *Henry VIII.* A. 2, S. 4.

When I did name her brothers, then freſh tears
Stood on her cheeks; as doth the honey dew
Upon a gather'd lily almoſt wither'd.
Titus Andronicus, A. 3, S. 1.

Oh, turn thy edged ſword another way;
Strike thoſe that hurt, and hurt not thoſe that help!
One drop of blood drawn from thy country's boſom,
Should grieve thee more than ſtreams of foreign gore;
Return thee, therefore, with a flood of tears,
And waſh away thy country's ſtained ſpots!
Henry VI. P. 1, A. 3, S. 3.

Oh, train me not, ſweet mermaid, with thy note,
To drown me in thy ſiſter's flood of tears;
Sing, ſyren, for thyſelf, and I will dote:
Spread o'er the ſilver waves thy golden hairs,
And as a bed I'll take thee, and there lie.
Comedy of Errors, A. 3, S. 2.

Her ſighs will make a battery in his breaſt;
Her tears will pierce into a marble heart;
The tyger will be mild, while ſhe doth mourn;
And Nero will be tainted with remorſe,
To hear, and ſee, her plaints, her briniſh tears.
Henry VI. P. 3, A. 3, S. 1.

—— I can ſmile, and murder while I ſmile;
And cry, content, to that which grieves my heart;
And wet my cheeks with artificial tears,
And frame my face to all occaſions.
Henry VI. P. 3, A. 3, S. 2.

— You are more inhuman, more inexorable,---
O, ten times more,---than tygers of Hyrcania.

See,

See, ruthleſs queen, a hapleſs father's tears:
This cloth thou dipp'dſt in blood of my ſweet boy,
And lo! with tears I waſh the blood away.

Henry VI. P. 3, A. 1, S. 4.

—— The hairy fool,
Much marked of the melancholy Jaques,
Stood on the extremeſt verge of the ſwift brook,
Augmenting it with tears. *As you like it*, A. 2, S. 1.

——— The big round tears
Cours'd one another down his innocent noſe
In piteous chaſe. *As you like it*, A. 2, S. 1.

——— The ſmiles of knaves
Tent in my cheeks; and ſchool-boys' tears take up
The glaſſes of my ſight! A beggar's tongue
Make motion through my lips: and my arm'd knees,
Who bow'd but in my ſtirrop, bend like his
That hath received an alms! *Coriolanus*, A. 3, S. 2.

—— I am weaker than a woman's tear,
Tamer than ſleep, fonder than ignorance;
Leſs valiant than the virgin in the night
And ſkill-leſs as unpractis'd infancy.

Troilus and Creſſida, A. 1, S. 1.

For myſelf,—foe as he was to me,
Might liquid tears, or heart-offending groans,
Or blood-conſuming ſighs recall his life,
I would be blind with weeping, ſick with groans,
Look pale as primroſe, with blood-drinking ſighs,
And all to have the noble duke alive.

Henry VI. P. 2, A. 3, S. 2.

If the river were dry, I am able to fill it with my tears; if the wind were down, I could drive the boat with my ſighs.

Two Gentlemen of Verona, A. 2, S. 3.

——— Within a month;
Ere yet the ſalt of moſt unrighteous tears

Had

Had left the flushing in her galled eyes,
She marry'd. *Hamlet*, A. 1, S. 2.

What! we have many goodly days to see!
The liquid drops of tears that you have shed,
Shall come again, transform'd to orient pearl;
Advantaging their loan, with interest
Oftentimes double gain of happiness.
Richard III. A. 4, S. 4.

— Neither bended knees, pure hands held up,
Sad sighs, deep groans, nor silver-shedding tears,
Could penetrate her uncompassionate sire.
Two Gentlemen of Verona, A. 3, S. 1.

A little month; or ere these shoes were old
With which she follow'd my poor father's body,
Like Niobe, all tears:—why she, even she,—
O heaven! a beast, that wants discourse of reason,
Would have mourn'd longer,—marry'd with my uncle,
My father's brother; but no more like my father,
Than I to Hercules. *Hamlet*, A. 1, S. 2.

——— She hath offer'd to the doom,
A sea of melting pearl, which some call tears.
Two Gentlemen of Verona, A. 3, S. 1.

Say, that upon the altar of her beauty
You sacrifice your tears, your sighs, your heart:
Write, till your ink be dry: and with your tears
Moist it again. *Two Gentlemen of Verona*, A. 3, S. 2.

There might you have beheld one joy crown another; so, and in such manner, that, it seem'd, sorrow wept to take leave of them; for their joy waded in tears. *Winter's Tale*, A. 5, S. 2.

His tears run down his beard, like winter drops
From eaves of reeds. *Tempest*, A. 5, S. 1.

——— Do not weep, good fools;
There is no cause: when you shall know your mistress

Has

Has deserv'd prison, then abound in tears,
As I come out. *Winter's Tale*, A. 2, S. 1.

Thou lov'st me not; for, brother, if thou didst,
Thy tears would wash this cold congealed blood,
That glues my lips, and will not let me speak.
Henry VI. P. 3, A. 5, S. 2.

Therefore great France
My mourning, and important tears [1], hath pitied.
Lear, A. 4, S. 4.

TEMPEST.

I have seen tempests, when the scolding winds
Have riv'd the knotty oaks; and I have seen
The ambitious ocean swell, and rage, and foam,
To be exalted with the threat'ning clouds:
But never till to-night, never till now,
Did I go through a tempest dropping fire.
Julius Cæsar, A. 1, S. 3.

——— Most degenerate king!
But, lords, we hear this fearful tempest sing,
Yet seek no shelter to avoid the storm:
We see the wind sit sore upon our sails,
And yet we strike not, but securely perish.
Richard II. A. 2, S. 1.

The owl shriek'd at thy birth, an evil sign;
The night-crow cry'd, aboding luckless time;
Dogs howl'd, and hideous tempests shook down trees;
The raven rook'd her on the chimney's top,
And chattering pies in dismal discords sung.
Henry VI. P. 3. A. 5, S. 6.

[1] ——— *important.*] In other places of this author for *importunate.* JOHNSON.

"Important tears" mean not that she was *whining* or *importunate:* beside, she had already mentioned her *mourning.* "Important tears" signify *the greatness*, the importance of her cause; a cause that had for its object no less than the preservation of her father's life, A. B.

THIEF.

THIEF.

Thieves for their robbery have authority,
When judges ſteal themſelves.
Meaſure for Meaſure, A. 2, S. 2.

——— I not deny,
The jury, paſſing on the priſoner's life,
May, in the ſworn twelve, have a thief or two
Guiltier than him they try.
Meaſure for Meaſure, A. 2, S. 1.

THOUGHT, THOUGHTS.

——— Thou doſt mean ſomething:
I heard thee ſay but now,—Thou lik'dſt not that,
When Caſſio left my wife; what didſt not like?
And, when I told thee—he was of my counſel
In my whole courſe of wooing, thou cry'dſt, indeed!
If thou doſt love me, ſhew me thy thought.
Othello, A. 3, S. 3.

Utter my thoughts? Why, ſay, they are vile and falſe;
As where's that palace whereinto foul things
Sometimes intrude not? who has a breaſt ſo pure,
But ſome uncleanly apprehenſions
Keep leets, and law-days, and in ſeſſion ſit
With meditations lawful? *Othello*, A. 3, S. 3.

Faſter than ſpring-time ſhowers, comes thought on thought,
And not a thought, but thinks on dignity.
My brain more buſy than the labouring ſpider,
Weaves tedious ſnares to trap mine enemies.
Henry VI. P. 2, A. 3, S. 1.

Thoughts tending to content, flatter themſelves,—
That they are not the firſt of fortune's ſlaves,
Nor ſhall not be the laſt: like ſilly beggars,

Who, ſitting in the ſtocks, refuge their ſhame,
That many have, and others muſt ſit there.
Richard II. A. 5, S. 5.

——— Now the biſhop
Turns inſurrection to religion:
Suppos'd ſincere and holy in his thoughts,
He's follow'd both with body and with mind;
And doth enlarge his riſing with the blood
Of fair king Richard. *Henry IV.* P. 2, A. 1, S. 1.

Leſt you ſhould not underſtand me well,
And yet a maiden hath no tongue but thought,
I would detain you here ſome month or two.
Merchant of Venice, A. 3, S. 2.

— That ſupernal judge, that ſtirs good thoughts
In any breaſt of ſtrong authority,
To look into the blots and ſtains of right—
That judge hath made me guardian to this boy.
King John, A. 2, S. 1.

If that thou couldſt ſee me without eyes,
Hear me without thine ears, and make reply
Without a tongue, uſing conceit alone,
Then, in deſpight of broad-ey'd watchful day,
I would into thy boſom pour my thoughts.
King John, A. 3, S. 3.

Sir, in this audience,
Let my diſclaiming from a purpos'd evil
Free me ſo far in your moſt generous thoughts,
That I have ſhot my arrow o'er the houſe,
And hurt my brother. *Hamlet*, A. 5, S. 2.

—— Thoughts are no ſubjects;
Intents, but merely thoughts.
Meaſure for Meaſure, A. 5, S. 1.

THUNDER.

THUNDER.

—— To the dread rattling thunder
Have I given fire, and rifted Jove's ſtout oak
With his own bolt. *Tempeſt*, A. 5, S. 1.

—— The thunder,
That deep and dreadful organ-pipe, pronounc'd
The name of Proſper. *Tempeſt*, A. 3, S. 3.

His legs beſtrid the ocean; his rear'd arm
Creſted the world; his voice was property'd
As all the tuned ſpheres, and that to friends;
But when he meant to quail and ſhake the orb,
He was as rattling thunder.
Antony and Cleopatra, A. 5, S. 2.

—— Thou all-ſhaking thunder,
Strike flat the thick rotundity o' the world!
Crack nature's moulds; all germins ſpill at once
That make ingrateful man! *Lear*, A. 3, S. 2.

TIME.

—— Theſe twenty years,
This rock, and theſe demeſnes, have been my world:
Where I have liv'd an honeſt freedom; paid
More pious debts to heaven, than in all
The fore-end of my time. *Cymbeline*, A. 3, S. 3.

Experience is by induſtry atchiev'd,
And perfected by the ſwift courſe of time.
Two Gentlemen of Verona, A. 1, S. 3.

Thou, Julia, thou haſt metamorphos'd me;
Made me neglect my ſtudies, loſe my time,
War with good counſel, ſet the world at nought.
Two Gentlemen of Verona, A. 1, S. 1.

Time is the nurſe and breeder of all good.
Two Gentlemen of Verona, A. 3, S. 1.

Still your fingers on your lips, I pray.
The time is out of joint;—O curſed ſpight!
That ever I was born to ſet it right!

Hamlet, A. 1, S. 5.

— Who would bear the whips and ſcorns of time,
The oppreſſor's wrong, the proud man's contumely,
The pangs of deſpis'd love, the law's delay,
The inſolence of office, and the ſpurns
That patient merit of the unworthy takes,
When he himſelf might his quietus make
With a bare bodkin? *Hamlet*, A. 3, S. 1.

——— From this time,
Be ſomewhat ſcanter of your maiden preſence;
Set your entreatments [1] at a higher rate,
Than a command to parley. *Hamlet*, A. 1, S. 3.

Let's take the inſtant by the forward top;
For we are old, and on our quick'ſt decrees
The inaudible and noiſeleſs foot of Time
Steals, ere we can effect them.

All's well that ends well, A. 5, S. 3.

Would he were waſted, marrow, bones, and all,
That from his loins no hopeful branch may ſpring
To croſs me from the golden time I look for!

Henry VI. P. 3, A. 3, S. 2.

——— Bloſſoming time,
That from the ſeedneſs the bare fallow brings
To teeming foyſon.

Meaſure for Meaſure, A. 1, S. 5.

—— O, let not virtue ſeek
Remuneration for the thing it was; for beauty, wit,

[1] *Set your entreatments at a higher rate,*
Than a command to parley.] *Entreatments* here mean *company*, *converſation*, from the French *entretien.* JOHNSON.

The meaning rather is, *Do not ſhew an inclination to liſten to him on every ſlight entreaty.* Polonius had ſaid immediately before—"Be ſomewhat ſcanter of your maiden preſence."

A. B.

High

High birth, vigour of bone, desert in service,
Love, friendship, charity, are subjects all
To envious and calumniating time.
Troilus and Cressida, A. 3, S. 3.

We did keep time, sir, in our catches.
Sneck up [1]! *Twelfth Night*, A. 2, S. 3.

In the spring time, the pretty rank time [2],
When birds do sing. *As you like it*, A. 5, S. 3.

TONGUE.

—— The duke, great Bolingbroke,—
Mounted upon a hot and fiery steed,
Which his aspiring rider seem'd to know,—
With slow, but stately pace, kept on his course,
While all tongues cry'd—God save thee Bolingbroke!
Richard II. A. 5, S. 2.

Think you a little din can daunt mine ears?
Have I not in my time heard lions roar?
Have I not heard great ordnance in the field,

[1] *Sneck up!*] "The modern editors, says Mr. Steevens, have regarded this unintelligible expression as the designation of a *hiccup*. But I think we might safely read, *sneak-cup*, i. e. one who takes his glass in a sneaking manner."

"Sneck-up," I think, should be written *sneb-up*. *Sneb* is an old word for *check*, or *rebuke*. See Spencer.

We now say *snub*, and *snap-up*. When it is remembered that Malvolio has taken upon him to admonish Sir Toby, the knight may very naturally call him *sneb-up*, i. e. reprover. They have not been talking of *drinking*, so that *sneak-cup* is hardly the word. A. B.

[2] —— *the pretty rank time.*] Thus the modern editors. The old copy reads,

"In the spring time, the pretty *rang* time."

I think we should read,

"In the spring time, the pretty *ring* time."

i. e. the aptest season for marriage. STEEVENS.

The true reading, perhaps, will be,

"—— the pretty *range* time."

i. e. the proper time for wandering about. A. B.

And

And heaven's artillery thunder in the ſkies?
And do you tell me of a woman's tongue?
Taming of the Shrew, A. 1, S. 2.

The tongues of mocking wenches are as keen
As is the razor's edge, inviſible,
Their conceits have wings,
Fleeter than arrows, bullets, wind, thought, ſwifter things.
Love's Labour Loſt, A. 5, S. 2.

Be not thy tongue thy own ſhame's orator;
Look ſweet, ſpeak fair, become diſloyalty;
Apparel vice, like virtue's harbinger:
Bear a fair preſence, though your heart be tainted.
Comedy of Errors, A. 3, S. 2.

He gives the baſtinado with his tongue;
Our ears are cudgell'd;
Zounds! I was never ſo bethumpt with words,
Since I firſt call'd my brother's father, dad.
King John, A. 2, S. 2.

—— I'll mountebank their loves,
Cog their hearts from them, and come home belov'd
Of all the trades in Rome. I'll return conſul,
Or never truſt to what my tongue can do
I' the way of flattery, further. *Coriolanus*, A. 3, S. 2.

Now my tongue's uſe is to me no more,
Than an unſtringed viol, or a harp;
Or like a cunning inſtrument cas'd up,
Or, being open, put into his hands
That knows no touch to tune the harmony.
Richard II. A. 1, S. 3.

[1] Your favour is well appear'd by your tongue.
Coriolanus, A. 4, S. 3.

[1] *But your favour is well appear'd by your tongue.*] This is ſtrange nonſenſe. We ſhould read,
" —— is well *appealed*,"
i. e. brought into remembrance. WARBURTON.

TOUCH.

Didſt thou but know the only touch of love,
Thou wouldſt as ſoon go kindle fire with ſnow,
As ſeek to quench the fire of love with words.
Two Gentlemen of Verona, A. 2, S. 7.

——— You muſt
Forget that rareſt treaſure of your cheek,
Expoſing it (but O, the harder heart!
Alack, no remedy) to the greedy touch
Of common kiſſing Titan; and forget
Your labour once and dainty trims, wherein
You made great Juno angry. *Cymbeline*, A. 3, S. 4.

Orpheus' lute was ſtrung with poets' ſinews;
Whoſe golden touch could ſoften ſteel and ſtones,
Make tigers tame, and huge leviathans
Forſake unſounded deeps to dance on ſands.
Two Gentlemen of Verona, A. 3, S. 2.

Ruffian, let go that rude uncivil touch.
Two Gentlemen of Verona, A. 5, S. 3.

If to preſerve this veſſel for my lord,
From any other foul unlawful touch [1],
Be—not to be a ſtrumpet, I am none.
Othello, A. 4, S. 2.

I ſhould read,
"——— is well *affear'd.*"
That is, *ſtrengthened*, *atteſted*, a word uſed by our author in Macbeth. JOHNSON.

"Appear'd" is, *made known*, *ſhewn*, and "favour" is *face*.

Your face is made known by your tongue, or your tongue ſpeaks for you, or, I know you by your tongue.

This paſſage does not, in my opinion, ſeem ſo nonſenſical as Dr. Warburton ſuppoſes it to be. A. B.

[1] *From any other foul unlawful touch.*] "Any *other* foul un-"lawful touch" muſt be wrong. The quarto reads, "bated "foul, &c." The true reading, I ſuppoſe, will be,
"From any *hated* foul unlawful touch." A. B.

TRAITOR,

TRAITOR, TREASON.

He, that temper'd thee, bade thee ſtand up,
Gave thee no inſtance why thou ſhouldſt do treaſon,
Unleſs to dub thee with the name of traitor.
If that ſame dæmon, that hath gull'd thee thus,
Should with his lion gait walk the whole world,
He might return to vaſty Tartar back,
And tell the legions—I can never win
A ſoul ſo eaſy as that Engliſhman's.

Henry V. A. 2, S. 2.

Our doubts are traitors,
And make us loſe the good we oft might win
By fearing to attempt.

Meaſure for Meaſure, A. 1, S. 5.

——— If ſhe be a traitor,
Why ſo am I; we ſtill have ſlept together,
Roſe at an inſtant, learn'd, play'd, eat together;
And whereſoe'er we went, like Juno's ſwans,
Still we went coupled, and inſeparable.

As you like it, A. 1, S. 3.

Thus do all traitors;
If their purgation did conſiſt in words,
They are as innocent as grace itſelf.

As you like it, A. 1, S. 3.

——— Her fair ſiſter,
Poſſeſs'd with ſuch a gentle ſovereign grace,
Of ſuch enchanting preſence and diſcourſe,
Hath almoſt made me traitor to myſelf:
But leſt myſelf be guilty of ſelf-wrong,
I'll ſtop mine ears againſt the mermaid's ſong.

Comedy of Errors, A. 3, S. 2.

Treaſon is not inherited, my lord;
Or, if we did derive it from our friends,
What's that to me? Miſtake me not ſo much,
To think my poverty is treacherous.

As you like it, A. 1, S. 3.

TRAVEL, TRAVELLER.

A traveller! By my faith, you have great reaſon to be ſad: I fear, you have ſold your own lands, to ſee other men's; then, to have ſeen much, and to have nothing, is to have rich eyes and poor hands.

As you like it, A. 4, S. 1.

You were beaten in Italy for picking a kernel out of a pomegranate; you are a vagabond, and no true traveller. *All's well that ends well*, A. 2, S. 3.

—— Our court you know is haunted
With a refined traveller of Spain;
A man in all the world's new faſhion planted,
That hath a mint of phraſes in his brain:—
A man of complements.

Love's Labour Loſt, A. 1, S. 1.

Thou didſt make tolerable vent of thy travel; it might paſs: yet the ſcarfs, and the bannerets, about thee, did manifoldly diſſuade me from believing thee a veſſel of too great a burden.

All's well that ends well, A. 2, S. 3.

——— Valentine, adieu!
Think on thy Protheus, when thou, haply, ſeeſt
Some rare note-worthy object in thy travel.

Two Gentlemen of Verona, A. 1, S. 1.

Farewell, monſieur traveller: look, you liſp, and wear ſtrange ſuits; diſable all the benefits of your own country; be out of love with your nativity, and almoſt chide God for making you that countenance you are. *As you like it*, A. 4, S. 1.

——— To importune you,
To let him ſpend his time no more at home,
Which would be great impeachment to his age [1],
In having known no travel in his youth.

Two Gentlemen of Verona, A. 1, S. 3.

TRUTH.

[1] —— *great impeachment to his age.*] *Impeachment* is *hindrance*— So in Henry V. "—— but

TRUTH.

I ſee a ſtrange confeſſion in thine eye:
Thou ſhak'ſt thy head; and hold'ſt it fear, or ſin,
To ſpeak a truth. *Henry IV.* P. 2, A. 1, S. 1.

—— Ornament is but the guiled ſhore [1]
To a moſt dangerous ſea; the beauteous ſcarf
Veiling an Indian beauty; in a word,
The ſeeming truth which cunning times put on
To entrap the wiſeſt. *Merchant of Venice*, A. 3, S. 2.

What in the world ſhould make me now deceive,
Since I muſt loſe the uſe of all deceit?
Why ſhould I then be falſe; ſince it is true
That I muſt die here, and live hence by truth?
King John, A. 5, S. 4.

In this, the antique and well-noted face
Of plain old form is much disfigured:
Makes ſound opinion ſick, and truth ſuſpected,
For putting on ſo new a faſhion'd robe.
King John, A. 4, S. 2.

Whom I moſt hated living, thou haſt made me,
With thy religious truth, and modeſty,
Now in his aſhes honour: peace be with him!
Henry VIII. A. 4, S. 2.

"—— but could be glad
"Without impeachment to march on to Calais."
STEEVENS.

I do not ſee how "impeachment" can, in this place, have the ſenſe of *hindrance*. In the quotation from Henry V. it certainly has that meaning, but here, I think, it ſignifies *diſcredit*, diſhonour. A. B.

[1] —— *the guiled ſhore.*] *i. e.* The *treacherous* ſhore. I ſhould not have thought that the word wanted explanation, but that ſome of the editors have rejected it, and read *gilded*.
STEEVENS.

"Guiled ſhore" is *deceived ſhore*. We muſt read *guiling ſhore*, i. e. deceitful. A. B.

Noble prince,
As there comes light from heaven, and words from breath,
As there is ſenſe in truth, and truth in virtue,
I am affianc'd this man's wife as ſtrongly
As words could make up vows.

Meaſure for Meaſure, A. 5, S. 1.

—— This is all as true as it is ſtrange:
Nay, it is ten times true, for truth is truth
To the end of reckoning.

Meaſure for Meaſure, A. 5, S. 1.

——— I rais'd him, and I pawn'd
Mine honour for his truth: who being ſo heighten'd,
He water'd his new plants with dews of flattery,
Seducing ſo my friends: and, to this end,
He bow'd his nature, never known before
But to be rough, unſwayable, and free.

Coriolanus, A. 5, S. 5.

While others fiſh with craft for great opinion,
I with great truth catch mere ſimplicity;
Whilſt ſome with cunning gild their copper crowns,
With truth and plainneſs I do wear mine bare.

Troilus and Creſſida, A. 4, S. 4.

——— Alas,
I am as true as truth's ſimplicity,
And ſimpler than the infancy of truth.

Troilus and Creſſida, A. 3, S. 2.

As true as ſteel, as plantage to the moon,
As ſun to day, as turtle to her mate,
As iron to adamant, as earth to the centre,—
Yet, after all compariſons of truth,
As truth's authentic author to be cited,
As true as Troilus ſhall crown up the verſe,
And ſanctify the numbers.

Troilus and Creſſida, A. 3, S. 2.

He's

He's quoted for a moſt perfidious ſlave,
With all the ſpots o' the world tax'd and deboſh'd,
Whoſe nature ſickens but to ſpeak a truth.
All's well that ends well, A. 5, S. 3.

——— If ſpeaking truth,
In this fine age, were not thought flattery,
Such attribution ſhould the Douglas have,
As not a ſoldier of this ſeaſon's ſtamp
Should go ſo general current through the world.
Henry IV. P. 1, A. 4, S. 1.

If circumſtances lead me, I will find
Where truth is hid, though it were hid indeed
Within the centre. *Hamlet*, A. 2, S. 2.

Hugh Capet alſo,—
To fine his title [1] with ſome ſhew of truth.
Henry V. A. 1, S. 2.

TUTOR.

What, I ſay,
My foot my tutor [2]? *Tempeſt*, A. 1, S. 2.

[1] *To fine his title, &c.*] This is the reading of the quarto 1608, that of the folio is, *to find his title*. I believe that *find* is right. The jury *finds* for the plaintiff, or *finds* for the defendant: to *find* his title is, to determine in favour of his title with ſome ſhew of truth. Dr. Warburton ſays, that *fine his title* is, to refine or improve it. JOHNSON.

Both the quartos read, to *fine* his title, *i. e.* to make it *ſhewy* or *ſpecious*, by ſome appearance of juſtice. STEEVENS.

"To fine his title" ſhould perhaps be—to *fix* his title, *i. e.* to ſettle his title; ſo that it ſhould not any longer be diſputed.
A. B.

[2] *My foot my tutor?*] This expreſſion I do not underſtand. It ſhould certainly be,—"My ſoot my tutor?" *Soot*, in old language, is *ſweet*; and may here be uſed as a word of endearment.

"What! my ſweeting become my tutor?"

He ſhortly after calls her *darling*. A. B.

TYRANT.

—— Why ſhould Cæſar be a tyrant then?
Poor man! I know he would not be a wolf,
But that he ſees, the Romans are but ſheep:
He were no lion, were not Romans hinds.

Julius Cæſar, A. 1, S. 3.

——— It is excellent
To have a giant's ſtrength; but it is tyrannous,
To uſe it like a giant.

Meaſure for Meaſure, A. 2, S. 2.

Hide not thy poiſon with ſuch ſugar'd words.
Lay not thy hands on me; forbear, I ſay;
Their touch affrights me, as a ſerpent's ſting.
Thou baleful meſſenger, out of my ſight!
Upon thy eye-balls murderous tyranny
Sits, in grim majeſty, to fright the world.

Henry VI. P. 2, A. 3, S. 2.

Ah me, I ſee the ruin of my houſe!
The tyger now hath ſeiz'd the gentle hind;
Inſulting tyranny begins to jut
Upon the innocent and awleſs throne.

Richard III. A. 2, S. 4.

Richard except, thoſe whom we fight againſt
Had rather have us win, than him they follow.
For what is he they follow? truly, gentlemen,
A bloody tyrant, and a homicide.

Richard III. A. 5, S. 3.

—— I'll not call you tyrant,
But this moſt cruel uſage of your queen
(Not able to produce more accuſation
Than your own weak-hing'd fancy) ſomething fa-
vours
Of tyranny. *Winter's Tale*, A. 2, S. 3.

——— O thou tyrant!
Do not repent theſe things; for they are heavier

Than all thy woes can ſtir: therefore betake thee
To nothing but deſpair. *Winter's Tale*, A. 3, S. 2.

A plague upon the tyrant that I ſerve!
Tempeſt, A. 2, S. 2.

U.

UNION.

——We grew together,
Like to a double cherry, ſeeming parted;
But yet a union in partition,
Two lovely berries molded on one ſtem.
Midſummer Night's Dream, A. 3, S. 2.

UNKINDNESS.

——Beloved Regan,
Thy ſiſter's naught: O Regan, ſhe hath tied
Sharp tooth'd unkindneſs, like a vulture here,—
I can ſcarce ſpeak to thee. *Lear*, A. 2, S. 4.

USE.

As ſurfeit is the father of much faſt,
So every ſcope by the immoderate uſe
Turns to reſtraint. *Meaſure for Meaſure*, A. 1, S. 3.

V.

VALOUR.

IN a falſe quarrel there is no true valour.
Much ado about nothing, A. 5, S. 1.

I never knew yet, but rebuke and check was the reward of valour. Do you think me a ſwallow, an arrow, or a bullet? Have I, in my poor and old motion, the expedition of thought? I have ſpeeded hither with the very extremeſt inch of poſſibility.
Henry IV. P. 2, A. 4, S. 3.

Then the vital commoners, and inland petty ſpirits, muſter me all to their captain, the heart; who, great and puff'd up with this retinue, doth any deed of courage; and this valour comes of ſherris.
Henry IV. P. 2, A. 4, S. 3.

You are the hare of whom the proverb goes,
Whoſe valour plucks dead lions by the beard.
King John, A. 2, S. 1.

Warlike and martial Talbot, Burgundy
Enſhrines thee in his heart: and there erects
Thy noble deeds, as valour's monument.
Henry VI. P. 1, A. 3, S. 2.

——— The deeds of Coriolanus
Should not be utter'd feebly.—It is held,
That valour is the chiefeſt virtue, and
Moſt dignifies the haver: if it be,
The man I ſpeak of cannot in the world
Be ſingly counterpois'd. *Coriolanus*, A. 2, S. 2.

What valour were it, when a cur doth grin,
For one to thruſt his hand between his teeth,

When

When he might ſpurn him with his foot away?
It is war's prize to take all 'vantages.

Henry VI. P. 3, A. 1, S. 4.

There is not work enough for all our hands;
Scarce blood enough in all their ſickly veins,
To give each naked curtle-ax a ſtain,
That our French gallants ſhall to-day draw out,
And ſheath for lack of ſport: let us but blow on
them,
The vapour of our valour will o'erturn them.

Henry V. A. 4, S. 2.

The better part of valour is—diſcretion: in the which better part, I have ſaved my life.

Henry IV. P. 1, A. 5, S. 4.

She did ſhew favour to the youth in your ſight, only to exaſperate you, to awake your dormouſe valour; to put fire in your heart, and brimſtone in your liver: you ſhould then have accoſted her.

Twelfth Night, A. 3, S. 2.

——— We have ſeen nothing:
We are beaſtly; ſubtle as the fox, for prey;
Like warlike as the wolf, for what we eat:
Our valour is, to chace what flies; our cage
We make a quire, as doth the priſon'd bird,
And ſing our bondage freely. *Cymbeline*, A. 3, S. 3.

——— To be furious,
Is, to be frighted out of fear: and in that mood,
The dove will peck the eſtridge; and I ſee ſtill,
A diminution in our captain's brain
Reſtores his heart: when valour preys on reaſon
It eats the ſword it fights with.

Antony and Cleopatra, A. 3, S. 11.

So full of valour that they ſmote the air
For breathing in their faces. *Tempeſt*, A. 4, S. 1.

——— Here I clip
The anvil of my ſword; and do conteſt

As hotly and as nobly with thy love,
As ever in ambitious ſtrength I did
Contend againſt thy valour. *Coriolanus*, A. 4, S. 5.

The compoſition, that your valour and fear makes in you, is a virtue of a good wing [1], and I like the wear well. *All's well that ends well*, A. 1, S. 1.

Mark then a bounding valour in our Engliſh;
That, being dead, like to the bullet's grazing,
Breaks out into a ſecond courſe of miſchief,
Killing in relapſe of mortality [2].
Henry V. A. 4, S. 3.

[1] *Is a virtue of a good wing.*] Mr. Edwards is of opinion, that a virtue of a good wing, refers to his nimbleneſs in running away. The phraſe, however, is taken from falconry, as may appear from Marſton's *Fawne*.—"I love my hawk for the *good-*"*neſs of his wing*, &c." Or it may be taken from dreſs. So in *Every Man Out of his Humour*—"I would have mine ſuch a "ſuit, ſuch ſtuff, ſuch wing, &c." Mr. Tollet obſerves, that a good wing, ſignifies a ſtrong wing in Lord Bacon's Natural Hiſtory. STEEVENS.

"A virtue of a good *wing*, and I like the *wear* well," is nonſenſe. For "wing" we muſt read *vigon*, a ſort of Spaniſh wool. The whole ſhould run thus—The compoſition that your valour and fear makes in you, is a vigon of good virtue, and I like the wear well.—*i. e.* Your valour and fear is a ſtuff of good manufacture, and I like the wear well. Without ſuch reading, where is the integrity of the metaphor? as Dr. Warburton would ſay. A. B.

[2] *Killing in relapſe of mortality.*] What it is to *kill in relapſe of mortality*, I do not know. I ſuſpect that it ſhould be read:
"Killing in *reliques* of mortality."
That the alluſion is, as Mr. Theobald thinks, *exceedingly beautiful*, I am afraid few readers will diſcover. The *valour* of a putrid body, that deſtroys by the ſtench, is one of the thoughts that do no great honour to the poet. JOHNSON.

"Mortality" is *ſickneſs*, "relapſe" is *return*, and the prepoſition "of" is uſed, as is common with the writers of Shakeſpeare's time, inſtead of *by*. The ſenſe of the paſſage is this—The *valour*, or rather the *power* of our Engliſh is ſuch, that being dead, they will yet *(in return)* deſtroy their enemies by breeding a ſickneſs—*by the ſtench which will ariſe from their bodies*. A. B.

VENGEANCE.

VENGEANCE.

Ariſe, black vengeance, from thy hollow cell!
Yield up, O love, thy crown, and hearted throne,
To tyrannous hate! ſwell, boſom, with thy fraught,
For, 'tis of aſpick's tongues! *Othello*, A. 3, S. 3.

Thou doſt, in thy paſſages of life,
Make me believe, that thou art only mark'd
For the hot vengeance and the rod of heaven,
To puniſh my mis-treadings.
Henry IV. P. 1, A. 3, S. 2.

VICTORY.

—— Victory, with little loſs doth play
Upon the dancing banners of the French;
Who are at hand, triumphantly diſplay'd,
To enter conquerors. *King John*, A. 2, S. 2.

A victory is twice itſelf, when the atchiever brings home full numbers.
Much ado about nothing, A. 1, S. 1.

——— At his nurſe's tears
He whin'd and roar'd away your victory;
That pages bluſh'd at him, and men of heart
Look'd wondering each at other.
Coriolanus, A. 5, S. 5.

Methought their ſouls, whoſe bodies Richard murder'd,
Came to my tent, and cry'd—On! victory!
I promiſe you, my heart is very jocund
In the remembrance of ſo fair a dream.
Richard III. A. 5, S. 3.

A thouſand hearts are great within my boſom:
Our ancient word of courage, fair Saint George
Inſpire us with the ſpleen of fiery dragons!
Upon them! victory ſits on our helms.
Richard III. A. 5, S. 3.

VILLAIN.

Villain, be ſure thou prove my love a whore,
Be ſure of it; give me the ocular proof;
Or, by the worth of mine eternal ſoul,
Thou hadſt been better have been born a dog,
Than anſwer my wak'd wrath. *Othello*, A. 3, S. 3.

Which is the villain? let me ſee his eyes;
That when I note another man like him,
I may avoid him.
Much ado about nothing, A. 5, S. 1.

Write down—that they hope they ſerve God:—and write God firſt; for God defend but God ſhould go before ſuch villains!
Much ado about nothing, A. 4, S. 1.

When rich villains have need of poor ones, poor ones may make what price they will.
Much ado about nothing, A. 3, S. 3.

Is he not approved in the height a villain, that hath ſlander'd, ſcorn'd, diſhonour'd my kinſwoman? O, that I were a man!
Much ado about nothing, A. 4, S. 1.

An evil ſoul, producing holy witneſs,
Is like a villain with a ſmiling cheek;
A goodly apple rotten at the heart.
Merchant of Venice, A. 1, S. 3.

I like not fair terms, and a villain's mind.
Merchant of Venice, A. 1, S. 3.

If a Jew wrong a Chriſtian, what is his humility? revenge: If a Chriſtian wrong a Jew, what ſhould his ſufferance be by Chriſtian example? why, revenge. The villainy, you teach me, I will execute; and it ſhall go hard, but I will better the inſtruction.
Merchant of Venice, A. 3, S. 1.

—— A ruſh

——— A rush will be a beam
To hang thee on; or, wouldst thou drown thyself,
Put but a little water in a spoon,
And it shall be as all the ocean,
Enough to stifle such a villain up.

King John, A. 4, S. 3.

Trust not those cunning waters of his eyes,
For villainy is not without such rheum:
And he, long traded in it, makes it seem
Like rivers of remorse and innocency.

King John, A. 4, S. 3.

——— O, how this villainy
Doth fat me with the very thought of it!
Let fools do good, and fair men call for grace,
Aaron will have his soul black like his face.

Titus Andronicus, A. 3, S. 1.

——— Trust not the physician;
His antidotes are poison, and he slays
More than you rob: take wealth and lives together;
Do villainy, do, since you profess to do't,
Like workmen: I'll example you with thievery.

Timon of Athens, A. 4, S. 3.

——— A hungry lean-fac'd villain,
A meer anatomy, a mountebank,
A thread-bare juggler, and a fortune-teller;
A needy, hollow-ey'd sharp-looking wretch,
A living dead man. *Comedy of Errors*, A. 5, S. 1.

——— Since I cannot prove a lover,
To entertain these fair well-spoken days,---
I am determined to prove a villain,
And hate the idle pleasures of these days.

Richard III. A. 1, S. 1.

——— They whet me
To be reveng'd on Rivers, Vaughan, Grey;
But then I sigh, and with a piece of scripture,
Tell them---that God bids us do good for evil.

And

And thus I clothe my naked villainy
With old odd ends, ſtol'n forth of holy writ.
Richard III. A. 1, S. 3.

O moſt pernicious woman!
O villain, villain, ſmiling, damned villain!
My tables,—meet it is, I ſet it down,
That one may ſmile, and ſmile, and be a villain;
At leaſt, I am ſure, it may be ſo in Denmark.
Hamlet, A. 1, S. 5.

——— Am I a coward?
Who calls me villain? breaks my pate acroſs?
Plucks off my beard, and blows it in my face?
Tweaks me by the noſe? gives me the lye i' the throat
As deep as to the lungs? who does me this?
Ha! why I ſhould take it: for it cannot be,
But I am pigeon-liver'd, and lack gall
To make oppreſſion bitter; or, ere this,
I ſhould have fatted all the region kites
With this ſlave's offal. *Hamlet*, A. 2, S. 2.

—— I lov'd my niece;
And ſhe is dead, ſlander'd to death by villains;
That dare as well anſwer a man, indeed,
As I dare take a ſerpent by the tongue.
Much ado about nothing, A. 5, S. 1.

I'll make one; an I do not, call me villain, and baffle me[1]. *Henry IV.* P. 1, A. 1, S. 2.

——— Love him, feed him,
Keep in your boſom: yet remain aſſur'd,
That he's a made-up villain[2].
Timon of Athens, A. 5, S. 1.

VIRGIN.

[1] *And baffle me.*] Mr. Tollet ſays, that *to baffle* means, to treat a perſon with the greateſt ignominy imaginable; but I rather think that *to baffle* is, in this place, to *mock*, to *laugh at*. Befler, Fr. A. B.

[2] ——— *a made-up villain.*] That is, a villain that adopts qualities

VIRGIN.

Hail, virgin, if you be; as thoſe cheek-roſes
Proclaim you are no leſs!
Meaſure for Meaſure, A. 1, S. 5.

VIRTUE.

—— 'Tis not to make me jealous,
To ſay,—my wife is fair, feeds well, loves company,
Is free of ſpeech, ſings, plays, and dances well;
Where virtuè is, theſe are more virtuous.
Othello, A. 3, S. 3.

Do you think, I do not know you by your excellent wit? can virtue hide itſelf?
Much ado about nothing, A. 2, S. 1.

It is moſt expedient for the wiſe (if Don Worm, his conſcience, finds no impediment to the contrary) to be the trumpet of his own virtues, as I am to myſelf. *Much ado about nothing*, A. 5, S. 2.

My heart laments, that virtue cannot live
Out of the teeth of emulation.
Julius Cæſar, A. 2, S. 3.

There is no vice ſo ſimple, but aſſumes
Some mark of virtue on his outward parts.
Merchant of Venice, A. 3, S. 2.

——— For you,
I would be trebled twenty times myſelf;

qualities and characters not properly belonging to him; a hypocrite. JOHNSON.

I rather believe that by "a made-up villain" we are to underſtand, a man who is ſkilled or complete in rogueries. Dr. Johnſon conſiders *made-up* in the ſenſe of *counterfeit*, but he is ſurely wrong. If any one, of bad character, adopts qualities and manners that do not properly belong to him, we cannot ſay that he counterfeits the villain, but on the contrary, that he counterfeits the honeſt man. A. B.

A thousand times more fair, ten thousand times
More rich; that to stand high in your account,
I might in virtues, beauties, livings, friends,
Exceed account. *Merchant of Venice*, A. 3, S. 2.

Virtue is bold, and goodness never fearful.
Measure for Measure, A. 3, S, 1.

——— If I am
Traduc'd by ignorant tongues,—which neither know
My faculties, nor person, yet will be
The chronicles of my doing,—let me say,
'Tis but the fate of place, and the rough brake
That virtue must go through.
Henry VIII. A. 1, S. 2.

——— If our virtues
Did not go forth of us, 'twere all alike
As if we had them not.
Measure for Measure, A. 1, S. 1.

——— Most dangerous
Is that temptation, that doth goad us on
To sin in loving virtue.
Measure for Measure, A. 2, S. 2.

Virtue he had, deserving to command:
His brandish'd sword did blind men with his beams;
His arms spread wider than a dragon's wings;
His sparkling eyes, replete with wrathful fire,
More dazzled and drove back his enemies,
Than mid-day sun, fierce bent against their faces.
Henry VI. P. 1, A. 1, S. 1.

My love till death, my humble thanks, my prayers;
That love, which virtue begs, and virtue grants.
Henry VI. P. 3, A. 3, S. 2.

Myself have often heard him say, and swear,—
That this his love was an eternal plant;
Whereof the root was fix'd in virtue's ground,
The leaves and fruit maintain'd with beauty's sun.
Henry VI. P. 3, A. 3, S. 3.

—— Your virtues, gentle maſter,
Are ſanctified and holy traitors to you.
As you like it, A. 2, S. 3.

—— Of late this duke
Hath ta'en diſpleaſure 'gainſt his gentle niece;
Grounded upon no other argument,
But that the people praiſe her for her virtues.
As you like it, A. 1, S. 2.

The only ſoil of his fair virtue's gloſs,
(If virtue's gloſs will ſtain with any ſoil)
Is a ſharp wit, match'd with too blunt a will.
Love's Labour Loſt, A. 2, S. 1.

——— All his virtues,—
Not virtuouſly on his own part beheld,—
Do, in our eyes, begin to loſe their gloſs;
Yea, like fair fruit in an unwholeſome diſh,
Are like to rot untaſted.
Troilus and Creſſida, A. 2, S. 3.

——— For the time I ſtudy,
Virtue, and that part of philoſophy
Will I apply, that treats of happineſs
By virtue 'ſpecially to be atchiev'd.
Taming of the Shrew, A. 1, S. 1.

From loweſt place when virtuous things proceed,
The place is dignify'd by the doer's deed:
Where great additions ſwell, and virtue none,
It is a dropſied honour.
All's well that ends well, A. 2, S. 3.

You are more ſaucy with lords, and honourable perſonages, than the heraldry of your birth and virtue gives you commiſſion.
All's well that ends well, A. 2, S. 3.

Any thing, that's mended, is but patch'd: virtue, that tranſgreſſes, is but patch'd with ſin; and ſin, that amends, is but patch'd with virtue.
Twelfth Night, A. 1, S. 5.

The charieſt maid is prodigal enough,
If ſhe unmaſk her beauty to the moon:
Virtue itſelf 'ſcapes not calumnious ſtrokes:
The canker galls the infants of the ſpring,
Too oft before their buttons be diſclos'd,
And in the morn and liquid dew of youth
Contagious blaſtments are moſt imminent.
Hamlet, A. 1, S. 3.

——— Forgive me this my virtue:
For, in the fatneſs of theſe purſy times,
Virtue itſelf of vice muſt pardon beg;
Yea, curb, and woo, for leave to do him good.
Hamlet, A. 3, S. 4.

O, throw away the worſer part of it,
And live the purer with the other half.
Good night: but go not to mine uncle's bed;
Aſſume a virtue, if you have it not.
Hamlet, A. 3, S. 4.

But virtue, as it never will be mov'd,
Though lewdneſs court it in a ſhape of heaven;
So luſt, though to a radiant angel link'd,
Will ſate itſelf in a celeſtial bed,
And prey on garbage. *Hamlet*, A. 1, S. 5.

Virtue is of ſo little regard in theſe coſter-monger times, that true valour is turn'd bearherd: pregnancy[1] is made a tapſter, and hath his quick wit waſted in giving reckonings.
Henry IV. P. 2, A. 1, S. 2.

[1] *Pregnancy.*] *Pregnancy* is readineſs. STEEVENS.
"Pregnancy" is ſomething more than readineſs. It means *livelineſs, great abilities.* A. B.

VOWS.

VOWS.

[1] It is the purpose that makes strong the vow;
But vows to every purpose must not hold.
Troilus and Cressida, A. 5, S. 3.

'Tis not the many oaths, that make the truth;
But the plain single vow, that is vow'd true.
What is not holy, that we swear not by
But take the highest to witness.
All's well that ends well, A. 4, S. 2.

Your vows, to her and me, put in two scales,
Will even weigh; and both as light as tales.
Midsummer Night's Dream, A. 3, S. 2.

Is all the counsel that we two have shar'd,
The sister's vows, the hours that we have spent,
When we have chid the hasty-footed time
For parting us,—O, and is all forgot?
Midsummer Night's Dream, A. 3, S. 2.

Why should you think that I should woo in scorn?
Scorn and derision never come in tears:
Look, when I vow, I weep; and vows so born,
In their nativity all truth appears.
Midsummer Night's Dream, A. 3, S. 2.

Unheedful vows may heedfully be broken;
And he wants wit, that wants resolved will
To learn his wit to exchange the bad for better.
Two Gentlemen of Verona, A. 2, S. 6.

[1] *It is the purpose.*] The mad prophetess speaks here with all the coolness and judgment of a skilful casuist. JOHNSON.
Dr. Johnson is right. But was he to be told that *reason* is frequently found in *madness?* He might, indeed, have learnt it from our author:
"O matter and impertinency mixt!
"Reason in madness!"
See King Lear. A. B.

——— Let there be no honour,
Where there is beauty; truth, where semblance; love,
Where there's another man: the vows of women
Of no more bondage be, to where they are made,
Than they are to their virtues.
Cymbeline, A. 2, S. 4.

Men's vows are women's traitors! All good seeming,
By the revolt, O husband, shall be thought
Put on for villainy; not born, where't grows;
But worn, a bait for ladies. *Cymbeline*, A. 3, S. 4.

VOYAGE.

As far as I see, all the good our English
Have got by the late voyage, is but merely
A fit or two o' the face [1]. *Henry VIII.* A. 1, S. 3.

[1] *A fit or two o' the face.*] A fit of the face seems to be what we now term a *grimace*, an artificial cast of the countenance. JOHNSON.

"A fit o' the face" seems rather to be a resemblance. He means that they had caught the manners of the French. It appears to be of the same import as *trick o' the face*, which we now use, and which means nothing more than a *likeness*. A. B.

W.

WAR, WARS.

——I HAVE be-dimm'd
The noon-tide ſun, call'd forth the mutinous winds,
And 'twixt the green ſea and the azur'd vault
Set roaring war. *Tempeſt*, A. 5, S. 1.

Who does i' the wars more than his captain can,
Becomes his captain's captain: and ambition,
The ſoldier's virtue, rather makes choice of loſs,
Than gain, which darkens him.
Antony and Cleopatra, A. 3, S. 1.

—— Will you again unknit
This churliſh knot of all-abhorred war?
And move in that obedient orb again,
Where you did give a fair and natural light,
And be no more an exhal'd meteor,
A prodigy of fear, and a portent
Of broached miſchief to the unborn times?
Henry IV. P. 1, A. 5, S. 1.

——— Let them come;
They come like ſacrifices in their trim,
And to the fire-ey'd maid of ſmoky war,
All hot, and bleeding, will we offer them:
The mailed Mars ſhall on his altar ſit,
Up to the ears in blood.
Henry IV. P. 1, A. 4, S. 1.

In thy faint ſlumbers, I by thee have watch'd,
And heard thee murmur tales of iron wars:
Thy ſpirit within thee hath been ſo at war,
And thus hath ſo beſtirr'd thee in thy ſleep,

That beads of ſweat have ſtood upon thy brow,
Like bubbles in a late-diſturbed ſtream.
Henry IV. P. 1, A. 2, S. 3.

No more the thirſty entrance of this ſoil
Shall daub her lips with her own children's blood;
No more ſhall trenching war channel her fields,
Nor bruiſe her flow'rets with the armed hoofs
Of hoſtile paces. *Henry IV.* P. 1, A. 1, S. 1.

Either be patient, and entreat me fair,
Or with the clamorous report of war
Thus will I drown your exclamations.
Richard III. A. 4, S. 4.

Grim-viſag'd War hath ſmooth'd his wrinkled front,
And now,—inſtead of mounting barbed ſteeds,
To fright the ſouls of fearful adverſaries,—
He capers nimbly in a lady's chamber,
To the laſcivious pleaſing of a lute.
Richard III. A. 1, S. 1.

——— O War, thou ſon of hell,
Whom angry heavens do make their miniſter,
Throw in the frozen boſoms of our part
Hot coals of vengeance!
Henry VI. P. 2, A. 5, S. 2.

This is Monſieur Parolles, the gallant militariſt (that was his own phraſe) that had the whole theorique of war in the knot of his ſcarf, and the practice in the chape of his dagger.
All's well that ends well, A. 4, S. 3.

—— Poor lord! is't I
That chaſe thee from thy country, and expoſe
Thoſe tender limbs of thine to the event
Of the none-ſparing war?
All's well that ends well, A. 3, S. 2.

'Tis

[1] 'Tis not the roundure of your old fac'd walls
Can hide you from our meſſengers of war.
King John, A. 2, S. 1.

——— His preſent gift
Shall furniſh me to thoſe Italian fields,
Where noble fellows ſtrike: war is no ſtrife
To the dark houſe, and the deteſted wife.
All's well that ends well, A. 2, S. 3.

You ſhall find in the regiment of the Spinii, one captain Spurio, with his cicatrice, an emblem of war, here on his ſiniſter cheek; it was this very ſword entrench'd it. *All's well that ends well*, A. 2, S. 1.

Were half to half the world by the ears, and he
Upon my party, I'd revolt, to make
Only my wars with him: he is a lion
That I am proud to hunt. *Coriolanus*, A. 1, S. 1.

Think'ſt thou, that I will leave my kingly throne,
Wherein my grandſire, and my father, ſat?
No: firſt ſhall war unpeople this my realm;
Ay, and their colours—often borne in France;
And now in England, to our heart's great ſorrow;
Shall be my winding-ſheet.
Henry VI. P. 3, A. 1, S. 1.

This battle fares like to the morning's war,
When dying clouds contend with growing light;
What time the ſhepherd, blowing of his nails,
Can neither call it perfect day, nor night.
Henry VI. P. 3, A. 2, S. 5.

——— What would you have, you curs,
That like nor peace, nor war? the one affrights you,

[1] *'Tis not the rondure.*] *Rondure* means the ſame as the French *rondeur*, i. e. the circle. STEEVENS.

To ſuppoſe that by "rondure" Philip means the *roundneſs* of their walls, that he is merely deſcribing them *as a circle*, were highly abſurd. By *rondure* we are to underſtand the *round*, the *whole extent of the walls*. A. B.

The other makes you proud. He that trusts to you,
Where he should find you lions, finds you hares;
Where foxes, geese. *Coriolanus*, A. 1, S. 1.

Away, my disposition, and possess me
Some harlot's spirit! my throat of war be turn'd,
Which quired with my drum, into a pipe
Small as an eunuch, or the virgin voice
That babies lulls asleep! *Coriolanus*, A. 3, S. 2.

——— You, lord archbishop,
Wherefore do you so ill translate yourself,
Out of the speech of peace, that bears such grace,
Into the harsh and boist'rous tongue of war?
Turning your books to graves [1], your ink to blood,
Your pens to lances; and your tongue divine
To a loud trumpet, and a point of war?
Henry IV. P. 2, A. 4, S. 1.

Be copy now to men of grosser blood,
And teach them how to war!—And you, good yeomen,
Whose limbs were made in England, shew us here
The mettle of your pasture; let us swear
That you are worth your breeding.
Henry V. A. 3, S. 1.

[1] *Turning your books to graves.*] For graves Dr. Warburton very plausibly reads *glaives*, and is followed by Sir T. Hanmer. JOHNSON.

We might perhaps as plausibly read *greaves*, i. e. armour for the legs: a kind of boots. Ben Jonson employs the word in his *Hymenæi*.

"Upon their legs they wore silver *greaves*."

I know not whether it be worth adding, that the metamorphosis of *leathern covers of books* into greaves, *i. e. boots*, seems to be more appposite than the conversion of them into instruments of war. STEEVENS.

"Glaives" is unquestionably the true reading. The metamorphosis (as Mr. Steevens calls it) of the *covers of books* into *boots*, is certainly more easy than the changing of them into *swords*. But "*turning* your books to glaves," is not to be taken literally:—the meaning is, *quitting your books to take up arms.*
A. B.

——— Mothers

— Mothers ſhall but ſmile, when they behold
Their infants quarter'd with the hands of war;
All pity choak'd with cuſtom of fell deeds:
And Cæſar's ſpirit, ranging for revenge,
With Até by his ſide, come hot from hell,
Shall in theſe confines, with a monarch's voice,
Cry havock, and let ſlip the dogs of war.

Julius Cæſar, A. 3, S. 1.

—— Take heed how you impawn our perſon,
How you awake the ſleeping ſword of war;
We charge you, in the name of God, take heed:
For never two ſuch kingdoms did contend,
Without much fall of blood. *Henry V.* A. 1, S. 2.

—— Thy threat'ning colours now wind up,
And tame the ſavage ſpirit of wild War;
That, like a lion foſter'd up at hand,
It may lie gently at the foot of Peace.

King John, A. 5, S. 2.

—— This commodity,
This bawd, this broker, this all-changing word,
Clapt on the outward eye of fickle France,
Hath drawn him from his own determin'd aid,
From a reſolv'd and honourable war,
To a moſt baſe and vile-concluded peace.

King John, A. 2, S. 2.

—— O, farewell!
Farewell the neighing ſteed and the ſhrill trump,
The ſpirit-ſtirring drum, the ear-piercing fife,
The royal banner; and all quality,
Pride, pomp, and circumſtance of glorious war!

Othello, A. 3, S. 3.

He never did fall off, my ſovereign liege,
But by the chance of war[1]. *Henry IV.* P. 1, A. 1, S. 3.

—— The

[1] *He never did fall off, my ſovereign liege, But by the chance of war.*] A poor apology for a ſoldier and

——— The mean time, lady,
I'll raiſe the preparation of a war
Shall ſtain your brother [1].

Antony and Cleopatra, A. 3, S. 4.

O, wi-

and man of honour, that he fell off, and revolted by the chance of war. The poet certainly wrote,

"But 'bides the chance of war."

i. e. He never did revolt, but *abides* the chance of war, as a priſoner. WARBURTON.

The plain meaning is, he came not into the enemy's power but by the chance of war. To *'bide* the chance of war may well enough ſignify, to ſtand the hazard of a battle, but can ſcarcely mean to endure the ſeverity of a priſon. JOHNSON.

Notwithſtanding the attempt of Dr. Johnſon to explain the preſent reading, I cannot help thinking that the paſſage is corrupt. The poet may have written,

"He never did fall off, my ſovereign liege,
"But *try'd* the chance of war."

The meaning will then be, that Mortimer neither revolted to the enemy, nor hung back during the fight: that he did his utmoſt. A. B.

[1] *I'll raiſe the preparation of a war Shall ſtain your brother.*] Thus the printed copies. But ſure, Antony, whoſe buſineſs here is to mollify Octavia, does it with a very ill grace: and 'tis a very odd way of ſatisfying her, to tell her, the war he raiſes, ſhall *ſtain*, i. e. caſt an odium upon her brother. I have no doubt but we muſt read, with the addition only of a ſingle letter,

"Shall *ſtrain* your brother,"

i. e. ſhall lay him under conſtraints; ſhall put him to ſuch ſhifts, that he ſhall neither be able to make progreſs againſt, or to prejudice me. THEOBALD.

I do not ſee but *ſtain* may be allowed to remain unaltered, meaning no more than *ſhame* or *diſgrace*. JOHNSON.

"Stain," I think, is right, only that it ſhould be printed 'ſtain for *ſuſtain*, or *ſupport*. The context will warrant this reading. Antony ſays, that if he loſes his honour, he loſes himſelf: ſtill, adds he, to ſhew you how much I am inclined to be well with Cæſar, yourſelf ſhall go between us, and I will make preparation to ſupport him, if he be ſo minded as to act with me. "*So your deſires are yours,*" continues he, *i. e. you have your wiſhes for a perfect reconciliation: be quick, and, if poſſible, effect it.* To this Octavia returns him thanks, which ſhe would certainly not have done, had he inſinuated that he meant to *ſhame* or *diſgrace* her brother. *When it appears to you*, proceeds Antony, *where this begins* (*i. e.* where there is any fault), turn

O, wither'd is the garland of the war,
The soldier's pole [1] is fall'n; young boys, and girls,
Are level now with men.
Antony and Cleopatra, A. 4, S. 13.

WARRIOR.

—— Tell the constable,
We are but warriors for the working-day:
Our gayness, and our gilt, are all besmirch'd
With rainy marching in the painful field.
Henry V. A. 4, S. 3.

—— Thou shalt be fortunate,
If thou receive me for thy warlike mate [2].
Henry VI. P. 1, A. 1, S. 2.

WAVES.

—— Like Arion on the dolphin's back,
I saw him hold acquaintance with the waves,
So long as I could see. *Twelfth Night*, A. 1, S. 2.

WEARINESS.

—— Weariness
Can snore upon the flint, when resty sloth
Finds the down pillow hard. *Cymbeline*, A. 3, S. 6.

turn your displeasure that way. From all which we may infer, that he was willing to assist Cæsar, if in honour he could do so. The poet wrote *'stain* on account of the metre. A. B.

[1] *The soldier's pole.*] He at whom the soldiers pointed, as at a pageant held high for observation. JOHNSON.

Perhaps by "soldier's pole," is meant the *standard*—the principal military ensign. A. B.

[2] *If thou receive me for thy warlike mate.*] "Mate" should be *meet*. *Meet* is here used as a substantive, and in the sense of *equal*—one who may be allowed to enter the lists with him. A. B.

WELCOME.

WELCOME.

Sir, you are very welcome to our houſe:
It muſt appear in other ways than words,
Therefore I ſcant this breathing courteſy.
Merchant of Venice, A. 5, S. 1.

A hundred thouſand welcomes: I could weep,
And I could laugh; I am light, and heavy. Welcome.
A curſe begin at very root of's heart,
That is not glad to ſee thee!
Coriolanus, A. 2, S. 1.

— Therefore as a ſtranger give it welcome.
There are more things in heaven and earth, Horatio,
Than are dreamt of in your philoſophy.
Hamlet, A. 1, S. 5.

—— — Hermione,
How thou lov'ſt us, ſhew in our brother's welcome;
Next to thyſelf, and my young rover, he's
Apparent to my heart. *Winter's Tale*, A. 1, S. 2.

——— Pray you, bid
Theſe unknown friends to us welcome; for it is
A way to make us better friends, more known.
Winter's Tale, A. 4, S. 3.

WIDOW.

Arm, arm, you heavens, againſt theſe perjur'd kings!
A widow cries; be huſband to me, heavens!
Let not the hours of this ungodly day
Wear out the day in peace. *King John*, A. 3, S. 1.

And will ſhe yet abaſe her eyes on me,
That cropp'd the golden prime of this ſweet prince,
And made her widow to a woful bed?
On me, whoſe all not equals Edward's moiety?
Richard III. A. 1, S. 2.

— See

——— See what now thou art.
For happy wife, a moſt diſtreſſed widow;
For joyful mother, one that wails the name;
For one being ſu'd to, one that humbly ſues;
For queen, a very caitiff crown'd with care:
For one that ſcorn'd at me, now ſcorn'd of me;
For one being fear'd of all, now fearing one;
For one commanding all, obey'd of none.
Richard III. A. 4, S. 4.

——— A poor petitioner,
A care-craz'd mother to a many ſons,
A beauty-waning and diſtreſſed widow,
Even in the afternoon of her beſt days,
Made prize and purchaſe of his wanton eye,
Seduc'd the pitch and height of all his thoughts
To baſe declenſion. *Richard III.* A. 3, S. 7.

If a man do not erect in this age his own tomb ere he dies, he ſhall live no longer in monument, than the bell rings, and the widow weeps.
Much ado about nothing, A. 5, S. 2.

WIFE.

If ſhe come in, ſhe'll ſure ſpeak to my wife:---
My wife! my wife! what wife? I have no wife:
O inſupportable! O heavy hour!
Methinks, it ſhould be now a huge eclipſe
Of ſun and moon; and that the affrighted globe
Should yawn at alteration. *Othello*, A. 5, S. 2.

WINDS.

I am a feather for each wind that blows.
Winter's Tale, A. 2, S. 3.

Thou ſhalt be as free
As mountain winds. *Tempeſt*, A. 1, S. 2.

——— The

——— The elements
Of whom your ſwords are temper'd, may as well
Wound the loud winds, or with bemock'd-at ſtabs
Kill the ſtill-cloſing waters, as diminiſh
One dowle that's in my plume. *Tempeſt*, A. 3, S. 3.

Blow, winds, and crack your cheeks! rage! blow!
You cataracts, and hurricanoes, ſpout
Till you have drench'd our ſteeples, drown'd the cocks!
You ſulphurous and thought-executing fires,
Vaunt couriers to oak-cleaving thunder-bolts,
Singe my white head! *Lear*, A. 3, S. 2.

The ſouthern wind
Doth play the trumpet to his purpoſes;
And, by his hollow whiſtling in the leaves,
Foretells a tempeſt, and a bluſtering day.
Henry IV. P. 1, A. 5, S. 1.

How like a younker, or a prodigal,
The ſkarfed bark puts from her native bay,
Hugg'd and embraced by the ſtrumpet wind!
How like a prodigal doth ſhe return;
With over-weather'd ribs, and ragged ſails,
Lean, rent, and beggar'd by the ſtrumpet wind!
Merchant of Venice, A. 2, S. 6.

To be impriſon'd in the viewleſs winds,
And blown with reſtleſs violence round about
The pendant world.
Meaſure for Meaſure, A. 3, S. 1.

Therefore the winds, piping to us in vain,
As in revenge, have ſuck'd up from the ſea
Contagious fogs; which falling in the land,
Have every pelting [1] river made ſo proud,
That they have over-borne their continents.
Midſummer Night's Dream, A. 2, S. 2.

WINE.

[1] ——*pelting*.] The meaning is plainly *deſpicable*, *mean*, *ſorry*, *wretched*,

WINE.

O thou invisible spirit of wine, if thou hast no name to be known by, let us call thee---devil! O, that men should put an enemy in their mouths, to steal away their brains! that we should, with joy, revel, pleasure, and applause, transform ourselves into beasts! *Othello*, A. 2, S. 3.

WISDOM.

—— Wisdom wishes to appear most bright,
When it doth tax itself.
Measure for Measure, A. 2, S. 4.

The amity that wisdom knits not, folly may easily untie. *Troilus and Cressida*, A. 2, S. 3.

—— Full oft we see
Cold wisdom waiting on superfluous folly.
All's well that ends well, A. 1, S. 1.

Thus do we of wisdom and of reach,
With windlaces, and with assays of bias,
By indirections find directions out;
So, by my former lecture and advice,
Shall you, my son: you have me, have you not?
Hamlet, A. 2, S. 1.

WIT.

Sometimes I have no more wit than a Christian, or an ordinary man has: but I am a great eater of beef, and, I believe, that does harm to my wit.
Twelfth Night, A. 1, S. 3.

wretched, but as it is a word without any reasonable etymology, I should be glad to dismiss it for *petty*; yet it is undoubtedly right. JOHNSON.

"Pelting" should be *palting*. See note on King Lear.
A. B.

Fat paunches have lean pates; and dainty bits
Make rich the ribs, but bankerout the wits.

Love's Labour Lost, A. 1, S. 1.

—— Gentle, ſweet,
Your wit makes wiſe things fooliſh: when we greet
With eyes beſt ſeeing heaven's fiery eye,
By light we loſe light.

Love's Labour Lost, A. 5, S. 2.

—— The world's large tongue
Proclaims you for a man replete with mocks;
Full of compariſons, and wounding flouts;
Which you on all eſtates will execute,
That lie within the mercy of your wit.

Love's Labour Lost, A. 5, S. 2.

None are ſo ſurely caught, when they are catch'd,
As wit turn'd fool: folly, in wiſdom hatch'd,
Hath wiſdom's warrant.

Love's Labour Lost, A. 5, S. 2.

This fellow picks up wit, as pigeons peas;
And utters it again, when Jove doth pleaſe:
He is wit's pedlar. *Love's Labour Lost*, A. 5, S. 2.

Folly in fools bears not ſo ſtrong a note,
As foolery in the wiſe, when wit doth dote;
Since all the power thereof it doth apply,
To prove, by wit, worth, in ſimplicity.

Love's Labour Lost, A. 5, S. 2.

You have a nimble wit; I think it was made of Atlanta's heels. Will you ſit down with me? we two will rail againſt our miſtreſs, the world, and all our miſery. *As you like it*, A. 3, S. 2.

A good ſherris-ſack hath a two-fold operation in it. It aſcends me into the brain; dries me there all the fooliſh, and dull, and crudy vapours which environ it; makes it apprehenſive, quick, forgetive, full of nimble, fiery, and delectable ſhapes; which deliver'd deliver'd o'er to the voice (the tongue), which is the birth, becomes excellent wit.

Henry IV. P. 2, A. 4, S. 3.

A good old man, ſir; he will be talking; as they ſay, when the age is in, the wit is out.

Much ado about nothing, A. 3, S. 5.

Diſdain and ſcorn ride ſparkling in her eyes,
Miſpriſing what they look on; and her wit
Values itſelf ſo highly, that to her
All matter elſe ſeems weak.

Much ado about nothing, A. 3, S. 1.

[1] That I had no angry wit to be a lord.

Timon of Athens, A. 1, S. 1.

WITCH.

Saint Withold footed thrice the wold;
He met the night-mare, and her nine-fold;
Bid her alight,
And her troth plight,
And, aroynt thee, witch, aroynt thee[2]!

Lear, A. 3, S. 4.

[1] *That I had no angry wit to be a lord.*] This reading is abſurd and unintelligible. But as I have reſtored the text, *that I had ſo hungry a wit to be a lord*, it is ſatirical enough of conſcience. Viz. I would hate myſelf, for having no more wit than to covet ſo inſignificant a title. WARBURTON.

The meaning may be, I ſhould hate myſelf for patiently enduring to be a lord. This is ill enough expreſſed. Perhaps ſome happy change may ſet it right. I have tried, and can do nothing, yet I cannot heartily concur with Dr. Warburton. JOHNSON.

Perhaps we may read,
"*So* angry wit."
Shakeſpeare may uſe *angry* in the ſenſe of *perverſe, untoward*. A. B.

[2] —— *aroynt thee, witch, aroynt thee!*] We ſhould read the line thus:

"Aroynt

[1]Aroynt thee, witch! the rump-fed ronyon[2] cries.
Macbeth, A. 1, S. 3.

WOE, WOES.

Now the wasted brands do glow,
Whilst the scritch-owl, scritching loud,
Puts the wretch, that lies in woe,
In remembrance of a shroud.
Midsummer Night's Dream, A. 5, S. 2.

"Aroynt thee, witch, aroynt thee, *right*."
i. e. depart forthwith. WARBURTON.

"Aroynt thee, witch, aroynt thee!" *i. e.* scab take thee, witch, scab take thee! *See note on Macbeth.*

There is no occasion for Dr. Warburton's reading, "aroynt "thee right," or *depart forthwith*. How *aroynt* could ever be supposed to have the sense of *depart*, I have not been able to discover. A. B.

[1] *Aroynt thee.*] *Aroint*, or avaunt, be gone. POPE.

I had met with the word *aroint* in no other author, till looking into Heern's Collections, I found it in a very old drawing, that he has published, in which St. Patrick is represented visiting hell, and putting the devils into great confusion by his presence, of whom one, that is driving the damned before him with a prong, has a label issuing out of his mouth, with these words, OUT OUT, ARONGT, of which the last is evidently the same with *aroint*, and used in the same sense as in this passage. JOHNSON.

The commentators are agreed that *aroint* is the same as *avaunt*; but they have totally mistaken the meaning of the word. "Royne" is *scab*, a term of reproach, and frequently used as such by our earlier writers. We must therefore read,

"Aroint the witch!"

i. e. scab take, or scab catch the witch. "Aroint" is formed by the same analogy as *arouse*, *aright*, &c. but improperly.

"Out out, arongt," as instanced by Dr. Johnson, means *out out, scab!* A. B.

[2] ——— *ronyon cries.*] *i. e.* A scabby or mangy woman. Fr. *Rogneux*, *royne*, scurf. STEEVENS.

I do not think Mr. Steevens has rightly explained the word. Bailey says, that *ronyon* means a fat, bulky woman. It seems in this place, however, to have the sense of *snarler*, from *rogonner*, Fr. to snarl, to growl, to grumble. A. B.

—I have

—— I have fed upon this woe already,
And now excess of it will make me surfeit.
Two Gentlemen of Verona, A. 3, S. 1.

Here can I sit alone, unseen of any,
And, to the nightingale's complaining notes,
Tune my distresses, and record my woes.
Two Gentlemen of Verona, A. 5, S. 3.

That unmatch'd form and feature of blown youth,
Blasted with ecstasy; O, woe is me!
To have seen what I have seen, see what I see!
Hamlet, A. 3, S. 1.

——— We pray you, throw to earth
This unprevailing woe; and think of us
As of a father: for, let the world take note,
You are the most immediate to our throne;
And, with no less nobility of love [1]
Than that which dearest father bears his son,
Do I impart toward you. *Hamlet*, A. 1, S. 2.

—— Wise men ne'er wail their present woes,
But presently prevent the ways to wail.
To fear the foe, since fear oppresseth strength,
Gives, in your weakness, strength unto your foe,
And so your follies fight against yourself.
Richard II. A. 3, S. 2.

—— One that was a woful looker-on,
[2] When as the noble duke of York was slain.
Henry VI. P. 3, A. 2, S. 1.

 —— Our

[1] *And with no less nobility of love.*] *Nobility* for *magnitude.* WARBURTON.
Nobility is rather *generosity.* JOHNSON.
"Nobility of love" may mean, *true and virtuous love.* A. B.

[2] *Ah, one that was a woful looker-on,*
When as the noble duke of York was slain.] "When as" should be printed as a single word, *whenas.* It means nothing more than *when: as* is added for the sake of the metre. So "*whereas*"

——— Our eſcape
Is much beyond our loſs: our hint of woe [1]
Is common. *Tempeſt*, A. 2, S. 1.

WOMAN.

Women will love her, that ſhe is a woman
More worth than any man; men, that ſhe is
That rareſt of all women. *Winter's Tale*, A. 5, S. 1.

If, one by one, you wedded all the world,
Or, from the all that are, took ſomething good,
To make a perfect woman: ſhe, you kill'd,
Would be unparallel'd. *Winter's Tale*, A. 5, S. 1.

——— E'en a woman; and commanded
By ſuch poor paſſion as the maid that milks,
And does the meaneſt chares. It were for me
To throw my ſceptre at the injurious gods;
To tell them that this world did equal theirs,
Till they had ſtolen our jewel.
Antony and Cleopatra, A. 4, S. 13.

Theſe dangerous unſafe lunes o' the king! beſhrew
them!
He muſt be told on't, and he ſhall: the office
Becomes a woman beſt; I'll take't upon me:
If I prove honey-mouth'd, let my tongue bliſter.
Winter's Tale, A. 2, S. 2.

" *whereas*" is frequently printed for *where*. So in our author's poem—" Wholeſome Counſel."
Whenas thine eye hath choſe the dame, A. B.

[1] ——— *our hint of woe.*] *Hint* is that which recalls to the memory. The cauſe that fills our minds with grief is common. Dr. Warburton reads *ſtint* of woe. JOHNSON.
I would read, " Our hent of woe." *Hent*, in Chaucer and Spencer, is, *got*, *caught*, *laid hold of*. " Our hent of woe" may therefore mean, *the woe that ſeizes or preys on us*. A. B.

——— However

—— However we do praiſe ourſelves,
Our fancies are more giddy and unfirm,
More longing, wavering, ſooner loſt and worn,
Than women's are. *Twelfth Night*, A. 2, S. 4.

— Women are as roſes; whoſe fair flower,
Being once diſplay'd, doth fall that very hour.
Twelfth Night, A. 2, S. 4.

Fear not; he bears an honourable mind,
And will not uſe a woman lawleſsly.
Two Gentlemen of Verona, A. 5, S. 3.

You muſt forget to be a woman; change
Command into obedience; fear, and niceneſs,
(The handmaids of all women, or, more truly,
Women its pretty ſelf) into a waggiſh courage;
Ready in gybes, quick-anſwer'd, ſaucy, and
As quarrellous as the weazel. *Cymbeline*, A. 3, S. 4.

——— Heaven and earth!
Muſt I remember? why, ſhe would hang on him,
As if increaſe of appetite had grown
By what it fed on: and yet, within a month,—
Let me not think on't;—frailty, thy name is woman!
Hamlet, A. 1, S. 2.

A woman mov'd, is like a fountain troubled,
Muddy, ill-ſeeming, thick, bereft of beauty;
And, while it is ſo, none ſo dry or thirſty
Will deign to ſip, or touch one drop of it.
Taming of the Shrew, A. 5, S. 2.

Let it not be believ'd for womanhood!
Think we had mothers; do not give advantage
To ſtubborn critics—apt without a theme,
For depravation—to ſquare the general ſex
By Creſſid's rule. *Troilus and Creſſida*, A. 5, S. 2.

Make the doors upon a woman's wit, and it will out at the caſement; ſhut that, it will fly with the ſmoak out at the chimney.

As you like it, A. 4, S. 1.

——— In that day's feats,
[1] When he might act the woman in the scene,
He prov'd best man i' the field.
Coriolanus, A. 1, S. 2.

Do you not know I am a woman? when I think,
I must speak. *As you like it*, A. 3, S. 2.

The duke is made protector of the realm;
And yet shalt thou be safe? Such safety finds
The trembling lamb, environed with wolves.
Had I been there, which am a silly woman,
The soldiers should have toss'd me on their pikes,
Before I would have granted to that act.
Henry VI. P. 3, A. 1, S. 1.

Women are soft, mild, pitiful, and flexible;
Thou stern, obdurate, flinty, rough, remorseless.
Bidst thou me rage? why, now thou hast thy wish;
Wouldst have me weep? why, now thou hast thy will.
Henry VI. P. 3, A. 1, S. 4.

I cannot be a man with wishing, therefore
I will die a woman with grieving.
Much ado about nothing, A. 4, S. 1.

One woman is fair; yet I am well: another is wise; yet I am well: another virtuous; yet I am

[1] *When he might act the woman in the scene.*] It has been more than once mentioned, that the parts of women were, in Shakespeare's time, represented by the most smooth faced young men to be found among the players. STEEVENS.

This does not appear to me to have any allusion to plays or players. "When he might act the woman in the scene," seems to mean, that from his extreme youth, little was expected from him in the field: yet at the time when he was only sixteen years of age, and when he would not have been censured had he shewn the fear and timidity of a woman, he proved himself an hero. Beside, it is Cominius who speaks, and not Shakespeare. A. B.

well:

well: but till all graces be in one woman, one woman ſhall not come in my grace.

Much ado about nothing, A. 2, S. 3.

I grant, I am a woman; but, withal,
A woman that lord Brutus took to wife:
I grant, I am a woman; but, withal,
A woman well-reputed; Cato's daughter.
Think you, I am no ſtronger than my ſex,
Being ſo father'd, and ſo huſbanded?

Julius Cæſar, A. 2, S. 1.

All women ſhall pardon me: becauſe I will not do them the wrong to miſtruſt any, I will do myſelf the right to truſt none; and the fine is, for the which I may go the finer I will live a bachelor.

Much ado about nothing, A. 1, S. 1.

——— My ſometime general,
I have ſeen thee ſtern, and thou haſt oft beheld
Heart-hard'ning ſpectacles; tell theſe ſad women,
'Tis fond to wail inevitable ſtrokes,
As 'tis to laugh at them. *Coriolanus*, A. 4, S. 1.

——— With immodeſt hatred,
The child-bed privilege deny'd, which 'longs
To women of all faſhion;—laſtly, hurried
Here to this place, i' the open air, before
I have got ſtrength of limit[1].

Winter's Tale, A. 3, S. 2.

[1] *I have got ſtrength of limit.*] I know not well how ſtrength of limit, can mean *ſtrength to paſs the limits* of the child-bed chamber, which yet it muſt mean in this place, unleſs we read in a more eaſy phraſe, *ſtrength of limb.* JOHNSON.

"Strength of limit" ſhould, perhaps, be ſtrength *or* limit. *Limit* for the uſual, or appointed, or *ſettled time*, for quitting her chamber. A. B.

WORD.

W O R D.

What ſaid he? How look'd he? Wherein went he? What makes he here? Did he aſk for me? Where remains he? How parted he with thee? And when ſhalt thou ſee him again? Anſwer me in one word.

As you like it, A. 3, S. 2.

—Hear me, Hubert! drive theſe men away,
And I will ſit as quiet as a lamb;
I will not ſtir, nor wince, nor ſpeak a word,
Nor look upon the iron angerly:
Thruſt but theſe men away, and I'll forgive you.

King John, A. 4, S. 1.

[1] ——— Theſe haughty words of hers
Have batter'd me like roaring cannon-ſhot,
And made me almoſt yield upon my knees.

Henry VI. P. 1, A. 3, S. 3.

Gregory, o' my word, [2] we'll not carry coals.

Romeo and Juliet, A. 1, S. 1.

That

[1] ——— *theſe haughty words of hers*
Have batter'd me like roaring cannon ſhot.] How theſe lines came hither I know not. There is nothing in the ſpeech of Joan haughty or violent; it is all ſoft entreaty and mild expoſtulation. JOHNSON.

"Haughty" does not here mean *violent* or *vehement*, but *great*, *important*. He ſays, in the next ſcene, his haughty courage, *i. e.* his great, his diſtinguiſhed valour. A. B.

[2] —— *we'll not carry coals.*] Dr. Warburton very juſtly obſerves, that this was a phraſe formerly in uſe, but as he has given no inſtances in ſupport of his declaration, I thought it neceſſary to ſubjoin the following:

Naſh, in his *Have with you to Saffron Walden*, ſays, "We "will *bear no coles.*" So in Marſton's Antonio and Melida, "He has had wrong; and if I were he, *I would bear no coles.*" Again in May-day, "You muſt ſwear by no man's beard but "your own, for that may breed a quarrel; above all things, "you muſt *carry no coals.*" And again in the ſame play, "Now my ancient being a man of an *un-coal carrying* ſpirit."

STEEVENS.

A quibble

That in the captain's but a cholerick word,
Which in the ſoldier is flat blaſphemy.
Meaſure for Meaſure, A. 2, S. 2.

WORLD.

——— World, world, O world!
But that thy ſtrange mutations make us hate thee,
Life would not yield to age. *Lear*, A. 4, S. 1.

I am ſorry, I muſt never truſt thee more,
But count the world a ſtranger for thy ſake.
Two Gentlemen of Verona, A. 5, S. 3.

Why, let the ſtrucken deer go weep,
The hart ungalled play:
For ſome muſt watch, while ſome muſt ſleep;
Thus runs the world away. *Hamlet*, A. 3, S. 2.

——— O God! O God!
How weary, ſtale, flat, and unprofitable
Seem to me all the uſes of this world!
Hamlet, A. 1, S. 2.

I care not for thee, Kate; this is no world,
To play with mammets [1], and to tilt with lips:
We muſt have bloody noſes, and crack'd crowns,
And paſs them current too.
Henry IV. P. 1, A. 2, S. 3.

A quibble on *coal*, Eng. and *colle*, Fr. *Colle* is what we call *ſham*, *bam*, *impoſition*. "We'll not carry coles," or *colles*,—*i. e.* We'll not be *impoſed on*. We'll not be *bamboozled*. A. B.

[1] ——— *mammets*.] *Puppets*. JOHNSON.
"Mammets" are undoubtedly *puppets*. But why ſhould Hotſpur be thought ſo very ungallant as to call his lady a puppet? I am rather inclined to think that the poet wrote *mammels* (*mammelles*, Fr.)
"To play with mammels, and to tilt with lips."
In this reading there is that *integrity of expreſſion*, which otherwiſe we may look for in vain. A. B.

2 You,

You, in my respect, are all the world:
Then how can it be said, I am alone,
When all the world is here to look on me?
Midsummer Night's Dream, A. 2, S. 2.

—— The spring, the summer,
The childing autumn, angry winter, change
Their wonted liveries; and the 'mazed world,
By their increase, now knows not which is which.
Midsummer Night's Dream, A. 2, S. 2.

—— Nay, had she been true,
If heaven would make me such another world,
Of one entire and perfect chrysolite,
I'd not have sold her for it. *Othello*, A. 5, S. 2.

O, world, thy slippery turns! Friends now fast sworn,
Whose double bosoms seem to wear one heart,
Whose hours, whose bed, whose meal, and exercise,
Are still together, who twin, as 'twere, in love
Unseparable, shall within this hour
On a dissension of a doit, break out
To bitterest enmity. *Coriolanus*, A. 4, S. 4.

O my good lord, the world is but a word [1];
Were it all yours, to give it in a breath,
How quickly were it gone!
Timon of Athens, A. 2, S. 2.

[1] *O my good lord, the world is but a world.*] The folio reads:
"—— but a word,"
And this is right. The meaning is, as the world itself may be comprised in a word, you might give it away in a breath.
WARBURTON.

I think the reading—"the world is but a world," meaning *that the goods of this world are in our possession, and that we may dispose of them as we think proper*, the more forcible of the two. If, however, we must admit the change of *world* to *word*, it would be better to read,
"O my good lord, the world's but *as* a word."
In the Merchant of Venice, Anthonio says,
"I hold the world but as the world." A. B.

I saw

I ſaw young Harry,—with his beaver on,
His cuiſſes on his thighs, gallantly arm'd,
Riſe from the ground like feather'd Mercury,
And vaulted with ſuch eaſe into his ſeat,
As if an angel dropt down from the clouds,
To turn and wind a fiery Pegaſus,
And witch the world with noble horſemanſhip.

Henry IV. P. 1, A. 4, S. 1.

—— He doth beſtride the narrow world,
Like a Coloſſus; and we petty men
Walk under his huge legs, and peep about
To find ourſelves diſhonourable graves.

Julius Cæſar, A. 1, S. 2.

——— Ye gods, it doth amaze me,
A man of ſuch a feeble temper ſhould
So get the ſtart of the majeſtick world,
And bear the palm alone.

Julius Cæſar, A. 1, S. 2.

Thou ſeeſt the world, Volumnius, how it goes;
Our enemies have beat us to the pit:
It is more worthy, to leap in ourſelves,
Than tarry till they puſh us.

Julius Cæſar, A. 5, S. 5.

Come, Antony, and young Octavius, come,
Revenge yourſelves alone on Caſſius,
For Caſſius is a weary of the world:
Hated by one he loves; brav'd by his brother;
Check'd like a bondman; all his faults obſerved,
Set in a note-book, learn'd, and conn'd by rote,
To caſt into my teeth. *Julius Cæſar*, A. 4, S. 3.

I hold the world but as the world, Gratiano;
A ſtage, where every man muſt play a part.

Merchant of Venice, A. 1, S. 1.

You

You have too much refpect upon the world:
They lofe it, that do buy it with much care.
Merchant of Venice, A. 1, S. 1.

I am too high-born to be property'd,
To be a fecondary at control,
Or ufeful ferving-man, and inftrument,
To any fovereign ftate throughout the world.
King John, A. 5, S. 2.

About the hour of eight, (which he himfelf
Foretold, fhould be his laft) full of repentance,
Continual meditations, tears, and forrows,
He gave his honours to the world again,
His bleffed part to heaven, and flept in peace.
Henry VIII. A. 4, S. 2.

— Good old man; how well in thee appears
The conftant fervice of the antique world,
When fervice fweat for duty, not for meed!
As you like it, A. 2, S. 3.

Oh, what a world is this, when what is comely
Envenoms him that bears it!
As you like it, A. 2, S. 3.

Inveft me in my motley; give me leave
To fpeak my mind, and I will through and through
Cleanfe the foul body of the infected world,
If they will patiently receive my medicine.
As you like it, A. 2, S. 7.

All the world's a ftage,
And all the men and women merely players:
They have their exits, and their entrances;
And one man in his time plays many parts.
As you like it, A. 2, S. 7.

He's gentle; never fchool'd, and yet learned; full of noble device; of all forts enchantingly beloved; and, indeed, fo much in the heart of the world, and

and eſpecially of my own people, who beſt know him, that I am altogether miſpriſed.

As you like it, A. 1, S. 1.

His nature is too noble for the world:
He would not flatter Neptune for his trident,
Or Jove for his power to thunder. His heart's his mouth,
What his breaſt forges, that his tongue muſt vent:
And, being angry, doth forget that ever
He heard the name of death. *Coriolanus*, A. 3, S. 1.

Why are our bodies ſoft, and weak, and ſmooth,
Unapt to toil and trouble in the world;
But that our ſoft condition, and our hearts,
Should well agree with our external parts?

Taming of the Shrew, A. 5, S. 2.

You muſt die: the general ſays, you that have ſo traiterouſly diſcovered the ſecrets of your army, and made ſuch peſtiferous reports of men very nobly held, can ſerve the world for no very honeſt uſe.

All's well that ends well, A. 4, S. 3.

We muſt ſuggeſt the people, in what hatred
He ſtill hath held them; that, to his power, he would
Have made them mules, ſilenc'd their pleaders, and
Diſproperty'd their freedoms: holding them,
In human action and capacity,
Of no more ſoul, nor fitneſs for the world,
Than camels in their war. *Coriolanus*, A. 2, S. 1.

Hadſt thou, like us, from our firſt ſwath, proceeded
The ſweet degrees that this brief world affords
To ſuch as may the paſſive drugs of it
Freely command, thou wouldſt have plung'd thyſelf
In general riot. *Timon of Athens*, A. 4, S. 3.

I, that

I, that am
Deform'd, unfiniſh'd, ſent before my time
Into this breathing world, ſcarce half made up,
And that ſo lamely and unfaſhionably,
That dogs bark at me, as I halt by them;—
Why I, in this weak piping time of peace,
Have no delight to paſs away the time;
Unleſs to ſpy my ſhadow in the ſun,
And deſcant on mine own deformity.

Richard III. A. 1, S. 1.

This is the excellent foppery of the world! that, when we are ſick in fortune (after the ſurfeit of our own behaviour), we make guilty of our diſaſters, the ſun, the moon, and the ſtars; as if we were villains by neceſſity; fools, by heavenly compulſion; knaves, thieves, and treachers, by ſpherical predominance; drunkards, liars, and adulterers, by an inforc'd obedience of planetary influence; and all that we are evil in, by a divine thruſting on.

Lear, A. 1, S. 2.

WORM.

——— Thou art by no means valiant;
For thou doſt fear the ſoft and tender fork
Of a poor worm[1]. *Meaſure for Meaſure*, A. 3, S. 1.

[1] ——— *the ſoft and tender fork*
Of a poor worm.] *Worm* is uſed for any creeping thing or *ſerpent.* Shakeſpeare ſuppoſes falſely, but according to the vulgar notion, that a ſerpent wounds with his tongue, and that his tongue is *forked.* He confounds reality and fiction; a ſerpent's tongue is *ſoft*, but not *forked* nor hurtful. If it could hurt, it could not be ſoft. JOHNSON.

Shakeſpeare could never ſuppoſe that a ſerpent wounds with his tongue, or he would not have ſaid, the "ſoft and tender "fork." He inſinuates that the tongue of the ſerpent is exactly the reverſe of hurtful; but that men are apt to be frightened by appearance, or alarmed from vulgar prejudice. "Fork" is not *forked*, but uſed ſimply for *tongue.* A. B.

WORTH.

WORTH.

—— 'Twas you incens'd the rabble:
Cats, that can judge as fitly of his worth,
As I can of thoſe myſteries which heaven
Will not have earth to know. *Coriolanus*, A. 4, S. 2.

——— It ſo falls out,
That what we have we prize not to the worth,
Whiles we enjoy it; but being lack'd and loſt,
Why, then we rack the value[1].
Much ado about nothing, A. 4, S. 1.

WRONG.

—— The wrongs I have done thee, ſtir
Afreſh within me: and theſe thy offices,
So rarely kind, are as interpreters
Of my behind-hand ſlackneſs!
Winter's Tale, A. 5, S. 1.

——— I cannot forget
The wrong I did myſelf: which was ſo much,
That heirleſs it hath made my kingdom; and
Deſtroy'd the ſweet'ſt companion, that e'er man
Bred his hopes out of. *Winter's Tale*, A. 5, S. 1.

—— Such is the infection of the time,
That, for the health and phyſic of our right,
We cannot deal but with the very hand
Of ſtern injuſtice and confuſed wrong.
King John, A. 5, S. 2.

——— Love all, truſt a few,
Do wrong to none.
All's well that ends well, A. 1, S. 1.

1 —— *we rack the value.*] *i. e.* We exaggerate the value. The alluſion is to *rack-rents*. STEEVENS.

It were better to read,
"—— reck the value."
i. e. Rate it according to its worth. A. B.

Y.

YOUTH.

NOW all the youth of England are on fire,
And ſilken dalliance in the wardrobe lies;
Now thrive the armourers, and honour's thought
Reigns ſolely in the breaſt of every man:
They ſell the paſture now to buy the horſe;
Following the mirror of all Chriſtian kings,
With winged heels, as Engliſh mercuries.

Henry V. A. 2, *Chorus.*

——— By his light,
Did all the chivalry of England move
To do brave acts; he was, indeed, the glaſs
Wherein the noble youth did dreſs themſelves.

Henry IV. P. 2, A. 2, S. 3.

——— There is my hand;
You ſhall be as a father to my youth:
My voice ſhall ſound as you do prompt mine ear;
And I will ſtoop and humble my intents
To your well-practis'd wiſe directions.

Henry IV. P. 2, A. 5, S. 2.

——— Turn two mincing ſteps
Into a manly ſtride; and ſpeak of frays,
Like a fine bragging youth; and tell quaint lies,
How honourable ladies ſought my love,
Which I denying, they fell ſick and dy'd.

Merchant of Venice, A. 3, S. 4.

——In

——— In her youth
There is a prone and ſpeechleſs dialect,
Such as moves men.

Meaſure for Meaſure, A. 1, S. 3.

It is a pretty youth;—not very pretty:—
But, ſure, he's proud; and yet his pride becomes him:
He'll make a proper man.

As you like it, A. 3, S. 5.

At which time would I, being but a mooniſh youth, grieve, be effeminate, changeable, longing, and liking; proud, fantaſtical, apiſh, ſhallow, inconſtant, full of tears, full of ſmiles; for every paſſion ſomething, and for no paſſion truly any thing.

As you like it, A. 3, S. 2.

— In my youth I never did apply
Hot and rebellious liquors in my blood;
Therefore my age is as a luſty winter,
Froſty, but kindly. *As you like it,* A. 2, S. 3.

I beſeech your majeſty to make it
Natural rebellion, done i' the blade of youth;
When oil and fire, too ſtrong for reaſon's force,
O'erbears it, and burns on.

All's well that ends well, A. 5, S. 3.

—— Such extenuation let me beg,
As in reproof of many tales deviſ'd,—
By ſmiling pick-thanks and baſe news-mongers,
I may, for ſome things true, wherein my youth
Hath faulty wander'd and irregular,
Find pardon on my true ſubmiſſion.

Henry IV. P. 1, A. 3, S. 2.

O, Harry, thou haſt robb'd me of my youth:
I better brook the loſs of brittle life,
Than thoſe proud titles thou haſt won of me;

They wound my thoughts, worſe than thy ſword my fleſh,
But thought's the ſlave of life, and life time's fool.
Henry IV. P. 1, A. 5, S. 4.

Ceaſe to perſuade, my loving Protheus;
Home-keeping youth have ever homely wits.
Two Gentlemen of Verona, A. 1, S. 1.

——— If ſhe muſt teem,
Create her child of ſpleen; that it may live,
And be a thwart [1] diſnatur'd torment to her!
Let it ſtamp wrinkles in her brow of youth;
With cadent tears fret channels in her cheeks;
Turn all her mother's pains, and benefits [2],
To laughter and contempt; that ſhe may feel
How ſharper than a ſerpent's tooth it is
To have a thankleſs child! *Lear*, A. 1, S. 4.

[1] ——— *thwart.*] *Thwart*, as a noun adjective, is not frequent in our language; it is however to be found in Promos and Caſſandra, 1578, "Sith fortune thwarte doth croſs my joys with "care!" HENDERSON.

Thwart is an adjective, and is very common with the earlier writers: it is ſometimes employed as a ſubſtantive, as—"a "thwart" for an *abortion.* A. B.

[2] *Turn all her mother's pains, and benefits, To laughter and contempt.*] Her "mother's pains" here ſignifies, not bodily ſufferings, or the throes of child-birth, but *maternal cares*; the ſolicitude of a mother for her child. Mr. Roderic is miſtaken in ſuppoſing that the ſex of this child is aſcertained by the word *her*, which clearly relates, not to Goneril's iſſue, but to herſelf. "Her mother's pains" means, the pains ſhe takes as a mother. MALONE.

Mr. Malone's obſervation is very juſt. I would, however, read "mother-pains"—the ſenſe will then be clearer. It is the mark of the genitive caſe which obſcures the meaning. A. B.

—— There

——— There is Siward's ſon,
And many unrough youths [1], that even now
Proteſt their firſt of manhood. *Macbeth*, A. 5, S. 2.

——— Choak his days
With barbarous ignorance, and deny his youth
The rich advantage of good exerciſe [2].
King John, A. 4, S. 2.

Do you ſet down your name in the ſcroll of youth, that are written down old with all the characters of age? Have you not a moiſt eye? a dry hand? a yellow cheek? a white beard? a decreaſing leg? an increaſing belly? Is not your voice broken? your wind ſhort? your chin double? your wit ſingle [3]? and every part about you blaſted with antiquity?
Henry IV. P. 2, A. 1, S. 2.

[1] ——— *unrough youths.*] An odd expreſſion. It means ſmooth-faced, unbearded. STEEVENS.

"Unrough" is ſurely *unhardy*; ſuch as have never experienced the fatigues of war. A. B.

[2] ——— *good exerciſe.*] In the middle ages, the whole education of princes and noble youths conſiſted in martial exerciſes, &c. Theſe could not be eaſily had in a priſon, where mental improvements might have been afforded, as well as any where elſe; but this ſort of education never entered into the thoughts of our active, warlike, but illiterate nobility. PERCY.

If, in the middle ages, the *whole education* of princes and noble youths conſiſted in martial exerciſes, &c.—what is meant by the following paſſage?

"——— to choak his days
"With barbarous ignorance." A. B.

[3] *Your wit ſingle.*] We call a man ſingle-witted, who attains but one ſpecies of knowledge. This ſenſe I know not how to apply to Falſtaff, and rather think that the Chief Juſtice hints at a calamity always incident to a grey-haired wit, whoſe misfortune is, that his merriment is unfaſhionable. His alluſions are to forgotten facts; his illuſtrations are drawn from notions obſcured by time; his *wit* is therefore *ſingle*, ſuch as none has any part in but himſelf. JOHNSON.

"Single" is *poor*, *weak*. *Single beer* is the weakeſt kind of malt liquor. A. B.

And,

And, like a gallant in the brow of youth [1],
Repairs him with occaſion?

Henry VI. P. 2, A. 5, S. 3.

[1] —— *gallant in the brow of youth.*] *The brow of youth* is an expreſſion not very eaſily explained. I read, the *blow of youth*—the bloſſom, the ſpring. JOHNSON.

The *brow of youth* is the *height* of youth, as the brow of a hill is its ſummit. STEEVENS.

"Brow of youth." We may, perhaps, read *browſe of youth.* The metaphor from the *browſe wood*, or early ſhoots of trees. A. B.

F I N I S.

Printed in Dunstable, United Kingdom

71961445R00271